Bed & Breakfast
American Style – 1985

FOURTH EDITION

Private Homes, Guest Houses, Mansions, Farmhouses, Country & Village Inns, Small Hotels, Seaside & Mountain Lodges

Northeast, West Coast, Northwest, Southwest, Middle West, Rocky Mountains, South, Middle Atlantic, Eastern Canada

Norman T. Simpson

THE BERKSHIRE TRAVELLER PRESS
Stockbridge, Massachusetts

OTHER BOOKS BY NORMAN T. SIMPSON

Country Inns and Back Roads, North America
Country Inns and Back Roads, Continental Europe
Country Inns and Back Roads, Britain and Ireland

COVER: Britt House, San Diego, California, by Jan Lindstrom
BOOK DESIGN AND DRAWINGS: Jan Lindstrom

Library of Congress Catalogue Card Number 81-65526
ISBN 0-912944-92-7

Printed in the United States of America by The Studley Press Inc., Dalton, Massachusetts
Published by Berkshire Traveller Press, Stockbridge, Massachusetts 01262.
413-298-3636

CONTENTS

Preface **7**

Is Owning a B&B for You? **9**

PREFACE

In a manner that is so characteristic of our times, a bed-and-breakfast fever has literally swept through America. Only a few years ago, I explained in the first edition of this book that the term "bed and breakfast" or "B&B" had been associated almost entirely with the British. It evoked the image of the thrifty English housewife who tucked away a few extra shillings by renting out her two extra bedrooms and offering a bit of breakfast in the bargain.

No longer is the B&B a British institution. In typical fashion, Americans have turned B&Bs into an American phenomenon. B&Bs are popping up here, there, and everywhere, like daffodils in spring. They have become our new and thriving cottage industry.

A far cry from a distant cousin of the 1920s and '30s—the "tourist home" with its threadbare carpets, skimpy towels, and creaky beds—today's B&B is, at the least, comfortably and attractively furnished, and at the most, opulently outfitted, with all manner of blandishments, such as jacuzzis, hot tubs, breakfast in bed, shoe-shine service, and the like, to tickle the fancies of its guests.

The American B&B "movement" is elastic, stretching to include everything from the small private home, like the British housewife's, with a couple of extra bedrooms tucked under the eaves, to imposing mansions with chandeliers and parquet floors, to rustic lodges on lakes or by the sea, to country inns and small hotels that offer a complimentary breakfast along with room service.

The main distinction between a B&B *home* and a B&B *inn* is not simply one of size; the atmosphere is obviously more intimate in a home where the hosts are living and where the guests usually share the living and dining rooms with the host family. The personal souvenirs, bibelots, photographs, bric-a-brac, and such, all reinforce the sense of being in someone's home. Sometimes "someone's" home even becomes a "friend's" home.

In a B&B inn, there are usually more bedrooms and at least one common room exclusively for the guests. The innkeepers often have private and separate living quarters.

Most of the time, in host homes, B&B means the bathrooms are shared, although there may be a bedroom or two with its own bath. However, just as country inns have become more responsive to the American public's preference for privacy, so have many host homes converted to private baths. There is a segment of inn-goers who have no problems with shared bathrooms—I, among them. Basically, B&B inns have more private bathrooms.

There is also a variety in the kinds of breakfasts offered and the manner in which they are served. In some instances, a lavish, full breakfast is served, but even the continental breakfasts could include homemade breads, pastries, and preserves. In small places guests might eat with the family in the kitchen or dining room; there are sometimes outside porches or terraces where breakfast can be enjoyed in the sunshine; of if you have a taste for luxury, there are a few places where you can be served breakfast in bed. Some places have dining rooms where dinner is served regularly, and others will provide it on special request. There are a few exceptions where breakfast is not available, but which, for a variety of reasons, I felt should be included.

Swimming pools, tennis courts, or other recreational facilities are not common features among B&B homes, but can be found at some of the larger places and more often at inns. However, even a small B&B might be surrounded by grounds with nature and cross-country ski trails. Some places provide various kinds of indoor diversions beyond books and magazines, with television and video tape libraries, record collections, board games, jigsaw puzzles, chess, backgammon, and such. All of which can be a great boon when your vacation gets rained out.

Inclusion in this book is not based on budget considerations, although most places have rates that compare favorably with nearby commercial facilities.

Rates for two people for one night are supplied in the Index and are intended as guidelines and not to be considered as firm quotations. They often include the low off-season rates as well as the high on-season rates, and in some cases, there is an added tax and service charge. The best policy, of course, is to call ahead and get all the details in advance of your visit. Also, because some places offer various kinds of plans, be sure to specify the B&B rate when you make your reservation.

I have personally visited 90% of the B&Bs covered in this edition. The remainder were researched by Betty Lowry, Owen Johnson, Evelyn Herburger, Carol Rabin, Virginia Rowe, and Carol Kelsey, all professional travel writers. Virginia Rowe is the managing editor, and Susan Zucco is our alert and efficient typesetter.

I will be interested in receiving any comments, complaints, or criticisms you may have about the lodgings I have described herein, and, where necessary, will take up the matter with the proprietors.

Some of the inns have been written about more extensively in my book *Country Inns and Back Roads, North America*.

IS OWNING A B&B FOR YOU?

The answer to that question has many "ifs." If you presently own your home free of mortgage entanglements and if you have a source of *other* income that would not be affected by the economic climate or the seasonal lag of travelers, then the answer *might* be yes.

Some B&B proprietors have painted rosy pictures of steady income and interesting, considerate guests beating a path to their doors. They have been fortunate enough to be located in an area where there is no dip in patronage during the off-season and to have had an 85% occupancy rate in a sufficient number of bedrooms to create a healthy profit.

I might add that in those popular (usually resort) areas described above, the market for buildings that might be used as B&Bs is so inflated I shudder to think of the people who have invested their life savings and mortgaged their future under circumstances that are very uncertain. Under-capitalization is a big problem.

Bear in mind that I am talking about individuals who will be buying property to convert into a B&B accommodation rather than those fortunate few who own easily adaptable property in an ideal tourist area where local codes are flexible.

Unless you are able to generate a sufficient amount of income from other sources allowing you to cover expenses during slack periods when there is insufficient cash flow from your bedroom rentals, you could have several months of discouragement and despair.

With those heavily cautionary remarks out of the way, I will simply suggest that there are a number of obvious questions you should ask yourself, such as what are your feelings about having people using your home and your belongings; do you enjoy having people in your home; are you comfortable and relaxed in your dealings with people; are you prepared to give up privacy; can you handle problems with equanimity? These are only a few of the points to be considered in deciding if owning a B&B is for you.

May I suggest an excellent book on this subject: *How to Open a Country Inn* written by Karen Etsell and Elaine Brennan, owners of the Bramble Inn on Cape Cod, which is listed in this book. Their book is available from your bookstore or directly from The Berkshire Traveller Press, Stockbridge, Massachusetts 01262. ($9.95 postpaid).

Note: Listings are arranged alphabetically by state and then
by name of inn. The Index lists towns alphabetically
within each state.

GUSTAVUS INN
Gustavus, Alaska

I have personally visited each of the bed-and-breakfast accommodations recommended in this book with two exceptions, the Gustavus Inn in Alaska and the California Guest House in Nelson, New Zealand. Eventually, I will visit each of them, but I hope that any readers who visit either of them will send me a postcard.

The Gustavus Inn is, according to its excellent brochure, located in southeastern Alaska fifty air miles from Juneau at the gateway to Glacier Bay. A three-day stay is encouraged to allow the traveler to enjoy the fishing, bicycling, kayaking and country life of the area—especially a visit by boat to the many tidewater glaciers in Glacier Bay National Park. There are several different package tours which include all meals and in some cases round-trip Alaska Airlines jet flights between Juneau and Gustavus, as well as an overnight boat trip aboard the *Glacier Bay Explorer*.

It's obvious that one just doesn't stop at the Gustavus Inn for bed-and-breakfast, but it is an original Alaskan homestead offering meals and it sounds like a definite open window to an Alaskan life-style.

The inn brochure mentions clean, but small, bedrooms accommodating singles, doubles, and twins. Singles may be asked to share. They have a limit of sixteen houseguests to assure personal attention to each. All baths are "down the hall."

The inn is open from May first to October first and I'd suggest you telephone for more of the tremendously intriguing information that is available. Reservations, of course, are very necessary.

GUSTAVUS INN, Box 31-B, Gustavus, Alaska 99826; May thru Sept.: 907-697-3311. Oct. thru April: 907-586-2006. A country inn located on the edge of a great glacier area and Glacier Bay National Park in Alaska. Breakfast, lunch, and dinner served daily. Full American plan available, as well as special package rates. Open May 1 to Oct. 1. Quite enjoyable for children. All descriptions of Alaskan adventures available including many sidetrips. David and JoAnn Lesh, Innkeepers.

Directions: Alaska Airlines has twice-daily connecting service to Gustavus from Juneau during the summer months. Charter service is available from Gustavus, Haines, Skagway, Juneau, and Sitka. Private boats find moorage in the Salmon River at Gustavus or Bartlett Cove. Especially essential to get full information directly by telephone or letter before planning further.

For rates, see Index.

THE LODGE ON THE DESERT
Tucson, Arizona

The Lodge on the Desert is a sophisticated resort that started in the fall of 1936 in the desert outside Tucson. Gradually, the city grew up around it, and today its six acres are separated from the Tucson residential area by a great hedge of oleander.

Lodging rooms are one- and two-story adobe buildings built in the style used by the Pueblo Indians, and the furnishings are all in a distinctive Southwest style.

The center of activity is the pool area marked by three great palm trees. Here, guests may sit in the sun and enjoy the magnificent view of the mountains. The adjoining lounge area has a large library, where often guests gather in the evening to play cards and socialize.

Lunch and dinner are part of the amenities.

A very pleasant continental breakfast is included in the B&B rate and consists of fruit juices, a choice of breads or toast, and a beverage. Selections may also be made from the breakfast à la carte menu at an additional cost. Breakfast may be taken on the individual terraces connected with each of the rooms or suites.

The high season at the Lodge on the Desert is from November 1 to May 1, and it is often necessary to reserve even a one-night stay well in advance.

THE LODGE ON THE DESERT, 306 N. Alvernon Way, Tucson, Ariz. 85733; 602-325-3366. A 40-room luxury inn within the city limits. Near several historic, cultural, and recreational attractions. American and European plans available in winter; European plan in summer. Breakfast, lunch, and dinner served to travelers every day of the year. Swimming pool and lawn games on grounds. Tennis and golf nearby. Attended, leashed pets allowed. Schuyler and Helen Lininger, Innkeepers.

Directions: Take Speedway exit from I-10. Travel about 5 mi. east to Alvernon Way, turn right (south) onto Alvernon (¾ mi.). Lodge is on left side between 5th St. and Broadway.

For B&B rates, see Index.

AMBER HOUSE
Sacramento, California

Sacramento, the capital city of one of America's largest states, has many fine inns. Among the best is the completely air-conditioned Amber House, operated by two young men, Bill McOmber and Robert O'Neil.

Only a few blocks east of the capitol, the house sits on a street lined with towering elm trees, distinquished by its clinker brick front, shiny redwood porch, tan awnings, and handsome brass nameplate.

Robert's colorful, stained glass creations sparkle in every room and classical music lilts through the house. A working fireplace and a boxed beam ceiling dominate the impressive living room, where complimentary wine is served late afternoon.

There are four double-bedded rooms, two with private baths, all handsomely and individually furnished. The light and airy Sun Room is lined with windows on three sides and features an antique white iron bed. The Lindworth Room's private bath boasts a 70-year-old porcelain tub with brass and ivory fixtures.

A full and varied breakfast consisting of seasonal fresh fruits, homemade pastry or quiche, or Robert's special cranberry kuchen is served in the formal dining room, or guest's room, on stunning Limoges china, with sterling silver and crystal accessories.

Sightseeing in the city includes the completely restored state capitol, the Railroad Museum, and Old Town.

AMBER HOUSE, 1315-22nd St., Sacramento, CA 95816; 916-444-8085. A 4-guestroom (2 private baths) handsomely restored bed-and-breakfast inn 7 blocks from the State Capitol. Open year-round. City sightseeing: Railroad Museum, Old Town. No children. No pets. No smoking. Off-street parking; also airline limousine terminal or local train station pick-up service available. Bill McOmber and Robert O'Neil, Innkeepers.

Directions: From the Capitol, take East Capitol to 22nd St.; turn right for a half block.

For B&B rates, see Index.

THE BATH STREET INN
Santa Barbara, California

When this 1875 private home was redesigned and reconstructed in order to make it a bed-and-breakfast inn, a great deal of care was taken to preserve the Victorian atmosphere of the original building and at the same time to incorporate security and safety features which conformed to the strictest modern standards.

Each guest accommodation has its individual charm: a small front suite has a quaint flower-hung balcony; a luxurious rear bedroom has a delightful garden bath; the third-floor guest rooms adjoin a library and parlor aerie looking out to Santa Barbara's spectacular Santa Ynez Mountains.

In the morning a leisurely continental breakfast is served in the sunny dining room or in one of the garden patios.

The beach is a short drive or bike ride away, and bikes are provided upon request.

The Bath Street Inn is in a quiet residential area of Santa Barbara, and it is a very warm outreaching place with many, many books and magazines in evidence. The innkeepers, Susan Brown and Nancy Stover, obviously have a great deal of interest in the arts.

THE BATH STREET INN, 1720 Bath Street, Santa Barbara, Ca. 93101; 805-682-9680. A 7-bedroom (private baths) bed-and-breakfast inn in a very pleasant residential area of a beautiful southern California city. Open year-round. Ideally located for all of the historic, natural, and cultural points of interest in and near Santa Barbara. Not suitable for children. No pets. Susan Brown and Nancy Stover, Innkeepers.

Directions: From Rte. 101, take Mission St. off-ramp east 1 block to Castillo, turn right 3 blocks; left on Valerio 1 block; right on Bath (Bath is one-way). Inn is on the right, parking in the rear.

For B&B rates, see Index.

BEAZLEY HOUSE
Napa, California

The key to a well-run bed-and-breakfast establishment is the personal touch. Carol and Jim Beazley, former residents of Nevada, exemplify this principle with their warmth and enthusiastic hospitality at their Beazley House.

Built in 1902 as the residence of a prominent Napa surgeon, and opened by the Beazleys in 1981 as the first bed-and-breakfast in Napa, Beazley House is situated on a quiet corner in a residential neighborhood. It was recently added to the list of Historic Houses.

The large comfortable living room with its antiques is the setting for afternoon sherry and tea, served from a teacart in front of the fireplace. The unusual "light" windows with eighteen tiny panes make it a sunny and inviting place for guests to visit or play games. The Beazleys' teenage daughter plays the cello for guests on Sundays in the adjacent Music Room. The formal dining room, its attractive redwood paneling stained to look like mahogany, is the scene for the continental breakfast, featuring fresh fruits, fruit juice, homemade muffins, jams, cheese, and coffee or tea.

A staircase with a window seat and half-round stained glass window leads to four attractive upstairs bedrooms, ranging in size from a large suite with fireplace and beautiful brass and porcelain bed to a small sunporch overlooking the lush back garden. All are charmingly decorated with wallpapers, print curtains, and antiques. One room has a private bath; the others share baths.

The Carriage House, completed in 1983, offers an additional five bedrooms, each with its own entrance, one with wheelchair access. Special features in these open-beam-ceiling rooms include fireplaces, double-paned windows, private cedar-lined bathrooms, some with double bathtubs complete with jacuzzis, and iron and brass queen- and king-sized beds with bright, handmade quilts.

BEAZLEY HOUSE, 1910 First St., Napa, CA 94559; 707-257-1649. A 9-guestroom bed-and-breakfast inn (many rooms with private bath), in the heart of the wine country. Open year-round. Many recreational activities in the area. Children over twelve are welcome. No pets. No smoking. Carol and Jim Beazley, Innkeepers.

Directions: Take Rte. 29 into Napa; then the Calistoga fork to the Central Napa-First Street exit. Turn left on Second Street for 0.3 mi., and turn left on Warren and left onto First Street. The inn is at the corner of First and Warren. Ample parking.

For B&B rates, see Index.

THE BED AND BREAKFAST INN
San Francisco, California

San Francisco now has several interesting bed and breakfast establishments, but for many years there was only one: The Bed and Breakfast Inn, located on Charlton Court, just off Union Street in one of the more conservative and least tourist-oriented areas.

The lodging rooms are named after various parts of London and each room provides an entirely different experience. Many have completely different sets of sheets, pillow cases and towels, and there are many varieties of beds, from those with carved Victorian headboards to traditional shiny brass bedsteads.

There are flowers everywhere, thermos jugs of ice water, many books, baskets of fruit, down pillows, and gorgeous coverlets and spreads.

The Bed and Breakfast Inn is within easy walking distance of Fisherman's Wharf and many of the San Francisco attractions, including connections with the cable car.

Since some of the bedrooms have their own patio, breakfast can be enjoyed in a delicious privacy by guests in those rooms. The continental offerings include orange juice, hot croissants, and fresh ground coffee, and are frequently taken in the dining room because the atmosphere is so conducive to good conversation.

THE BED AND BREAKFAST INN, Four Charlton Court, San Francisco, Ca. 94123; 415-921-9784. A 9-room European-style pension in the Union Street district of San Francisco. Convenient to all of the Bay area recreational, cultural, and gustatory attractions. Continental breakfast is the only meal offered. Open daily year-round. Not comfortable for small children. No pets. No credit cards. Robert and Marily Kavanaugh, Innkeepers.

Directions: Take the Van Ness Exit from Route 101 and proceed to Union Street. Charlton Court is a small courtyard street halfway between Laguna and Buchanan, off Union.

For B&B rates, see Index.

BIG RIVER LODGE
Mendocino, California

This section of the northern California coast is one of the most satisfying travel experiences in North America, and a particular treat is an evening walk in the sharp, clean air on the Mendocino headlands while the dazzling sunset highlights the rugged coastline. Mendocino itself is now designated as a historic site and the restoration and architecture conform to the general feeling of the 1800s. Wandering through the town is like an expedition into the past.

It was a particular pleasure to visit Joan and Jeff Stanford at the Big River Lodge. I had met them a few years earlier when they were the innkeepers at a bed-and-breakfast inn in Carmel, but now they had relocated most happily in Mendocino and had an unusually attractive bed-and-breakfast hostelry that had begun life as a rather so-so motel.

The situation certainly provides a great advantage because there is a beautiful view of the sea and some of the town of Mendocino. Each of the lodging rooms opens onto a deck that is lined with all varieties of flowers. All have chairs and a table so that guests can enjoy the splendid view, particularly of the sunsets.

The lodging rooms that look like anything but a motel, have books, plants, secretaries, local art, and many interesting paintings. There are comforters and attractive tablecloths, four-poster beds, antiques, and antique reproductions.

Joan and Jeff will make dinner reservations, advise guests on galleries and sights to be seen. They have walked all of the walks, and they also provide bicycles at no additional charge.

As a final touch, each bedroom has its own woodburning fireplace.

BIG RIVER LODGE, P.O. Box 487, Mendocino, Ca. 95460; 707-937-5615. A 23-bedroom (all private baths) elegantly rustic lodge, just a couple of minutes from the center of Mendocino with ocean and village views and woodburning fireplaces. Open every day in the year. Continental breakfast is the only meal served; however, ample advice is available about restaurants in the area. Centrally located to enjoy all of the historic, scenic, and artistic attractions of the Mendocino-Fort Bragg coast. Joan and Jeff Stanford, Proprietors.

Directions: From San Francisco, follow coastal Hwy. 1 north to Mendocino, or follow Rte. 101 to Cloverdale; 128 to coastal Hwy. 1 and then north. Two miles north of Little River (just to the south of Big River) turn east on Comptche-Ukiah Rd. and look for the Big River Lodge Sign.

For B&B rates, see Index.

BRITT HOUSE
San Diego, California

The British Queen Victoria lent her name to a distinctive type of 19th-century architecture that flourished first in England, but it remained for American designers to bring it to full flower.

One of the more beautiful Victorian mansions is the Britt House which has been lovingly restored and maintained by innkeepers Daun Martin and Robert Hostick.

An outstanding feature of the house is a lavish, two-and-a-half-story stained-glass window adjacent to the winding staircase leading to the second floor.

There are nine large bedrooms, each decorated differently with antiques, wallpapers reminiscent of the Victorian era, fresh flowers and plants, and original drawings by Robert Hostick.

The inn is fortunately within walking distance of Balboa Park and the famous San Diego Zoo.

The attractive lodging rooms are most appropriate in which to enjoy an intimate breakfast. Daun is busy early in the morning preparing individual baskets, which have freshly squeezed orange juice, two eggs, shirred or scrambled, freshly ground coffee, spiced or regular tea, homemade yeast breads with sweet butter and jam.

BRITT HOUSE, 406 Maple St., San Diego, Ca. 92103; 619-234-2926. A 9-room bed-and-breakfast inn with shared baths located just a short distance from Balboa Park with its world-famous zoo. Breakfast and afternoon tea included in room rate. (Special dinners can be arranged with advance notice). Open all year. Museum of Art, Man and Natural History, Reuben H. Fleet Space Theater, and the beaches, desert country, and Mexico (13 mi.) nearby. Sauna on grounds; jogging, biking, skating, bicycles nearby. No pets. Not particularly suitable for young children. Daun Martin, Innkeeper.

Directions: Take Airport-Sassafrass turnoff coming south on Hwy. 5. Proceed on Kettner. Turn left on Laurel; left on Third; right on Nutmeg; right on Fourth St., and come down one block to the corner of Fourth and Maple.

For B&B rates, see Index.

BURGUNDY HOUSE
Yountville, California

Here's an inn with a most rich and varied past. Burgundy House was built by Charles Rouvegneau around the 1870s and was used as both a brandy distillery and a boarding house. Rouvegneau constructed the walls by using enormous native fieldstone, measuring over twenty inches thick, found in the hills around the area. In keeping with the construction of those days, heavy hand-hewn wooden beams and posts were used throughout the structure. When Burgundy House no longer operated as a distillery, its various subsequent functions were as a school, a speakeasy, and a bordello. Bob and Mary Keenan bought this old building in 1975, and they began renovating and restoring it so that it might be used as an antique shop. Customers who came to browse and shop for antiques were so intrigued by the building that the Keenans decided they should take overnight guests. Soon thereafter, the shop became an inn.

There are five bedrooms sharing two baths on the second floor and one double-bedded room with private bath and a downstairs patio. Each room has walls of exposed fieldstone, and is individually decorated with antique beds and eclectic furniture from 'round the world. Surrounding the inn are three cottages and a larger building, all decorated in special themes—the Mayor's House, the Little Cottage, the Justice Court, and Bordeaux House.

Depending on the weather in the valley, breakfast is served either before the blazing fire in a small, cozy room next to the front parlor or outside in the lovely garden. The menu consists of an assortment of pastries, juice, fruit, tea or coffee.

Burgundy House, which is surrounded by vineyards, has extraordinary vistas in every direction one looks, of the mountains, the vines, and the valley. It's a peaceful and tranquil setting, and yet one is close to many restaurants and attractions in the valley.

BURGUNDY HOUSE. 6711 Washington St., Yountville, CA 94599; 707-944-2855. A 9-guestroom (6 baths) circa 1870 guest house in the heart of the wine country. Continental breakfast included with lodgings. Open all year. No telephone or television. Children over 12 permitted in the cottages. No pets. Mary and Bob Keenan, Innkeepers.

Directions: Take Highway 101 north from San Francisco to Highway 29. Take turnoff to Yountville. Turn right to California St. and left to Washington St.

For B&B rates, see Index.

CARTER HOUSE
Eureka, California

Eureka is an up-and-coming community. I've been visiting it off and on for about ten years, and it is definitely emerging as an area of considerable interest.

Symbolic, perhaps, of this emergence is the Carter House, a handsome redwood Victorian home that looks old but was actually completed in 1982. It is an architectural re-creation of the Murphy House, which was destroyed by the 1906 earthquake. The Victorian decor is further enhanced by marble and hardwood floors, oriental carpets, potted plants, and fresh-cut flowers.

The first floor has been set aside as an art gallery where the works of thirty different artists are displayed. The three bedrooms, furnished in handsome Victorian antiques, are located on the third floor, and offer views of the Eureka marina and the extraordinary Carson mansion.

Breakfast includes a fresh tart or pastry, fruit compote, and homemade bran muffins; lox and bagels are offered when salmon is in season. Hors d'oeuvres are served in the early evening, and tea and cookies are served following the dinner hour.

The Carter House is just a few steps from Old Town Eureka, where there are many beautifully restored turn-of-the-century buildings. This downtown restoration ranks with some of the best I have ever seen, and is not as commercial as many.

So, Old Town Eureka and the Carter House are making Eureka a really compelling stop for the traveler on Route 101. If arriving by bus or train, arrangements can be made for a ride to the Carter House in a shiny black Bentley—the Carter House is definitely a class act.

CARTER HOUSE, Third & L St., Eureka, Ca. 95501; 707-445-1390. A 3-bedroom (private and shared baths) bed-and-breakfast accommodation on the third floor of a recently re-created 1884 Victorian mansion in northern California. A full breakfast is the only meal served. Open all year. Conveniently located to visit many of the recreational, cultural, and natural attractions of Humboldt County. No pets. Mark and Christi Carter, Proprietors.

Directions: Eureka is approx. 200 mi. north of San Francisco on Rte. 101, the main north/south highway running the entire length of the West Coast.

For B&B rates, see Index.

CHALET BERNENSIS INN
St. Helena, California

Lace curtains, doilies, handmade quilts, ornate brass or iron beds, and early American and Victorian furnishings characterize the homelike theme at the Chalet Bernensis, a Victorian home built in 1884.

Guests can relax on the wide porch, picnic on the lovely grounds, browse in the antique shop, go hot-air ballooning, biking, gliding, visit the mineral hot springs, the Robert Louis Stevenson and Silverado museums, as well as the many wineries nearby.

An unusual feature of this inn is the replica of the original water tank tower in which there are four guest rooms, each with a private bath, air conditioning, and fireplaces. There is also an antique shop.

Breakfast can be homemade bran muffins or scones, juice, fresh fruit, coffee, tea, and homemade jams and jellies. There are no facilities to amuse children. Pets are not permitted and smoking is discouraged.

Because of its beauty and proximity to the Bay Area, the California wine country has become an extremely popular holiday and vacation area during recent years. There are many small towns nestled in the valley including Calistoga and Napa. Principal among the diversions is a tour of the wineries, although Lake Berryessa, which is a man-made lake formed by Monticello Dam, provides 169 miles of shoreline for picnicking, fishing, swimming, water-skiing, boating, speedboat rides, and excursion trips.

CHALET BERNENSIS INN, 225 St. Helena Hwy., St. Helena, Ca. 94574; 707-963-4423. A 14-guestroom bed-and-breakfast inn (nine rooms have private baths). Open year-round. Breakfast the only meal served. Conveniently located to enjoy all of the wine country natural, historical, and cultural attractions. No children. No pets. No smoking in rooms. Jack and Essie Doty, Innkeepers.

Directions: Follow Rte. 101 north from San Francisco, turn east on Rte. 37 and then north on Rte. 29 through Napa and continue on to St. Helena.

For B&B rates, see Index.

GATE HOUSE INN
Jackson, California

Not only miners rushed to the mother lode country of California's Sierras when gold was first discovered, but also merchants and traders to meet the needs of those miners. One such family was the Chichizolas, who established a general store in Jackson, offering supplies, clothing, food, hardware, and whatever else was needed. The success of this family's efforts was later evidenced by the construction in the early 1890s of the largest and most pretentious Victorian home in the area.

In 1981, Ursel and Frank Walker bought the home (only its third owners) to offer a bed-and-breakfast inn with the same service and attention to guests that had typified their previous years as owners of the Palace Restaurant in nearby Sutter Creek, acknowledged to have been the finest in the gold country.

All rooms in the inn are beautifully decorated and furnished, some with original Early American wallpaper in floral designs still in perfect condition. Light fixtures are Italian imports, installed when the house was constructed, as is the marble in the living room fireplace. Marble-topped chiffoniers and sinks are prominent in the bedrooms.

A unique and separate accommodation is in the "Summerhouse," originally the caretaker's quarters and later the summerhouse for the private residence.

A full breakfast with coddled eggs, fresh fruit and juices, accompanied by an assortment of pastries and muffins, is served in the morning on Ursel's bone china and antique crested bronzeware.

GATE HOUSE INN, 1330 Jackson Gate Rd., Jackson, CA 95642; 209-223-3500. A 5-guestroom turn-of-the- century bed-and-breakfast inn, including a separate cottage (all private baths) 45 mi. southeast of Sacramento and 2 mi. from Amador County Airport. A full breakfast is the only meal served, but four restaurants are within walking distance. Open all year. More than 20 excellent Amador County wineries are nearby, featuring fine chardonnay, zinfandel, and Johannisberg Riesling. Also old and historic mining towns, museums, antique stores, gold-panning, golf, skiing, and water sports nearby. Regretfully, no children. No pets. No smoking. No credit cards. Ursel and Frank Walker, Innkeepers.

Directions: From either north or south on Hwy. 49, turn off on Jackson Gate Rd. just north of its intersection with Hwy. 88 from Stockton to the west.

For B&B rates, see Index.

THE GINGERBREAD MANSION
Ferndale, California

When an entire village is given Historical Landmark status by a state government as a result of its well-preserved and colorfully painted Victorian shops, homes, and farmhouses, a visit there is very much in order. Then, when the most photographed building in that village is a bed-and-breakfast inn, you know it must be something special.

Yet "special" is a minimal word to describe the Gingerbread Mansion, with its widow's walk, weathervanes, turrets, gables, and intricately carved finials and spoolwork. It is all made even more pleasing to the eye by the exterior tones of soft peach and gold, the well-groomed hedges and topiaries, and a formal English-style garden with brick walkways and a magnificent holly tree.

Built in 1899 by a local physician in an unusual combination of Queen Anne and Eastlake architectural styles, the mansion has had a varied past as a private home, a hospital, a rest home, and an apartment building, until it was purchased by its present two young innkeepers Wendy Hatfield and her husband, Ken Torbert.

Now beautifully restored with period pieces and replicas of Victorian wallpaper the mansion has four very comfortable second-floor bedrooms that share two large baths. One of these is as spectacular as the mansion itself, with a claw-footed tub on a raised platform, surrounded on three sides by a white, spindle-posted railing.

An inviting lounge with fireplace and a separate adjoining well-stocked library are on the main floor, as is the breakfast room, where Wendy has a full continental offering each morning with freshly squeezed orange juice, a seasonal fruit plate, a cheese tray, and an assortment of home-baked breads with locally made jams.

THE GINGERBREAD MANSION, 400 Berding St., Ferndale, CA 95536; 707-786-4000. A 4-guestroom spectacular Victorian mansion in a historic landmark village, 20 mi. south of Eureka in northern California. Continental breakfast included in room rate. Open all year. Village sightseeing, including antique shops and crafts, all within walking distance. Bicycles available. Children over 10 by prior arrangement. No pets. No smoking. Wendy Hatfield and Ken Torbert, Innkeepers.

Directions: Turn off U.S. 101 at the Ferndale exit, 20 mi. south of Eureka. Ferndale is 5 mi. west. At the mint green Bank of America building, turn left for one block.

For B&B rates, see Index.

THE GLENBOROUGH INN
Santa Barbara, California

Jo Ann Bell and Pat Hardy, proprietors of this bed-and-breakfast inn in the residential section of Santa Barbara feel so enthusiastic about their occupation that they, along with four other innkeepers, have formed the Innkeepers Guild of Santa Barbara. If you think you want to be an innkeeper I'd suggest that you write to them for further information about frequent seminars.

Guests at the Glenborough Inn are invited to a late afternoon-early evening get together with hot mulled cider or wine and hors d'oeuvres on the parlor sideboard or a cool glass of Pat's wine punch or iced tea on the shady lawn.

All of the rooms enjoy the softness and warmth of plants and fresh flowers. Rooms have delightful old quilts, many turn-of-the-century wall hangings and samplers, and here and there a Norman Rockwell reproduction.

One of the features at the Glenborough is the outdoor, fully enclosed hot tub with large, fluffy bath towels for spa users. This is available for private use by reservation.

Breakfast served in bed, in the guest's room, or sometimes enjoyed outside on the lovely grounds, is served on fine china or handmade pottery and silver with linen napkins. Incidentally, smoking is not allowed in the main house.

THE GLENBOROUGH INN, 1327 Bath Street, Santa Barbara, Ca. 93101; 805-9661-0589. A 4-bedroom 1906 home (shared baths) and a 4-bedroom 1880s cottage (private baths) including 2 fireplace suites. Private hot tub use included with room rate. Open all year. Within walking distance of the many historic, natural, and cultural advantages of Santa Barbara. Children and pets discouraged; smoking and non-smoking rooms. Jo Ann Bell and Pat Hardy, Innkeepers.

Directions: From Rte. 101 take off-ramp at Carrillo. Go east to Bath Street and turn left; go 3½ blocks to inn.

For B&B rates, see Index.

GLENDEVEN
Little River, California

This section of northern California on Highway 1 is rapidly becoming a weekend and mid-week vacation area for residents of the Bay area. The drive up the coast with its tremendous cliffs and headlands is most spectacular. The coastal towns afford interesting excursions into shops and restaurants.

Janet de Vries explained that Glendeven was originally built by a man from the state of Maine, one Isaiah Stevens, in 1867. I must say that he picked a very gracious location and today this Victorian house is a cheerful bed-and-breakfast home.

The center of activity is the living room which has a fireplace, a piano, and windows along the south side with an extraordinary view of the headlands. It is obvious that both Jan and Janet de Vries are involved in contemporary arts and crafts as evidenced by the ceramics, the paintings, and the numerous gallery notices.

The lodging rooms have quite unusual furnishings with a generous number of French antiques as well as contemporary decorations. The recently completed East Wing Suite has its own fireplace and a view of the bay.

The continental breakfast is generous, including fresh fruit, or baked apple, muffins, and coffee cake. (There is always something baked.) There are also hard-boiled eggs fresh from the chickens that are kept in the rear of the property.

GLENDEVEN, 8221 No. Highway One, Little River, Ca. 95456; 707-937-0083. A 6-bedroom bed-and-breakfast home (four with private baths). Open year-round except for Christmas Eve and Christmas Day. Most convenient for enjoyable excursions to the northern California coastal towns. A couple of mi. south of Mendocino. Breakfast is the only meal served. No pets. No credit cards. Jan and Janet de Vries, Proprietors.

Directions: Either follow coastal Hwy. 1 all the way from San Francisco skirting the shores of the Pacific, or follow Rte. 101 to Cloverdale; Rte. 128 to Hwy. 1, and then proceed north to Little River.

For B&B rates, see Index.

THE GOSBY HOUSE INN
Pacific Grove, California

Pacific Grove is a delightful oceanside resort and residential area situated on the famous Monterey Peninsula where the waters of the Pacific Ocean and Monterey Bay converge. Four miles of freely accessible sandy beaches and a rocky, coved shoreline afford unsurpassed enjoyment to young and old alike—for the sunbather, swimmer, skin diver, beachcomber, fisherman, or artist. It is a paradise of coastal wonders and marine life, with seals, seabirds, sea otters, emigrating whales, and coastal flora. The beautiful Monarch butterflies spend their winters here.

It is also the location of a bed-and-breakfast establishment that should delight the eclectic imagination of any Victorian enthusiast—The Gosby House Inn.

The exterior has all of the turn-of-the-century delights: a cupola with a conical roof, several different gabled sections, stained-glass windows, and many different types of siding.

The interior, including the many bedrooms, has quite a few original Victorian pieces along with some excellent reproductions. There are several old framed newspapers adorning the walls and decorative Victorian prints in the bedrooms. Ten bedrooms have their own fireplaces.

The reception area has a display case with some lovely dolls dressed in period costumes of various kinds; the building is on the National Historic Register.

THE GOSBY HOUSE INN, 643 Lighthouse Ave., Pacific Grove, Ca. 93950; 408-375-1287. A 23-bedroom bed-and-breakfast inn (2 share bath). Within a short distance of the Pacific Ocean in a relatively quiet residential section. Open year-round. Convenient for visits to Cannery Row in Monterey, Old Fisherman's Wharf, Carmel, 17-mile Drive, Pebble Beach. Smoking is not permitted.

Directions: From Highway 1, take the Pebble Beach-Pacific Grove Exit (Rte. 68 west) 5 mi. to Pacific Grove and follow Forest Ave. 3 mi. to Lighthouse Ave. Turn left 3 blocks.

For B&B rates, see Index.

GRAMMA'S BED & BREAKFAST INN
Berkeley, California

Not all of the proliferating California bed-and-breakfast establishments are being run by enterprising couples or families bent on staking out a claim on a new way of life.

Gramma's, which is in the university community of Berkeley, is a good example of the fact that bed-and-breakfast is now becoming a business. This nineteen-room, restored Tudor mansion is a small specialty hotel that has some of the comforts of a home, including handmade quilts, special soaps manufactured in Berkeley, and homebaked bread made by a local lady who takes pride in her work.

The living room area is shared by all the guests and there is a fireplace and late afternoon wine and cheese.

The bedrooms are most comfortable with a sort of commercial country-inn theme, and there's a rather lavish buffet-style breakfast served every morning. The Sunday brunch is even more lavish, and is available to houseguests at half the full price.

Gramma's is just a few moments from downtown San Francisco and it has proven to be an excellent place in which to stay for many women business executives while they are in the Bay area.

GRAMMA'S BED & BREAKFAST INN, 2740 Telegraph Ave., Berkeley, Ca. 94705; 415-549-2145. A 19-bedroom specialty hotel adjacent to the University of California in a residential section of Berkeley. Open year-round. Transportation available to San Francisco. Convenient for all of the Bay area cultural, historical, and natural attractions. No pets.

Directions: For first-time guests, I would suggest telephoning Gramma's (415-549-2145).

For B&B rates, see Index.

27

GRAPE LEAF INN
Healdsburg, California

Healdsburg, Geyserville, and Cloverdale are just a few moments apart on Route 101, which leads to upper northern California.

In Healdsburg, the Grape Leaf Inn, at one time a private home, is located on a rather quiet residential street. Proprietor Terry Sweet has furnished this restored eighty-two-year-old home to reflect the turn of the century.

The first thing that impressed me upon walking into the entry hall was the combination dining-living room with its very comfortable couch, love seat, fireplace, and lots of plants and flowers.

The seven comfortably furnished bedrooms, all with private baths, are named after the wines of the Alexander Valley. One of the main reasons that people come to Healdsburg is to visit the wineries. Within a twenty-minute drive of the inn there are thirty-three wineries that are still family-owned. During the wintertime especially, you can go right into the winery and talk to the winemaker. There is also a canoe company nearby where rental canoes are available for day-trips on the Russian River, which runs through Healdsburg.

Full breakfast served by Kathy Cookson, resident innkeeper, includes freshly ground coffee that is roasted nearby, fresh orange juice, fresh fruit, eggs prepared in a variety of ways, and home-baked muffins or coffee cake. In addition, in the afternoon, Sally pours a red or white local premium quality wine to be enjoyed with Sonoma County cheeses.

GRAPE LEAF INN, 539 Johnson St., Healdsburg, Ca. 95448; 707-433-8140. A 7-bedroom bed-and-breakfast home at the northern border of the Sonoma wine country. Open year-round. Breakfast is the only meal served. Conveniently located to visit all of the cultural and historic attractions and wineries. Night tennis, bicycles, canoe trips, and other recreation nearby. Terry Sweet, Proprietor; Kathy Cookson, Innkeeper.

Directions: From San Francisco, follow Rte. 101 exiting at Healdsburg Ave. (the 2nd exit from Healdsburg) and continue in the same direction for 4 traffic lights. Turn right at Grant St., go 2 blocks to Johnson St. and turn right. Grape Leaf is on the right with a small, unobtrusive sign.

For B&B rates, see Index.

THE GREEN GABLES INN
Pacific Grove, California

If you're ever planning to be in Pacific Grove, by all means telephone in advance in the hope that there will be accommodations available at the Green Gables.

Located right on the water on Ocean View Boulevard, this many-gabled Victorian beauty with its white fence and well-kept garden, can only be described as "delicious."

Large bay window alcoves, antique furnishings, and a unique fireplace framed by stained glass panels make the living room a gracious gathering place for guests.

The six bedrooms in the main house are exceptionally comfortable and have leaded casement windows with a view of the Pacific Ocean as it crashes on the great rocks. There are four additional bedrooms in the carriage house.

A generous breakfast is served in a lovely little dining room with its own view of the ocean, too. There is a substantial main course, which could be a quiche, a fritata, Belgian waffles, or crepes, combined with fresh fruits, homemade breads, juices, and coffee or tea.

A complimentary social hour is held in the afternoon, when hors d'oeuvres, wine, sherry, and hot cider are offered.

THE GREEN GABLES INN, 104 Fifth St. (corner of Ocean View Blvd.), Pacific Grove, Ca. 93950; 408-375-2095. Ten guest rooms available in this home by the bay. Open all year. Breakfast included. Conveniently located for all the Monterey Peninsula recreational, cultural, and historic attractions, including the famous golf courses and Cannery Row. Not suitable for children. No pets. No credit cards. No smoking. Roger and Sally Post, Owners; Shawn Quinn, Innkeeper.

Directions: Exit Hwy. 1 on Rte. 68 west; continue to Pacific Grove (5 mi.) and then follow Forest Ave. to Ocean Blvd. and then turn right on 5th St.

For B&B rates, see Index.

THE GREY WHALE INN
Fort Bragg, California

Fort Bragg is located on Route 1 on the exciting north coast, where forest meets the sea, just nine miles north of Mendocino village. Guests at the Grey Whale can enjoy beachcombing amid the twisted driftwood, whale-watching as the giant grey whales migrate within sight of shore, attend a salmon barbecue in July, along with such other diversions as the Footlighters' Gaslight Gaieties summer theater.

A walk on the secluded unspoiled miles of beaches has something very special for everyone. There's something special, too, about the Grey Whale which, for many years, was the Redwood Coast Hospital. The rooms and corridors are spacious, and in one of the oceanview suites, an old gimbaled surgery lamp is a reminder of the building's past.

The large suites with kitchens are ideal for an extended bed-and-breakfast experience. One spacious first-floor room has superior facilities for the guest in a wheelchair.

Breakfast at the inn is served buffet style in a cozy breakfast room from 7:30 to 11:00 A.M., and includes fruit juice, prizewinning homemade breads and coffee cakes, fresh fruit, yogurt or cheese, and hot beverages.

THE GREY WHALE INN, 615 No. Main St., Fort Bragg, Ca. 95437; 707-964-0640. A 13-room inn located on Hwy. #1 at the north end of Fort Bragg. Continental breakfast included in room rates. (Only meal served.) Open every day in the year. Many natural, historic, and recreational attractions within a short distance. Available by Greyhound Bus and Skunk Train. Beachcombing, scuba diving, fishing, and hiking nearby. John and Colette Bailey, Innkeepers.

Directions: From the south, follow Hwy. 101 to Cloverdale, take Rte. 128 west to Hwy. #1, and follow north to Fort Bragg. Alternate route: Exit Hwy. 101 at Willits, then west on Rte. 20 to Fort Bragg. Driving time from San Francisco, 4 hrs. Another alternate: Hwy. 1 along the coast. Driving time from San Francisco: 6 hrs.

For B&B rates, see Index.

THE HAPPY LANDING
Carmel-by-the-Sea, California

Just a half a block from Ocean Avenue, the principal shopping street of Carmel, stands The Happy Landing, a collection of English-type pink cottages built around a courtyard with a delightful lily pond and a gazebo where weddings and receptions are often held.

Built in 1925 as a family retreat, this early Comstock-designed group of buildings has evolved into one of Carmel's entrancing accommodations. They are in keeping with the Carmel tradition of individual and family comfort.

There are nine of these little cottages set amongst the rose trellises, and almost all of them have cathedral ceilings and individual fireplaces. Some are furnished in wicker and others have antiques and brass. The pink theme is continued throughout, even to the pink towels. When you open your curtains in the morning, it is the signal that you are ready to have breakfast brought to your room by Aiko, the Japanese maid. It consists of various breakfast breads, fresh fruit, juice, and coffee or tea. Many guests sit out in the garden enjoying the Carmel sunshine and the ubiquitous birds.

Although the Happy Landing is not on Carmel Bay, it is possible to get a glimpse of the bay through the trees. Views of both the ocean and the garden can be enjoyed from the large reception room with its stone fireplace, where tea is served in the afternoon.

THE HAPPY LANDING, Box 2619, Monte Verde between 5th and 6th Streets, Carmel, Ca. 93921; 408-624-7917. A 7-guestroom (private baths) bed-and-breakfast inn; including 2 suites with king-sized beds. Open every day of the year. In a very quiet section of Carmel, a short distance from the beach and a pleasant walking distance to shops and restaurants. Conveniently located for drives through Pebble Beach and Big Sur. No pets. Bob Alberson, Dick Stewart, and Jewell Brown, Innkeepers.

Directons: Take the Ocean Ave. exit from Hwy. 1 and continue to Monte Verde. Turn right for 1½ blocks. The Happy Landing Inn is next to the Christian Science Church.

For B&B rates, see Index.

THE HEIRLOOM
Ione, California

Slightly west of the famous California towns of Jackson and Sutter Creek, lies the country village of Ione. Well off the main road, in a beautiful garden setting, is the town's historical center—a brick antebellum mansion with classic columns and wisteria-entwined porticos. Built in 1863 by a Virginian, the windows are deep-set in Southern style, a fan transom covers the front entrance, and the living room is all in off-white paneling. A Colonial staircase and mantel complete the background for the antique furnishings in this charming home.

The four seasons provide themes for the decor of the guest rooms, and innkeepers Patricia Cross and Melisande Hubbs have used jonquil yellow in the Springtime room, seafoam and dusty rose for Summer, maple-leaf colors for Autumn, and Winter is evoked with burgundy and blue. Three of the rooms have balconies and there are double and king- and queen-sized beds. A handcrafted adobe (rammed earth) cottage, with Early American primitive furnishings, a woodburning stove, and a skylight is called the Room for All Seasons.

Usually attired in long skirts with aprons, Patricia and Melisande serve their guests a full breakfast. A typical meal will offer fresh orange juice, home-baked breads or popovers, an entrée of crêpes, soufflés, quiche, or eggs Benedict, and the very best of coffees. Breakfast may be enjoyed in bed or on the balcony, in the garden, or in the fireside dining room.

On arrival in late afternoon, guests are served sherry, white wine, or tea. Guests will find fresh flowers, fruit, and candy in their rooms.

THE HEIRLOOM, 214 Shakeley Lane, P.O. Box 322, Ione, CA 95640; 209-274-4468. A 5-guestroom (2 private baths) historic bed-and-breakfast inn (circa 1863) in the heart of the gold rush country in the foothills of the Sierra Nevadas, west of Jackson and Sutter Creek. Open year-round. Bicycles available for exploring country roads. Historic sites, antiquing, wineries nearby. No children under 12. No pets. No credit cards. Patricia Cross and Melisande Hubbs, Innkeepers.

Directions: From Hwy. 88 or 16 take Hwy. 124 to Ione. Watch for the Heirloom sign on left. A short lane leads to the inn.

For B&B rates, see Index.

HERMITAGE HOUSE
San Francisco, California

Extensive scrubbing, oiling, painting, paperhanging, and updating plumbing and wiring have brought this 1903 home of Judge Charles Slack back up to snuff. When Hermitage House, a four-story Greek Revival mansion, was purchased by the Binkleys in 1978, it had been used as a drug rehabilitation center and was much in need of restoration and care. Innkeeper Marian Binkley was skillful in her renovation, as she kept much of the mansion's original character and beauty intact, and then transformed the building into a cozy and convenient inn.

Hermitage House has six bedrooms with baths, four of which have working fireplaces. Not only are the rooms beautifully papered with floral patterns and attractive turn-of-the-century furniture, but the beds are four-postered or brass. Each room has a special name, such as Game Room, Guinevere, or Green Gables; but one of the most interesting bedrooms is Judge Slack's study on the top floor of the house. It is noteworthy for its high, beamed ceiling, walls lined with bookshelves, a massive stone fireplace, and a dormered window, providing a special vista of the Twin Peaks district of San Francisco.

The cheery breakfast room, off the main entrance, is where the morning fare is served buffet style. Each morning there is a buffet filled with freshly squeezed orange juice, a variety of cold cereals, an assortment of rolls and croissants, fruits, tea, coffee, and chocolate. I was given a tour of the kitchen, where Marian Binkley pointed with pride to the original 1900 Wedgewood stove. Marian boasts, "It's in grand condition and I only had to get two new gadgets for it—a self-lighter and a thermostat!"

HERMITAGE HOUSE, 2224 Sacramento St., San Francisco, CA 94115; 415-921-5515. A 6-guestroom bed-and-breakfast inn located in the city's Pacific Heights district, with limited off-street parking facilities for guests. Continental breakfast only. Open all year. Convenient local public transportation (the bus stops at the corner) to many districts in the city. Walking distance to Union Street and Fillmore. Children discouraged. No pets. Ted and Marian Binkley, Innkeepers.

Directions: Take Van Ness exit from Rte. 101 to Sacramento St. Inn is between Laguna and Buchanan Streets.

For B&B rates, see Index.

HILL HOUSE INN
Mendocino, California

Query knowledgeable Californians as to the beauties of their state's 800-mile Pacific Ocean frontage, and you will hear unanimous praise for the coasts of Big Sur and Mendocino County. While Big Sur provides a picturesque drive, it is generally accommodation-less, but Mendocino offers both spectacular scenery and the best of creature comforts—and high on the list is the Hill House Inn.

One's first view of the inn, across the quarter-mile of open, green-belt land separating it from Highway 1, is a bit startling, for the three low-profile buildings provide an outward appearance not unlike what one would expect in New England or on the East Coast. The pleasing olive-painted siding, trimmed in white and topped by dark grey roofs, appears most inviting, and this feeling is immediately confirmed when you step into the central reception building with its comfortable couches, flowers and greenery, large fireplace, and neatly patterned wallpaper.

As they are shown to their rooms, guests invariably stop to admire the colorful flower beds and the luxuriant plantings in the atrium areas within each of the two guest buildings.

The decor of the bedrooms is a proper mix of modern and Victorian furnishings and offers either two double beds or a single king-sized bed; some rooms have fireplaces. Marble-topped end tables with excellent reading lights flank the beds, while a color TV is discreetly concealed in a cabinet. There are comfortable chairs and a combination writing and breakfast table placed in front of view windows overlooking either the ocean or the gardens.

A continental breakfast of fresh juice, hot bread or muffins, and your choice of hot drinks is brought to your room each morning. Each evening, decanters of sherry in the lounge area await the pleasure of inn guests.

HILL HOUSE INN, P.O. Box 625, Mendocino, CA 95460; 707-937-0554. A 44-guestroom New England-style inn (private baths) in historic Mendocino county, overlooking the Pacific Ocean. Continental breakfast included. Open all year. Shops, galleries, restaurants, and Mendocino Headlands State Park nearby. Children welcome. No pets. Monte and Barbara Reed, Owners; Julie Beck, Manager.

Directions: From either north or south on Hwy. 1, take Little Lake Exit towards the ocean, one block to Lansing, then right to the top of the hill.

For B&B rates, see Index.

HOPE-MERRILL HOUSE
Geyserville, California

The Hope-Merrill House is one of the most impressive renovations and restorations I have seen. Earlier "modernizations" had installed new windows and lowered ceilings that covered up the original Gothic arches over the bay windows throughout the house—all of which had to be torn out and the moldings retrimmed. Turn-of-the-century wainscoting is a highlight of the interior—it is known as Lincrusta-Walton and is the same wainscoting that has been restored in the state capitol. Even the original silk-screened wallpapers are custom-designed.

This loving effort extends to the very elegant bedrooms that are decorated with Victorian carved headboards, a wicker chaise lounge, a free-standing mirror, a marble top dresser, and nice old sepia and tinted prints. One room has wallpaper designed from a set of random mathematical tables that simulate the positions of stars as you would see them in the sky. The bathrooms are equally elegant with lots of pictures on the walls.

Bob and Rosalie Hope also own the Hope-Bosworth House, located immediately across Geyserville Avenue, so if one house is filled, there is a good chance you can be accommodated in the other one. The Hope-Bosworth House has four rooms and a very pleasant atmosphere.

HOPE-MERRILL HOUSE, 21253 Geyserville Ave. (P.O. Box 42). Geyserville, Ca. 95441; 707-857-2945. A 5-bedroom restored Victorian home. Some with private baths. Reservations can also be made for the Hope-Bosworth House which is across the street and has 4 bedrooms and a very pleasant atmosphere. Conveniently located to enjoy all of the wine country, cultural, scenic and historical attractions. No pets. Not suitable for children. Bob and Rosalie Hope, Proprietors.

Directions: From San Francisco, take Rte. 101 north 80 mi. to the Geyserville exit, drive east 1 block to Old Redwood Hwy. and turn left on Geyserville Ave. (Old Redwood Hwy.) and go 1 mi. north. The two houses are across the road from each other.

For B&B rates, see Index.

THE HOUSE OF SEVEN GABLES
Pacific Grove, California

It is difficult to imagine a more dramatic marine outlook than that afforded to the guests of the House of Seven Gables. Above the shoreline of Monterey Bay, it has an unobstructed view from large picture windows of the bay's half-moon-shaped beach, stretching far, far into the distance. Commercial and private fishing boats from nearby Old Fisherman's Wharf are constantly passing in review, assuring one that this is real life and not just some painter's fantasy.

Between early December and late February, migratory gray whales cavort below the windows, sending up spouts of vapor, then revealing broad backs before sounding into the deep waters of the bay with a final wave of huge tails. Ever since Lucie Chase, a well-to-do civic leader, built this showplace Victorian home in 1886—parking her electric car in front to further display her affluence—these huge creatures have used this protected water as a haven to break their long journey between the Sea of Cortez and the Arctic Ocean. Even if your visit is at a different time of the year, you will always enjoy a performance by the frisky California sea otters and the proliferating marine bird life.

Mornings, seated in loge-view seats, praising Nora Flatley's sumptuous breakfast of fresh orange juice, a huge family-style bowl of mixed fresh fruits, crisp croissants, and a hot apple cobbler, guests are treated to a show few people ever see.

Seven Gables has been the Flatleys' home for many years. Their children, who now operate the house as an inn, have modernized only the baths. The old comfortable rooms are furnished with English and French antiques, with most rooms further enhanced by the filtered light of antique Tiffany-quality, stained glass windows.

THE HOUSE OF SEVEN GABLES, 555 Ocean View Blvd., Pacific Grove, CA 94950; 408-372-4341. A 14-guestroom Victorian bed-and-breakfast inn on the ocean front of the Monterey Peninsula. All rooms with private baths and ocean views. Breakfast included in room rate. Open all year. Convenient to Monterey golf courses, Cannery Row, Carmel, Big Sur, Butterfly Trees, 17-Mile Drive. Adults only. No pets. No smoking. No credit cards. The John Flatley Family, Owners and Innkeepers.

Directions: From Hwy. 1, take the Pebble Beach- Pacific Grove exit (Rte. 68 west). Continue 5 mi. to Pacific Grove and follow Forest Ave. to its end at Ocean View Blvd. Turn right 2 blocks to Fountain.

For B&B rates, see Index.

THE INN AT UNION SQUARE
San Francisco, California

There are probably few inns in America that deliberately strive to be inconspicuous in their outward appearance, or find their entrance commonly mistaken for that of an antiquarian bookstore occupying the ground floor. Yet at a very select location in San Francisco, directly across from the Post Street entrance of the Westin St. Francis Hotel on Union Square, amidst fine shops, international airline ticket offices, and some fifty steps from the cable cars, is the Inn at Union Square.

Only a neat awning and brass plate identify the inn, formerly a 60-room hotel that Norm and Nan Rosenblatt (she an interior decorator by profession) completely remodeled into a very comfortable 27-room inn, all with Georgian furniture, colorful fabrics, private facilities, direct dial telephones, and TV's concealed within stylish armoires.

For guest convenience, each of the four floors has its own common room with fireplaces, icemakers, and refrigerators. It is here or in the guest's room that a continental breakfast of fresh fruits and juices, scones, croissants, and hot drinks is served in the morning, with the latest news and financial papers.

As security is paramount in any centrally located, metropolitan inn, 24-hour desk and concierge service is provided. Access to upper floors is by a keyed elevator.

Most of the well-furnished guest rooms are above adjacent buildings and face east, so natural lighting, while brightest in the morning hours, continues throughout the day. The overlook is made even more pleasing by the colorful flower garden on the neighboring roof. Turndown bed service is provided in the evenings and shoes will be given a gratis shine if placed in the hallway upon retiring.

The inn staff assures constant attention to guests. Earliest possible reservations are necessary.

THE INN AT UNION SQUARE, 440 Post St., San Francisco, CA 94102; 415-397-3510. A 27-guestroom bed-and-breakfast inn in the very heart of San Francisco's fine shops, hotels, and theaters. All rooms with private baths, concealed TV's, and direct dial telephones. Breakfast only meal served. Open year-round. Cable cars a few steps away. Valet parking if desired. Minimal accommodations for children; inquire in advance. No pets. Advance reservations a must. Norm and Nan Rosenblatt, Innkeepers.

Directions: At the Union Square corner of Post and Powell, across from Post St. entrance to St. Francis Hotel.

For B&B rates, see Index.

THE JABBERWOCK
Monterey, California

The whimsy of Lewis Carroll and his Jabberwock poem from *Alice in Wonderland* is matched by the imagination of Barbara and Jim Allen, proprietors of the Jabberwock. They have turned a towered and turreted former convent, built in 1911, into a seven-bedroom bed-and-breakfast inn. Unique touches abound, starting in the foyer with the gumball machine and shoe-shiner set among antiques and oriental rugs, along with a needlepoint wallhanging of the Jabberwock poem.

Opened in March of 1982, Jabberwock is the only bed-and-breakfast in Monterey. Its unique setting overlooking Monterey Bay offers guests a magnificent view. Situated on a quiet corner, the large lot includes a lush garden with a waterfall and ponds.

The homey living room with its wallpaper, antiques, and dark green rug is the place where homemade cookies and milk are set out for the guests after dinner. A glassed-in sunporch with comfortable rattan chairs for reading and tables for puzzles and games offers a wonderful view of Monterey Bay. Fresh flower arrangements adorn all the rooms.

The dining room, with its fireplace and charming wallpaper, has a mirror on the table to help guests read the breakfast menu, printed backwards. Breakfast is Barbara's specialty and she uses made-up names, such as "Razzleberry Flabjous" or "Snarkleberry Flumptious." Breakfast can also be served in the guest's room.

A lovely stained-glass window on the landing helps lead the guests to the bedrooms on the second and third floor, each decorated with flowered wallpapers, antique furniture, goosedown quilts, and lace-trimmed sheets. Some rooms have fireplaces and telescopes or binoculars.

THE JABBERWOCK, 598 Laine St., Monterey, CA 93940; 408-372-4777. A 7-guestroom bed-and-breakfast inn (3 rooms with private bath, 4 share baths) overlooking Monterey Bay. Open year-round. Minimum two nights on weekends, 3 nights at special times, i.e. Monterey Jazz Festival, Crosby Tournament. Mature teenagers accepted. No credit cards. No pets. Jim and Barbara Allen, Innkeepers.

Directions: From San Francisco, take Del Monte Ave. off Highway 1 into Monterey, following signs to Cannery Row through the tunnel to Lighthouse Ave. Turn left on Hoffman and left on Laine. Pick-up service at Monterey Airport.

For B&B rates, see Index.

JOSHUA GRINDLE INN
Mendocino, California

A New Englander searching for a place to remind him of his home should pay a visit to Mendocino. Not only is the spectacular coastal scenery reminiscent of New England, but many of the wooden Victorian homes resemble those built in the Northeast.

In the 1870s, Joshua Grindle, a native of Maine, came to Mendocino to try his hand in the lumber business. He built a beautiful Italianate-style house for his bride in 1879, and went to work at a nearby mill.

Californians Gwen and Bill Jacobson, although not New Englanders, were also taken by the beauty of Mendocino and were delighted to be able to buy the Grindle house in 1977, which they then turned into a gracious bed-and-breakfast inn.

The Joshua Grindle Inn's five guest rooms in the main house all have private baths and are exquisitely decorated with early American furnishings, handmade quilts from New England, etchings, and oil paintings. In a cottage adjacent to the inn are two other bedrooms complete with Franklin fireplace. A recently completed watertower houses two more guest rooms, each with fireplace.

The main visiting room off the entrance is beautifully wallpapered, has a baby grand piano and a fireplace decorated with tiles made in England. Here on a chest there is always a bowl of fresh fruit and sherry provided by the Jacobsons. Hospitality abounds in the dining room, where guests may relax at a long pine table while Gwen serves up a delicious, full continental breakfast, complete with fresh fruit, homemade breads, eggs, coffee, and tea.

As the inn is only a few short blocks from the main street, it is best to set aside time to walk, browse, and explore the many little alleys, paths, shops, art galleries, and historic buildings that make up Mendocino. The inn offers bikes, too, for those who wish to combine sightseeing with a little exercise!

JOSHUA GRINDLE INN, 44800 Little Lake, Mendocino, CA 95460; 707-937-4143. A 9-guestroom (private baths) attractive Victorian inn on California's northern coast. Continental breakfast included in room rate. Open all year. Many cultural, recreational, and historic attractions nearby. No telephone, no television. Children discouraged. No pets. No credit cards. Gwen and Bill Jacobson, Innkeepers.

Directions: Starting from San Francisco, travel on Hwy. 101 north to Cloverdale, then Rte. 128 and take Hwy. 1 north to Mendocino. Alternate route is to take scenic Hwy. 1 north to Mendocino.

For B&B rates, see Index.

LA RESIDENCE
Napa, California

In a two-acre country setting with large, old magnolias and California live oaks, a few miles north of Napa, sits La Residence, a three-story Gothic Revival- style house with a Southern flavor. Built in 1870 by Harry C. Parker, a New Orleans river pilot who came to California during the 1849 gold rush, this beautiful house with its wide, columned porch has been turned into a very special bed-and-breakfast inn by its proprietor, Barbara Littenberg.

With her background as both fashion designer and archaeologist, and influenced by English country inns, Barbara has decorated La Residence in the style of a nineteenth-century country house, with fresh flowers in each room, antique armoires, sofas and queen-size replicas of brass and cast-iron beds covered with quilted eyelet or floral spreads and ruffled pillows. Each bedroom has its own sitting area.

Several of the seven bedrooms have marble or brick fireplaces and all have large windows. Four rooms have private baths. Two large second-floor rooms have french doors leading to the balcony at the front of the house. The smaller, but cozy and charming third-floor rooms have wallpapered eaves. There is central air conditioning throughout.

An additional building completed in 1984, the Barn, has eight rooms with private baths and fireplaces. Furnished in English pine furniture with English chintzes and French fabrics, each room has a sitting area. The country French dining room is the setting for the complimentary continental breakfasts of fresh orange juice, cheese and cold cuts, croissants, tea or coffee, as well as for dinners. The kitchen in the main house is available to guests for preparing snacks.

LA RESIDENCE, 4066 St. Helena Highway North (Hwy. 29), Napa, CA 94558; 707-253-0337. A 7-guestroom (4 private baths) Gothic Revival country house just north of Napa in the wine country. Also 8 guestrooms (private baths) in the Barn. Wheelchair access to some rooms. Continental breakfast included in rate. Open all year. Minimum stay of 2 nights on weekends. Convenient to wineries and all the other attractions of the Napa Valley. No telephones or television. No children. No pets. Barbara Littenberg, Innkeeper.

Directions: Take Highway 29 beyond Napa, past Salvador Rd., turn right at Bon Apetit Restaurant, where a sign will take you to the inn, which faces the highway.

For B&B rates, see Index.

LARKMEAD COUNTRY INN
Calistoga, California

Tucked away off Larkmead Lane, midway between Highway 29 and the Silverado Trail, is Larkmead Country Inn, perhaps one of the valley's most peaceful retreats and best-kept secrets. The country inn is incognito; there are no signs, but the clue is that it's adjacent to the famous Kornell Winery. And after entering through two massive fieldstone gates, there is another hint - just next to the house is a wooden plaque that reads, "Parking near the Loggia." Now you'll know you've found your new home!

The house, which is almost completely surrounded by vineyards and a number of magnolias and sycamore trees, is a large clapboard Victorian built in 1918 by Mr. Elmer Salmina. Larkmead Vineyards, before the house was built, were owned by San Francisco's Lillie Coit, the lady best known for her fascination with the fire brigade and Coit Tower, built in her memory. In 1979, Gene and Joan Garbarino bought the house as their home, and soon after decided it would be perfect as a bed-and-breakfast inn.

A flight of stairs leads to the living room, which is tastefully furnished in European antiques, Persian carpets, and interesting oils and etchings. This understated elegance gives one the feeling of visiting in the home of a well-to-do relative. Yet one cannot help but feel comfortable in these genteel surroundings, as Joan and Gene and their able innkeeper assistant, Pat Lewis, are extremely adept at making one feel at home.

The four guest rooms, all with private baths, are named after wines—Chablis, Beaujolais, Chenin Blanc, and Chardonney. Each room is tastefully decorated with beautiful wallpaper, fabrics, and antiques, and all have spectacular views.

A continental breakfast, complete with sterling silver and china, is served either in the guest's room or in the stately dining room adjacent to the living room.

LARKMEAD COUNTRY INN, 1103 Larkmead Lane, Calistoga, CA 94515; 707-942-5360. A 4-guestroom Victorian home in the Napa Valley. Continental breakfast. Open all year. Central air conditioning. Close to many famous wineries. No pets. No credit cards. Gene and Joan Garbarino, Innkeepers.

Directions: From Hwy. 29, go 4 1/2 mi. north of St. Helena; turn right on Larkmead Lane.

For B&B rates, see Index.

THE PELICAN INN
Muir Beach, California

The thin line on your map (probably red in color) that runs adjacent to the Pacific Ocean along most of the length of California is the famous Coastal Route 1. After you cross the Golden Gate Bridge in San Francisco, follow Route 101 north to the Mill Valley exit, turn left at the traffic lights, and there is Route 1 waiting for you to enjoy its curves and undulations all the way to Rockport where it goes inland and becomes part of Route 101 again at Leggett. This scenic route offers spectacular views of the Pacific at almost every turn of the road. There are several B&Bs located on this road and among them I have chosen three.

The first is actually about twenty minutes from the Golden Gate Bridge and is as romantic a country inn as can be imagined this side of England's west country.

The innkeeper, Charles Felix, is as he proudly announces "the son of a publican" and with his distinctive white hair and moustache, there's no mistaking him as he moves among the patrons in the low-ceilinged dining room with its heavy exposed posts and beams, beautiful old tables, hutches, and sideboards. These have been sent over from England and many of them are almost two hundred years old. At one end of the dining room there is a great brick Inglenook fireplace complete with a chamber for smoking hams.

The six Tudor-style lodging rooms have exposed beams, white plaster walls, Hogarth prints and English countryside scenes, as well as half-tester beds, and a profusion of fresh flowers.

The breakfast is full and hearty in the true English style complete with "bangers" (sausages), bacon and eggs, broiled tomatoes, and other things dear to the heart of a Briton. The coffee pot is always available and an English tea is served throughout the day.

THE PELICAN INN, Muir Beach, Ca. 94965; 415-383-6000. A 6-room English inn on the northern California coast, 8 mi. from the Golden Gate Bridge. Price of lodging includes breakfast. Lunch and dinner served Tues. thru Sun. Swimming, tennis, backroading, walking, and all San Francisco attractions nearby. Charles and Brenda Felix, Innkeepers.

Directions: From Golden Gate Bridge follow Rte 101 north to the Stinson Beach-Hwy. 1 North exit, turn left at traffic lights and follow Hwy. #1 about 5 or 6 mi. to inn.

For B&B rates, see Index.

PETITE AUBERGE
San Francisco, California

The attractions of San Francisco, combined with the comforts of a centrally located inn, just three blocks from Union Square, and appropriately named Petite Auberge, add up to an assured formula for enjoyment in everyone's "favorite city."

Sally and Roger Post, owners of three other successful inns on the Monterey Peninsula, purchased an old, five-story hotel, gutted its insides, and then fashioned a 26-room, truly French- style country inn. From the moment I walked into the attractive entrance area with its antique carousel horse and multi-colored helium balloons tied to the neck, a Post-owned-inn trademark, I knew a unique lodging experience was at hand. The female staff, outfitted in chic Pierre Deux dresses, carried out the French theme to perfection.

Before being shown to my room, I inspected the lower guest lounge, with its comfortable seating arrangement around the fireplace, and the adjacent breakfast room, with tables for two and four opening onto a small, flowered courtyard. A sumptuous breakfast buffet is offered each morning with fresh fruits, cereals, and fresh breads and pastries from the inn's own kitchen. An icemaker and refrigerator, the latter containing gratis soft drinks, are always available for guests to use.

The bedrooms are reached by an old-fashioned cage elevator, its brass bars shined to perfection and affording a view of each floor as you ascend. My room was comfortably furnished with an inviting, quilted bed coverlet, windows draped and louvered, a gas fireplace, and the TV cleverly concealed within an armoire. A small sign informed me my shoes would be carefully shined were I to set them in the hallway before retiring. After dinner at a small nearby restaurant, I found my bed neatly turned down with a fresh flower on the pillow. Needless to say, you are well cared for at the Petite Auberge.

PETITE AUBERGE, 863 Bush St., San Francisco, CA 94108; 415-928-6000. An exceptional French-style 26-guestroom bed-and-breakfast inn (all private baths) just 3 blocks from San Francisco's most fashionable department stores, shops, theaters, and hotels. Cable cars 1 1/2 blocks away. TV and telephones all rooms; 18 with fireplaces. No pets. Earliest possible advance reservations necessary. Karen Tropper, Manager and Innkeeper.

Directions: Between Taylor and Mason on Bush Street.

For B&B rates, see Index.

PUDDING CREEK INN
Fort Bragg, California

Rumor has it that there might be jewels buried on the grounds around Pudding Creek Inn! Could be, as the inn—actually two homes connected by an enclosed garden court—was built in 1884 by a Russian count, who is said to have fled his homeland with riches that were not his own! Marilyn and Gene Gundersen bought the property in the 1970s and soon after they set about restoring and redecorating it. In 1980, they opened the home as a bed-and-breakfast inn.

Pudding Crest Inn has ten guest rooms, all with private baths, and two have original working fireplaces. The rooms, cozy and comfortable, are attractively decorated in a country style and many are paneled in redwood, the native wood lumbered in this area.

On the main floor is a country store and an old-fashioned kitchen, complete with the original cast-iron stove and hand water pump. A continental breakfast, consisting of fresh fruit, juice, Marilyn's delicious homemade coffee cakes and breads, and coffee and teas, is served in this kitchen or in the enclosed court. The enclosed garden area, separating one house from the other, has a little fountain and an abundance of fuchsias, ferns, impatiens, and begonias. In the early evening it's an ideal place to relax and meet the other inn guests and enjoy a glass of wine, compliments of the Gundersens.

Pudding Creek is in a convenient location on Main Street in the north part of Fort Bragg. The ocean, the famous Skunk Train Depot, shops, and restaurants are within easy walking distance of the inn. And the city has much to brag about when it comes to nearby scenic excursions and recreational activities. There is boating, diving, tennis, whale-watching, and fishing. And don't forget, when you feel lucky and adventurous, you could strike it rich by uncovering the count's hidden treasure!

PUDDING CREEK INN, 700 North Main St., Fort Bragg, CA 95437; 707-964-9529. A 10-guestroom (private baths) inn on Ft. Bragg's main street. Continental breakfast included. Open all year. Restaurants nearby. Skunk Railroad, and all the diversions offered by a seaside town nearby. No telephones, no televisions. Children over 10 welcome. No pets. Marilyn and Gene Gundersen, Innkeepers.

Directions: Driving from the south, take Hwy. 101 to Cloverdale, then Rte. 128 west to Hwy. 1, and continue north to Fort Bragg. Inn is located at the north end of the city.

For B&B rates, see Index.

RED CASTLE INN
Nevada City, California

This section of California, which is reached most conveniently by Interstate 80, the main highway between the California coast and Reno, Nevada, has already accumulated enough history to last a millennium.

The lure for gold brought thousands of men and women from all over the world to this section beginning in 1849, and today the vacationer is drawn once again into these foothills to visit some of the remarkably well-preserved and restored miners' camps.

Nevada City, with an approximate elevation of 2,800 feet is one of the several towns and villages on Route 49 that has a very unique history associated with the gold rush.

Some of the miners and businessmen struck it rich and a prime example of how the gold was reinvested can be found in the Red Castle which was built in 1860 by a mine owner and civic leader who crossed the plains in 1849.

Today it is a thoroughly enjoyable bed-and-breakfast inn and innkeepers Jerry Ames and Chris Dickman have augmented the already outstanding Gothic Revival house with a very impressive collection of period antiques.

A visit to the Red Castle Inn would be a most unusual and rewarding experience regardless of its location, but the fact that it's in the gold country of California makes it even more so.

RED CASTLE INN, 109 Prospect St., Nevada City, Ca. 95959; 916-265-5135. An 8-room inn located on a hill overlooking one of the great gold rush communities in the foothills of the Sierra Nevada Mountains. Approximately 2800 ft. altitude. Lodgings include continental breakfast (the only meal served). Open year-round. There are numerous historic, cultural, and recreational attractions, all within a very short distance. No recreation on grounds. Hiking, golf, xc skiing nearby. No diversions for small children. German and Spanish are spoken. Jerry Ames and Chris Dickman, Innkeepers.

Directions: Nevada City is on Rte. 49, the Gold Rush Highway. Eastbound: When arriving in town, take Broad St. turnoff. Turn right, and then right again up the hill to the Exxon station. Take a hard left into Prospect St. Westbound: Take Coyote St. turnoff. Turn left down the hill, and left on Broad St., right on Sacramento; up the hill to the Exxon station and a hard left into Prospect.

For B&B rates, see Index.

ROCK HAUS BED AND BREAKFAST INN
Del Mar, California

Ideally situated in the heart of the village of Del Mar, a few furlongs from the Del Mar Race Track and minutes from La Jolla, Rancho Santa Fe, and the Torrey Pines Golf Course, the Rock Haus Bed and Breakfast Inn, an early California, bungalow-style house, has served variously as a private home, a place of worship, a gambling parlor, a hotel, and now as an excellent bed-and-breakfast inn.

Most of the six upstairs guest rooms enjoy a pleasant view of the water. One room, the Whale Watch Room, has a raised bed so guests can watch for those strange, wonderful creatures and also enjoy a beautiful sunset.

The decorations and furnishings reflect Carol and Tom Hauser's preoccupation with the beautiful, tasteful things of life. Furthermore, many of the unique paintings were done by Carol's mother.

The living room at Rock Haus has a low, peaked ceiling, cream walls, and brown beams. Through the living room is the veranda, closed in with glass, also overlooking the Pacific. Breakfasts are served on the veranda and include fresh fruit, juice, muffins, breads, and coffee or tea.

Del Mar is located on AMTRAK, and the inn provides courtesy pick-up at the station.

ROCK HAUS BED AND BREAKFAST INN, 410 15th St., Del Mar, CA 92014; 619-481-3764. An 8-guestroom (2 with private baths; 6 share 3 baths) bed-and-breakfast inn just 2 blocks from the ocean in one of southern California's attractive towns. The Huntsman's Room has a private fireplace. Breakfast, included in the room rate, is the only meal served. Open year-round. Memorial Day to Labor Day, 2-night minimum stay required on weekends. Conveniently located to enjoy all of the many historic, natural, and cultural attractions of southern California. No children. No pets. No smoking. Carol and Tom Hauser, Innkeepers.

Directions: Once in Del Mar inquire for 15th Street.

For B&B rates, see Index.

ROSE VICTORIAN INN
Arroyo Grande, California

California inns come in all shapes, sizes and colors—but probably the most imposing is the Rose Victorian Inn. Originally a private home, this four-story house of Victorian Italian stick architecture was built by Charles and Henrietta Pitkin in 1885. It is located in the quiet, rural community of Arroyo Grande, midway between San Francisco and Los Angeles on California's central coast.

The mansion, painted in four shades of rose, is surrounded by more than 200 multi-colored rose bushes, all within a white picket fence. A rose arbor and gazebo are popular spots for weddings and receptions.

Each of the eight bedrooms, equipped with queen- or king-sized beds, is named after a variety of rose and decorated accordingly. They are bright and sunny and some have a glimpse of the ocean on clear days.

A hearty breakfast, served in the formal dining room, consists of croissants with meaty fillings, eggs Benedict or Florentine, rotated to offer variety. A restaurant behind the inn is open to the public for dinner and Sunday brunch, and offers menus that include fresh vegetables from the inn's garden, and a wide selection of entrees, reputed to be "the best food in the county." A gift and antique shop is also on the premises.

Surfing, sport fishing, beach walking at nearby Pismo Beach and visiting the area's excellent wineries offer plenty to do.

ROSE VICTORIAN INN, 789 Valley Rd., Arroyo Grande, CA 93420; 805-481-5566. An 8-guestroom (private and shared baths) Victorian mansion on the central California coast. Full breakfast and dinner included in room rate. Open all year. Restaurant open to the public for dinner Tues. thru Sun. and Sun. brunch. Surfing, sport fishing, beach walking, wineries nearby. Children over 16 welcome. No pets. No smoking except in restaurant. Ross and Diana Cox, Innkeepers.

Directions: From south: Take Los Berros Rd. exit from Hwy. 101 to Valley Rd. Inn on the immediate right. From north: Take the Fair Oaks exit from Hwy. 101, turn right at Fair Oaks and turn left on Valley Rd.

For rates, see Index.

SAN ANTONIO HOUSE
Carmel, California

Carmel has been described as one of the jewels of the California coastline. Nature has provided the setting—the surging Pacific Ocean, a crescent-shaped sweep of sandy beach, a dramatic shoreline embroidered with the delightful and colorful flora that abounds in the region.

Fortunately, the planners of Carmel have also intelligently augumented this heaven-bestowed natural beauty with protective laws that should preserve Carmel's beauty indefinitely.

Couple all of the above with the attractive shops, stores, galleries, and restaurants, and it will become evident why Carmel is such a popular destination for holiday-seekers.

Located just one block from the beach, the newly renovated San Antonio House, a circa 1900 three-story brown shingle quite reminiscent of New England, can provide a bed-and-breakfast experience that is entirely in keeping with the Carmel ambience. Set in a gentle grove of Monterey pines, with a handsome, large holly tree, colorful gardens and stone terraces, this little cottage has four spacious suites, all of which have their own woodburning fireplaces and refrigerators. Guests will also find a decanter of sherry, a coffee pot and fresh ground coffee and tea. Each of these rooms has been most tastefully furnished with antiques by Karen Levett, who, with her husband, Dennis, has carefully supervised the rejuvenation of this quiet, conservative, small guest house.

Continental breakfast is served in your suite and this is one of the few places where the word "continental" is truly defined, since the breakfast features two kinds of cheeses, juices, warm, freshly made breads or muffins, hard-boiled eggs, and fresh fruit. There is even a special breakfast salami, as well.

If you are planning a visit to Carmel, the San Antonio house would be a wonderful place to stay.

SAN ANTONIO HOUSE, San Antonio Road, Carmel, Ca. 93921; 408-624-4334. A graceful bed-and-breakfast inn with four guest suites. Continental breakfast served to houseguests only. Open all year. Conveniently located for the beach, the shops and galleries of Carmel, and all of the recreational offerings of the area. Karen and Dennis Levett, Bob Anderson, Innkeepers.

Directions: Turn into Ocean Ave. from Rte. 1, and proceed toward the ocean, turning left on San Antonio. There is a discreet sign in front of the inn.

For B&B rates, see Index.

THE SANDPIPER INN AT-THE-BEACH
Carmel-by-the-Sea, California

Carmel-by-the-Sea! Even the name has a melodious, inviting sound and I can assure many of our readers who have never visited Carmel that it is an experience to be treasured. South of San Francisco and north of Big Sur on U.S. 1, the California coastal highway, Carmel's gentle weather, beautiful homes and *chic* shops make it a very popular vacation area and I would suggest that reservations be made well in advance for even a short stay.

The Sandpiper Inn, fifty yards from Carmel Beach, is in many respects similar to a British country house. In fact, both Irene and Graeme Mackenzie are Scottish. There are country house touches, including great pots of flowers and overflowing window boxes and eye-catching quilts and pleasant draperies and colorful pictures.

Accommodations are in fifteen handsomely furnished rooms and cottages all with comfortable beds and private bathrooms. Some have views of Carmel Beach and others have woodburning fireplaces.

Guests congregate in front of the beautiful stone fireplace in the living room which has a distinctive cathedral ceiling. Many of them have come to Carmel to test the challenge of the area's famous golf courses.

Breakfast may be served in a number of different places. For example, it may be enjoyed by the fire in the living room/library or it can be taken on a tray to the bedroom or the patio. Breakfast leads off with sugar-free chilled orange juice, two hot fresh-baked danish pastries, and a wide assortment of breakfast beverages.

THE SANDPIPER INN at-the-Beach, 2408 Bayview Ave. at Martin St., Carmel-by-the-Sea, Ca. 93923; 408-624-6433. A 15-room bed-and-breakfast inn near the Pacific Ocean. Open all year. Breakfast only meal offered. Carmel and Stuarts Cove beaches, Old Carmel Mission, Point Lobos State Reserve, 17-Mi. Drive, and Big Sur State Park nearby. Ten-speed bicycles available; jogging and walking on beach. Arrangements to play at nearby private golf and tennis clubs with pools and hot tub. Children over 12 welcome. Please no pets. Graeme and Irene Mackenzie, Innkeepers.

Directions: From the north, on Hwy. 1 turn right at Ocean Ave. through Carmel Village and turn left on Scenic Dr. (next to ocean), proceed to end of beach to Martin St. and turn left.

For B&B rates, see Index.

THE SEAL BEACH INN & GARDENS
Seal Beach, California

The Seal Beach Inn & Gardens is a classic, old world, French Mediterranean-style bed-and- breakfast inn located in a lovely little seaside village. Each one of the twenty-four rooms of the inn is unique, with a character of its own, filled with antiques and objets d'art.

Location is a bonus, for the inn is just 300 yards from the beach and, via the freeway, only a short distance from all major Southern California attractions, such as Disneyland, Knott's Berry Farm, Marineland, Universal Studios tour, and others.

A complimentary continental breakfast, consisting of freshly baked croissants, muffins, and strudels, along with fresh- squeezed orange juice and imported blends of coffee, is served each morning in the tea room or by the pool. The inn also features lovely garden areas replete with fascinating architectural artifacts.

THE SEAL BEACH INN & GARDENS, 212 5th St., Seal Beach, CA 90740; 213-493-2416. A 24-guestroom classic country inn located in a quiet seaside village, 300 yards from beach. Breakfast only meal served. Open all year. Swimming pool. Near Disneyland, Knott's Berry Farm, Lion Country Safari, Catalina Island (20 mi. offshore) with California mountains and lakes two hours away. Long Beach Playhouse, Music Center, tennis, biking, skating, golf, parks nearby. No pets. Marjorie and Jack Bettenhausen, Innkeepers.

Directions: From Los Angeles Airport take Freeway 405 south to Seal Beach Blvd. exit. Turn left toward the beach, right on the Pacific Coast Highway; left on 5th St. in Seal Beach, which is the first stoplight after Main St. Inn on corner of 5th and Central Ave.

For B&B rates, see Index.

THE SHAW HOUSE INN
Ferndale, California

The Shaw House, built in 1854 by the founder of Ferndale, is very much in place in this preserved-restored Victorian village, which is a historic landmark.

Recognized in an architectural guide as "a perfect Victorian Gothic Revival Cottage," the gabled entrance is flanked by two smaller gables on each side. The house has seven gables altogether. The wide clapboards are tastefully accentuated by blue trim, and the house sits back from the main street behind a discreet, low, white fence.

Innkeeper Velna Polizzi moved to Ferndale from Santa Cruz a few years ago and started renovating and decorating this handsome house. There are five bedrooms; three share one bath. The honeymoon suite has its own bath, as well as a honeymoon bed that has always been in this house. Velna explains that Mr. Shaw was a justice of the peace, and when he married couples he let them stay in his bed.

The inn abounds with splendid antiques, fresh flowers, magazines, and fruit, and the bedrooms have a very pleasant cozy feeling nestled underneath the gables. The library is exceptional, with thousands of books on every subject from antiques to zoology.

Breakfasts are on the generous side and always include a hot dish, sometimes fresh ranch eggs with bacon or local sausage. There is always a protein and a fruit dish. This is served in the dining room or, on exceptionally pleasant days, on the little deck overlooking the Francis Creek.

Ferndale, besides having many crafts studios, shops, galleries, and restaurants, also boasts a village playhouse. There are pleasant hiking trails nearby, and many walks within the town from which to enjoy its historic homes and delightful gardens.

THE SHAW HOUSE INN, P.O. Box 250, 703 Main St., Ferndale, Ca. 95536; 707-786-9958. A 5-bedroom bed-and-breakfast inn (shared baths) in a most pleasant town just south of Eureka. Open all year. Conveniently located to enjoy the many recreational, cultural, and historic attractions of the northern California coast. Adults only. No pets. No smoking. No credit cards. Velna Polizzi, Innkeeper.

Directions: Leave Highway 101 at the directional sign for Ferndale, which is to the west.

For B&B rates, see Index.

THE SPRECKELS MANSION
San Francisco, California

Amongst the prestigious families of San Francisco's late 19th century, none had greater prominence than that of sugar baron, Claus Spreckels. In 1898 he built a stately mansion of the Colonial Revival style on the northern slope of the city's Twin Peaks, directly across the green, expansive lawns of Buena Vista Park. For more than eighty years it has been maintained as a single family home with a succession of artistic people in residence, including Jack London. Even in a city with more than a thousand Victorian buildings, San Franciscans have always looked upon the home with reverence and awe. When advertised for sale in 1979, two talented young men, Jeffrey Ross and Jonathan Shannon, were first in line for its acquisition and have since turned it into a spectacular inn.

As I ascended the front steps to the columned portal area, I experienced a sense of anticipation that was further heightened by the Corinthian columns, Meissen chandeliers, and leaded, stained glass windows in both the hall and parlor.

The bedrooms all have queen-sized beds and most have working fireplaces, for there are seven fireplaces in all, including one in front of the free-standing tub of the Sugar Baron Suite bathroom.

A handsome Edwardian building next door, built in 1897 as a wedding present for one of the Spreckels children, has also been acquired and is now part of the inn.

Each morning trays and breakfast baskets of fresh juice, croissants, and coffee are brought to the bedrooms, and wine is served in the library in early evening.

THE SPRECKELS MANSION, 737 Buena Vista West, San Francisco, CA 94117; 415-861-3008. A 10-guestroom (8 with private baths) imposing and elegant Victorian mansion and an adjacent, equally grand Edwardian mansion on quiet, residential Buena Vista Hill, above San Francisco. Breakfast, included in room tariff, is the only meal served, but recommendations to the many fine restaurants are available. Open year-round. Within 15 min. of the city: Union Square, the Waterfront. Golden Gate Park with its museums and gardens nearby. No children. No pets. No cigars. Direct-dial telephones in all rooms. Jeffrey Ross and Jonathan Shannon, Proprietors.

Directions: Head west on Market St. to Haight, then a right turn to Buena Vista West, adjacent to Buena Vista Park. Wind up the hill to Spreckels Mansion, 737 Buena Vista West.

For B&B rates, see Index.

SUTTER CREEK INN
Sutter Creek, California

Located in California's gold rush country on Route 49, the Sutter Creek Inn was the first B&B inn that I visited in California, and that was back in 1967.

Since that time, innkeeper Jane Way, who is also a graphologist, has become one of the outstanding keepers of such accommodations on the West Coast, and is well known for having a very comfortable and unusual inn.

The building is a replica of a New Hampshire house and was built in this gold rush town during the second half of the 19th century. A beautiful, colorful living room is filled with books and music. Many of the bedrooms have fireplaces, some have canopied beds, some are tailored and simple, and all have private baths.

It is surrounded by green lawns, a grape arbor, and impressive gardens.

Guests are called to breakfast at 9 A.M. when a melodious bell peals forth. Everyone troops into the big kitchen and dining room to sit around the harvest tables. Breakfasts are different each morning, and I've enjoyed such appetizing dishes as scrambled eggs, french toast, pancakes, and the like. Conversation is apt to be animated since everyone easily gets acquainted and is eager to share his or her gold country adventure.

SUTTER CREEK INN, 75 Main St., Box 385, Sutter Creek, Ca. 95685; 209-267-5606. A 17-room New England village inn with a 4-star Mobil rating on the main street of a historic mother lode town, 35 mi. from Sacramento. Lodgings include breakfast. Open all year. Water skiing, riding, fishing, and boating nearby. No children under 15. No pets. Mrs. Jane Way, Innkeeper.

Directions: From Sacramento, travel on the Freeway (50) toward Placerville and exit at Power Inn Rd. Turn right and drive one block, note signs for Rte. 16 and Jackson. Turn left on Fulsom Rd., approx. ¼ mi., follow Rte. 16 signs to right for Jackson. Rte. 16 joins Rte. 49.

For B&B rates, see Index.

TOLL HOUSE INN
Boonville, California

The hilly, partially wooded pastureland between the northern California towns of Boonville and Ukiah for more than a century was the domain of pioneer sheep ranchers. One of the largest was the 2,400-acre spread of the Miller family, who, in 1912, built a headquarters home six miles from Boonville and an access road. The Millers exacted a charge for the use of this road by muleskinners hauling redwood logs to inland mills, so the home became known as the Toll House.

In 1981, Beverly Nesbitt purchased the building as a home and an inn, transforming it into a gracious and restful place, which quite appropriately can be described as the "quintessence of quiescence." The comfortable lounge, the bright and cheery breakfast room, the ascending staircase, and guest rooms are all tastefully decorated in floral prints.

Large redwood patios seem to beckon from every window, and an inviting hammock and secluded hot tub, the latter surrounded by trees, lawn, and colorful flower beds, compete for guest attention.

The professional kitchen in the house would be envied by many restaurants, as one of its former owners, an amateur chef, left nothing to be desired, even including a huge walk-in refrigerator and freezer. This is Beverly's pride and joy, and she turns out what seems to be a never-ending stream of breakfast delicacies each morning, with fresh breads, waffles, pancakes, omelettes, and fresh fruits and juices of the season.

THE TOLL HOUSE INN, P.O. Box 268, Hwy. 253, Boonville, CA 95415; 707-895-3630. A 4-guestroom (2 with private bath and fireplace) former ranch house in the secluded Bell Valley and the Mendocino wine country of northern California. Full breakfast included. Open all year. Dinner available by prior arrangement. Hot tub, sundeck, garden, birdwatching on grounds. Wineries, Mendocino, the Skunk Railway, and Fort Bragg nearby. No children under 10. No pets. No credit cards. Smoking discouraged. Beverly Nesbitt, Innkeeper.

Directions: From the north on U.S. 101, exit Rte. 253 south of Ukiah. Watch for inn on your right about 6 mi. north of Boonville. From the south on U.S. 101 exit Rte. 128 on the northern outskirts of Cloverdale. Upon reaching Boonville, turn right on Rte. 253 and the inn will be on your left after 6 mi.

For B&B rates, see Index.

UNION STREET INN
San Francisco, California

San Francisco is truly one of the great places in the world to visit, or even to live in. It's a good, clean city, easy to get around in, has some great restaurants and is filled with lighthearted people.

While there are some spiffy hotels, to me the way to visit San Francisco is to stay in an elegant B&B and that exactly describes the Union Street Inn and its proprietor Helen Stewart.

Helen is a former San Francisco schoolteacher who restored this handsome turn-of-the-century Edwardian building, using tones and textures that not only are of the period, but also increase the feeling of hospitality.

The bedrooms have intriguing names such as Wildrose, Holly, English Garden, and Golden Gate. Some have private bathrooms and others have shared bathrooms.

During most of the months of the year it's possible to enjoy breakfast on the wooden deck which overlooks the garden. Helen Stewart calls it continental, but it seems pretty hearty to me. There's freshly squeezed orange juice, freshly ground coffee, fresh-baked croissants and an assortment of homemade jams and jellies, including kiwi, pomegranate, wild grape, and assorted plums.

The inn is located in the city's most pleasant shopping and entertainment areas and it's an easy walk to Fisherman's Wharf, Ghirardelli Square, Pier 39, and other downtown San Francisco attractions.

UNION STREET INN, 2229 Union St., San Francisco, Ca. 94123; 415-346-0424. A 5-room bed-and-breakfast inn; 3 rooms share 2 baths. Convenient to all of the San Francisco attractions including the cable car line. Breakfast only meal served. Open every day except Christmas and New Year's. Well-behaved young children are welcome; no accomodations for infants. No pets. Helen Stewart, Innkeeper.

Directions: Take the Van Ness exit from Rte. 101 to Union St.; turn left. The inn is between Fillmore and Steiner on the left side of the street.

For B&B rates, see Index.

VAGABOND'S HOUSE
Carmel-by-the-Sea, California

For most of our Eastern readers, Carmel, California, represents a kind of Arthurian grail, an objective to be achieved, a place to be visited sometime "when we can get away."

Let me assure you that the whole of Monterey Peninsula, which includes Pacific Grove, Monterey, Pebble Beach, Del Monte, Carmel, and Carmel Valley, is just about as beautiful and enjoyable as you can imagine. The sea, beaches, golf courses, mountains, trees, and the flowers, as well as the beautiful homes, make it an Elysian experience. However, there are times when it can be quite crowded.

The Vagabond House, at the corner of Fourth and Dolores Street in Carmel, provides an almost magic withdrawal. It has a three-sided courtyard with many beautiful trees, flowers, and shrubs, and accommodations are in twelve completely different cottage rooms or suites, many of which have their own woodburning fireplaces. These are pleasingly furnished with Early American maple furniture, quilted bedspreads, and antique clocks. Most rooms have kitchens supplied with coffee pots and fresh ground coffee for brewing.

The innkeepers have outdone themselves with a full European breakfast, featuring juices, fresh fruits in season, including strawberries with powdered sugar, kiwis with cream cheese, home-baked muffins and bread, strawberry-whipped butter, jams and jellies, hard-boiled eggs in a silver bowl, and Monterey jack cheese—all of which can be enjoyed in the guest rooms or shared with other guests in the courtyard.

A word of caution: advance reservations are almost always necessary at the Vagabond's House.

VAGABOND'S HOUSE, Fourth & Dolores Streets, P.O. Box 2747, Carmel, Ca. 93921; 408-624-7738 or 408-624-7403. A 12-room village inn serving a full European breakfast to houseguests only. No other meals served. Open every day of the year. Not ideal for children. Attended, leashed pets allowed. Bike renting, golf, natural beauty and enchanting shops nearby. Dennis and Karen Levett, Bruce Indorato, Innkeepers.

Directions: Turn off Hwy. 1 onto Ocean Ave.; turn right from Ocean Ave. onto Dolores, continue 2½ blocks. Parking provided for guests.

For B&B rates, see Index.

VICTORIAN FARMHOUSE
Little River, California

The drive on Highway 1 as it bends and twists on the Mendocino coastline promises the traveler vistas of amazing diversity and beauty. It's a combination of rocky cliffs and sandy beaches alongside sand dunes, forest, and grassland. An inviting stop two miles south of Mendocino is the community of Little River and the Victorian Farmhouse. This house was built by the Dennens in 1877, just at the time Peterson's shipyard was prospering. The shipyards have vanished, but the farmhouse has been completely restored and refurbished by Thomas and Jane Szilasi, and is now a quiet and lovely bed-and-breakfast retreat for the wayfarer.

There are two rooms upstairs, named after the original owners, John Dennen and Emma Dora. Both have views of the orchard and the ocean and share a sitting room. There are also two rooms, each with private bath and fireplace, downstairs in the house. They are both smartly decorated and have private entrances. To reach these rooms, one wanders through a beautiful terraced garden filled with flowers. It's Tom's work of love and it is evident that he has the greenest of thumbs. This lovely, tranquil setting is enhanced by vistas of the apple and pear orchard, and of the ocean.

The Szilasis strive to give their visitors as much privacy as is desired, and a delicious breakfast of fresh fruits, juices, fresh-baked breads, and coffee on elegant chinaware is served in each room.

VICTORIAN FARMHOUSE, Hwy. 1, P.O. Box 357, Little River, CA 95456; 707-937-0697. A 4-guestroom (private baths) Victorian mansion on the Mendocino coast between Mendocino and Elk. Continental breakfast. Open all year. Skunk Railroad, wineries, shops and galleries, canoeing, nature walks, deep sea fishing, golf, horseback riding, whale watching, and much more nearby. No children under 16. No pets. No credit cards. Tom and Jane Szilasi, Innkeepers.

Directions: Two mi. south of Mendocino on the east side of Hwy. 1.

For B&B rates, see Index.

VINTAGE TOWERS
Cloverdale, California

Cloverdale is on Highway 101 at the northern end of the Sonoma County wine country and at the beginning of the Mendocino wine country and coastal redwood area. Route 128 branches west at Cloverdale to the coastal Route 1, Little River, Mendocino, and Fort Bragg. Route 128 east goes into Calistoga and St. Helena, and then continues on over the mountains and is a very picturesque back road.

Vintage Towers is a very pleasant Victorian Queen Anne restoration now on the National Register of Historic Places. Proprietors Tom and Judy Haworth have taken great pains to develop some unusual decor in each of the seven rooms. One is a circus room with a poster from the Altouf Circus and very gay decorations that give it a nice light feeling. The Wicker Tower Suite has a big wicker bedstead and other wicker furniture, and is done in shades of green and white and pale green. Still another room is called the Calico Tower with Renaissance Revival antiques as part of the motif, a twisty, old-fashioned fire escape, and a private balcony.

There's a music room with a player piano, a trumpet, and an old wind-up Victor talking machine, as well as a library where guests can gather.

Breakfast, served in the formal dining room, in the veranda, or in the garden gazebo, consists of egg dishes, fresh pastries, and fruit from their orchard. On Sunday, a full brunch includes champagne.

VINTAGE TOWERS, 302 North Main St., Cloverdale, Ca. 95425; 707-894-4535. A 7-bedroom bed-and-breakfast home in a restored, towered Queen Anne Victorian house. Located in a quiet residential area. Open year-round. Some shared baths. Breakfast the only meal served. Arrangements can be made for tubing trips down the Russian River; also bicycle trips to several local wineries. One hour from the coast. Conveniently located for many cultural, historical, and scenic attractions. Chauffeured limo for airport pick-up and winery tours. Tom and Judy Haworth, Proprietors.

Directions: From Hwy. 101, turn east on First St. and then turn left on Main St. for three blocks.

For B&B rates, see Index.

WASHINGTON SQUARE INN
San Francisco, California

A two-story doctor's office and a pharmacy, both rundown and dilapadated, had a facelift and new lease on life when Norm and Nan Rosenblatt bought them in 1978. The facelift was, in fact, total refurbishing under the guidance of owner-interior decorator Nan Rosenblatt, and the end result was the creation of a charming bed-and-breakfast inn.

Fresh flowers are set in each of the fifteen rooms, ten of which have private baths. The rooms, which vary in size, are a happy blend of antique and contemporary furniture, each decorated in a different color scheme with fabrics of bright, cheery floral patterns. The Rosenblatts are supportive of local artists and, as a result, the inn is filled with original works of talented native painters.

The inn's spacious lobby is dominated by an antique desk, brass chandeliers, and a delicately carved fireplace. It's an ideal place for guests to gather and they do in the later afternoon between 3:30 and 6:00. It is then time for tea served with cucumber sandwiches and homemade shortbread. In the morning, guests may choose between having their breakfast served in bed on a tray complete with a fresh flower, or meeting with others in the lobby to savour freshly squeezed orange juice, hot, flaky croissants, and Italian coffee or herb tea.

Guests are really made to feel welcome and may call upon the inn's manager to make dinner reservations, direct them to the nearest bus, or obtain theater tickets—and if a guest leaves his shoes outside the door at night, he'll find them polished the next morning! The inn has many pluses, among which is its ideal location in the center of the city's North Beach, the colorful Italian district, and across the street from the park, where there's usually something interesting going on!

WASHINGTON SQUARE INN, 1660 Stockton St., San Francisco, CA 94133; 415-981-4220. A 15-guestroom inn (10 with private baths) midway between Union Square and Fisherman's Wharf. Continental breakfast and afternoon tea included. Open year round. Children permitted. No pets. Norm and Nan Rosenblatt, Innkeepers.

Directions: From Rte. 101 take Broadway exit. Turn right onto Columbus Ave. Take right at Stockton and travel 2 blocks to inn, which is at the corner of Filbert and Stockton Sts.

For B&B rates, see Index.

WHALE WATCH INN BY THE SEA
Gualala, California

Whale Watch is a contemporary and newly constructed inn, perched on sheer rock cliffs above the Pacific Ocean on one of the most beautiful sections of northern California's rugged coastline.

If you are fortunate enough to be at one of the inn's many vantage points during winter or early spring, you will observe the two-way migrations of the great gray whales, first southward from their homes in Arctic waters to the birthing deeps of the Gulf of California, and then northward again with their newly born calves. Thus the name, Whale Watch.

A perpendicular staircase, securely fastened to the rock cliff wall, leads to the sheltered rocks and beach below.

The main building, all paneled redwood and glass, has a large hexagonal lounge with free-standing fireplace and flue rising to the center of the peaked ceiling.

A full continental breakfast is served each morning, either here or on the ocean-view, wide deck, and consists of fresh fruit and juices, freshly baked breads or croissants, yogurt or cheese, and a selection of coffee and teas. Even when the Pacific "acts up," and this might enshroud the lounge in wind, fog, or rain, coziness is not lost with a blazing fireplace, comfortable couches, leather chairs, taped stereo music, and myriad games, puzzles, and books.

An adjacent building offers two studio apartments and two suites, all redwood paneled, artfully decorated, with free- standing fireplaces, and fully equipped kitchens. Skylights add to the natural lighting, as do the private decks with their patio furniture, greenery-filled planters, and ocean overview. Guests may choose to enjoy breakfast baskets in their rooms and make unlimited quantities of coffee in their well-stocked kitchens. Eleven more rooms are being added for occupancy in early spring.

WHALE WATCH INN BY THE SEA, 35100 Hwy. 1, Gualala, CA 95445; 707-884-3667. A 17-guestroom (private baths) contemporary, redwood, small inn on rock cliffs over the Pacific Ocean, about 3 hrs. north of San Francisco, in northern California. Extended continental breakfast included. Open all year. Whale watching in winter or early spring. No children. No pets. No smoking in rooms. Aurora Hayes, Innkeeper.

Directions: On the ocean side of Hwy. 1, at Anchor Bay, 5 mi. north of Gualala.

For B&B rates, see Index.

THE WINE COUNTRY INN
St. Helena, California

The sunny Napa Valley of California is one of the happy experiences for San Franciscans and others who wish to make a quick escape from city cares.

In 1975 when Ned and Marge Smith built the Wine Country Inn, which is fashioned after the inns of New England, it was the first such accommodation in the valley. Each of its rooms is oriented to rural views and many overlook the nearby vineyards. Combining the old and the new, all rooms are individually decorated with country antique furnishings and lovely fresh colors reflecting the seasonal moods of the valley.

Jim Smith, now the innkeeper, reports that over the last several years the Napa Valley has become one of the nation's centers for fine dining. Seventeen restaurants within a ten-mile radius of the inn offer outstanding cuisine of various countries and styles.

On beautiful mornings, of which there are many in the Napa Valley, guests may enjoy their continental breakfast on the patio, sitting around the harvest table in the common room, or they can take a tray to their bedrooms. Although the hot sticky buns are my choice, there are many other types of breakfast treats including nut bread, pumpkin bread, raisin-bran muffins, and a selection of fine fruits in season. Breakfast is always a good time to get to know other guests.

THE WINE COUNTRY INN, 1152 Lodi Lane, St. Helena, Ca. 94574; 707-963-7077. A 25-bedroom country inn in the Napa Valley, about 70 mi. from San Francisco. Continental breakfast served to houseguests; no other meals served. Open daily except Dec. 19-25. This inn is within driving distance of a great many wineries and also the Robert Louis Stevenson Museum. Golf and tennis nearby. Not suitable for children. No pets. Jim Smith, Innkeeper.

For B&B rates, see Index.

BRIAR ROSE BED & BREAKFAST
Boulder, Colorado

The enthusiasm for bed-and-breakfast accommodations has reached through all parts of North America, including Colorado. However, the Briar Rose can puff with pride over being the first bed-and-breakfast inn in the most interesting city of Boulder.

The Briar Rose is a lovely little Queen Anne cottage with brick-work on the bottom and fancy shingles up above, with some very attractively ornamented windows. The entryway has a cozy fireplace on the left and a bright sitting room on the right, with carefully chosen Victorian and Regency furniture that blends well with the architecture of the building.

With the recent addition of a small building off the garden, the Briar Rose has eleven bedrooms, six of which have private baths. There are many special touches such as beautiful down comforters on all the beds, baskets of fruit, and many flowers. Several of the rooms have their own private patios.

Breakfast on the sunporch at Briar Rose includes warm, fresh croissants, pastries, European-style yogurt, fresh orange juice, and market-blend coffee. Dinner is available on request, consisting of a single-entrée meal that also includes a salad and simple sweet for dessert. It is not a public restaurant, but arrangements can be made to accommodate the guests.

Visitors to Boulder have unusual opportunities, not only to enjoy its proximity to the great mountains nearby, but also to participate in the very active arts programs for which the community is justly well known. There are regular concert series and chamber music concerts, including occasional informal offerings on Sunday afternoons at the Briar Rose!

BRIAR ROSE BED & BREAKFAST, 2151 Arapahoe Ave., Boulder, Colo. 80302; 303-442-3007. An 11-bedroom inn located in a quiet section of a pleasant, conservative Colorado city, approx. 1 hr. from Denver. Some bedrooms with shared baths. Open all year. Breakfast included in lodging rate. Evening meal available upon request. Afternoon tea served. Convenient for all of the many recreational, cultural, and historic attractions nearby. Limousine service available to and from Denver airport. Emily Hunter, Innkeeper.

Directions: From Denver follow I-25 north and Rte. 36 to Boulder. Turn left on Arapahoe Ave. Briar Rose is on the right on the corner of 22nd St.

For B&B rates, see Index.

THE HEARTHSTONE INN
Colorado Springs, Colorado

The Hearthstone Inn is a magnificent Queen Anne mansion near Pike's Peak in the Colorado Rockies. It is rapidly becoming one of the showplaces of the community. An elaborate building when it was a private home in the 1880s, it has been lovingly restored by Ruth Williams and Dorothy Williams.

The exterior is trimmed in lavender, plum, peach, and bittersweet, all authentic Victorian colors. Dorothy and Ruth bought the dilapidated building in 1977, and as a result of a complete, authentic renovation it has been included on the National Register of Historic Places. In 1982 they were able to acquire the turn-of-the-century home next door, and this has now been restored and refurbished and is a part of the inn.

All of the bedrooms, halls, and landings have their own special decor and each antique piece has been chosen with great care. The quilts on the beds are all handmade.

Careful attention is paid to ensure a completely different breakfast each morning, which is served in the sunny dining room.

The Hearthstone is an excellent center for enjoying all the wonderful advantages of the Pike's Peak area.

THE HEARTHSTONE INN, 506 N. Cascade Ave., Colorado Springs, Co. 80903; 303-473-4413. A 26-room bed-and-breakfast inn within sight of Pike's Peak, located in the residential section of Colorado Springs. A full breakfast is included in the price of the room; only meal served. Open every day all year. Convenient to spectacular Colorado mountain scenery as well as the Air Force Academy, Garden of the Gods, Cave of the Winds, the McAllister House Museum, Fine Arts Center, and Broadmoor Resort. Golf, tennis, swimming, hiking, backroading, and Pike's Peak ski area nearby. Check innkeepers for pet policy. Dorothy Williams and Ruth Williams, Innkeepers.

Directions: From I-25 (the major North/South Hwy.) use Exit 143 (Uintah St.) travel east (opposite direction from mountains) to third stop light (Cascade Ave.). Turn right for 7 blocks. The inn will be on the right at the corner of St. Vrain and Cascade. A big Victorian house, tan with lilac trim.

For B&B rates, see Index.

OUTLOOK LODGE
Green Mountain Falls, Colorado

Outlook Lodge is a country Victorian inn literally on the lower slopes of Pike's Peak. It is only fifteen miles from Colorado Springs, but worlds apart in a great many other ways. The village is at an altitude of almost eight thousand feet, and the inn is next to the historic "Church in the Wildwood."

Impy Ahern, the innkeeper, shows a genuine interest in each of her guests and has an amplitude of friendliness and enthusiasm.

There are bowls of fruit in the twelve bedrooms, hanging plants, bookcases, and dresser scarves which enhance the Victorian atmosphere.

A typical breakfast consists of a choice of two kinds of fruit juices (one always being freshly sqeezed orange juice), fresh fruits, such as strawberries, kiwi, melon, and so forth, homemade breads and other hot offerings, such as scones, cinnamon rolls, and muffins.

Outlook Lodge is convenient to wonderful sightseeing opportunities during all seasons of the year. These include Pike's Peak, The Cog Railway that runs to the top, the old gold-mining town of Cripple Creek, and the Air Force Academy. Back roads have magnificent pine-scented views of the impressive mountain scenery.

OUTLOOK LODGE, 6975 Howard, Green Mountain Falls, Colo. 80819; 303-684-2303. A 12-room rustic lodge on the slopes of Pike's Peak, 15 mi. from Colorado Springs. European plan. All lodgings include continental breakfast. No other meals served. Open from June 1st through Labor Day weekend. Immediately adjacent to all the copious mountain recreational activities as well as the U.S. Air Force Academy; Colorado Springs Fine Arts Center; Cripple Creek Gold Camp. Tennis, swimming, horseback riding, lake fishing, backroading, all nearby. Impy Ahern, Innkeeper.

Directions: Green Mountain Falls is 15 mi. west of Colorado Springs on U.S. 24. Outlook Lodge is located next to the historic Church in the Wildwood.

For B&B rates, see Index.

BEE AND THISTLE INN
Old Lyme, Connecticut

The quiet and peaceful atmosphere of historic Old Lyme encourages guests of the Bee and Thistle to remain for more than one night. That's why it is most appropriate that dinner is served every evening except Tuesday.

Situated in the historic district of the village, the old inn, built in 1756, has yellow clapboards, a garrison roof, and is set well back from the street. It has many fireplaces, antiques, and comfortable bedrooms. It recalls early-American gracious living.

A carved staircase leads to the second-floor bedrooms, all but two of which have private baths, and some have canopy or four-poster beds.

Breakfast (à la carte) is on the porches, or before the fire in the little dining room, and includes freshly squeezed orange juice, a variety of fruits, homemade bigger-than-life muffins, and delicious omelettes. Lunch is also offered with soups, chowders, and other seasonal dishes.

Dinners include hearty New England fare prepared to order and served in a romantic candlelit setting.

The Lieutenant River flows through the back of the property. Bicycles are available and there are several good jogging routes to follow, as well.

BEE AND THISTLE INN, 100 Lyme St. (Rte. 1), Old Lyme, Ct. 06371; 203-434-1667. A 10-bedroom (2 rooms with shared bath) inn located in an as-yet-unspoiled Connecticut village, near the border of Rhode Island. À la carte breakfast served daily. Lunch and dinner daily, except Tuesday. Sunday brunch. Open year-round. Conveniently located to visit Gillette Castle, Goodspeed Opera House, and Essex Steam train and train rides. Mystic Seaport, Essex Village, Ivoryton Summer Theater nearby. No pets. Bob and Penny Nelson, Innkeepers.

Directions: Coming north on I-95 take a left at the bottom of Exit 70. At the first light take a right. At the second light, take a left and then follow Rte. 1 (Lyme Street) to inn.

For Lodging rates, see Index.

BISHOP'S GATE
East Haddam, Connecticut

Guests might fancy they hear the strains of delightful music, so close is Bishop's Gate to the Goodspeed Opera House. And there's more than simply physical proximity (down the hill and around the corner) that forms a bond with the Goodspeed; hostess Julie Bishop has had a long and intimate association with it, as evidenced by her gallery of photographs of stage celebrities who have appeared there.

In her cozy 1818 Colonial house, tucked into a niche in the bustling village of East Haddam, Julie offers the most special of bed-and-breakfast experiences with her own buoyant and infectious brand of hospitality. The recently renovated and redecorated rooms are beautifully furnished with family heirlooms and antiques and oriental rugs adorning the wide pine floorboards.

Four sparkling bedrooms boast working fireplaces; one has a lovely Jenny Lind spool bed with a fishnet canopy; and there is a smashing suite with a cathedral beamed ceiling, an outside sun deck, and a luxurious dressing room and bath with a stall shower and a sauna.

The kitchen-dining room with its Colonial dutch oven and fireplace with a crane is the scene of the breakfast gathering at a long harvest table, where guests might enjoy such delightful offerings as homebaked apple crisp or freshly baked scones with jams and jellies.

East Haddam offers a number of diversions with fine shops and restaurants, tennis, golf, and river cruises—not to mention the musicals at the Goodspeed Opera House from April to the end of November. And, of course, there are the historic and fascinating communities of Essex, Old Lyme, Mystic, and Old Stonington, all within an easy drive.

BISHOP'S GATE, Goodspeed Landing, East Haddam, Ct. 06423; 203-873-1677. A 6-bedroom (2 with shared baths) Colonial home within walking distance of the famed Goodspeed Opera House. Open year-round. Continental breakfast included with room charge. Convenient to all the historic, cultural, and recreational attractions that abound in the area. Not suitable for children under 6. No pets. No credit cards. Julie Bishop, Hostess.

Directions: From NYC or Boston, take I-95 to Exit 69 and Rte. 9. Continue on Rte. 9 to Exit 7 and East Haddam. Just past the Goodspeed Opera House, bear left up the hill on Rte. 149. At the crest of the hill, turn right at the sign for Bishop's Gate, driving down a short hill to parking area in the rear of the building.

For B&B rates, see Index.

THE CANDLELIGHT
Kent, Connecticut

Route 7 is one of the most scenic and enjoyable ways to go from New York City or Connecticut north to the Berkshires and beyond. I would suggest using Route 22 and branching off to the east at Wingdale and picking up Route 7 at Gaylordsville proceeding north.

The Candlelight is a very pleasant stop for bedroom accommodations in the most attractive town of Kent, Connecticut, which, among other things, is the homeground of the artist and author Eric Sloane. In fact, he designed the folder which gives the town history and supplies some most valuable facts about the region.

Kent is also the location of the Kent School and the South Kent School. As a result there are some weekends when there are never any rooms available at the Candlelight; these include Memorial Day weekend, June 7, October 11, and October 26 (or the nearest weekends to those dates).

Because there is a constant flow of prospective students to these schools, The Candlelight is also busy at other times throughout the year, and it is well to reserve ahead. Mr. and Mrs. Edwards told me they have visitors from all over the world who are anxious to place their sons or daughters at these schools.

The four bedrooms at The Candlelight share one and a half baths. They are very pleasantly furnished and it is, indeed, like being in someone's private home.

Breakfasts are not served at The Candlelight, but it so happens that I had breakfast in the little local restaurant which is just about five minutes away on foot. It is very acceptable. An excellent lunch and dinner are served at the Fife and Drum restaurant on the main street of this picturesque Connecticut village.

The road which runs alongside the Housatonic River makes this an exceptionally enjoyable drive. It's worth an overnight stop at The Candlelight just to make the remainder of the journey by daylight.

THE CANDLELIGHT, Kent, Connecticut 06757; 203-927-3407. A 4-room guest house on Rte. 7 in the picturesque Housatonic Valley. One and one-half shared baths available. Call ahead for reservations in order to avoid disappointments. No pets. No credit cards. Albert and Helen Edwards, Proprietors.

Directions: Kent is about two and a half hours from New York City on Rte. 7. It sits on the east side of the main street, back of a rather broad lawn and it is almost across the street from a white carpenter Gothic church.

For Lodging rates, see Index.

67

CURTIS HOUSE
Woodbury, Connecticut

A great many of the houses in Woodbury, including several built in the 1600s, are of white clapboard. In such an atmosphere it is hardly surprising that Woodbury is well known for its many antique shops and small galleries. It is also the site of the Glebe House, the birthplace of American Episcopacy. Woodbury's churches today are classic in their simplicity and are beautifully restored and maintained by active members.

In such a setting it's not strange to find the Curtis House which is distinguished by a large sign designed by Wallace Nutting, who has included many of the Woodbury buildings in his book, *Connecticut the Beautiful.*

The Curtis House, under the watchful eye of its genial innkeeper, Chet Hardisty, has been serving locals and travelers longer than any other inn in Connecticut, vying for this reputation with the Griswold Inn in Essex.

There are many comfortable four-poster beds above stairs, wide pine boards underfoot, and many early artifacts made in Connecticut adorn the rooms.

Lunches and dinners are hearty affairs and this makes it a convenient first stop from New York City.

The continental breakfast is a "help-yourself arrangement" served in the lounge or dining room.

CURTIS HOUSE, Route 6 (Main St.), Woodbury, Conn. 06798; 203-263-2101. An 18-room village inn, 12 mi. from Waterbury. Open year-round. European plan. Lodgings include continental breakfast. Lunch and dinner served daily except Christmas. Antiquing, skiing, tennis, horseback riding nearby. Lodgings not adaptable to young children. No pets. The Hardisty Family, Innkeepers.

Directions: From N.Y. take Sawmill River Pkwy. to I-84. Take Exit 15 from I-84 in Southbury. Follow Rte. 6 north to Woodbury. From Hartford take I-84 to Exit 17, follow Rte. 64 to Woodbury.

For B&B rates, see Index.

GRISWOLD INN
Essex, Connecticut

On I-95 at New Haven, on what we refer to as the "New England Corridor," the traveler is faced with the choice of either following I-91 north to Sturbridge and on to Maine on I-495, or following I-95 to the eastern end of Connecticut and across Rhode Island and north to Boston and beyond. One of the reasons to take the latter course would be to stop at Essex, Connecticut, to enjoy the Griswold Inn.

The main building of the inn was the first three-story structure in Connecticut, and, with the exception of the removal of the second-floor gallery, the building has remained structurally unchanged for two centuries.

During the War of 1812, the inn was occupied by British mariners who burned the entire Essex fleet.

Today, Essex is mainly a residential, yachting, and holiday area and is particularly well known for its unusual number of very pleasant shops and boutiques.

In summer, sailors from the world over make Essex a port of call.

Guests are comfortably ensconced in antique-furnished country inn lodging rooms. Breakfasts are informal and guests can wander down to the library-dining room and help themselves to orange juice, coffee, and toasted english muffins.

The dinner menu is basically American with a wide selection of fish, beef, and lamb dishes. Every Sunday a Hunt Breakfast is served featuring great tables of fried chicken, herring, lamb, kidneys, eggs, creamed chipped beef, and the inn's own brand of 1776® sausage.

GRISWOLD INN, Main St., Essex, Conn. 06426; 203-767-0991. A 22-room inn in a waterside town, steps away from the Connecticut River, and located near the Eugene O'Neill Theatre, Goodspeed Opera House, Ivoryton Playhouse, Gillette Castle, Mystic Village, Valley Railroad and Hammonasset State Beach. All rooms with private baths. European plan. Complimentary continental breakfast served daily to inn guests. Lunch and dinner served daily to travelers. Hunt breakfast served Sundays. Closed Christmas Eve and Christmas Day. Day sailing on inn's 44-foot ketch by appointment. Bicycles, tennis, and boating nearby. Victoria and William G. Winterer, Innkeepers.

Directions: From I-95 take Exit 69 and travel north on Rte. 9 to Exit 3, Essex. Turn right at stoplight and follow West Ave. to center of town. Turn right onto Main St. and proceed down to water and inn.

For B&B rates, see Index.

THE HOMESTEAD INN
Greenwich, Connecticut

Forty-five minutes from Manhattan on the much-traveled NYC-New Haven-Boston corridor, the Homestead Inn sits in a quiet, residential area surrounded by old trees and lovely homes. A sophisticated inn with antique-filled rooms and old chestnut beams, it was originally a 1799 farmhouse that had been Victorianized and made into an inn a hundred years ago. Neglected and tired in 1979, it was purchased by its present owners and completely renovated by the eminent New York City designer, John Saladino. Now it has lovely bedrooms, each with its own bath, cozy public rooms, and a famous French restaurant that serves dinner seven nights per week and luncheon Monday through Friday. Continental breakfast—croissants, preserves, orange juice, and coffee—is served on the sunny enclosed porch, and is included in the price of the rooms.

Patronized by a variety of travelers: executives visiting the many corporate headquarters in the area, inn-lovers on their way through New England, European tourists, and escapees from the hectic pace of New York City—the Homestead extends a warm welcome to those who seek a sophisticated country charm at the very gateway to New England.

THE HOMESTEAD INN, 420 Field Point Rd., Greenwich, CT 06830; 203-869-7500. A 13-guestroom, elegant inn located in the residential area of a suburb, 45 min. from New York City in one direction and New Haven in the other. Continental breakfast included in room rate. Luncheon served Mon. thru Fri. Dinner served daily, save for a few holidays. Located a short distance from Connecticut countryside, shore scenes, and many corporate headquarters. Easily accessible by train or car from NYC. Lodgings not adaptable for young children. No pets. Lessie B. Davison, Nancy K. Smith, Innkeepers.

Directions: Rte. I-95 to Exit 3 to Greenwich. Off ramp, turn west toward the railroad bridge and take a left (just before the bridge) onto Horseneck Lane. Drive to the end, and turn left onto Field Point Rd. The inn is 1/4 mi. on your right.

For B&B rates, see Index.

THE INN AT CHESTER
Chester, Connecticut

Here's a place early-bird risers will appreciate. Because inn-keeper David Joslow had to suffer boredom and impatience waiting for breakfast in his far-flung travels, he determined this would never happen in his inn. Consquently, early risers at the Inn at Chester are able to enjoy a real bargain in the form of a special early-morning repast of two eggs, toast, and coffee served upstairs from 6:30 to 7:30 every morning. This is in addition to the later breakfasts available in the dining room at "more normal" hours.

The original clapboard farmhouse has evolved in style and size far beyond its 1778 origins, and today the inn fuses such diverse elements as period and antique furnishings, barnboard siding, and a thirty-foot stone wall with a fireplace into an eclectic, contemporary look.

Bedrooms in the original building have a quaint, old-fashioned feeling with under-the-eaves ceilings, while those in the new wing seem more modern. All are tastefully furnished and have private baths.

Diversions of all kinds abound both inside and out, with a billiard table in the game room, an exercise room and sauna, a tennis court, trails that lead into Cockaponset State Forest, and nearby Cedar Lake, to which inn guests are given a beach pass.

Meals in the several handsome dining rooms are definitely top-drawer, prepared by an accomplished chef with everything made from scratch, including the freshest of produce and home-baked breads and pastries. The cornsticks are scrumptious.

THE INN AT CHESTER, 318 Main St. (Rte. 148), Chester, Ct. 06412; 203-526-9494. A 22-bedroom inn 5 mi. from the town of Chester. European plan. Breakfast not included in room tariff. Breakfast, lunch, and dinner served daily to travelers. Sunday brunch at 11:30 A.M. Open year-round. Many recreational and cultural activities, including backroading, antiquing, sailing, golf, and fishing nearby. Tennis, nature walks, xc skiing (when there is snow) on grounds. Children welcome (cribs available). David Joslow, Innkeeper; Betsy Wettish, Manager.

Directions: From NYC or Boston on I-95, take Exit 69; take Route 9 north to Exit 6. Turn left on Rte. 148 and continue 3 mi. Inn is on right. From Hartford on I-91, take Rte. 9 south to Exit 6. Turn right on Rte. 148 and continue 3 mi.

For Lodging rates, see Index.

OLD RIVERTON INN
Riverton, Connecticut

Riverton is a small, late 18th- and early 19th-century village typical of the many that thrived in northwest Connecticut 150 or more years ago. Today, besides the Old Union Church which is now the museum, visitors to Riverton can enjoy several excellent antique shops, craft galleries, the Hitchcock factory store, the Seth Thomas factory outlet, and especially the Old Riverton Inn, which has been providing for the "hungry, thirsty, and sleepy" since 1796.

The inn was restored in 1937, much as it might have been at its original opening. However, the popularity of this village inn necessitated the addition of a wing and some remodeling. The combination of the old floors and fireplaces and the old hemlock beams with modern decor has created a very pleasant atmosphere.

The many visitors to the Hitchcock Chair Factory, which is just a short stroll across the river, find it most convenient to plan either luncheon or dinner at this inn. Overnight visitors have the added advantage of a full complimentary breakfast of bacon, eggs, toast, juice, and coffee.

It is well to note that the Old Riverton Inn dining rooms are closed on Mondays, but open all the remaining days of the week. Overnight accommodations are available every evening.

Traditional furniture for every room may be found in the Hitchcock Chair Factory store in Lambert Hitchcock's original factory.

The area abounds in wonderful scenic drives, including trips to the Saville Dam, the Granville State Forest, and the village of Winchester.

OLD RIVERTON INN, Route 20, Riverton, Ct. 06065; 203-379-8678. A restored 18th-century inn about 3½ miles northeast of Winstead, Ct., in a most pleasant northwest Connecticut village. Complimentary breakfast offered to overnight guests. Lunch and dinner served every day except Mon. Open year-round, except first 2 weeks in Jan. A few steps from the Hitchcock Chair Factory Store and several other small shops. Excellent for browsing. Cross-country skiing, white-water canoeing, downhill skiing, golfing, tennis, backpacking, hunting, nearby. Mark and Pauline Telford, Innkeepers.

Directions: Riverton is located 3½ mi. northeast of Winstead on Rte. 20. Winstead is on Rte. 44, the main road from Salisbury to Hartford.

For B&B rates, see Index.

SHORE INNE
Groton Long Point, Connecticut

Even if Mystic, Connecticut, with its restored seaport, marine life aquarium, museum, submarine memorial, and many interesting shops, were not nearby, the Shore Inne is a delightful place to stay overnight or for as long as two weeks.

This white clapboard building overlooks the water, and there's even a beautiful copper beech tree shading some wooden benches, tables, and chairs, where you can eat lunch and enjoy the ocean view.

Innkeeper Helen Ellison says, "My location is unique and superb and the beaches here are as beautiful as you'll find in Connecticut. It's not the Caribbean, but the water is pure, the beach is lovely, there are eight tennis courts nearby, and we're just three-and-a-half miles from Mystic Seaport.

"We're solidly booked in advance during July and August, but June, September, and October are more quiet and we can probably accommodate a certain number of people who want to stay for just one night. Of course, they frequently stay longer when they realize how unusual we are."

Helen has had so many requests for her buttermilk bran muffins served piping hot every morning that she's happy to supply every guest with a copy of the recipe. It's quite simple—I've made them myself.

SHORE INNE, 54 East Shore Rd., Groton Long Point, Ct. 06340; 203-536-1180. A 7-bedroom waterside guest house in a very quiet residential area (3 rooms with private baths). Open every day from March 15 to Nov. 15. Continental breakfast is the only meal served. Mystic Seaport, Mystic Marine Life Aquarium, Fort Griswold, Coast Guard Academy, swimming, fishing, sunning, biking, tennis nearby. No pets. Helen Ellison, Proprietor.

Directions: Going east on I-95 take Exit 88 and turn right on Rte. 117 to Rte. 1, then left. Turn right on Rte. 215 (do not go toward Noank). Take first left after the Yankee Fisherman Restaurant to East Shore Rd. Park in rear off Middlefield St.

For B&B rates, see Index.

SILVERMINE TAVERN
Norwalk, Connecticut

The Silvermine Tavern at various times has served as a country inn, a gentleman's country seat, and a town meeting place. It has a very large outdoor dining area overlooking the Silvermine River and the mill pond with ducks and swans. Summer terrace dining among the oaks, maples, pines, and poplar trees is very popular. I like the Silvermine in the winter, also, when the many fireplaces are crackling and the candles create a romantic feeling.

Some of the New England dishes on the menu include Indian pudding, bread pudding, honeybuns, native scrod, lobster, scallops, and oysters.

On the second floor, which is reached by a winding staircase, there are typical country inn bedrooms without televisions or telephones. There are other lodging rooms to be found in nearby buildings that are a part of the tavern complex.

The continental breakfast in the dining room fortunately includes the famous honeybuns as well as juice, fresh fruit, and lots of coffee. During clement weather it's fun to wander out on the deck and look over the mill pond.

SILVERMINE TAVERN, Perry Ave., Norwalk, Ct. 06850; 203-847-4558. A 10-room country inn in the residential section of Norwalk. Long Island Sound and beaches 6 mi. away. European plan includes continental breakfast. Lunch and dinner served to travelers daily. Open year-round. Closed Christmas Day and Tuesdays during winter. Golf, tennis, and fishing nearby. Francis C. Whitman, Innkeeper.

Directions: From New York or New Haven via I-95, take Exit 15. Pick up the new Rte. 7 going north. At the end of Rte. 7 (approx. 1 mi.) turn right, go to first stoplight, turn right. At next stoplight by firehouse turn right onto Silvermine Ave. Proceed down Silvermine Ave. about 2 mi. to Tavern. From I-84 and Danbury take old Rte. 7 south to Norwalk. At the first traffic light south of the Merritt Pkwy. (approx. ½ mi.) turn right onto Perry Ave. Continue 2½ mi. to the Tavern. From the Merritt Pkwy., take Exit 39 onto Rte. 7 and follow above directions.

For B&B rates, see Index.

WEST LANE INN
Ridgefield, Connecticut

Nestled among the gently rolling wooded hills which are graced with small lakes and streams, Ridgefield is located on the outermost reaches of New York City suburbia. There are many fascinating antique shops, historic sites, the Aldrich Museum of Contemporary Art, the Hammond Museum, and a host of interesting countryside shops.

The West Lane Inn with its broad lawn and flowering shrubs is set among majestic old maples. The lobby has rich oak paneling and deep pile carpeting. A fire is often crackling on the hearth. The original building was constructed as the home of one of the wealthy landowners of the early 1800s.

Each of the somewhat oversized bedrooms has either one king-sized or two queen-sized beds. All have a full private bath and some are equipped with working fireplaces.

Breakfast may be taken in the breakfast room, the lodging rooms, or on the very pleasant porch. A continental breakfast is included in the room charge. Hearty "breakers of the fast" may enjoy melon, yogurt, berries, poached eggs, cereals, English muffins, bagels and cream cheese, and other offerings at an additional charge.

The West Lane is a very convenient overnight stop for travelers in and out of upper New England and New York City.

WEST LANE INN, 22 West Lane, Ridgefield, Conn. 06877; 203-438-7323. A 14-room inn in a quiet residential village in southwest Connecticut. Approx. 1 hour from N.Y.C. Open every day in the year. Light snacks available until 10:30 p.m. Convenient to many museums and antique shops. Golf, tennis, swimming, and xc skiing and other outdoor recreations available nearby. No pets. Maureen Mayer, Innkeeper.

Directions: From New York: follow I-684 to Exit 6, turn right on Rte. 35, 12 mi. to Ridgefield. Inn is on left. From Hartford: Exit I-84 on Rte. 7 south and follow Rte. 35 to Ridgefield.

For B&B rates, see Index.

THE WHITE HART INN
Salisbury, Connecticut

Northwestern Connecticut has names like Litchfield, Kent, Cornwall Bridge, Sharon, and Salisbury. There are winding roads, picket fences, old colonial houses, horses, high hedges, and there is an obvious appreciation for fine leathers and imported tweeds.

The village of Salisbury sums it up very nicely, and plump in the middle of it is the White Hart Inn with its adjoining Country Store. This inn is a rambling old place with many fireplaces and chimney corners.

Originally built in the 1800s as a private residence, the inn's three-building complex has been in continuous service since 1867. Today's accommodations are all complete with private baths, air conditioning, radios, color cable TV, and telephones.

There is much in the area to tempt the overnight guest to remain for several days, including backroading among beautiful lake country.

In addition to the directions below, it is possible to reach the White Hart from Route 22 in New York State by turning east for a few miles at Wingdale to join Route 7 at Gaylordsville, then proceed north to Canaan on a road that leads past the very photogenic Housatonic River. Salisbury is just a few miles to the west on Route 44.

WHITE HART INN, Salisbury, Conn. 06068; 203-435-2511. A 25-room village inn, 55 mi. west of Hartford. European plan. Breakfast (not included in room rate), lunch, dinner served to travelers daily. Alpine and xc skiing, ski-jumping, golf, swimming nearby. John Wain, Owner; Susan G. Redmond, Gen. Manager.

Directions: Exit the Taconic Pkwy. at Millbrook, N.Y. Proceed east on U.S. 44 to Salisbury. Inn is at junction of U.S. 44 and 41.

For Lodging rates, see Index.

THE HOMESTEAD GUESTS
Bethany Beach, Delaware

This is a homey kind of house with an electronic organ in the parlor, a collection of miniature pitchers, and a cockateel holding forth on the front porch. Proprietor Mrs. Rogers explained that this bird should not be confused with his larger cousin, the cockatoo.

This old house offers three country-type bedrooms that share one bath. Although breakfast is not available, Bethany Beach is such a popular place that I thought The Homestead should be included as a possible overnight or longer stay.

The big attraction here is the beach and after a day of sun it would also be fun to use the backyard barbecue and picnic table. Mrs. Rogers provides a refrigerator for her guests, and as she says, "People can keep breakfast things right here."

THE HOMESTEAD GUESTS, 721 Garfield Pkwy., Bethany Beach, Del. 19930; 302-539-7248. A 3-bedroom home serving as a guest house (sharing 1 bath) about 2 mi. inland from Bethany Beach. Open from May to Oct. No meals served, but refrigerator and cooking facilities are available. No pets. Mrs. Alton Rogers, Proprietor.

Directions: The Homestead is on the north side of Rte. 26 about ½ mi. west of Rte. 1.

For Lodging rates, see Index.

SEA-VISTA VILLA
Bethany Beach, Delaware

Many readers in Washington, D.C., Baltimore, and Philadelphia need no introduction to the Delaware shore. They are aware of the fact that the beaches are extremely attractive and popular. That was why I felt particularly fortunate in discovering the Sea-Vista Villa, the personal residence of Dale Duvall, located on the shores of a small lake just about five blocks from the beach at Bethany Beach.

The residence is a townhouse in the country with all modern conveniences. The guest bedroom for use by B&B travelers is bright and airy, and includes a full breakfast served by the host.

The tennis courts and swimming pool are available to guests in season, as is a canoe on the salt pond.

Advance reservations are definitely required and Mr. Duvall will provide the most explicit directions at that time. There are also some delightful housekeeping villas available by the week from Memorial Day to Labor Day.

SEA-VISTA VILLA, Box 62, Bethany Beach, Delaware; 202-223-0322, 305-539-3354. A 1-bedroom private townhouse made available for B&B guests. The host serves a full breakfast. Within convenient distance of the beach and also other outdoor sports. Tennis courts, swimming pool. Open from May to Thanksgiving. No credit cards. No pets. Children welcome at housekeeping villas. Dale M. Duvall, Host.

For B&B rates, see Index.

CHALET SUZANNE
Lake Wales, Florida

The title of this book says "American Style," but here at Chalet Suzanne, I think it might be better to refer to "World Style," because there are several different types of accommodations to be found including Bavarian, Swiss, Oriental, French, English, Turkish, and Chinese.

All of this didn't happen by accident. Back in the 1930s Bertha Hinshaw was a world traveler and thought it would be fun to bring whole sections of rooms and small houses back to central Florida to add to her growing collection of lodging and restaurant facilities.

Today, Chalet Suzanne is known the world over, not only for its funky architecture, but also for its restaurant, one of the ten top-rated in the country, where its equally famous chicken Suzanne may be found on both the lunch and dinner menus. There is also the Chalet Suzanne Soup Factory, where the most delicious soups and sauces are concocted and canned. And there is an airstrip.

The breakfasts, which are available at various à la carte prices, include fruit, any style of eggs, bacon, ham or sausage, and the specialty—tiny Swedish pancakes served with lingonberries imported from Sweden. Breakfasts are served in the dining room, on the patio, at poolside, or in the individual bedrooms.

Expect to be surprised at Chalet Suzanne, but never bored.

CHALET SUZANNE, P.O. Box AC, Lake Wales, Fla. 33853; 813-676-6011. A 30-room phantasmagoric country inn and gourmet restaurant, 4 mi. north of Lake Wales, between Cypress Gardens and the Bok Singing Tower near Disney World. European plan. Open daily for lodgings year-round. Dining room open from 8 A.M. to 9:30 P.M. daily. Closed Mondays May thru Nov. Pool on grounds. Golf, tennis, riding nearby. Not inexpensive. The Hinshaw Family, Innkeepers.

Directions: From Interstate 4 turn south on U.S. 27 toward Lake Wales. From Sunshine State Pkwy. exit at Yeehaw Junction and head west on Rte. 60 to U.S. 27 (60 mi.). Proceed north on U.S. 27 at Lake Wales. Inn is 4 mi. north of Lake Wales on Country Road 17A.

For Lodging rates, see Index.

HOTEL PLACE ST. MICHEL
Coral Gables, Florida

Tucked away in the midst of Coral Gables' many stylish boutiques and modern, glass, corporate office buildings is a delightful and unexpected European-style inn. The Hotel Place St. Michel is an anachronism in this setting, but a relaxing oasis and fortunate serendipity for those who first discover it.

Built in 1926, this intimate thirty-room, three-story hotel was once known as the Sevilla and hosted many discriminating travelers of that period. Complete restoration as the Hotel Place St. Michel by owners Stuart Bornstein and Alan Potamkin has retained the architectural integrity of this landmark. The gleaming hand-tiled floors, soaring arches, and vaulted ceilings are evidence of their success.

All of the guest rooms have an individual character, and each contains authentic antiques carefully culled from shops in Scotland, England, and France. Highly polished armoires, writing desks, and nightstands eclectically harmonize with color television sets tastefully mounted atop treadle sewing machine bases. White lace curtains frame the windows and paddle fans whirr from the high ceilings. Freshly cut flowers scent the rooms and antique gold-and-white telephones sit on the night tables.

A continental breakfast of freshly baked croissants with an assortment of marmalades and jams, fruit juices, and hot coffee are included with the room rate and may be enjoyed in the lobby-level dining room or the more informal cafe-style lounge. If you wish to take breakfast in your room, room service will oblige.

HOTEL PLACE ST. MICHEL, 162 Alcazar, Coral Gables, FL 33134; 305-444-1666. A charming 30-room restored 1926, European-style hotel in the heart of Coral Gables, 7 min. from Miami International Airport and 10 min. from downtown Miami. All rooms with private baths and air conditioning. Continental breakfast included in room tariff. Open year-round. Dining room open daily for breakfast, luncheon, and dinner. Sunday brunch. Within 3 blocks of shopping mecca of Miracle Mile, and easy walking distance to theaters, galleries, and boutiques. Children welcome. No pets. Stuart Bornstein and Alan Potamkin, Owners and Proprietors.

Directions: Follow I-95 south into U.S. 1 (Dixie Hwy.). Continue south to Ponce de Leon Blvd. Right turn onto Ponce, continuing to 2135 Ponce. Right turn onto Alcazar.

For B&B rates, see Index.

THE 1735 HOUSE
Amelia Island, Florida

This is the ideal answer for a stop on the way north or south through Florida. Amelia Island is at the northernmost point of the scenic ocean drive of Route A1A. It's just a fifteen-mile detour from I-95.

Unquestionably, the outstanding feature of The 1735 House is its situation directly on the seashore. It's about fifteen steps across the sand to the ocean.

There are six bedrooms and, in some cases, bunk beds for families traveling with children. A complimentary breakfast basket with fresh fruit, juice, fresh-baked goods, and beverage, as well as the morning paper, is furnished each morning.

The innkeepers are David and Susan Caples whom I first met a number of years ago when I spoke at the Cornell Hotel School where they were enrolled in the graduate program.

In addition to being a good overnight stop, The 1735 House is an ideal place to stay for travelers continuing on to Cumberland Island. The unusual recreational opportunities on Amelia Island make it an excellent place to stay for three or four nights as well.

THE 1735 HOUSE, 584 So. Fletcher (Rte. A1A), Amelia Island, Fla. 32034; 904-261-5878. A 6-bedroom country inn located directly on the beach near Fernandina, Florida. Open year-round. Breakfast only meal served. Convenient to golf, tennis, swimming, fishing, sailing, boating, and the historic seaport of Fernandina Beach. Free pick-up service is provided at the Jacksonville or Fernandina Beach Airports or the Marine Welcome Station. David and Susan Caples, Innkeepers.

Directions: Amelia Island is located near the Florida/Georgia border. It is 15 mi. east of the Yulee exit on I-95 and 35 miles north of Jacksonville.

For B&B rates, see Index.

OLD ILLIOPOLIS HOTEL
Illiopolis, Illinois

I'll never forget my visit to the Old Illiopolis Hotel. I'll tell you why as soon as I share the important details of this truly unique establishment, which was built at the same time that the Great Western Railroad came through Illiopolis, and was used as a stopover for the railroad crew and passengers.

The owners of this unusual Midwestern landmark are James Browne and Kathleen Jensen-Browne. Mrs. Jensen-Browne is a special education teacher at the school and her husband is an assistant professor of management at nearby Millikin University.

The old-fashioned parlor on the first floor sets the tone with a loveseat, a working player piano and lots of piano rolls, and groups of great photographs of the family. The kitchen has a high, beamed ceiling, and a big, round table. There is all manner of interesting paraphernalia on the walls, including an old cornet, a few photographs, and a mounted butterfly collection.

Abovestairs there are five smallish, very comfortable bedrooms, sharing two bathrooms. Each room is individually decorated and offers a real touch of yesteryear. I couldn't help but feel that the house has grown along with the times. There are pictures of various national and international notables covering the past 100 years.

Breakfast is taken in the wonderful kitchen, where everybody sits around the table and enjoys rolls, fruit juice, milk, hard-boiled eggs, whole-wheat toast, and there is more than enough to eat. Breakfast can be served in the bedrooms, also.

It may be of interest to add that I met several engaging members of the community and, in addition to being presented with a key to the town by Mayor Ed Bliler, I was interviewed by two radio stations and my visit was covered by three newspapers and a TV crew. Don't tell me that small towns are sleepy and out of date.

OLD ILLIOPOLIS HOTEL, 608 Mary St., Box 66, Illiopolis, Ill. 62539; 217-486-6451. A 5-bedroom bed-and-breakfast hotel (sharing two bathrooms). Open all year except Christmas. Telephone in evening after 4 P.M. No smoking in any of the bedrooms. No credit cards. James Browne and Kathleen Jensen-Browne, Proprietors.

Directions: Turn off I-72 and proceed into the town, turning right on Matilda Street. Turn left on 5th St. and right on Mary St. The hotel is right across the street from the public library.

For B&B rates, see Index.

INDIANA STATE PARK INNS

In my experience, some of the best places to stay in the Indiana countryside are the inns in the state parks, which are maintained by the state.

There are six of these inns and each of them has something special to recommend it. For example, the Potawatomi Inn in Angola has an indoor swimming pool, sauna, and jacuzzi, with riding stables, hiking, boating, and other outdoor sports. In winter there is even a refrigerated toboggan run and cross-country skiing.

At Turkey Run Inn there are four tennis courts for guests and you can hike to the beautiful covered bridge area.

Spring Mill State Park also has an early pioneer village and gristmill, and it is near the Virgil Grissom Memorial.

The Canyon Inn, located in the McCormick's Creek State Park, has horseback rides, hiking trails, and forest paths, as well as a pool.

In Brown County, the Abe Martin Lodge, along with individual cabins, is located in 15,000 acres of bluegreen, heavily pine forested, rolling hills, and flowering dogwood and redbud trees.

The Clifty Inn is in Clifty Falls State Park in beautiful Madison, and from the verandas is a view of the Ohio River. It is reminiscent of the days of Mark Twain.

All of these inns are open year-round and offer very acceptable accommodations. Many of them have swimming pools as well. Accommodations and food are under the European plan and breakfast is not included with the cost of the room.

Turkey Run Inn, Turkey Run State Park — 317-597-2211
P.O. Box 444, Marshall, In. 47859

Canyon Inn, McCormick's Creek State Park — 812-829-4881
P.O. Box 71, Spencer, In. 47460

Spring Mill Inn, Spring Mill State Park — 812-849-4081
Box 68, Mitchell, In. 47446

Potawatomi Inn, Pokagon State Park — 219-833-1077
R.R. 2, Box 37, Angola, In. 46703

Abe Martin Lodge, Brown County State Park — 812-988-4418
P.O. Box 25, Nashville, In. 47448

Clifty Inn, Clifty Falls State Park — 812-265-4135
P.O. Box 387, Madison, In. 47250

For Lodging rates, see individual listings in Index.

OPEN HEARTH BED AND BREAKFAST
Bristol, Indiana

Open Hearth is an unusually attractive bed-and-breakfast inn. It is actually a guest house at Echo Valley Farm, just below the Michigan border in northern Indiana.

There are three bedrooms, a cozy living room with a fireplace and walls decorated with prints by Indiana artists, and a kitchen. There are paths to follow, birds to watch, farm animals to enjoy.

There is a beautiful, large pond with a gazebo on one corner, where it is great fun to sit and watch the fish and ducks.

This is a wonderful place to bring children. Michele and Dick Goebel have children of their own and the place has all kinds of farm and domestic animals, including—according to a late bulletin—nine baby lambs.

Michele is the daughter of Arletta Lovejoy of the nearby Patchwork Quilt Country Inn, and she can make arrangements for her guests to dine there every evening except Sunday and Monday. Also, Michele and Arletta give guided tours through the Amish heritage country.

Incidentally, Michele is a marvelously innovative cook and gives cooking classes in the Open Hearth kitchen.

Breakfasts include some of Michele's own recipes, including pecan sticky buns, apple-raisin coffee cake made with oatmeal, zucchini and oatmeal muffins, as well as homemade jams and jellies.

OPEN HEARTH BED AND BREAKFAST, 56782 State Rd. 15, Echo Valley Farm, Bristol, In. 46507; 219-848-5256. A 3-bedroom (shared bathroom) bed-and-breakfast home located in the beautiful rolling farmland of northern Indiana. Accommodations are in a separate small house adjacent to the main house. Accommodations available Mon. through Sat. nights. Most conveniently located for many of the area's points of interest including quilt shops, cheesemaking, buggy shops, summer theaters, winter skiing, snowmobiling, and country fairs. Children welcome. No pets. No alcoholic beverages; no smoking in guest rooms. Dick and Michele Goebel, Proprietors.

Directions: Just ⅛ mi. north of the intersection of U.S. 20 and Indiana Rte. 15.

For B&B rates, see Index.

PATCHWORK QUILT BED AND BREAKFAST
Middlebury, Indiana

Patchwork Quilt, which has long been in *Country Inns and Back Roads* as a prime example of the best in American farm cookery, has now added overnight accommodations and bids fair to set new standards for such establishments.

There are three bedrooms. One called "The Treetop" features a canopied bed, a hand-painted armoire, and a turquoise velvet chair. It is panelled in white and turquoise and has a beautiful print above the Franklin fireplace. Another room, known as "The Meadow," is panelled in wattled walnut hardwood. The Early American cannon-ball bed has a mini-canopy made from an apricot quilted counter-pane. A leather-top lady's pigeon-holed desk and wall unit displays Pigeon Forge pottery.

Breakfast on the farm is served in a very pleasant little room with windows looking out over the fields and orchards. It is a most generous continental-style breakfast, featuring freshly baked breakfast cake or roll every day and generous helpings of fruit and orange juice.

The Patchwork Quilt Country Inn dining room has gained national fame for its prizewinning recipes for both chicken and strawberries. It is open by reservation every evening except Sunday and Monday.

PATCHWORK QUILT BED AND BREAKFAST, 11748 C.R. #2, Middlebury, Ind. 46540; 219-825-2417. A 3-bedroom bed-and-breakfast inn (shared bath) located near the Michigan border of Indiana in an interesting Amish community. Rooms available every night in week. Dinner at Patchwork Quilt by reservation nightly except Sunday and Monday. Conveniently located for the Shipshewana auction and flea market. Not convenient for children. No pets. No alcoholic beverages; no smoking in guest rooms. No credit cards. Milton and Arletta Lovejoy, Innkeepers.

Directions: From east or west, exit Indiana Toll Rd. at Middlebury (Exit 107) and go north ¼ mi. to County Rd. #2 and proceed west 1 mi. to inn. From Middlebury, follow Indiana Rte. 13 for 8 mi. north to County Rd. #2 and west 1 mi.

For B&B rates, see Index.

THE ROCKPORT INN
Rockport, Indiana

Rockport is a small community on the Ohio River, ten miles north of Owensboro, Kentucky, and thirty miles east of Evansville, Indiana.

The area in and around Rockport is rich in Lincoln lore, since Honest Abe grew up near here. In fact, he left for New Orleans on his famous trip from Rockport.

The Rockport Inn, a full-service inn, was built as a private residence about 1855. It was expanded into a rooming house about 1870 and then into a small hotel about 1920. The building recently has been thoroughly renovated, with as much of the original design and spirit being retained as has been feasible and possible. It is one of the oldest structures in the area.

There are six bedrooms of varying sizes. Each has a private bath and air conditioning, which can be quite welcome in this part of the world. There are four dining rooms of different sizes, and the furnishings both upstairs and down are turn-of-the-century.

At the time of my visit, breakfast and lunch were served during the week, and dinner was served Wednesday through Saturday. There is also a Saturday brunch.

The Rockport Inn is probably the most unique lodging experience of its kind in southern Indiana.

THE ROCKPORT INN, Third at Walnut St., Rockport, In. 47635; 812-649-2664. A 6-bedroom village inn in a small Ohio River town in southern Indiana. Breakfast is not included in room rate. Breakfast and lunch served Mon. thru Fri. Dinner served Wed. thru Sat. No meal is served on Sun. Open year-round. Excellent backroading along the river especially to the east. Emil and Carolyn Faith Ahnell, Innkeepers.

Directions: Rockport is on Rte. 66 between Evansville and Cannelton in southern Indiana. It is just north of Owensboro, Kentucky. The inn is in the business section of town.

For Lodging rates, see Index.

THE BEAUMONT INN
Harrodsburg, Kentucky

The Bluegrass Parkway, I-64, and I-75 all converge in the vicinity of Lexington, Kentucky, which is a place well-known for its predilection for fast and beautiful horses.

Fortunately, Routes 127 and 68 provide an enjoyable and quick journey to Harrodsburg where there are two very pleasant and unusual inns that offer bed and breakfast. One of these is the Beaumont Inn.

It is hard to imagine an atmosphere more steeped in Kentucky history and tradition than this lovely old red brick inn with its majestic white pillars and climbing ivy.

The front hall is adorned with many pictures of Robert E. Lee, and the sitting rooms have stunning rose decorations around each wall and are graced by elegant fireplaces.

The bedrooms are large, commodious, and air conditioned and are furnished with the same attention to detail.

In Kentucky, the Beaumont Inn is famous for its menu and I hope that everyone traveling with this book will plan on arriving in time for dinner.

The full breakfast, which is included in the B&B rate, includes all kinds of juices and fruits in season, cereal, any style of eggs, sausage or bacon, grits, hot biscuits, strawberry preserves, and probably the most famous of all: lacy-edged cornmeal batter cakes served with an old-fashioned brown-sugar syrup.

THE BEAUMONT INN, Harrodsburg, Ky. 40330; 606-734-3381. A 29-bedroom destination-resort inn in the heart of Kentucky's historic bluegrass country. European plan. B&B rates also available. Lunch and dinner served to travelers; all three meals to house-guests. Open every day from early March thru November 30. Tennis, swimming pool, shuffleboard on grounds. Golf courses and a wide range of recreational and historic attractions nearby. No pets. The Dedman Family, Innkeepers.

Directions: From Louisville: Exit 48 from east I-64. Go south on Ky. 151, to U.S. 127 south to Harrodsburg. From Lexington: U.S. 60 west, then west on Bluegrass Parkway to U.S. 127. From Nashville: Exit I-65 to Bluegrass Parkway near Elizabethtown, Ky., then east to U.S. 127. From Knoxville: Exit north I-75 at Mt. Vernon, Ky., then north on U.S. 150 to U.S. 127. Use bypass at Danville, Ky. Go north on U.S. 127 to Beaumont Inn entrance which is on east side of highway as you enter Harrodsburg.

For B&B rates, see Index.

DOE RUN INN
Brandenburg, Kentucky

Pioneer America lives at the Doe Run Inn. I'm sure that it has changed very little in the last 165 years. The building with the huge, four-foot-thick limestone blocks on the outer walls was made to repel Indian attacks. The tremendous front door could withstand almost any attempt to break in, and the huge fireplace still sends warmth radiating through the room.

The building was originally a gristmill. An old record shows a payment made to Abraham Lincoln's father who worked as a stonemason on the building.

Lodging rooms have antique beds, tables, and chairs that would be at home in a museum. Just a few have private baths. The rooms are much the same as they have been for the past 50 years, and there has been very little modernization because there's very little that can be done with such an old building.

The inn overlooks twin streams rushing through the verdant woods.

My, oh my, those homemade biscuits with jelly, served with country ham and red-eye gravy with a side order of hash-browns, is just the way to begin the day. In the summertime, breakfast is served on the open porch with the sweet morning sounds of the birds.

DOE RUN INN, Rte. 2, Brandenburg, Ky. 40108; 502-422-2982. A 17-room country inn (5 rooms with private bath; 12 rooms with shared baths) reminiscent of the backwoods on Rte. 448, 4 mi. south of Brandenburg, 38 mi. south of Louisville. Near Fort Knox. Breakfast is not included in room rate. European plan. Breakfast, lunch and dinner served to travelers daily. Closed Christmas Eve and Christmas Day. Hiking, swimming and fishing nearby. J. Michael Brown, Innkeeper.

Directions: From Louisville take 64W through Indiana to 135 S. Cross the toll bridge to Kentucky and follow 1051 to the dead end. Turn right on 448 and follow signs to Doe Run Inn.

For B&B rates, see Index.

THE INN AT PLEASANT HILL
Shakertown, Kentucky

The Inn at Pleasant Hill is in a restored Shaker community in one of the most beautiful sections of central Kentucky.

The Shakers were members of a religious sect with some rather advanced social ideas. They lived in communal dedication to their religious beliefs of celibacy, public confession of sins (which culminated in the frenetic dances which gave them the name of Shakers), renunciation of worldliness, and common ownership of property.

The inn front desk is located in the Trustees House, one of 25 or more buildings clustered along the single country road. The lodging rooms, most on the second floor and some on the third floor, are situated in various restored and preserved Shaker shops and communal buildings. Each has the austere furniture characteristic of Shaker design.

Shakers may have had several interesting abstentions, but eating was not one of them. A full country buffet breakfast is served including fruit juice, fresh fruits, baked fruits, bacon and sausage, eggs, grits, cereal, hot biscuits and muffins, all of which are made in the inn kitchen. The waitresses wear simple Shaker dress.

INN AT PLEASANT HILL, Shakertown, Ky., P.O. address: Rte. 4, Harrodsburg, Ky. 40330; 606-734-5411. A 72-room country inn in a restored Shaker village on Rte. 68, 7 mi. northeast of Harrodsburg, 25 mi. southwest of Lexington. European plan. Breakfast, lunch, dinner served daily to travelers. Open year-round. Suggest contacting Inn about winter schedule. Closed Christmas Eve and Christmas Day. Ann Voris, Innkeeper.

Directions: From Lexington take Rte. 68 south toward Harrodsburg. From Louisville, take I-64 to Lawrenceburg and Graeffenburg exit (not numbered). Follow Rte. 127 Bypass south to Harrodsburg and Rte. 68 northeast to Shakertown.

For Lodging rates, see Index.

THE ALTENHOFEN HOUSE
Blue Hill, Maine

No doubt the average traveler on Routes 1 and 3 between Bucksport and Ellsworth, Maine, is unaware of the fact that the Blue Hill Peninsula to the south offers many attractive Maine scenes and views, and also some splendid accommodations.

One of these is the Altenhofen House, built in 1815 and recently restored. It has spacious rooms with private baths, and open fireplaces abound.

The house is in two parts, one with mellowed red bricks and impressive columns, and the other, an added white clapboard and red brick wing. It is situated on a little peninsula of thirty acres with a private shoreline. There is also a very pleasant swimming pool on the grounds.

The innkeepers and owners are Peter and Brigitte Altenhofen. Peter is still an airline captain, but is to be found at the inn a great deal of the time.

Incidentally, the Altenhofen House is within a very short drive of Acadia National Park. To me, the entire Blue Hill Peninsula is one glorious backroading experience.

THE ALTENHOFEN HOUSE, Peters Point, Blue Hill, ME 04614; 207-374-2116. An elegantly restored 1815 mansion with 8 guestrooms all with private baths. Breakfast served to houseguests. Closed Jan. to April. Exceptional opportunities for all types of holiday activities, including swimming in the pool or the sea, sailing, windsurfing, fishing, tennis, golf, horseback riding, and guided hunting; seaplane facilities at front door. Kids and pets are welcome. Peter and Brigitte Altenhofen, Hosts.

Directions: Coming east on U.S.1, follow Rte. 15 to Blue Hill and then Rte. 176 toward East Blue Hill.

For B&B rates, see Index.

BLACK POINT INN
Prouts Neck, Maine

The Black Point Inn is one of the few remaining American plan hotels of the kind that flourished in New England for about one hundred years. It has quiet dignity, personal service, attention to details, ocean bathing, excellent tennis courts, a golf course, exceptional food, and an unpretentious elegance. Men wear coats for dinner and many of the ladies enjoy wearing gay summer dresses. Dressing up is part of the fun.

Prouts Neck became popular as a summer resort in the middle of the nineteenth century. In 1886, there were half a dozen summer cottages, and one of them was occupied by Charles Savage Homer, whose son, Winslow, became one of America's best-known artists. He must have gotten his inspiration for some of those great paintings of the Maine coast just from walking on the rocks and the beaches at Prouts Neck.

Although the Black Point is for the most part a full American plan inn, there are a few weeks at the beginning and end of the season when bed-and-breakfast guests may be accommodated. In my opinion these also happen to be the most ideal times for vacationing on the Maine coast. Please note that bed-and-breakfast accommodations are available at the Black Point only between May 1 and June 1, and October 1 and November 1.

BLACK POINT INN, Prouts Neck, Me. 04070; 207-883-4311. An 80-room luxury resort-inn on Rte. 207, 10 mi. south of Portland. American plan. Breakfast, lunch, and dinner served to travelers. B&B rates available May 1 to June 1; Oct. 1 to Nov. 1. Fresh water whirlpool, heated salt water pool, bicycles, sailing, dancing, golf, tennis and ocean bathing all within a few steps. No pets. Normand H. Dugas, Innkeeper.

Directions: From Maine Tpke. take Exit 7. Turn right at sign marked Scarborough and Old Orchard Beach. At second set of lights turn left on Rte. 207. Follow 4.3 miles to Prouts Neck.

For B&B rates, see Index.

BLUE HARBOR BED & BREAKFAST
Camden, Maine

The town of Camden, first visited in 1605 by English Captain George Weymouth, and permanently settled in 1768, is one of the busiest places on the northern coast of Maine. Even during the dead of winter (when, incidentally, the Blue Harbor Bed & Breakfast is also open) there is a bustle of activity in the center of town and along the town dock from which the famous Windjammer cruises depart. June is probably the best month to visit—the weather is usually fair and it isn't terribly crowded.

Blue Harbor Bed & Breakfast is at the south end of Camden, just a few minutes from many fine restaurants and shops. Each of the seven guest bedrooms is individually decorated with Maine country furniture, handmade, hand-tied bed quilts, and ruffled country curtains. All of the rooms will accommodate at least two guests and some larger rooms, up to four. Five of the guest rooms have shared baths, two have a semi-private bath, and a private suite is available.

Thomas and Lorraine Tedeschi do not offer televisions or radios in the bedrooms; however, soft music plays in the sitting rooms, where there is all sorts of comfortable furniture and lots of books and magazines.

Lorraine prepares warm muffins, fresh fruits and fruit juices, homemade breakfast breads and freshly brewed coffee and tea, all served on the sun porch at no additional charge.

For an even longer stay, the Blue Harbor Bed & Breakfast has a most friendly atmosphere.

BLUE HARBOR BED & BREAKFAST, 67 Elm St. (U.S. Rte. 1), Camden, ME 04843; 207-236-3196. A 7-guestroom bed-and-breakfast inn (semi-private and shared baths) in a busy harbor village. Breakfast is included in the room rate. Open all year. Conveniently situated to enjoy the dozens and dozens of recreational, cultural, and historical attractions of the area. Just a few moments from Rockland and other ferry terminals. No credit cards. No pets. Non-smokers, please. Thomas and Lorraine Tedeschi, Innkeepers.

Directions: Blue Harbor Bed & Breakfast is at the south end of Camden on Rte. 1.

For B&B rates, see Index.

BLUE HILL INN
Blue Hill, Maine

Blue Hill is on the east Penobscot peninsula which extends into Penobscot Bay south of U.S. 1 between Bucksport and Ellsworth. The village of Blue Hill nestles underneath a mountain at the head of Blue Hill Bay. There are beautiful homes, historic landmarks, handcraft and pottery shops, and the Kneisel School of Music.

The Blue Hill Inn, built in 1832 right in the center of the village, is as neat and tidy a New England inn as can be found anywhere. The country-inn bedrooms are roomy and have attractive, appropriate furniture and private baths. The many chairs and sofas in the living room invite getting acquainted with the other guests.

The inn is open all year and serves both breakfast and dinner; the latter including succulent chowders, homemade bread or popovers, and a different entrée each evening, such as roast beef, roast lamb, or roast pork. A full country-style breakfast can be had for three dollars and a continental breakfast is also available.

The inn is the focal point for day-trips to the picturesque harbor towns on the peninsula, as well as Mt. Desert Island and the Acadia National Park. Reservations for the summer season and weekends almost any time of the year must be made well in advance.

BLUE HILL INN, Blue Hill, Me. 04614; 207-374-2844. An 11-bedroom traditional village inn in the center of picturesque Blue Hill on the Maine coast. Open year-round. Closed Christmas. Breakfast and dinner available. Historic landmarks, Kneisel School of Music concerts, the famous Rowantrees and Rackliffe Pottery studios in Blue Hill. Tennis, golf, and beach facilities are available nearby. Exploring and cross-country skiing in Acadia Nat'l Park nearby; day trips to Deer Isle, Northeast Harbor, and Seal Harbor. No pets. Rita and Ted Boytos, Innkeepers.

Directions: From U.S. 1 take Rte. 15 to Blue Hill.

For Lodging rates, see Index.

93

THE BRADLEY INN
Pemaquid Point, New Harbor, Maine

One of the busiest travel corridors in the Northeast is Route 1 which is one of the main roads up the New England coast from Massachusetts through Newburyport and on to Portsmouth, New Hampshire, York, Ogunquit, Kennebunkport, and the other southern Maine seacoast villages, to Camden, Ellsworth, Calais, and into New Brunswick, Prince Edward Island, and Nova Scotia. I have tried to provide a number of overnight B&B suggestions along the way, some of which are just a few miles off the main road.

A visit to the Bradley Inn on the rock-bound coast of Maine is in many respects a step backward in time. The twelve bedrooms all share bathrooms and conveniences "down the hall."

The old-fashioned dining room provides dinners not only for guests, but for many people in the immediate area who consider the Bradley "their inn."

Travelers arriving in the evening can count on enjoying a wonderful dinner. I hope that many will take an extra hour and a half and visit the Pemaquid Lighthouse which is located on a rocky point actually within walking distance of the inn.

A varied continental breakfast is served to inn guests year-round.

THE BRADLEY INN, Rte. 130, Pemaquid Point, New Harbor, Me. 04554; 207-677-2105. A 12-room country inn (no private baths) located near the Pemaquid Lighthouse on Maine's rocky coast, 15 mi. from Damariscotta. Rooms and continental breakfast available year-round to inn guests. Dinner served every day during the summer and on weekends during the winter. Restaurant is closed Christmas Eve, Christmas Day, Jan. and Feb. Tennis, swimming, golf, canoeing, backroading, woodland walks, xc skiing, as well as many cultural and historic attractions available nearby. Smoking allowed only in common rooms on first floor. No pets. Edwin and Louine Ek and Grandma, Innkeepers.

Directions: From South: Maine I-95 to Brunswick/Bath coastal Rte. 1 Exit. Follow Rte. 1 through Brunswick, Bath, and Wiscasset. Exit Business Rte. 1 at Damariscotta. Turn right at top of hill (white church), follow Rte. 130, 14 mi. to Pemaquid Pt. From north: Rte. 1; exit at Business Rte. 1, Damariscotta. Turn left at white church onto Rte. 130. Follow 130, 14 mi. to Pemaquid Pt.

For B&B rates, see Index.

THE BRANNON-BUNKER INN
Damariscotta, Maine

The U.S. 1 coastal route traveler, hunched foward over the steering wheel, intent on reaching Bar Harbor, Calais, New Brunswick, or Nova Scotia would do well to take one of the several local byways that lead down to the end of the peninsulas along the rocky coast of Maine. For instance, Route 129 is such a road, and it passes the Brannon- Bunker Inn with its spacious front lawn, trees planted along the highway, and the pleasant look of an old Maine homestead.

The entrance leads into a low-ceilinged breakfast room furnished with many of the accouterments of bygone days. Beyond the breakfast room is a large room with a whitewashed fireplace, an old school clock, a corner cupboard, and a chess set. I realized that I was walking around in a barn that had been converted into an inn. In one corner of the room is the guest kitchen with a refrigerator that guests can share for lunch and dinner.

Bedrooms have a real New England country look—ruffled curtains at the windows and an assortment of twin and double beds. There are lots of books everywhere.

One of the things that guests enjoy is walking behind the inn down to the river at low tide to watch the seals at play. It's a good place for sunning and lazing away the day in a lawn chair, if you like.

A light breakfast that includes warm homemade muffins is served.

The inn is just a short distance away from a golf course.

THE BRANNON-BUNKER INN, Rte. 129, Damariscotta, ME 04543; 207-563-5941. An 8-guestroom village inn on the Damariscotta River; 5 rooms share 2 baths and 3 rooms have private baths. Open from May 1 thru Columbus Day. Continental breakfast included with lodgings. Breakfast only meal served. Many good restaurants in the area. All water sports, excursion boats, sightseeing, tennis, golf nearby. Only minutes away from Boothbay Harbor, Wiscasset, and Camden-Rockland activities. Jeanne and Joe Hovance, Innkeepers.

Directions: From U.S. 1 turn south on Rte. 129 at Damariscotta. The inn is on Rte. 129, 5 min. away from U.S. 1.

For B&B rates, see Index.

THE BREEZE INN
East Machias, Maine

I would indeed be remiss if I failed to point out the Breeze Inn to our readers who are traveling either north or south on Route 1 en route to or from northern Maine, New Brunswick, Prince Edward Island, and Nova Scotia.

The little sign out in front of the Breeze Inn is one of the reasons I stopped at the big turn in the road at East Machias.

This is a real up-country, State-of-Maine inn, that's really a throwback to the days when people maintained "Tourist Homes." In fact, the Breeze Inn is like a tourist home of fifty years ago. It's been a family home for Esther and Dick Lyford for many years.

There are five clean, very pleasant rooms on the second floor, all of which share one bathroom; however, every effort is made to make the visitor feel at home, and coffee and doughnuts are served on the front porch every morning.

It's a home of photographs of children and grandchildren on almost every available space on the wall. Downstairs in the living room there's a big color TV and a Bible open on the table to Psalms 121. I might add that there were a couple of other uninviting-looking brick motels within a few minutes, but I'm certainly glad to point out this real "State of Maine" experience to our readers.

THE BREEZE INN, Rte. 1, East Machias, Maine 04630; 207-255-8453. A 5-guestroom (shared bath) accommodation on Rte. 1 between Ellsworth and Calais, Maine. Coffee and doughnuts served in the morning. No pets. No credit cards. Esther and Dick Lyford, Proprietors.

Directions: East Machias is about 3 mi. north of Machias on Rte. 1.

For B&B rates, see Index.

BREEZEMERE FARM
Brooksville, Maine

The East Penobscot Bay region of Maine, south of Mt. Desert Island and north of Penobscot Bay, is one of the most unspoiled places where trees, birds, flowers, and marine life abound. There are beautiful homes, historic landmarks, craft shops, golf, tennis, swimming, horseback riding, antiquing, and sailing.

Right in the spirit of this as-yet-to-be-discovered area is Breezemere Farm, an inn on sixty acres at the head of Orcutt Harbor.

The day begins with a big country breakfast including Breezemere granola and other treats such as blueberry pancakes with genuine maple syrup. The bedrooms are in the main house or in some nearby cottages.

Of particular interest to families with young people is the lodge, a good-sized building with a giant fireplace used for all kinds of indoor recreation. It's great for the occasional rainy day, and the front porch looks right down into the little harbor. It even has an inside shuffleboard court.

Even if only staying for one night, be sure to get there in time for dinner—and remember, don't tell a soul about East Penobscot Bay; we'll keep it our own little secret.

BREEZEMERE FARM, Box 290, Brooksville, Me. 04617; 207-326-8628. A circa 1850 saltwater farm. A 7-bedroom farmhouse plus 6 cottages. Sixty acres of farm and blueberry fields and forest at the head of Orcutt Harbor. Shared baths in the inn. Large farm breakfast included with the lodgings. Dinner by reservation. Open from Memorial Day to Oct. 15. In Aug., 3-day minimum stay. Bicycles, rowboats, Day Sailer, Hobiecat, woodland and coastline exploring, clamming and musseling, shuffleboard, and indoor recreation on grounds. Charter boat tours, golf, tennis, craft and antique shops nearby. Pets allowed in cottages only. Joan and Jim Lippke, Innkeepers.

Directions: From Bucksport via Rtes. 1 or 3, take Rte. 175 to No. Brooksville. Turn right onto 176W. The first right after Cape Rosier Rd. is Breezemere Farm.

For B&B rates, see Index.

THE CAPTAIN LORD MANSION
Kennebunkport, Maine

Kennebunkport is a picturesque seacoast village that contains an unusual number of stately homes built in the late 18th and early 19th centuries. Its quiet tree-shaded streets and the nearby river where there are many ocean-going fishing boats, provide visitors with an honest "New England" experience.

The Captain Lord Mansion, which is listed on the National Register, was built during the War of 1812 by ships' artisans who were idled by the British blockade. With its three stories topped by a cupola, it is the most impressive structure in Kennebunkport today. There are at least twenty-four rooms in the mansion, and sixteen have been set aside as lodging rooms. All of them have their own private baths. Eleven have working fireplaces.

All of the bedrooms are named for ships built by the original owner. They are individually decorated with fine antiques. Some rooms overlook the river and the Arundle Yacht Club, and others have a view of the extensive gardens and historic homes in the quiet residential neighborhood.

At breakfast everyone gathers around the great table in the kitchen for some of Bev's homemade muffins, hot breads, and boiled eggs. This is where plans are hatched (no pun intended) for the day's activities, as well as selecting a restaurant for the evening meal.

As one might imagine, advance reservations are almost always necessary at the Captain Lord Mansion.

THE CAPTAIN LORD MANSION, Box 527, Kennebunkport, Me. 04046; 207-967-3141. A 16-bedroom inn located in a mansion in a seacoast village. Near the Rachel Carson Wildlife Refuge, the Seashore Trolley Museum, The Brick Store Museum, and lobster boat tours. Lodgings include breakfast. No other meals served. Open year-round. Bicycles, hiking, xc skiing, deep sea fishing, golf, indoor swimming, and tennis nearby. No children under 12. No pets. No credit cards. Bev Davis and Rick Litchfield, Innkeepers.

Directions: Take Exit 3 (Kennebunk) from the Maine Turnpike. Take left on Rte. 35 and follow signs through Kennebunk to Kennebunkport. Take left at traffic light at Sunoco station. Go over drawbridge and take first right onto Ocean Ave., then take fifth left off Ocean Ave. The mansion is on the second block on the left. Park behind building and take brick walk to office.

For B&B rates, see Index.

THE CAPTAIN'S HOUSE
Newcastle, Maine

As I mentioned in the account of my visit to elfinhill in Newcastle, the Captain's House is right next door and also enjoys a view of the Damariscotta River.

Cathy and Kirk Schlemmer are two young people who decided to settle in this part of Maine and share their house with bed-and-breakfast guests. As would be expected, the house originally belonged to a sea captain, who built it in the early 1800s.

There are four guest rooms with one bath downstairs and one upstairs. The house is adorned with a profusion of plants and many of the bright quilts created by Cathy. At the time of my visit there was a baby boy who was four months old.

Breakfasts feature yeast breads made by Kirk, quick breads by Cathy, homemade granola, juice, fresh fruit, eggs, blackberry jam, and apple cider, and they are served in the dining room. Both the living room and the dining room have a very pleasant view of the river. Incidentally, three of the bedrooms also enjoy this river view.

THE CAPTAIN'S HOUSE, Rte. 1, Box 19, River Rd., Newcastle, ME 04553; 207-563-1482. A 4-guestroom (shared baths) bed-and-breakfast guest house just off Rte. 1 in Newcastle. Open year-round. A full breakfast is included in the room rate. No pets. No credit cards. No smoking. Cathy and Kirk Schlemmer, Proprietors.

Directions: About 6½ mi. past Wiscasset, on Rte. 1, turn right, following signs for Newcastle and River Road; watch for sign on the left, 8/10 of a mi. from Rte. 1.

For B&B rates, see Index.

THE CARRIAGE HOUSE INN
Searsport, Maine

U.S. 1 is one of the principal routes to northern Maine and continues on into New Brunswick, Prince Edward Island, and Nova Scotia. There are some very attractive Maine towns en route, including Bath, Wiscasset, and Camden.

North of Camden, to the east between the stands of trees and an occasional motel, is beautiful Penobscot Bay. In Searsport, which would be an ideal stop for the weary traveler, there are two bed-and-breakfast places directly across U.S. 1 from each other. I'm certain if you called Nancy, Susan, or Bruce at the Carriage House and they. were full they would recommend the Homeport, and vice versa with Mrs. Johnson.

I think each inn is equally comfortable, hospitable, and friendly, although they differ in some interesting ways.

The Carriage House shares the spotlight with the Maine House, and this truly impressive building is now an antique shop. During past years the property was owned by the late Waldo Peirce, a renowned Maine painter, and was used as his summer home and studio.

Built during the mid-19th century, this mansion has high ceilings and large, cheerful bedrooms with appropriate furnishings.

The kitchen-brunch room is one of the most interesting rooms in the house. It has tongue-and-groove walls and ceiling that create a very cozy feeling. In addition to the continental breakfast, coffee and tea are available for guests at any time.

THE CARRIAGE HOUSE, East Main St., Searsport, Maine 04974; 207-548-2289. A 6-bedroom guest house in an impressive Victorian mansion. Lodgings include continental breakfast; coffee or tea available at all times. All of the Penobscot Bay recreation and natural attractions are easily accessible. Open all year. Nancy Noqueira, Susan and Bruce Atkinson, Proprietors.

Directions: The Carriage House is on U.S. 1 in Searsport.

For B&B rates, see Index.

CHARMWOODS
On Long Lake, Naples, Maine

Route 302 connects with I-89 at Barre, Vermont, swings across New Hampshire, providing a spectacular journey through Crawford Notch into North Conway, and then cuts into the lake country of Maine through Fryeburg. It is a very favorite road for Canadians.

A very pleasant overnight stop on this road would be Charmwoods, a unique type of guest house set in an area of great natural beauty on Long Lake in Naples, Maine.

Once a private lakefront estate, Charmwoods radiates all the flavor and ambience of the Maine woods, but is a mere 2½-hours' drive from downtown Boston.

The focus of activity at Charmwoods is frequently in the commodious and gracious living room with its massive fieldstone fireplace and panoramic view of lake and mountains. In fact, every handsomely appointed bedroom suite enjoys a view of the lake.

A "glorified" continental breakfast, which is included in the B&B rate, is served either in the dining room or on the terrace overlooking the lake. It is one of the most congenial hours of the day, as I discovered when I realized that two hours had gone by!

CHARMWOODS, Naples, Me. 04055; 207-693-6798 (winter: 617-469-9673). Four bedrooms, all with private baths, plus guest cottage. Located on the west shore of Long Lake, approx. ½ hr. from Maine Tpke. Open early June through Oct. Breakfast is the only meal served (to houseguests only). Tennis, swimming, boating, canoeing, shuffleboard, and horseshoes on grounds; horseback riding, golf, nearby. Summer playhouse just down the road. Not suitable for children under 12. No pets. No credit cards. Marilyn and Bill Lewis, Innkeepers.

Directions: From Boston: follow Rte. 1 north to I-95 to Exit 8 (Portland-Westbrook). Turn right and follow Riverside St. 1 mi. to Rte. 302. Turn left (west) to Naples. Charmwoods is just beyond the village on the right with an unobtrusive sign. From North Conway, N.H.: follow Rte. 302 through Bridgton. Charmwoods sign and driveway off Rte. 302 just west of Naples village.

For B&B rates, see Index.

CLEFTSTONE MANOR
Bar Harbor, Maine

I had three letters of recommendation before I visited this inn, and I must say that every one of them was absolutely correct.

Each of the eighteen guest rooms is individually furnished with tasteful antiques chosen by the owners, Don and Phyllis Jackson. There are three large rooms for guests to enjoy—a living room with a fireplace, a large dining room, and a very light and airy sunroom. All of the bedrooms are exceptionally attractive and comfortable with handmade crafts in each, and every bed is supplied with a down comforter for those cool, Maine nights.

A continental breakfast is included in the room rates, and Phyllis bakes homemade blueberry, bran, and cinnamon muffins, as well as raisin bread to go with the fruit, orange juice, and coffee. Four o'clock is teatime and guests are invited to sample herbal teas and homemade Scottish shortbread. Everyone gathers in the sunroom and shares their activities of the day. At 8:00 P.M., there is additional refreshment offered, including several types of cheeses and crackers.

Cleftstone Manor is an excellent place to stay for several days to enjoy all of the many attractive features of the Mount Desert area, and it is just 500 yards from the Bluenose Ferry to Nova Scotia. If it served the evening meal I would certainly include it in *Country Inns and Back Roads, North America.*

CLEFTSTONE MANOR, Eden St., Bar Harbor, Me. 04609; 207-288-4951. An 18-guest room (12 with private bath) elegant country inn within walking distance of the Bluenose Ferry to Nova Scotia. Open May 15 through mid-October. Continental breakfast, afternoon tea, and evening refreshments included in room rate. Ideal for honeymooners and longer stays to enjoy many of the natural, historical, and cultural attractions of Mt. Desert Island. Hot-air balloon flights are also available through the inn. The Jackson Family, Innkeepers.

Directions: Follow Rte. 3 to Bar Harbor. The inn is on the right-hand side, plainly marked.

For B&B rates, see Index.

THE COUNTRY CLUB INN
Rangeley, Maine

Rangeley, Maine is one of those places in the world which has a special kind of charisma. There are few locations that offer such beauty and grandeur in all seasons. The combination of wide skies, vast stretches of mountain woodland, and the placid aspect of Rangeley Lake were drawing people to this part of western Maine long before the roads were as passable and numerous as they are today.

The Country Club Inn sits at a high point overlooking all of the marvelous panorama of lake, sky, and mountains. The cathedral-ceilinged living room has heavy beams, wood paneling, many, many different types of sofas, rocking chairs, and armchairs. I saw several jigsaw puzzles in various states of completion, a huge shelf of books, and a great moose head over one of the two fireplaces.

An 18-hole par 70 golf course is just a few steps from the front door and there is excellent fishing for square-tailed trout and landlocked salmon in all of the Rangeley Lakes. And, of course, magnificent cross-crountry skiing on the grounds, downhill skiing on nearby Saddleback Mountain, and all the other wintertime diversions.

The dining room has a spectacular view of the lake and mountains and the full hearty breakfasts fortify the vacationer for a lovely day in the outdoors. At breakfast there are hot muffins made from blueberries grown on the nearby hillside, as well as a choice of pancakes, corned beef hash, eggs any style, and homefries.

THE COUNTRY CLUB INN, P.O. Box BB, Rangeley, Maine 04970; 207-864-3831. A 25-room resort-inn on Rangeley Lake in Maine's beautiful western mountain-lakes country, 45 mi. from Farmington. European, modified American plans. Open late May to mid-Oct.; and mid-Dec. to mid-Mar. Breakfast, lunch, and dinner served to travelers. Near many cultural, historic, and recreational attractions. Swimming pool and lake swimming, horseshoes, bocci, and 18-hole golf course on grounds. Fishing, saddle horses, water skiing, canoeing, tennis nearby. XC skiing on grounds; downhill skiing on nearby Saddleback Mt. Bob and Sue Crory, Innkeepers.

Directions: From Maine Tpke.: take Auburn Exit 12 and follow Rte. 4 to Rangeley. From Vt. and N.H.: take I-91 to St. Johnsbury; east on Rte. 2 to Gorham, and Rte. 16 north to Rangeley.

For B&B rates, see Index.

CRESCENT BEACH INN
Cape Elizabeth, Maine

The state of Maine is many things to many people, and for some people it's the opportunity to stay in a real old-fashioned inn and be within at least a short walk of the water.

The Crescent Beach Inn on Cape Elizabeth, south of Portland, provides the kind of homey atmosphere and warm hospitality that has typified Maine seacoast accommodations for many, many years. It also has the additional advantage of having private access to the warm sands of Crescent Beach, immediately in front of the inn.

Fortunately, this inn has been acquired by a group of individuals who are interested in preserving the qualities that make this part of Maine so pleasant.

During the summer swimming months, the Crescent Beach Inn is extremely popular, particularly with families, because the ocean and the broad lawns provide an excellent place for children to play. In addition, Crescent Beach State Park offers more sandy beaches and picnic tables, and the Two Lights State Park lures seascape addicts and history buffs.

The inn has several different types of guest rooms; I'd suggest asking for one with a sea view as your first choice; however, all are most pleasant.

Breakfast is included in the room rate and dinner is served. I enjoyed an excellent sirloin steak.

Crescent Beach Inn offers a different, rather nostalgic Maine experience. It's just a short distance from the Maine Turnpike, which should not deter the traveler en route to or from more northern points from staying overnight or even longer.

CRESCENT BEACH INN, Rte. 77, Cape Elizabeth, ME 04107; 207-799-1517. A 20-guestroom (some with private baths) old-fashioned Maine seacoast hotel a few minutes from the Maine Turnpike. Open from Memorial Day through Oct. 31. Continental breakfast included in room rate. Dinner served. Convenient for side trips to the Old Port area of Portland, as well as many cultural, historical, and natural attractions nearby. Excellent for children. Belinda Waterhouse, Innkeeper.

Directions: Take Exit 7 off the Maine Turnpike and turn right onto Rte. 1. Continue 1/2 mi. and turn left onto Pleasant Hill Rd. Continue to the end of the road and turn left again onto Spurwink Rd. Stay on Spurwink until you reach the Spurwink Church on your left. Bear right onto Rte. 77 and the inn will be on your right about, 2 mi.

For B&B rates, see Index.

DOCKSIDE GUEST QUARTERS
York, Maine

There's something very romantic about awakening in the morning to the sound of sea gulls and the chug-chug of fishing boats putting out to sea. That's what the guests at the Dockside Guest Quarters enjoy, because it is located right on the harbor of York, Maine, and the action begins at dawn when the lobster and fishing boats head out to sea guided by hundreds of shore birds.

This section of southern Maine is a very happy combination of seaside life and a generous dollop of history.

The Dockside Guest Quarters includes the original New England homestead of the 1880s, called the Maine House, as well as several other cottage buildings of a contemporary design, each with its own porch and water view.

One of the uncrowded times to visit is in late May and early June when it's fun to wander along York beach, enjoy golf and tennis, or perhaps rent a sailboat for scooting around the harbor.

The Dockside Dining Room, an excellent restaurant on the grounds of the inn is an excellent place to dine after a long day of travel.

On nice mornings, guests bring their continental breakfast, consisting of fruit juices, fresh doughnuts and coffee cake, as well as bread and preserves, to the sunny porch on the ocean side of the Maine House. It's a good time to get acquainted.

DOCKSIDE GUEST QUARTERS, Harris Island Rd., York, Maine 03909; 207-363-2868. An 18-room waterside country inn 10 mi. from Portsmouth, N.H. Some studio suites in newer multi-unit cottages. York Village is a National Historic District. American plan available. Continental breakfast served to houseguests only. Dockside Dining Room serves lunch and dinner to travelers daily except Mondays. Open from Memorial Day weekend in May through Columbus Day in Oct. Lawn games, shuffleboard and badminton, fishing, sailing, and boating from the premises. Golf, tennis, and swimming nearby; safe and picturesque paths and roadways for walks, bicycling, and jogging. Credit cards are not accepted for any amounts over fifty dollars. Personal checks accepted for payment of food and lodgings incurred by registered guests. David and Harriet Lusty, Innkeepers.

Directions: From U.S. 1 or I-95, take Exit at York to Rte. 1A. Follow 1A thru center of old York Village, take Rte. 103 (a side street off Rte. 1A leading to the harbor), and watch for signs to the inn.

For B&B rates, see Index.

DRAGONWICK INN
Belfast, Maine

Clean, bright, larger-than-average rooms are two of the mental pictures I conjure up when I think of the Dragonwick Inn. The inn is a white clapboard sitting up on a little knoll off Route 3, the road from Belfast to Augusta, and just a little over a mile from Route 1, the principal north-south road on the Maine coast.

There are sixty acres of quiet woods and fields, where guests may go hiking or cross-country skiing, and a natural pond offers a refreshing dip or ice skating in the winter months. By the way, if you like the taste of fresh raspberries, they're for the picking in the patch out back.

Breakfast is served either at hearthside in the large country kitchen, or on the sun porch through the french doors.

Innkeeper Steve Swayze pointed out that the original structure, built in 1803 with later additions, was believed to have been constructed as a tavern, but later became a farm. He and his wife, Elizabeth, have completed total restoration of the main house, preserving the very comfortable country atmosphere, which includes three sitting rooms on the first floor.

As is the case with many B&B owners, Steve and Elizabeth,, originally from Syracuse, New York, were inspired to have their own place by visiting inns and deciding they wanted to change their location and lifestyle.

"So far, we've found it very interesting and rewarding," is their comment.

Dragonwick is only a mile and a half from the town of Belfast, a working town, where visitors may catch a glimpse of true Maine life steeped in tradition and pride in one's work. Shops provide tourists with the opportunity to indulge themselves in fine wares and treasured collectibles.

DRAGONWICK INN, Rte.3, Belmont Ave., Belfast, ME 04915; 207-338-3988. A 7-guestroom (2½ shared baths) bed-and-breakfast inn just a short distance from Penobscot Bay and the town of Belfast. Breakfast, the only meal served, is included in the room rate. Open all year. No pets. No credit cards. Steve and Elizabeth Swayze, Innkeepers.

Directions: Leave the Maine Turnpike at Brunswick. Follow Rte. 1 to Belfast, turn left on Rte. 3 for 1.3 mi. Alternate route: leave I-95 in Augusta and follow Rte. 3 to Belfast.

For B&B rates, see Index.

ELFINHILL
Newcastle, Maine

The twin villages of Newcastle and Damariscotta face each other across the Damariscotta River, about six and one-half miles north of Wiscasset. Elfinhill is the first of two bed-and-breakfast inns on the River Road about a half-mile from Route 1. My notes about the Captain's House, immediately next door, are also in these pages.

Elfinhill is unique, if for no other reason, because Ms. Emma Stephenson is originally from Kent, England, and as she says, "We are a true British-American-style B&B."

Of course, I was intrigued by the name "elfinhill," and with a twinkle in her eye she pointed out the biggest elf I'd ever seen, seated in the garden in the rear of the inn. He's five feet eight inches tall with a jolly smile, red cheeks, yellow hat, blue pants, red jacket, and a big yellow tie. Emma explained that he was obtained when the Danbury Fair in Connecticut closed a few years ago.

There are three bedrooms here with shared bathrooms. At breakfast time, Emma says, she specializes in coffee cakes. There are blackberries from the garden and fresh fruit in season, along with cheeses, homemade preserves and jellies and, of course, a wide choice of coffee and English teas. Incidentally, she also does a brisk business in specialty baking.

Elfinhill enjoys a very pleasant view of the Damariscotta River, and I must point out that it was through her generosity that I learned about the Mill Pond Inn, also located in Damariscotta.

ELFINHILL, 20 River Rd., Newcastle, ME 04553; 207-563-1886. A 3-guestroom (shared baths) bed-and-breakfast accommodation with a real British air about 6 mi. north of Wiscasset. Open all year. Breakfast is included in the room rate. Conveniently located to enjoy the many natural and recreational attractions on the Pemaquid and Boothbay peninsulas. Second floor area is non-smoking. No pets. No credit cards. Personal checks accepted. Emma Stephenson, Innkeeper.

Directions: About 6½ mi. past Wiscasset, on Rte. 1, turn right, following signs for Newcastle. Take River Rd. and watch for Elfinhill on the left, 6/10 of a mi. from Rte. 1.

For B&B rates, see Index.

ENGLISH MEADOWS INN
Kennebunkport, Maine

English Meadows Inn is a 19th-century Victorian farmhouse that has been operating as an inn for over eighty years. From Route 35 it's easy to identify the inn by the lilac-tree-lined drive and a weathervane in the shape of a whale.

From the front yard it's possible to look across the trees and fields to the tower of the church in Dock Square in Kennebunkport where there is a collection of shops, restaurants, churches, and galleries, as well as deep-sea fishing boats.

When I first visited this inn I was greeted enthusiastically by two friendly dogs, Ramona and Buttons, who seemed to lead me naturally to the sideporch where I could look through the large windows into a spotlessly clean kitchen. And it was here, the next morning, I enjoyed one of Claudia Kelly's wonderful full New England breakfasts.

Claudia is the daughter of Gene and Helene Kelly who came to Kennebunkport a few years ago and turned this Victorian gem into a trim bed-and-breakfast inn.

There are fourteen lodging rooms furnished with brass and iron beds, hooked rugs, early quilts, and wonderful prints.

The Kelly family's interest in antiques is reflected in their own Whaler Antiques Shop which has country furniture and accessories, and wicker folk art.

ENGLISH MEADOWS INN, R.F.D. 1, Route 35, Kennebunkport, Maine 04046; 207-967-5766. A 14-bedroom bed-and-breakfast inn (2 have private baths, 12 share 6 baths), just a short distance from the center of Kennebunkport. A full breakfast is the only meal offered. Open from April to the end of October. A beautiful beach which is spectacular in all weather nearby, as well as some splendid shopping, antiquing, and backroading. No credit cards. The Kelly Family, Innkeepers.

Directions: Use Exit 3 from Maine Turnpike. (If coming north slow down and be sure you take the correct turn.) Follow routes 35 and 9A to Kennebunkport. The inn is on the right-hand side 5 mi. before reaching Kennebunkport.

For B&B rates, see Index.

GOOSE COVE LODGE
Deer Isle, Maine

Although Goose Cove Lodge is a modified American plan inn, George and Elli Pavloff have set aside a few weeks at the beginning and end of the season to offer the readers of this book a delightful bed-and-breakfast experience. See the dates in the italicized paragraph below.

Goose Cove Lodge, like most of the other bed-and-breakfast inns included in this book, represents an unusual, and distinctive accommodation. Located on a gorgeous bay and secluded cove, the bedrooms are in individual cabins and cottages tucked into a wooded hillside. They all have private bathrooms and fireplaces that are particularly welcome during the late spring and mid-fall.

A combination of the really spectacular beauty of the place, as well as its privacy, combine to make Goose Cove Lodge something quite special. Innkeeper Elli Pavloff says, "It is one of the very special places with a magic all its own—there aren't many places that are still unspoiled."

I had better emphasize that Sunset, Maine, is not really on the road to anywhere except the fishing village of Stonington, a few miles away. The reader will see from the directions that one wouldn't just happen to be "driving by," but would be making a special effort to drive down the Penobscot Bay Peninsula, across the bridge, and into Deer Isle.

Please note that bed-and-breakfast rates and accommodations are available only at certain times during the year.

GOOSE COVE LODGE, Sunset, Deer Isle, Me. 04683; 207-348-2508. A 22-room (60 people) resort-inn on beautiful Penobscot Bay approx. 1 hr. from Rte. 1 at Bucksport. Open May 1 to mid-Oct. B&B rate available May 1 to mid-June; mid -Sept. to mid-Oct. Modified American plan mid-June to mid-Sept. Meals served to houseguests only. Swimming, boating, canoeing, hiking, and birdwatching all available at the inn. Other outdoor sports, including backroading, golf, tennis, etc., nearby. Especially adaptable for children of all ages. Elli and George Pavloff, Innkeepers.

Directions: From Bucksport, drive 4 mi. north on Rte. 1 and turn right at Rte. 15 down the Blue Hill Peninsula to Deer Isle Village. Turn right in village at sign to Sunset, Maine. Proceed 3 mi., turn right at Goose Cove Lodge sign. Follow dirt road 1½ mi. to inn.

For B&B rates, see Index.

GRANE'S FAIRHAVEN INN
Bath, Maine

Bath is one of those interesting communities on U.S. 1 (the coastal route) leading to Camden, Mt. Desert, and points north into Canada.

Somewhat separated from the rather interesting downtown section of Bath on the Kennebec River where the world's largest naval crane can be seen for miles around, is Grane's Fairhaven Inn, overlooking this selfsame river.

It has beautiful plantings on green lawns, cross-country ski trails leading into the woods, and a very quiet and pleasant aspect.

The building dates to about 1790 and was lived in by members of the same family for 125 years. The present owners, Jane Wyllie and Gretchen Williams, have done much to preserve the original warmth and Maine-coast ambience.

There are several places to curl up quietly with a book or listen to music in the sitting rooms, and the bedrooms are all furnished with appropriate country-inn furniture.

A full breakfast is available each morning—plenty of fresh fruits, hot and cold cereal, homemade jam or marmalade, piping hot biscuits, muffins, or bread, bacon and eggs, and various types of soufflés and omelets on occasion.

GRANE'S FAIRHAVEN INN, No. Bath Rd., Bath, Me. 04530; 207-443-4391. A 9-bedroom old country home with shared baths on 27 acres of woods and fields on the Kennebec River. Open year-round. Full country breakfast available. Hiking, nature walks, cross-country skiing, snowshoeing on grounds. Swimming, golfing, picnicking, tennis, boating, fishing nearby. Performing Arts Center offers Fri. & Sat. concerts (classical, jazz, bluegrass). Jane Wyllie and Gretchen Williams, Innkeepers.

Directions: From U.S. 1 south in Bath follow signs for Congress Ave., turning right off U.S. 1 and right again on Congress Ave. At 4-street intersection, take Oak Grove (first street on left). Follow Oak Grove 1½ miles and turn right immediately beyond large barn. Look for inn sign ½ mile on left.

For B&B rates, see Index.

GREY ROCK INN
Northeast Harbor, Maine

Grey Rock Inn on Mt. Desert Island on the upper coast of Maine was built as a private estate in the early 1900s. The inn has an alpine setting of evergreens and berry bushes and has quite a few woodland walks on the property.

The bedrooms are quite large, many with handsome brass beds, which are turned down for guests each night. Each room faces the harbor and has its own bath. They are cool and shady in the summertime and most pleasantly decorated.

My first visit to Grey Rock came in 1974 when I discovered that Janet Millet is British, having been brought up in England. This means that very frequently she invites her guests to join her in the living room for a cup of tea in the late afternoon. The scene is most reminiscent of an English country-house hotel. Guests are frequently en route to New Brunswick by land or Nova Scotia by ferry. Many stay longer to enjoy the wonderful attractions at Acadia National Park.

Some of the real treats at the continental breakfast are the various kinds of muffins which are baked fresh every morning. These include blueberry, ginger pecan, date, raisin, and honey muffins, as well as prune danish, cranberry bread, cheeses, and croissants. English touches are provided with the marmalade preserves and tea. In summer, it's fun to breakfast on the porch.

GREY ROCK INN, Harborside Rd., Northeast Harbor, Me. 04662; 207-276-9360. A 9-bedroom village inn in the town of Northeast Harbor, adjacent to Acadia National Park and all of the attractions of this unusual region. European plan. Continental breakfast served to houseguests only. No other meals served. Small cottage available for minimum 4-night stay. Season from early spring to Nov. 1. Children 14 yrs. and older preferred. No pets. No credit cards. Janet Millet, Innkeeper.

Directions: Located on the right-hand side of Rte. 198 approaching the town of Northeast Harbor. Note sign for inn. Do not try to make a right-hand turn at this point, but proceed about one block, turn around and approach the inn on the left up the steep hill.

For B&B rates, see Index.

HARBOR LIGHTS TOURIST HOME
Southwest Harbor, Maine

Southwest Harbor is a very interesting working town at the far end of Mt. Desert Island in upper Maine. There is a sprinkling of people who have known about it but not told their friends for many years. A touch of very unusual glamour is the Hinkley Boatyard where what some people call the most splendid sailboats and yachts in the world are built. Casual visitors cannot get inside the yard but you can see enough from the outside.

These and other boatyards in Southwest Harbor are one of the reasons that Hilda Leighton keeps the Harbor Lights Tourist Home year-round. The boat people come up to negotiate the sale, to visit their boats while they are being built, and to get them when they are completed. The town is also a no-nonsense fishing village. There's something refreshing about real stores that are patronized by people who live there year-round.

Harbor Lights is a big yellow Victorian house with green shutters, a mansard roof, and a lovely kind of homey feeling about it as soon as you step in through the old front doors. For example, in the living room there's an organ and lots of pictures of Hilda's family. In the hallway there is a very big magazine rack with all kinds of magazines and paperbacks.

There seemed to be an endless number of sensibly furnished bedrooms.

I think I would like to visit there during the winter sometime. Can you imagine that harbor with about four inches of fresh snow?

HARBOR LIGHTS TOURIST HOME, Rte. 102, Southwest Harbor, Me. 04679; 207-244-3835. A 9-room Victorian village inn on Mt. Desert Island in a busy boat-building center, 20 mi. south of Ellsworth. Most rooms have private bath. No meals served; however, outdoor grill, refrigerator, and pinic tables available. Open year-round. Near Acadia National Park and all attractions in this resort region. Hilda Leighton, Proprietor.

Directions: Follow US #1 to Ellsworth, Rte. 3 to Rte. 102 on Mt. Desert Island to Southwest Harbor. Go through blinker in business district, and look for inn sign on left side; inn is across the street from yarn shop.

For Lodging rates, see Index.

HARTWELL HOUSE
Ogunquit, Maine

Ogunquit is a seaside village where the flavor of old Maine remains zesty and alive. Among other reasons that tourists flock to it every year are the beautiful beach and the Marginal Way that meanders at cliff's edge past innumerable picture-postcard Maine seascapes and fabulous rock formations.

In addition to the lure of the forest and the sea, there is summer theater, art galleries, boutiques, and many restaurants.

Hartwell House is on the road from the center of Ogunquit to Perkins Cove. It is a two-story, pleasantly designed building fronted with many Moorish arches. There are most pleasant gardens in the front and a considerable lawn in the rear.

There are nine accommodations, including two efficiency apartments; all have private baths and all are furnished entirely in Early American and English antiques featuring four-poster beds and handsome bedspreads.

It's withing walking distance of the beach and also on a minibus route that serves the town.

Breakfast is buffet-style with fruit salad, homemade breads and coffee.

HARTWELL HOUSE, P.O. Box 393, 116 Shore Rd., Ogunquit, Maine 03907; 207-646-7210. A 9-room inn providing a very compatible atmosphere for a limited number of guests (2 rooms may be rented as a complete apartment). Open year-round. The ocean, Perkins Cove, the Marginal Way, Ogunquit Playhouse all within walking distance. Fishing, golf, swimming, bicycles, sailing, nearby. Shared tennis and swimming pool privileges. Not suitable for children under 14. No pets. Trisha and Jim Hartwell, Innkeepers.

Directions: Follow I-95 north through New Hampshire to Maine; take last exit before Maine toll booth; north on Rte. 1, 7 mi. to center of Ogunquit. Turn right on Shore Road approx. ¾ of mi. Hartwell on right.

For B&B rates, see Index.

HAWTHORN INN
Camden, Maine

A converted Victorian home with light, airy rooms, fireplaces, spacious grounds, and a large deck offering a see-through-the-trees view of Camden Harbor, the Hawthorn Inn is set back from the road a bit and is within a one-block walk of Camden shops, restaurants and the town dock.

The center reception hall has an imposing staircase that goes up three stories, and is flanked on both sides by sitting rooms, one with a fireplace. During the winter, a cheery fire burns every night. There are successions of little sitting rooms and parlors in various places throughout the inn, and there is a piano. The pleasant bedrooms have hooked rugs and antique quilts, and two have private baths.

Fresh fruit and homemade muffins are part of the continental breakfast served in the sunny dining room. A full à la carte breakfast is available for an additional charge.

There is a rather pleasant association with the Shakespeare Theater, just a short walk away, as all of the opening night receptions for the dramatic productions are held at the Hawthorn Inn. The theater, by the way, performs both Shakespeare and other dramatists during the summer season.

There is insufficient space for all of the many attractions of Camden and vicinity to be noted. However, I'm sure the Hawthorn Inn will be glad to provide prospective guests with much information.

HAWTHORN INN, 9 High St., Camden, ME 04843; 207-236-8842. A 7-guestroom Victorian inn in the center of a harborside Maine village. Continental breakfast included in room rate. Full à la carte breakfast also available. Open all year. Conveniently located to enjoy the many cultural, scenic, and historic attractions in the area. Douglas and Jocelyn Morrison, Innkeepers.

Directions: On Rte. 1 in Camden, continue through the business district and around the curve on High St.

For B&B rates, see Index.

HILLTOP HOUSE
Boothbay Harbor, Maine

The traveler on U.S. 1, the coastal route through Maine, is in for a treat if he turns off on Route 27 and drives the twelve miles down the peninsula into Boothbay Harbor. There's much to see and enjoy and it is well worth an overnight stay and even more. I would advise stopping at the first information booth and getting a booklet and a map or two to help in getting oriented.

Hilltop House, as well as its neighboring guest house, Topside, is right down on the harbor at the top of McKown Hill. It is a real "down home" type of place with comfortable rooms, and the operating family has been here for forty years. It's a big old house with an inviting front porch and a tree with a swing on it, and some satisfying views of Boothbay Harbor.

A continental breakfast of hot muffins and coffee is included in the room rate.

I visited Boothbay Harbor shortly after Labor Day and although there were still quite a few people there, I can imagine that during July and August the one-way streets would be jammed. I can't see why anyone who can come to Maine in September and October would possibly want to go to this section of the Maine coast in July or August.

HILLTOP HOUSE, McKown Hill, Boothbay Harbor, Me. 04538; 207-633-2941. A 6-bedroom farmhouse lodging with shared baths (1 rm. with private bath) on a hill overlooking Boothbay Harbor; also a family unit with complete kitchen and bath. Open year-round. Continental breakfast included. All summertime activities within a 3-minute walk—sightseeing, fishing, excursion boats, antiquing nearby. Swimming beaches within easy driving distance. No credit cards. Mrs. Cora Mahr, Manager.

Directions: From Rte. 1 north of Bath, follow Rte. 27 to Boothbay Harbor and continue on through, watching for a sign for McKown Hill on the left.

For B&B rates, see Index.

THE HOMEPORT INN
Searsport, Maine

Searsport on Penobscot Bay is one of the antiquing centers of Maine. According to a little folder on the town there must be at least twenty antique shops plus a few galleries.

During the last century Searsport was well known as a lumbering port. Maine lumber was carried to many parts of the world.

The original owner of the Homeport Inn was a sea captain who provided his house with a widow's walk which, I understand, can be used today as a bedroom in an emergency.

The house itself befits such a sophisticated individual and a hundred or so years later the furnishings, I'm sure, would be most pleasing to him, including the impressive flocked wallpaper, marble fireplace, and crystal chandelier.

Abovestairs, the bedrooms are almost opulently furnished. Some beds have a canopy and there are attractive lace curtains and appropriate wall hangings. Six of the rooms have private baths.

Breakfast is served in a long narrow room, which at one time was a porch looking out over the fields to Penobscot Bay. In clement weather, breakfast can be enjoyed on the patio, with a view of the English garden, the fountain, and the bay. A full breakfast, along with homemade muffins, juices, and coffee, is offered.

The Homeport is right across U.S. 1 from the Carriage House, and I'm sure that both are equally comfortable. If you call one and it is full, I'm sure they'll recommend the other.

THE HOMEPORT INN, Searsport, Maine 04974; 207-548-2259. A 7-bedroom elegantly furnished New England sea captain's mansion. Convenient to recreational, cultural, and natural attractions in the Penobscot Bay area. Breakfast only meal served. Open year-round. Edith and Dr. George Johnson, Innkeepers.

Directions: Mrs. Johnson suggests, as an alternate to Rte.1, following Rte. I-95 to Augusta and then taking Rte. 3 to Belfast, just below Searsport.

For B&B rates, see Index.

HOMEWOOD INN ON CASCO BAY
Yarmouth, Maine

I think the best time to visit Maine is in September and October. The sun is still high, the water is still warm, and the principal roads are relatively free of the heavy traffic found in July and August.

That's why I was delighted to find my good friends Fred and Colleen Webster at the Homewood Inn offering bed-and-breakfast accommodations in June, September, and October.

Lodging rooms are in a group of waterside cottages overlooking scenic Casco Bay. In the early fall on chilly evenings they are very cozy with the crackling fires in the fireplaces.

There is much to do in the area, including shopping in Portland's Old Port Exchange, visiting L.L. Bean in Freeport, and the many state parks and museums up and down the Maine coast.

Recreation on the grounds includes a swimming pool, shuffleboard, croquet, saltwater swimming, tennis courts, and bike rentals. The inn also boasts the Maine Craft Shop run by Doris and Ted Gillette, who have taken special pains to seek out and display authentic "down east" crafts.

Late spring and early fall B&B guests can take advantage of the full breakfast as a part of their room rate. It is a welcome start for another day on the Maine coast.

HOMEWOOD INN, P.O. Box 196B Drinkwater Point, Yarmouth, Me. 04096; 207-846-3351. A 46-bedroom waterside inn on Casco Bay north of Portland. European plan. Breakfast and dinner served to travelers daily, except Mondays when steak or lobster cookout at night available (by advance reservation). Open early June to mid-Oct. B&B only available in June, Sept., and Oct. Bicycles (incl. tandems), pool, tennis, croquet court, hiking, saltwater swimming on grounds. Golf, riding, fishing, state parks, theater nearby. Fred and Colleen Webster, Ted and Doris Gillette, and Julie Webster Frank, Innkeepers.

Directions: From the south, take Exit 9 from Maine Tpke. (I-95) to Rte. 1-N, or Exit 17 from I-295 to Rte. 1-N, and follow signs to inn. From north (Brunswick area) from I-95, take "Yarmouth, Rte. 1" exit and follow signs to the inn.

For B&B rates, see Index.

KENNISTON HILL INN
Boothbay, Maine

It was the gracious, rather stately, white clapboard exterior of this inn, on a little knoll in a wonderful grove of trees on Route 27, between Boothbay and Boothbay Harbor, that originally attracted me. I'm delighted to say that both the interior, and the atmosphere generated by Paul Morrisette and Ellen Winn confirmed my initial impression.

Eight large, tastefully decorated rooms (four with fireplaces) have homelike accommodations, created by handmade quilts, delicately colored wallpaper, and something I always like to find at an inn—fresh flowers.

The entrance leads into a very impressive living room boasting a gorgeous fireplace with a big mantel and lots of interesting, fancy decorations. The small library with another fireplace is a sort of quiet little place for reading and games.

By virtue of Paul's experience as owner of the well-known Country Kitchen Restaurant in Brattleboro, Vermont, for many, many years, bed-and-breakfast guests are treated to what he assures me is "not a continental breakfast."

"Today we had a blend of orange juice, bananas, and lemon juice for a drink, followed by zucchini and walnut pancakes with spiced apples and raisins, and bacon and coffee."

One might say that Kenniston Hill Inn is the right combination of Maine and Vermont.

KENNISTON HILL INN, Rte. 27, Boothbay, ME 04537; 207-633-2159. An 8-guestroom 200-year-old colonial bed-and-breakfast inn (mostly private baths) 1 mi. from Boothbay Harbor. A full breakfast is included in the room rate. Open April thru Dec. Shopping, boat trips, fishing, golf, bicycling, restaurants, and theater nearby. No pets. Paul Morissette and Ellen Winn, Innkeepers.

Directions: The Kenniston Inn is located in Boothbay on Rte. 27. Turn off Rte. 1 just after Wiscasset, inn is on the left, 1 mi. from Boothbay Harbor.

For B&B rates, see Index.

LINCOLN HOUSE
Dennysville, Maine

There are two ways to travel from Maine to New Brunswick, one is to follow I-95 to Bangor and then take Route 9 cross-country to the border crossing at Calais. The other is to follow Route 1 through the Maine seaside towns and villages. This is an excellent opportunity to see Maine at its "down-east" best.

About 30 miles south of Calais and the same distance north of Machias, is the town of Dennysville, on the banks of the Dennys River, a habitat of the famous North Atlantic salmon. In 1787, Judge Theodore Lincoln, an ancestor of Abraham Lincoln, built the Lincoln House. It was and still remains the first and oldest house in the village.

In 1976, Mary Carol and Jerry Haggerty, the innkeepers, restored this home to its original simple elegance, naming it the Lincoln House Country Inn. They offer very pleasant accommodations for the overnight traveler en route to or from Canada or the longer-staying vacationer.

The first memorable experience is to walk into the lovely Keeping Room, where there is a most unusual fireplace with a built-in hot water heater, which was used during Colonial days. The experience into the past continues through the other sitting rooms, the guest bedrooms, and the adjacent barn pub, whose walls are decorated with memorabilia of many years ago, and also a dart board.

The kitchen is always handy for coffee and conversation, and the guests enjoy the use of the library and the living room with a Steinway grand piano.

The 95 wooded acres around the Lincoln House have many examples of wildlife, including bald eagles and osprey. Families of seal swim in the river, and deer abound on the old logging roads and nature trails.

To make things even more pleasant, travelers can enjoy a single entrée dinner each evening, and for overnight lodgers breakfast is also available at an additional cost.

LINCOLN HOUSE, Rte. 1, Dennysville, ME 04628; 207-726-3953. A 6-guestroom inn (sharing 4 baths) midway between Machias and Calais, Maine. Open all year for lodging by reservation. Breakfast and dinner served. Most convenient for northern Maine seacoast historic, natural, and recreational attractions. Mary Carol and Jerry Haggerty, Innkeepers.

Directions: Follow Rte. 1 north about 27 mi. from Machias, Maine. Look for inn signs.

For B&B rates, see Index.

MILL POND INN
Newcastle, Maine

Here's an inn that has its own resident American eagle, as well as loons, herons, otters, and all varieties of ducks. These furry and feathered friends can be seen from the deck, the Keeping Room, and many of the bedrooms overlooking the Mill Pond.

Three or four things remain in my mind after a June visit. I was impressed by the fresh flowers in all the rooms, as well as the rocking chairs and colorful afghans. I was also delighted to find oversized cotton bath towels.

There are beautifully furnished bedrooms and a handsome Keeping Room, used as the breakfast room, with walls of extra-wide wood paneling. A red brick fireplace now has a very efficient-looking Franklin stove that burns on chilly mornings.

Innkeeper Gloria Krellman fled the world of academe and found this really exceptional location overlooking the Mill Pond, just across the village street from the south end of Lake Damariscotta. It's actually in Newcastle, Maine, but the little community is called Damariscotta Mills. It's a grey-shingled house with white trim.

Gloria assures me that a full breakfast is served from 7:30 to 9:00 A.M.; from 9:00 to 9:30, it's possible to get coffee and rolls. I noticed that she was grinding her own coffee beans.

As lovely as the Mill Pond is and as attractive as the setting may be, I think the Mill Pond Inn would be a hit in any location.

MILL POND INN, RFD 1, Box 245, Newcastle, ME 04553; 207-563-8014. A 7-guestroom (5 with private baths) bed-and-breakfast inn a short distance from Rte. 1 in the Damariscotta/Newcastle area. Breakfast is included in the room rate. Open all year. Conveniently located to enjoy the unusual ambience of the mid-Maine coast historic, recreational, and cultural attractions. No credit cards. No pets. No smoking. Gloria Krellman, Innkeeper.

Directions: Coming north on Rte. 1, exit at Damariscotta/Newcastle. Follow signs to Rte. 215 north for 2 mi.

For B&B rates, see Index.

THE MOORELOWE
York Harbor, Maine

For the traveler going north on I-95 and the Maine Turnpike, York Harbor is the first exit after crossing the Piscataqua River Bridge between Portsmouth, New Hampshire, and southern Maine. This bridge, incidentally, is a very graceful span and is a welcome replacement for the drawbridge that was used for many years and quite frequently held up traffic.

York is a quiet, peaceful village and a very appropriate introduction for first-time travelers to Maine. The Historic District has a group of fine old buildings and historical sites, including the Old Gaol Museum, Jefferds Tavern, the Elizabeth Perkins House, and other splendid pre-Revolutionary dwellings.

The Moorelowe is a yellow building on the right-hand side of the main street with a generous enclosed front porch and lots of comfortable wicker furniture. It is the home of Mr. and Mrs. Kenneth Day and their dog Pudgy, and for someone looking for some authentic "down east" atmosphere, Mr. Day would be hard to top. He's about as laconic a man as I have ever met.

However, while I helped him make a bed he told me that people were always talking about how clean the rooms were and many of his guests have been returning for many years. Children are quite welcome and the beach is nearby.

Breakfast is not served here, but as Mr. Day said, "You can get breakfast anywhere."

The downstairs living room is right out of a New England sampler with a piano and lots of music and lots of photographs of the Day children and grandchildren.

I think the Moorelowe could be a lot of fun. However it *was* a bit disillusioning to discover that Mr. Day, who is a sort of walking advertisement for the state of Maine, was actually born and raised in Colrain, Massachusetts!

THE MOORELOWE, Route 1A, York Harbor, Maine 03911; 207-363-2526. A 7-room guest house (3 rooms with private baths). Breakfast not offered. Open June 1 to Sept. 30. York Beach, boats for fishing and pleasure trips nearby; tennis and golf within 10-min. drive. Convenient to all southern Maine attractions. No credit cards. Mr. & Mrs. Kenneth Day, Proprietors.

Directions: Use the York Exit from I-95. Follow 1A into village.

For Lodging rates, see Index.

THE MOORINGS
Southwest Harbor, Maine

The Moorings is an excellent place for far more than just a one-night stopover. It is a trim little inn located right on the fjord-like shores of Southwest Harbor. Among the pastimes that guests may enjoy are fishing, hiking, clamming, biking, sailing, rowboating, or canoeing, exploring, and picnicking.

The Moorings is also a sail inn, which means that people who are enjoying the beautiful waters of Mt. Desert Island may tie up for a few days and take their ease on land enjoying the comforts of the house.

The main house is the oldest in Southwest Harbor. All of the bedrooms have private baths and some have sitting rooms. Their names are copied from sailing vessels built in Maine: *Nirvana, Jupiter, Monarch,* and *Dauntless,* to name a few.

Decorations for the most part are maritime in nature, including duck decoys, lanterns, sea chests, sextants, binnacles, and many books on sailing.

Each bedroom (without housekeeping) has a tray for breakfast including orange juice, doughnuts, and coffee which can be enjoyed in the living room in front of the fireplace, outside on the lawn, or in the bedroom. There is also a small refrigerator for guests' use.

Most intriguing is the fact that the inn is located right next door to the Hinckley boatyards.

THE MOORINGS, Manset, Southwest Harbor, Me. 04679; 207-244-5523; 207-244-3210. A fjord-side country inn in a famous yacht-building and fishing port on Mount Desert Island. A variety of lodgings located in the main house, motel, cottages, and apartments. Immediately adjacent to a restaurant serving lunch and dinner. Open from May to October. Conveniently located to enjoy all of the Mount Desert Island recreational, cultural, and historic attractions. No credit cards. Betty and Leslie King, Innkeepers.

Directions: From Ellsworth, follow Rtes. 3 and 102 to Mount Desert Island and Southwest Harbor. Turn left on 102A; 1½ mi. on Shore Rd.

For B&B rates, see Index.

NEWAGEN SEASIDE INN
Cape Newagen, Maine

At the seaward tip of Southport Island, the Newagen Seaside Inn is a place where the exciting, rocky coast of Maine, so longed for by many of our West Coast readers, may be experienced in all of its awesome beauty. Several paths on the broad lawns lead to the ocean, or a sheltered cove with a saltwater swimming pool, or docks where there are working lobster boats and ducks and seabirds.

The island's known history dates back to a meeting between a British captin, Christopher Levett, and the Indian, Sagamor, in 1623. Indians destroyed the fort and settlement fifty years later.

Although I had seen the brochure in advance, the Newagen was somewhat larger than I had expected. The main inn, built in the early '40s, is in the style of a Colonial mansion with four square pillars at the entrance. It has twenty-five bedrooms, with private baths and a living room with a large fireplace. There is a smaller building with ten bedrooms and baths "down the hall," called the Little Inn, that offers bed-and-breakfast acommodations. Several cottages of varying sizes are within sight and sound of the crashing waves.

The Newagen is on the European plan, except for bed-and-breakfast rates available to guests in the Little Inn, and breakfast, lunch, and dinner are served in the traditional dining room. Innkeeper Heidi Larsen tells me everything is homemade, including breads, rolls, and cakes.

She showed me a little gazebo out on the lawn—"a beautiful place to get married," she said. In fact, she and her husband, Peter, were married there themselves!

NEWAGEN SEASIDE INN, Southport Island, Cape Newagen, ME 04552; 207-633-5242 (summer); 633-5558 (winter). A rather sedate 48-guestroom (private and shared baths) full-service inn on the tip of a small island beyond Boothbay Harbor. European plan, mid-June to mid-Sept., serving breakfast, lunch, and dinner. B&B rates available in the Little Inn. Swimming pool, lawn games, putting green, nature trails on grounds. Charter sailing, rowboating, and fishing from inn's dock. Golf and tennis nearby. Ideal for children. Heidi and Peter Larsen, Innkeepers.

Directions: From Rte. 1, follow Rte. 27 south through Boothbay Harbor, cross the drawbridge and continue around the island about 5 mi. to inn entrance.

For B&B rates, see Index.

OCEAN REEFS LODGE
Chamberlain, Maine

I was taking the shortcut from Waldoboro to New Harbor, Maine, near Pemaquid Point, when I happened to notice this pleasant little waterside bed-and-breakfast opposite Long Cove. It's a Maine lodge with a partly closed-in front porch, which provides an excellent view of the constant parade of water traffic. There are dozens of bobbing lobster pots, and you can watch the lobstermen come and pull them up to see if there's anything in them.

This is the rockbound coast of Maine, on a secluded road—an ambience that I must confess is hard to find.

Ocean Reefs has four rooms, each with its own private bath, and two cabins with a private bath in the house. It's not very fancy, but it's a great place for just getting off by yourself and being quiet and doing a little fishing, if you care to, or reading lots of books, or watching the cormorants diving for fish or floating on the surface of the Cove. There are even seals in the vicinity, off Ross and Haddock Islands nearby.

One can watch the Atlantic waves break over the reefs and make day trips to Camden, Reid State Park, Bailey's Island, Boothbay Harbor, and so forth. It's not far from L.L. Bean.

Ocean Reefs Lodge was open and operating during 1984; however, I'd like to suggest that anyone planning a trip there in 1985 telephone in advance. By the way, a continental breakfast is included in the room rate.

OCEAN REEFS LODGE, P.O. Box 105, Rte. 32, Chamberlain, Me. 04541; 207-677-2386. A 6-bedroom bed-and-breakfast waterside inn on a secluded Maine coast road, with an unusually pleasant view and situation. Open from mid-June to mid-Oct. Fishing, swimming and boating, and Maine coast attractions nearby. Be sure to telephone in advance.

Directions: Leave Rte. 1 at Damariscotta and follow Rte. 130 to Rte. 32 at New Harbor, then turn north.

For B&B rates, see Index.

OLD FORT INN
Kennebunkport, Maine

Kennebunkport is a Maine waterside town that still retains the atmosphere it had when clipper ships sailed from its shores. The lovely old sea captains' houses remain on its beautiful streets, and its winding river makes a real New England adventure.

The Old Fort Inn is a luxurious adult resort nestled in a secluded setting within walking distance of the ocean. Each of the colorful and beautifully decorated rooms has its own kitchen facilities, and maid service is provided.

Outdoor recreational facilities include a large fresh-water swimming pool, a private tennis court, and shuffleboard. Golf courses are only a few minutes away.

A continental breakfast served in the attractive lodge is included with the cost of the rooms.

OLD FORT INN, Old Fort Ave., Kennebunkport, Me. 04046; 207-967-5353. A 12-bedroom resort-inn in Kennebunkport within walking distance of the ocean in a historic Maine town. Includes a continental breakfast, and a full kitchen is provided with each bedroom. Daily maid service. Lodge and antique shop. Open from May 1 to Oct. 31. Heated pool, tennis court, shuffleboard on grounds. Bicycles, golf, salt water swimming and boating nearby. Not comfortable for children under 7. No pets. Sheila and David Aldrich, Innkeepers.

Directions: Take Exit 3 (Kennebunk) from the Main Turnpike. Take left on Route 35 and follow signs through Kennebunk to Kennebunkport. Take left at traffic light at Sunoco station. Go over drawbridge and take first right on Ocean Ave. Take Ocean Ave. to the Colony Hotel; turn left in front of the Colony, go to the Y in the road, go right ¼ mile on left.

For B&B rates, see Index.

OLDE GARRISON HOUSE
Cape Porpoise, Kennebunkport, Maine

Cape Porpoise, located just a few miles beyond Kennebunkport, is a real honest-to-goodness fishing village with a very paintable harbor, salt air, and gulls swooping down over returning fishing boats. Captain John Smith named it in 1614 for a school of porpoises he saw playing in the bay. What other small village boasts a plaque at the pier commemorating the repulse of the mighty British in 1782 by a small band of determined townspeople bent upon being masters of their own fate? Here at Cape Porpoise you'll find beauty, serenity, vistas, history, legends, deeds, and dire happenings.

There are no dire happenings at the Olde Garrison House overlooking the beautiful tidal cove in the front and a tidal marsh in the rear.

It is owned by Lyman Huff, who is a working lobsterman, and his wife Louise, both of whom are natives of Cape Porpoise.

Built in 1730, the house has very pleasant bedrooms and a simple kitchen where guests may use the refrigerator and boil water and toast toast. "Our guests seem to like it that way," Louise said, as she showed me through. "We have many people who have been returning for several years. There are four restaurants nearby and many more in Kennebunk."

Louise said that Mr. Huff was on a lobster boat at the time of my visit, but is a great talker and fills the guests with history and legends and wonderful stories about the state of Maine. In a time when it's hard to find a community that is not overrun with commercialism, Cape Porpoise has managed to hold its own, even though *some* travelers have found it.

OLDE GARRISON HOUSE, Cape Porpoise, Me. 04014; 207-967-3522. A 7-bedroom Cape Cod-type house overlooking a tidal cove in an unspoiled section of Kennebunkport. Two rms. with private baths; 5 rms. share 2 baths. Open from late May to Oct. 15. Advance reservations advised. Guests have the use of refrigerator and toaster and may boil water for breakfast. Many restaurants nearby. Sightseeing in historic, authentic fishing village, bicycle rentals, lobster boat tours nearby. All diversions available in Kennebunkport. No children under 10. No pets. No credit cards. Louise and Lyman Huff, Proprietors.

Directions: Follow Rte. 9 north from Kennebunkport for about 2 miles to Community Library in Cape Porpoise. Leaving Rte. 9, go straight on Pier Rd. and find Olde Garrison House on the left.

For Lodging rates, see Index.

THE PENTAGOET INN
Castine, Maine

Travelers hastening pell-mell across Maine on U.S. 1 between Bucksport and Ellsworth little realize that to the south lies the east Penobscot Bay region which has intriguing back roads, beautiful ponds, tidal basins, sequestered villages, historic landmarks, silversmiths, blacksmiths, wood carvers, and outdoor recreation of all kinds.

I'd suggest that the reader write to either the Pilgrim's Inn in Deer Isle, Maine, or Pentagoet Inn in Castine, for a special map showing all of the roads and enticements of this fascinating peninsula.

Castine is on the west side of one end of Route 175 and Route 166, thirty minutes from Route 1. In addition to being a fishing village and a stop on the famous Windjammer Cruises, it is also the home of the Maine Maritime Academy, and the location of the Pentagoet Inn.

Situated just one square from the town harbor, this gracious Victorian inn has a welcome warmth and dedicated sense of hospitality personified by its innkeeper, Natalie Saunders. She has supplemented the turn-of-the-century atmosphere with appropriate furniture and decorations, and a few fillips of her own.

A continental breakfast is included in the room rate. However, a full breakfast is available and features freshly baked-every-day bran muffins; in fact, Natalie starts baking them at six o'clock every morning. The remainder of the breakfast includes all kinds of eggs, pancakes, french toast, and similar day-strengthening offerings. On summer mornings, breakfast is served on the outside porch looking down into the harbor area.

THE PENTAGOET INN, Castine, Maine 04421; 207-326-8616. A 14-room inn in a seacoast village on the Penobscot Peninsula, 36 mi. from Bangor. Some rooms with shared baths. Breakfast and dinner served to travelers. Dinners are single entrée prix-fixe. Sunday brunch. Open every day in the year. Tennis, swimming, backroading, village strolling nearby. Clean, leashed pets permitted. Natalie Saunders, Innkeeper.

Directions: From south follow I-95 to Brunswick and use Rte. 1 exit. Follow Rte. 1 to a point 3 mi. past Bucksport. Turn right on Rte. 175 to Rte. 166 to Castine.

For B&B rates, see Index.

PILGRIM'S INN
Deer Isle, Maine

It may be stretching it a bit to drive the thirty miles from coastal Route 1 south into the Blue Hill Peninsula to reach Deer Isle and Pilgrim's Inn, but be assured that for anyone fortunate enough to book an overnight room, it is well worth the trip.

The twelve guest bedrooms are mostly quite large and little changed from Colonial days. Rooms feature richly hued pine floorboards, a woodstove, a queen-sized bed, antiques, old wooden furniture, and an unusual selection of books and magazines. Three rooms have private baths. The common room and the taproom have enormous fireplaces, and both the front parlors and the taproom have the original 1793 pine paneling.

Meals are served in the converted barn from mid-May to mid-October. There is always a full breakfast with a single menu that changes daily. Omelets, freshly baked pastry and blueberry pancakes are very popular. The maple syrup is genuine, the flowers are fresh and the hospitality is warm and friendly. During the winter, bed and breakfast is offered to the passing pilgrim.

PILGRIM'S INN, Deer Isle, Me. 04627; 207-348-6615. A 12 bedroom inn (some shared baths) in an island village on the Blue Hill Peninsula on the Maine coast. Modified American plan, May 21 to Oct. 23, includes hearty breakfast and a gourmet dinner. In season outside dinner reservations accepted. B&B rates available in winter. A 3-day minimum stay is required in August. Ten-speed bicycles available. Golf and tennis available for inn guests. The Deer Isle area is replete with all types of cultural and recreational advantages, including fishing, sailing, hiking and browsing. Jean and Dud Hendrick, Innkeepers.

Directions: From Boston, take I-95 to Brunswick exit. Take coastal Rte. 1 north past Bucksport. Turn right on Rte. 15 which travels to Deer Isle down the Blue Hill Peninsula. At the village, turn right on Main Street (Sunset Rd.) and proceed one block to the inn on the left side of the street, opposite the Harbor.

For B&B rates, see Index.

THE ROBERTS HOUSE
Wiscasset, Maine

The traveler bent on following Maine's rocky coast leaves I-95 at Brunswick and follows the fascinating convolutions of Route 1 through Bath, past the gigantic naval crane, and continues on a few more miles into Wiscasset, which is one of the most memorable villages in Maine.

The Roberts House sits right down in the village about three blocks from the river and is a beautiful 1799 house. There have been only four owners since that date and the bedrooms have their names on the doors.

The present owners are Ed and Alice Roberts, who have been coming here each summer for quite a number of years, leaving the gentler climate of Ventura, California. Now, with Ed retired, they are in Wiscasset most of the year, except when they decide to go off on a holiday themselves, now and then, as they put it, from November through May. If the magazines, books, paintings, and prints are any indication, they are certainly extremely literate and literary-minded. I found it very difficult to tear myself away.

The full country breakfast served to each houseguest includes homemade fresh muffins, omelets, and different varieties of pancakes with home ingredients.

Because it is such a snug house and is also the Robert's home, the guests, many of whom have returned for many years, soon get comfortably acquainted, sometimes in a lovely little sitting room with a fireplace and a piano, where there are spontaneous sing-alongs from time to time.

There's lots to see and do in Wiscasset and the Roberts House is a good place to use for a home base.

THE ROBERTS HOUSE, P.O. Box 413, Main St., Wiscasset, Me. 04578; 207-882-5055. A 4-bedroom (2 shared baths) 200-year-old home in downtown Wiscasset. A full country breakfast is the only meal served. Open June 1 to early Oct., and open by chance Nov. to June. Minimum stay 2 nights; if space available, 1-night stay O.K. Convenient for enjoyment of all of the recreational, cultural, and natural attractions which abound on this part of the Maine coast. School-age children. No pets. No credit cards; personal checks accepted. Ed and Alice Roberts, Proprietors.

Directions: The Roberts House sign is plainly visible on the west side of Main St. in Wiscassett.

For B&B rates, see Index.

THE SQUIRE TARBOX INN
Westport Island, Maine

Although Westport Island, which is on Maine's coast, is only eight miles from U.S. Route 1 at Wiscasset, it actually feels very much farther out of the way.

There are two types of guests at this inn: those who have learned that it's such a pleasant place to remain for a few days, and those who are en route to or from northern Maine, New Brunswick, Prince Edward Island or Nova Scotia.

The oldest part of this inn dates from 1763. It is quite small; nine guest rooms have been furnished with simple antiques, and three of them have private baths. A large hearth with original bake ovens, original floors, and wainscoting set the tone for this sedate white Colonial farmhouse.

The continental breakfast served in the dining room, or on the porch on sunshiny mornings, includes homemade breads and cakes.

The one principal difficulty for the bed-and-breakfast guest who may be rushing off to the Northeast or back to the city is the great temptation to stay at the Squire Tarbox for extra days.

THE SQUIRE TARBOX INN, Westport Island, R.D. #2, Box 2160, Wiscasset, Me. 04578; 207-882-7693. A 9-bedroom (6 rooms with shared baths) restored Colonial farmhouse on Rte. 144 in Westport, 8 mi. from Wiscasset. Modified American plan. All lodgings include continental breakfast. Breakfast served to houseguests only. Open from May 15 to end of Oct. Exploring, towns, beach, and harbors nearby. No pets. Bill and Karen Mitman, Innkeepers.

Directions: Take Rte. 1 north from Brunswick to Rte. 144, 7 mi. north of Bath. Follow Rte. 144 to Wiscasset-Westport Bridge. Inn is located 6 mi. south of bridge on Westport Island.

For B&B rates, see Index.

SURRY INN
Surry, Maine

On a beautiful, sunny day in June, I visited this neat little inn on Contention Cove, and was surprised and pleased to find that I had originally met Sarah Krinsky at the Barrows House in Dorset, Vermont. She and her husband, Peter, are making a very welcome country inn out of this home, which was originally built in 1834 and once served as a lodging for steamship and stage passengers from Boston and Bangor. Its rolling lawns slope down to a private beach on the cove near the old steamship landing.

There are eight, very attractive, light and airy guest rooms in the main house, many of them with a view of the Cove. They are furnished with an assortment of Maine upcountry furniture, some decorated with stenciling. There is stenciling around the window and door frames in one guest room, something I've never seen before. The pattern is repeated on the top of a painted chest.

Sarah went to some lengths to assure me the Surry Inn is a full-service inn, not only serving breakfast to houseguests, but also a rather extensive dinner to the public. I noted that the reviewer from the *Maine Times* has given it very good marks for freshly baked crusty bread and several main dishes, including scallops Nicoise. I'd like to go back some time and try the medallions of pork in ginger cream.

I'm delighted to report that the Surry Inn, bright as a new penny, has found dedicated innkeepers and should flourish for many years to come.

SURRY INN, P.O. Box 25, Surry, ME 04648; 207-667-5091. An 8-guestroom (most with private baths) country inn on the water about 5 mi. from Ellsworth on the Penobscot Peninsula. Open year-round. Breakfast is included in room rate. Dinners served every night. Conveniently located to enjoy all of the many recreational, cultural, and historic attractions in the area. Able to accommodate children. No pets. Sarah and Peter Krinsky, Innkeepers.

Directions: From the south: Follow Rte. 1 north; 7 mi. north of Buckport, turn right onto Rte. 176 (Surry Rd.) and follow it to its end. Turn left onto Rte. 172 and be at the inn in 2½ mi.

For B&B rates, see Index.

TOPSIDE
Boothbay Harbor, Maine

The subtitle for this place is "What a View," and from my vantage point looking out from the top floor of this three-story summer hotel at Boothbay Harbor, I could certainly re-echo the sentiments. It was truly an impressive view of the harbor, the fishing boats, sailboats, and moorings.

All of the bedrooms in the main building are cheerful, clean, and bright, and many have a water view. They all have private baths and each room is equipped with a four-cubic-foot refrigerator. Rooms are in other large cottages scattered around the rather spacious lawns with large porches that also share the view of the harbor.

Breakfast is not served at Topside; however, morning coffee is offered and there are several restaurants within walking distance recommended by the management.

TOPSIDE, McKown Hill, Boothbay Harbor, Me. 04538; 207-633-5404 (summer), 914-357-3820 (winter). A 9-bedroom summer hotel/motel located at a high point overlooking Boothbay Harbor. Open from May 15 to mid-Oct. Conveniently located for all of the recreational and cultural attractions. No pets. Rates particularly attractive after Labor Day. Mr. & Mrs. Newell J. Wilson, Owners/Managers.

Directions: From U.S. 1 follow Rte. 27 to Boothbay Harbor through the village and look for a sign on the left that says "McKown Hill."

For Lodging rates, see Index.

THE WATERFORD INNE
East Waterford, Maine

The Oxford Hills in southwestern Maine is another one of those very rare places which have not really been discovered as yet. It's just slightly off the regular tourist path, and as a result there's a wonderful unspoiled feeling about the forests, rolling fields, pleasant lakes, and small hidden villages that add to the fun of backroading.

The Waterford Inne sits atop a hill with sweeping views down the valley and to the ridge beyond. The house was built in 1825 and the five original bedrooms have been augmented by four rooms in a wing leading out to a handsome red barn.

The keepers of this inn are a mother and daughter from Oradell, New Jersey, Barbara and Rosalie Vanderzanden, for whom the inn is a second career.

The inn is open year-round, with the exception of eight weeks, beginning March 1. There is good cross-country and downhill skiing in this area.

A good night's sleep in the peaceful Oxford Hills usually generates hearty appetites which are more than satisfied with the full breakfasts which are prepared by Rosalie and served by Barbara.

THE WATERFORD INNE, Box 49, East Waterford, Maine 04233; 207-583-4037. A 9-room farmhouse-inn in the Oxford Hills section of southwest Maine, 8 mi. from Norway and south of Paris. Closed Mar. 1 to April 30. Breakfast and dinner served to travelers by reservation. European plan. Within a short distance of many recreational, scenic and cultural attractions in Maine and the White Mountains of New Hampshire. Cross-country skiing and badminton on grounds. Lake swimming, golf, rock hunting, downhill skiing, hiking, canoeing nearby. No credit cards. Alcoholic beverages not served. Well-behaved pets welcome. Rosalie and Barbara Vanderzanden, Innkeepers.

Directions: From Maine Turnpike: use Exit 11, follow Rte. 26 north approximately 28 mi. into Norway, then on Rte. 118 west for 8 mi. to Rte. 37 south (left turn). Go ½ mi., turn right at Springer's General Store, up the hill ½ mi. From Conway, New Hampshire: Rte. 16 to Rte. 302 east to Fryeburg, Me. Take Rte. 5 out of Fryeburg to Rte. 35 south, thence to Rte. 118, which is a left fork (with Rte. 35 going right). Continue on Rte. 118 east, past Papoose Pond camping area, then watch for right turn onto Rte. 37. Go ½ mi. to Springer's General Store. Take immediate right turn, ½ mi. up hill.

For B&B rates, see Index.

HISTORIC INNS OF ANNAPOLIS
Annapolis, Maryland

In the 1770s an innkeeper was required to provide stabling for at least ten horses plus a store of oats and hay. Bed and breakfast, one might say. Two hundred years later, the Historic Inns of Annapolis hearken back to their Revolutionary beginnings. The three historic inns are:

The Maryland Inn, advertised in 1784 as "an elegant brick house...one of the first houses in the state for a house of entertainment..." Its rooms now beautifully restored, it is an elegant restaurant serving continental cuisine, and a marvelous old tavern, featuring Charlie Byrd and other top jazz musicians year around.

The Robert Johnson House, the oldest portion of which dates to 1763, faces the grand old Maryland State Capitol, where General Washington resigned his commission in the Continental Armies in 1783.

The Governor Calvert House, with many rooms looking over either the State Capitol or lovely Colonial gardens, and with a new underground garage for "stabling"—without oats and hay.

A stay at the Historic Inns will encourage visitors to walk where Washington walked, from the harbor to the former site of Mann's Tavern and the Coffee House to the State Capitol, to visit the great Georgian mansions owned by signers of the Declaration of Independence, or to tour the U.S. Naval Academy. Every point of interest is an easy walk from any of the inns.

HISTORIC INNS OF ANNAPOLIS, Church and State Circles, Annapolis, MD 21401. Three 18th-century village inns in a historic seaport, 20 miles from Baltimore and Washington, D.C. Near U.S. Naval Academy and Chesapeake Bay. European plan. Breakfast, lunch and dinner served to travelers daily. Sunday brunch served year-round. Jazz Club, music Wed. through Sun. in the King of France Tavern. Tours arranged to historic and scenic points of interest. Tennis and sailing school available. No pets. Paul Pearson, Proprietor; Peg Bednarsky, Innkeeper.

Directions: From Baltimore, take Rte. 2 south to first directional turnoff "Washington/Annapolis." From Washington, take Rte. 50 east to Exit "Annapolis/Naval Academy. Rowe Blvd."

For B&B rates, see Index.

ROBERT MORRIS INN
Oxford, Maryland

The town of Oxford has a history far in advance of the Revolutionary War and it's always a marvel to me that this little village has managed to stave off the encroachments of contemporary living, such as the fast-food restaurant and the chain motel. I daresay it is much the same as it has been for the last 150 years, and even more. It is also accessible by a tiny auto ferry.

The Robert Morris Inn is on the banks of the Tred Avon River and was built prior to 1710 by ships' carpenters, using wooden-pegged paneling, ships' nails, and hand-hewn beams.

In addition to lodgings in the main building, guests are accommodated in the Lodge, located a short distance away on a point of land overlooking the bay. There are other accommodations in waterfront buildings as well, and some rooms have private porches overlooking the Tred Avon.

A full, à la carte breakfast is served in the warm-hued Tap Room, and features a great many unusual dishes, such as a seafood omelet, Eastern Shore scrapple, sausage, corn muffins, and toasted high-fiber granola.

Anyone wishing accommodations in the high summer season should reserve by March or April, even for midweek stays. If possible, arrive in time for dinner, it's worth it.

ROBERT MORRIS INN, Oxford, Md. 21654; 301-226-5111. A 36-room (28 rooms with private baths; 8 rooms with shared baths) village inn in a secluded Colonial community on the Tred Avon, 10 mi. from Easton, Md. European plan. Breakfast, lunch, and dinner served to travelers daily. Open year-round except Christmas. Tennis, golf, sailing, swimming, and bicycles nearby. No pets. Kenneth and Wendy Gibson, Innkeepers.

Directions: From Delaware Memorial Bridge, follow Rte. 13 south to Rte. 301 and proceed south to Rte. 50, then east on Rte. 50 to Easton. From Chesapeake Bay Bridge, follow Rte. 50-301 to Rte. 50 and proceed east to Easton. From Chesapeake Bay Bridge Tunnel, follow Rte. 13 north to Rte. 50 and proceed west to Easton. From Easton, follow Rte. 322 to Rte. 333 to Oxford and inn.

For B&B rates, see Index.

THE STRAWBERRY INN
New Market, Maryland

There are forty-six antique stores on Main Street in New Market and only one inn. There is only one full-scale restaurant, too—the family-style Mealey's, which is conveniently across the street. Things were considerably different a century ago when New Market was a thriving town, full of westward-bound travelers, and Main Street was part of the National Pike, stretching from Baltimore to St. Louis.

Now, there are day-trippers from Washington, D.C., and many from all points north, south, and west and only a few lucky travelers will have planned ahead to enjoy the extended ambience of antique-filled rooms at the cozy bed-and-breakfast inn. Incidentally, the choice room is the large "1776," a twin-bedded double on the first floor, though there are four others upstairs, each distinctive in its own way.

Breakfast arrived outside my door on a butler's tray at the hour I specified: juice, fruit, hot bread, croissants. The coffee pot had a silver strawberry on its lid. Fresh strawberries decorated strawberry-motif china, and of course there was strawberry jam.

Shops in New Market stay open weekends and close Mondays. Even Mealey's closes Mondays, so that's the day to save for the larger area's attractions: the old town in Frederick, Harper's Ferry, Baltimore's restored Inner Harbor.

THE STRAWBERRY INN, P.O. Box 237, 17 Main St., New Market, MD 21774; 301-865-3318. A 5-guestroom (all with private baths) air-conditioned B&B inn at the corner of Main St. and Strawberry Alley in the middle of New Market. Less than 1 hr. to Baltimore or Washington, D.C.; 6 mi. from Frederick. Breakfast is included and the only meal served, but a good restaurant across the street. Open all year. Advance reservations necessary. Sightseeing and antique shopping all around. No TV. No children under 7. No pets. No credit cards. Jane and Ed Rossig, Innkeepers.

Directions: Exit 8 from I-70 going north on Hwy. 75. Turn left almost immediately on Hwy. 144, which shortly becomes Main St., New Market. The Strawberry Inn is on your right in the center of town.

For B&B rates, see Index.

AUTUMN INN
Northampton, Massachusetts

Northampton is a beautiful, rather engaging town located on the banks of the Connecticut River and is a gateway to many intriguing travel possibilities. Route I-91, the north and south highway from New York to Vermont, intersects with Route 9 which leads eastward through Amherst, Brookfield, Ware, and Worcester, and west to Williamsburg, Goshen, and the Berkshires. It's a community where there is a very pleasant blending of "town and gown" since it is the home of Smith College. Four other colleges and prep schools are also nearby.

There couldn't be a better setting for the Autumn Inn than where it is located in the quiet residential area of Northampton, almost a part of the Smith campus. There are pleasantly landscaped grounds on all sides and a welcome heated swimming pool in the rear.

Innkeepers Vince and Irene Berger have really put a great deal of their own lifestyle into the Autumn Inn. For one thing they both are very much interested in art, and many of the bedrooms have prints, lithographs and collotypes by Norman Rockwell, Eric Sloan, Raymond Hull, and David Lee.

Particular care has been taken in furnishing the bedrooms, and each is done in a different theme. One room is furnished entirely with furniture from the Hitchcock chair and furniture factory in Connecticut, and still another from Heywood Wakefield in Vermont. Every bedroom has a private bath and an individually controlled temperature.

An à la carte breakfast is served in a pleasant dining room, and the menu offers a variety of appetizing items, including country pancakes served with melted butter and maple syrup, french toast, and various egg dishes. There is a tempting luncheon menu, too.

AUTUMN INN, 259 Elm St., Northampton, Massachusetts 01060; 413-584-7660. A 30-room inn located in one of western Massachusetts' most gracious towns. Breakfast and lunch served every day of the year. Smith College, The University of Massachusetts, Amherst College, Hampshire College, Mt. Holyoke College, Deerfield Academy, and Williston Academy, all within a short drive. Swimming pool. Downhill and xc skiing nearby. No pets. Vince and Irene Berger, Innkeepers.

Directions: From I-91 take the exit marked "Northampton Center" (Exit 18) turn west on Rte. 9 through the center of the town and look for a red brick building on the north side of the street.

For Lodging rates, see Index.

BAY BREEZE GUEST HOUSE
Monument Beach, Cape Cod, Massachusetts

I would imagine that most of the visitors to Cape Cod cross over one of the two bridges and then follow Route 6 out toward Provincetown, heading for the villages and communities on the south shore. Others turn south toward Woods Hole to catch the ferries to the islands.

An alternate possibility is to follow Route 28A to Monument Beach Village to get a taste of what Cape Cod was like at the turn of the century at the Bay Breeze Guest House.

You'll know you're in the right place when you get to the old railway station at Monument Beach and there, just across the tracks, is a rambling old guest house which is kept each summer by Joe Rogers, a former teacher and education counselor who says he's retired to work here harder than ever.

It's a big house where families formerly spent the summertime. Now Joe has turned it into a comfortable old guest house where there are complete kitchen facilities. You can borrow the dishes, have space in the refrigerator, and cook three meals a day if you really want to. There's also a bath and shower downstairs when you come off the beach.

The feeling here is of being in grandmother's house with bric-a-brac galore. The walls and ceilings are all tongue and groove, and the wall hangings are in the same genre.

Some of the bedrooms face the bay and accommodate three or four beds. It's a nice place for a family to spend a few days because it's just a few steps to the semi-private beach and a large grassy area for baseball and frisbee throwing.

This is a quiet and more serene aspect of Cape Cod.

BAY BREEZE GUEST HOUSE, P.O. Box 307, Monument Beach, Cape Cod, Ma. 02553; (summer) 617-759-5069 or (spring) 617-275-7551. A 7-bedroom guest house (share 3 bathrooms). Open from June through October. No meals served, but kitchen facilities and refrigerator are available. Convenient for all of the Cape Cod cultural, recreational, and historic attractions. Semi-private beach nearby, particularly safe for children. No pets. No credit cards. Joseph and Mildred Rogers, Proprietors.

Directions: Cross the Bourne Cape Cod Canal bridge, take right at the rotary at the end of the bridge and follow Shore Rd. to Monument Beach.

For Lodging rates, see Index.

BEECHWOOD
Barnstable Village, Massachusetts

Antiquers, whether searching for treasures or knowledge, will find both at Beechwood. Jeff and Bea Goldstein had a shop in Los Angeles for nine years, and Jeff is an expert restorer as well. Beechwood, a Queen Anne- style rambler, is undergoing a painstaking return to the 1880s, and visitors find themselves sharing the joy at each new acquisition. Furthermore, not only do Jeff and Bea know where all the best flea markets on the Cape are located, they have been known to go along with their guests.

Beechwood takes its name from two giant copper beech trees shading the veranda. Incidentally, a rocking chair on that veranda can provide instant spiritual transport to the nineteenth century as well as relaxation.

The five bedrooms, each with private baths, are individually themed. Three have working fireplaces, welcome additions on a cool Cape evening.

An "expanded continental" breakfast is served. This means not only juice, fruit, homemade breads and muffins, but hard-boiled eggs and cheese as well. Also included in the tariff is afternoon tea with cake or sandwiches. There are fine restaurants in the area for your other meals.

BEECHWOOD, 2839 Main St., Barnstable Village, Cape Cod, MA 02630; 617-362-6618. A 5-guestroom (each with private bath) bed-and-breakfast inn on the north shore of Cape Cod. Open all year. Breakfast and afternoon tea included in room rate. Mid-Cape location convenient for touring, antiquing. No children under 15. No pets. Jeff and Bea Goldstein, Innkeepers.

Directions: Leave Rte. 6 (Mid-Cape Hwy.) at Exit 6 and take Rte. 132 north to Rte. 6A (Main St.). Turn right. Beechwood is exactly 1.7 mi. on your right. It comes up after a slight curve, so slow down and signal at 1.5 mi.

For B&B rates, see Index.

THE BRAMBLE INN GALLERY AND CAFE
Brewster, Massachusetts

If ever there was an inn with individuality, without a single trace of sterotype, it is the Bramble Inn.

The "gallery" portion of the name is accounted for by the fact that the dining rooms are hung with watercolors, oil paintings, lithographs, pastels, and photography.

The basic colors in the dining rooms are pink and green. There are pink tablecloths and pink napkins held in place by very attractive flowered rosebud napkin rings. The walls and woodwork are sparkling white and the floorboards of differing widths have been refinished with a warm, brown patina. There are lots of plants hanging from the ceiling and much ivy to provide accents of green.

The lodging rooms at the top of the stairs have flowered wallpaper, antiques, country furniture, and share two baths. There is a definite tilt to the doors and floors adding to the fun. There are five additional lodgings, three with private baths, in the 1849 House just two doors away.

The Bramble is the home of an unusual dessert called Cape Cod Bramble, chopped raisins and cranberries gently sweetened and wrapped in a tender pastry and topped with ice cream. The dinner menu includes such entrées as Lobster Thermidor and Boeuf Bourguignon.

The inn's sunny porch is the setting for breakfast, featuring fresh fruit, homemade muffins, and coffee or tea.

The innkeepers, Karen Etsell and Elaine Brennan, are the authors of a book that is rapidly growing in popularity, *How to Open a Country Inn*. The Bramble was used as a model for many of the facts and figures quoted in the book.

THE BRAMBLE INN GALLERY AND CAFE, Rte. 6A, Main St., Brewster, Cape Cod, MA 02631; 617-896-7644. A 7-guestroom village inn and art gallery in the heart of one of Cape Cod's northshore villages. Lodgings include continental breakfast. Dinner served daily except Sundays. Open mid-April through October. Swimming, sailing, water sports, golf, recreational, and natural attractions within a short drive. Adjacent to tennis club. Small, intimate inn does not meet needs of most children. No pets. Elaine Brennan and Karen Etsell, Innkeepers.

Directions: Take Exit 10 from Rte. 6. Follow Rte 124 to Brewster to the intersection of Rte. 6A (4 mi.). Turn right, 1/10 mi. to inn.

For B&B rates, see Index.

THE BROOKFIELD HOUSE INN
West Brookfield, Massachusetts

In addition to being a Victorian enthusiast's delight, the Brookfield House Inn provides pleasant lodgings and a sumptuous dinner.

The dining room is one of the very few I've ever seen that has glass tops on the tables. This elegance is matched by hand-carved chairs as well as flocked wallpaper, many varieties of marble fireplaces, and molded ceilings.

The proprietors are Arlene and Nick Chios. Nick has had considerable experience in the restaurant business and for him and Arlene the opportunity to have their own place is the culmination of a long-cherished dream.

There are two bedrooms at this time: the Yellow Room, with a black walnut Victorian bedroom set and a marble-topped basin and counter, and the Pink Room, a very sunny room with similar Victorian furniture. Each of these shares a bathroom.

Nick himself will be delighted to prepare a special breakfast with a choice of omelets, french toast, eggs Benedict, or eggs any way. The coffee cakes are also homemade.

Some of Nick's dinner specialties are veal Brazil, beef Wellington, and roast duckling with a brandied sauce. Among his desserts are Black Forest mousse and amoretto cake.

West Brookfield is just a short, pleasant drive to Sturbridge Village.

THE BROOKFIELD HOUSE RESTAURANT AND INN, West Brookfield, Ma. 01585; 617-867-6589. An impressive Victorian mansion with restaurant of excellent local reputation and two lodging rooms, one with private bath. Open year-round with the exception of Christmas Eve and Day. Dinner is served Wed.-Sun. Sunday dinner is served from 12:00 to 8:00 P.M. A buffet lunch is offered Wed.-Fri. No pets. Arlene and Nick Chios, Proprietors.

Directions: Coming west on the Mass. Turnpike take Exit 8 (Palmer) and follow Rte. 67 to the end when it becomes Rte. 9. From the east on the Mass. Turnpike take Exit 9, and follow it to Sturbridge and then take Rte. 148 north, picking up Rte. 9; turn left into West Brookfield.

For rates, see Index.

BULL FROG BED & BREAKFAST
South Ashfield, Massachusetts

Lucky, indeed, the traveler who finds himself on Route 116, which starts in Adams, Massachusetts, runs across part of the Berkshires into the Pioneer Valley, and continues on through Amherst. I say lucky, because it's one of the best paved back roads that I've ever encountered. For one thing it passes through the village of Ashfield, in itself a real treat, with several unspoiled little shops, including Mr. Smither's Metal Restoration Emporium, and a bona fide country store. Interestingly, the town hall steeple is of Christopher Wren design.

Continuing east on Route 116, look for the sign saying "Bed and Breakfast" at a bend on the left-hand side of the road. This is where Lucille and Moses Thibault have decided to open up the second floor of their 225-year-old farmhouse to bed-and- breakfast guests.

The house is wonderfully furnished with country things, including many splendid country antiques. The guest has a choice of a bedroom with a king-sized bed or still another bedroom with two double beds. A spacious bath with shower is shared.

When I asked Lucille about breakfast, she replied, "Anything." This translates into any kind of eggs and bacon, homemade muffins, homemade jams and jellies, or even pancakes or french toast. I'll let her explain all that to her guests.

Like the nearby Parson Hubbard House, a few miles north, this is a real bed-and-breakfast-home experience. My guess is that there will be many people who seek it out for a second visit.

BULL FROG BED & BREAKFAST, South Ashfield, MA 01330; 413-628-4493. A 2-guestroom (shared bath) bed-and- breakfast home on an exceptionally beautiful paved back road in western Massachusetts. Open all year except Jan., Thanksgiving, Christmas, and New Year's. Room rate includes breakfast; only meal served. Convenient for visits to nearby Five College area in Amherst and Northampton and easily accessible to some splendid backroading adventures. Swimming pond on grounds, shared with frogs. Babies and young children easily accommodated. No pets. No credit cards. Lucille and Moses Thibault, Proprietors.

Directions: From I-91 (north and south) follow Rte. 116 through Conway and continue on looking for B&B sign on right. From Rte. 9 (east and west) turn off on Rte. 112 at Goshen. Continue to Rte. 116 passing through Ashfield and look for B&B sign on left.

For B&B rates, see Index.

THE CAPTAIN FREEMAN INN
Brewster, Massachusetts

Brewster in general, and the Captain Freeman Inn in particular, seem ideal for a family trip to the Cape. Breakwater Beach is an easy walk. There is a local Museum of Natural History and a Sealand. The general store with its potbelly stove and penny candy is just steps away from the inn, and the inn has its own swimming pool.

Captain Freeman built his elegant house in 1860, sparing no expense in adding architectural niceties such as the two-tone inlaid wood floors and imported plaster moldings. It became a guest house in 1944 and had since slipped into a discouraging condition, when John and Barbara Mulkey decided to give up the government hustle of Washington, D.C., for the quiet independence of a country inn. Their restoration is a continuing process, and the basic character of the house is being well maintained.

Children will love the trundle beds, and there is a crib for even the littlest visitor. Books and games fill the shelves of the cozy nook on the upstairs front landing.

Continental breakfast, served on the porch overlooking the pool or inside around an antique oak table, consists of juice, homemade muffins, or coffee cake, and coffee, tea or milk.

THE CAPTAIN FREEMAN INN, 15 Breakwater Rd., Brewster, MA 02631; 617-896-7481. A 10-guestroom inn (5 private and 2 shared baths) on the green in the center of Brewster, Cape Cod, about two hours from Boston. Open year-round. Continental breakfast included in rate. No other meals served. Many good restaurants in the area. Swimming pool. Beach, museums, shops, antiquing, all nearby. Children and pets welcome. John and Barbara Mulkey, Innkeepers.

Directions: Once on Cape Cod, take Rte. 6 (Mid-Cape Hwy.) to Exit 10 (Rte. 124). Follow Rte. 124 north to Brewster and Rte. 6A. Turn right on Rte. 6A, go 100 yards to Breakwater Rd. and turn left. The General Store is on the corner. Captain Freeman Inn is on the left.

For B&B rates, see Index.

CAPTAIN ISAIAH'S HOUSE
Bass River, Cape Cod, Massachusetts

This is one of those delightful homes built by a Cape Cod sea captain in the early 1800s. It is a gracious village guest house in an elegant old residential section of the Cape—a white clapboard home on a very quiet street a few steps from the Bass River.

The six guest rooms (four with working fireplaces) are airy and comfortable and furnished in antiques, including braided rugs, quilts, and Hitchcock chairs.

Breakfast includes at least two kinds of homemade bread, as well as blueberry buckle, a special crumb cake. Marge Fallows says, "We just leave it on the table and wander in and out of the dining room or garden chatting with people about what they are going to do as they get acquainted with each other. We're all very informal and on a first-name basis."

Like many other Americans who are guest-house enthusiasts, the Fallows traveled in Europe enough to know that for economy and comfort and meeting the locals, there's nothing like a B&B lodging. "We view ourselves as a kind of adult hostelry where guests receive more than they expect and depart feeling as though they have been visiting in a house of distant relatives who wanted them to enjoy themselves."

Captain Isaiah's House is a second career for this family, and they are still improvising to find out what things work best for both themselves and their guests.

I discovered that Marge and Alden Fallows at one time had been very close neighbors of mine in the Berkshires, and it was indeed a pleasure to renew our acquaintance under such very pleasant circumstances.

CAPTAIN ISAIAH'S HOUSE, 33 Pleasant St., Bass River, Ma. 02664; 617-394-1739. A 6-bedroom guest house (4 with fireplaces) sharing 4 full baths. Breakfast is the only meal served. Open from May to Oct. Conveniently located to enjoy all of the recreational, cultural, and historical attractions in the Falmouth-Hyannis-Chatham area of the Cape. No credit cards. Alden and Marge Fallows, Innkeepers.

Directions: Take Mid-Cape Highway (Rte. 6) to Exit 8 (So. Yarmouth). Turn right and go to traffic lights on Rte. 28, cross lights, and take second left at Akin Ave. Captain Isaiah's House is on the left at the corner of Akin and Pleasant Sts.

For B&B rates, see Index.

THE CAPTAIN'S HOUSE
Rockport, Massachusetts

It has always seemed a propitious sign when another guest sidles up and says, "I hope you won't tell anyone about this place—it's too good to share." That's the way it is at the Captain's House, a five-bedroom guest house in a secluded, residential section of Rockport. Yes, you can swim right off the rocks, and definitely, most of the rooms have spectacular ocean views. One even has a private sunporch.

Carole Dangerfield named the house for her sea-captain grandfather, whose portrait hangs in the dining room. "We were going to name each guest room for one of his ships," she says, "but in eighteen years we've never quite gotten around to it." No matter. The heritage is obvious.

Only a mile and a half south of the center of Rockport, the Captain's House has an ambience of total seclusion. There are inviting chairs in the large, handsome living room; bowls of fresh flowers everywhere. A help-yourself continental breakfast of home-baked sour cream coffee cake, juice, and tea or coffee is offered in a sunroom facing the sea.

The other guest is right. This place is too good to share.

THE CAPTAIN'S HOUSE, 109 Marmion Way, Rockport, MA 01966; 617-546-3825. A 5-bedroom (3 with private baths) guest house, a mile and a half from the center of Rockport. Breakfast only. Closed Dec. through March. Restaurants, galleries, and shops in town. Ocean swimming. No pets. Carole and George Dangerfield, Proprietors.

Directions: From the end of Rte. 128 (Boston's inner beltway) take Rte. 127A to Rockport. Marmion Way is on your right.

For B&B rates, see Index.

THE CAPTAIN'S HOUSE INN OF CHATHAM
Chatham, Cape Cod, Massachusetts

Dave and Cathy Eakin are typical of many people who have fled the so-called corporate life and sought out a new career in innkeeping. They were indeed fortunate to find an exceptional house with over two acres in Chatham, one of Cape Cod's most picturesque villages.

The site was chosen in 1839 by Captain Harding for his home, and the antiques that the Eakins had been collecting for years, including many family heirlooms from their home in Yardley, Pennsylvania, found a most appropriate setting.

The bedrooms are named after the ships in which the good captain sailed, and they are now adorned with handsome, flowered wallpapers and even some pictures of boats on which the captain sailed.

Besides comfortable bedrooms in the main house, there are additional accommodations in the Carriage House and in the Captain's cottage.

Cathy does all the baking for breakfast and she explains that she puts out two or three sweet breads, including Dutch Apple Loaf. She also makes homemade blueberry muffins. Breakfast is taken in the dining room, which has a splendid view of the lovely garden.

Dave and Cathy are both sailors and they have a 35-foot sailboat on which they love to sail with their guests when time permits.

The Captain's House is a real home-away-from-home and either Dave or Cathy are always on hand to attend to guests' special needs.

THE CAPTAIN'S HOUSE INN OF CHATHAM, 371 Old Harbor Rd., Chatham, Cape Cod, MA 02633; 617-945-0127. A 10- guestroom (all private baths) Cape Cod bed-and-breakfast inn. Additional accommodations are available in adjacent historic buildings. Open all year, but closed Jan. 2 to 31. Breakfast included in room rate. All of the historic, cultural, and scenic attractions of Cape Cod are most convenient. Beaches, golf, tennis courts, antiquing are nearby. No facilities for children under 12, except in weekly rental of Carriage House. No pets. Dave and Cathy Eakin, Innkeepers.

Directions: Follow the mid-Cape Hwy. (Rte. 6) to Exit 11 and follow Rte. 137 for 3 mi. until it intersects with Rte. 28, at which point take a left, heading toward Chatham for 2 or 3 mi. At the rotary with the Mobil and BP stations, look for a sign that says Orleans-Rte. 28 south. The inn is ½ mi. farther on the left.

For B&B rates, see Index.

CENTENNIAL HOUSE
Northfield, Massachusetts

Northfield is a very pleasant village in New England that you wouldn't find, except by accident, or if by some chance you were looking for a good preparatory school for your children. The main street is really Route 63, going north and south, with pleasant 19th-century homes set well back from the roadway. There are lots of big trees and lovely gardens.

The prep school here is Northfield Mt. Hermon, which has flourished for over a hundred years and definitely sets the tone of the village. It certainly sets the tone of Centennial House, because for many years it was the residence of the president of the school. At one time it was even used as a dormitory. However, the history of the house actually goes back to 1811.

Of particular interest is a wonderful, big living room with a marvellous fireplace, beautiful wood paneling, and heavy overhead beams that certainly invites visits in the winter. Off the living room is an extremely comfortable summer porch with quite a few rocking chairs overlooking the lawn and the western view. When weather permits, this is where the continental breakfast is served, which features three kinds of homemade bread.

The bedrooms are different sizes and shapes. I particularly remember the twin-bedded bedroom on the side with its own bath, and another very pleasant front bedroom with a big brass bed and an optionally shared bath.

Northfield is just a few miles to the east of I-91, and Centennial House would make a very pleasant, surprising, and accommodating overnight stop whether you are headed for the north or back to the city. Incidentally, Route 63 is an excellent back road continuing north, parallel to I-91, rejoining it near Walpole. It is well worth the few minutes more to make the journey.

CENTENNIAL HOUSE, 94 Main St., Northfield, Ma. 01360; 413-498-5921. A warm, inviting 6-room (3½ baths) bed-and-breakfast inn located in an attractive New England village. Includes continental breakfast. Open all year. Convenient for I-91 travelers. Within a few minutes of Northfield Mt. Hermon School. Skiing nearby. Marguerite L. Lentz, Proprietor.

Directions: Leave I-91 at Northfield exit, go east on Rte. 10, turn north on Rte. 63. Inn is in middle of the town across the street from fire station.

For B&B rates, see Index.

CHARLOTTE INN
Edgartown, Martha's Vineyard, Massachusetts

Like many other houses in Edgartown, which is on the far side of the island of Martha's Vineyard, the Charlotte Inn is a classic three-story white clapboard with a widow's walk.

Lodging rooms are individually furnished and great care has been exercised in their decoration. All of them are very quiet and have their own private baths. There is a warm feeling of hospitality and a most romantic atmosphere. Some rooms have working fireplaces for guests to enjoy during the winter and there are quite a few four-poster beds as well.

Many people visit during the so-called off-season, when Edgartown is delightfully quiet and has fewer visitors. Guests enjoy shopping in town, walking along the beaches, bicycling to the many interesting points on the island.

The room rate includes a continental breakfast, which is served in the dining room and might include English muffins or a selection of freshly baked pastries. A full breakfast is also available.

CHARLOTTE INN, So. Summer St., Edgartown, Martha's Vineyard Island, Ma. 02539; 617-627-4751. A 16-room combination inn-art gallery and restaurant located on one of the side streets in the village of Edgartown, just a few short steps from the harbor. European plan. Rooms available every day of the year. Continental breakfast served to inn guests. Chez Pierre restaurant open for lunch and dinner from mid-March through New Year's Day. Other island restaurants open year-round. Boating, swimming, beaches, fishing, tennis, riding, golf, sailing, and biking nearby. No pets. Gery and Paula Conover, Innkeepers.

Directions: Martha's Vineyard Island is located off the southwestern coast of Cape Cod. The Woods Hole-Vineyard Haven Ferry runs year-round and automobiles may be left in the parking lot at Woods Hole. Taxis may be obtained from Vineyard Haven to Edgartown (8 mi.). Check with inn for ferry schedules for all seasons of the year. Accessible by air from Boston and New York.

For B&B rates, see Index.

COBB'S COVE
Barnstable Village, Cape Cod, Massachusetts

The principal road from the mainland out to the end of Cape Cod (which is really an island) is Route 6. However, taking Route 6A, which runs along the northern shore of the Cape through Sagamore, Sandwich, Barnstable, Yarmouth, Dennis, and Brewster, rejoining Route 6 at the Orleans traffic circle, is a very pleasant and rewarding adventure.

Part of the fun would be to spend a night or two at Cobb's Cove, a very unusual bed-and-breakfast inn in the village of Barnstable.

The interior has exposed beams and beautiful wood with harmonizing accompanying colors of beige, yellow, and tan. Each of the six lodging rooms has a full bath including a whirlpool tub, a dressing room, air conditioning, and private telephone lines which are available for extended stays.

All around the house are shelves and corners filled with books and objects that indicate the eclectic interests of the innkeepers. There are groups of shells and fossils as well as minerals and gems. There are many, many books including quite a few dealing with the natural and human history of the Cape.

When warm weather arrives at the Cape, the full breakfasts, which are individually prepared, are enjoyed on the sunny terrace. For colder weather the library is ideal. Breakfast includes fresh fruit, eggs done to order, bacon, homemade breads, biscuits, and sometimes cornbread. It's a good time to confer with other guests and map out another delightful day on the Cape.

COBB'S COVE, Barnstable Village, Rte. 6A, Cape Cod, Ma. 02630; 617-362-9356. A 6-room secluded inn on Cape Cod's north shore. Lodgings include a full breakfast. Houseguests can arrange for dinner. Open every day in the year. Within a short distance of Cape Cod Bay and the Atlantic Ocean, the U.S. National Seashore, and Sandy Neck Conservatory, as well as many museums, art galleries, craft shops, and other attractions of the Cape. Active sports nearby. No facilities to amuse children at the inn. No pets. Credit cards not accepted. Evelyn Chester, Innkeeper.

Directions: From Rte. 6 (Mid-Cape Hwy.), turn left at Exit 6 on Rte. 132 to Barnstable. Turn right on Rte. 6A, approximately 3 mi. through Barnstable Village, past the only traffic light and turn left just past the Barnstable Unitarian Church, at small Cobb's Cove sign; then left at first driveway marked "Evelyn Chester."

For B&B rates, see Index.

COLONEL EBENEZER CRAFTS INN
Sturbridge, Massachusetts

Are you traveling on I-86 between New England and New York, or on the Massachusetts Turnpike, east and west from Boston or the Berkshires? Sturbridge is at the crossroads and hopefully you will arrive in time for afternoon tea, which is a regular feature at the Colonel Ebenezer Crafts Inn.

Assuming reservations have been made, stop first at the reception desk at the Publick House in Sturbridge to get directions to the inn which is about a mile away on top of a ridge in the residential district away from the highway.

This inn was originally a very picturesque home built in the colonial manner. It was named after one of the early patriots of Massachusetts, Colonel Ebenezer Crafts.

The living room really invites guests to get acquainted and there is a generously supplied bookcase and stacks of *National Geographics* which make wonderful bedtime reading.

Each of the ten lodging rooms is very light and airy and is furnished in either antiques or good reproductions.

Besides afternoon tea, guests at the inn can also enjoy dinner and lunch at the nearby Publick House as well. Old Sturbridge Village is just down the road.

The continental breakfast is one of the largest I've ever enjoyed. Besides the customary juices, there is also cranberry juice and apple cider in season. The pecan sweet rolls are made fresh every day, as are the blueberry and pumpkin muffins. In winter these are served in a cozy corner, and in the summer on the patio overlooking the swimming pool and garden. Be sure to ask for their scrumptious hot chocolate.

COLONEL EBENEZER CRAFTS INN, c/o Publick House, Sturbridge, Ma. 01566; 617-347-3313. A 10-room bed and breakfast inn in a historic village 18 mi. from Worcester. Old Sturbridge Village nearby. Lodging rates include continental breakfast and afternoon tea. (Lunch and dinner available at nearby Publick House.) Open year-round. Swimming pool on grounds. Tennis nearby. Buddy Adler, Innkeeper.

Directions: From Massachusetts Tpke.: take Exit 9, follow signs to Sturbridge on Rte. 131. From Hartford: follow I-84, which becomes I-86. Take Exit 3.

For B&B rates, see Index.

COLONIAL HOUSE INN
Plymouth, Massachusetts

Plymouth still lives, thanks to some entrepreneurs who have restored and recreated Plimoth Plantation where visitors are plunged into the life of Plymouth in 1627. They have also constructed *Mayflower II*, a full-scale reproduction of the type of ship that brought the Pilgrims to the New World in 1620.

I think both of these attractions considerably enhance a visit to the famous Plymouth Rock located on the water's edge in the town harbor.

The Colonial House Inn, just a short distance from Plymouth Rock, has been kept by Oscar and Olga Isaacs for thirty years. The bedrooms and public rooms have an Early American decor, and a swimming pool was added in recent years to the quiet, secluded grounds.

It's located within a short distance of all historical sites, beaches, restaurants, churches, and local entertainment.

Mrs. Isaacs informed me it is most necessary to have advance reservations, and if desired during the peak of the tourist season they should be made many weeks ahead.

Breakfast is not served, but there are several restaurants within a short distance.

COLONIAL HOUSE INN, 207 Sandwich St., Plymouth, Ma. 02360; 617-746-2087. A 5-bedroom guest house (private baths) 1 mi. south of Plymouth Center on Rte. 3A. Open year-round. No meals served, restaurants nearby. Conveniently located to visit Plimoth Plantation, the Mayflower II, *and Plymouth Rock. No pets. No credit cards. Oscar and Olga Isaacs, Proprietors.*

Directions: Plymouth is located on Rte. 3 south of Boston and north of Cape Cod. Sandwich St. is one of the main thoroughfares of the town.

For Lodging rates, see Index.

COUNTRY INN AT PRINCETON
Princeton, Massachusetts

Route 2, a portion of which has gained considerable fame as the trail used by the Mohawk Indians for many centuries before the arrival of the white man in New England, traverses the nothern part of Massachusetts near Boston to Williamstown and beyond. It passes quite near Princeton, Massachusetts, one of those delightful villages that have remained relatively undiscovered.

Built in 1890, this gambrel-roofed Queen Anne country mansion has country gardens, rolling lawns, fieldstone walls, and granddad maples. The veranda and garden terrace overlook the pine groves and across a fifty-mile mountainous panorama to the Boston skyline.

The inn is beautifully appointed with collectors' furnishings and antiques. The atmosphere is one of some formality, but also of a great deal of warmth.

There are six very romantic and spacious parlor-rooms provided to travelers. A continental breakfast is served in the privacy of these guest bedrooms, often in front of windows with ample views of the countryside or forest.

In addition to the special ambience and decor, the inn also offers an unusal dinner menu, including, filet mignon topped with a thick slice of goose liver paté and smothered in a rich, zesty truffle sauce, and fresh Atlantic salmon poached in a fish fume and served in a sauce of shallots, white wine, and fresh sorrel.

COUNTRY INN AT PRINCETON, 30 Mountain Rd., Princeton, MA 01541; 617-464-2030. A 6-guestroom late-Victorian mansion, 50 mi. from Boston and 14 mi. north of Worcester. Open all year except Christmas. Dinner reservations Wed. thru Sun. evenings. Sunday brunch. Closed Mon. and Tues. Near Wachusett Ski Resort, Audubon and Wildlife Society, Mt. Wachusett State Reservation. Tennis, swimming, fishing, hiking, nature trails nearby. Downhill and xc skiing 3 mi. Lodging for couples only, no accommodations for children. Sorry, no pets. Don and Maxine Plumridge, Innkeepers.

Directions: From Boston, follow Rte. 2 west to Rte. 31 south. From Conn. and Mass. Tpke. (90), follow Rte. 290 north to Rte. 190; then Exit 5 and continue on Rte. 140 to Princeton. At Rte. 62 turn left 4 mi., and turn right at post office and flashing light. With the town common on your left, the inn is 200 yards up Mountain Rd. on right.

For B&B rates, see Index.

DARR ANTIQUES AND GUEST HOUSE
Sheffield, Massachusetts

The deceptively ordinary-looking yellow clapboard sitting primly behind the white picket fence may fool you. Be prepared for a bit of "culture shock" when you walk into the foyer. You are stepping into a sleek, sophisticated world of classic Empire, Sheraton, and Hepplewhite furnishings, oriental rugs, chinoiserie, and African objets d'art.

Donald Andrew Cesario and Robert Randolph Stinson (find the name "Darr") have created a special environment here; one that is both elegant in decor and warm in hospitality. Their interests in antiques and entertaining have found perfect expression in this polished (in every sense) bed and breakfast and the fine antique shop attached to the back of the house.

Some examples of what makes this place special: the little decorated breakfast menu card that offers wide possibilities, including fruit, juice, puffed pancakes with apple, freshly baked coffeecakes, muffins, biscuits, bacon or ham, scrambled eggs du jour, which might have mushrooms, scallions, chives, or, as Don puts it, "whatever I have in the refrigerator..."

Abovestairs in the three bedrooms are lovely wallpapers covering moldings and ceilings as well as walls, fluffy comforters, and thick, wall-to-wall carpeting. The blue and yellow room has a sleigh bed and a marble topped chest, the "peach sherbet" room has a charming Victorian settee, and the dusty rose twin-bedded room has a pleasant private porch with plants and a grouping of outdoor furniture.

A New York townhouse in the Berkshires?

DARR ANTIQUES AND GUEST HOUSE, P.O. Box 130, Main St., Sheffield, MA 01257; 413-229-7773. A 3-guestroom (2 baths) elegant B&B home in a quiet village just north of the Connecticut border. A full breakfast included in the room rate. Open year-round. Minimum stay of 2 nights on busy summer weekends; however, a last-minute call might find 1 night available. Antiquing, nature and historical sites, restaurants, shopping, and all of the Berkshire attractions within easy driving distance. Well-behaved children acceptable. No pets. No credit cards. Donald Cesario and Robert Stinson, Hosts.

Directions: On Rte. 7 at the southern end of the Sheffield green, next to brick library. The only yellow house with a white picket fence.

For B&B rates, see Index.

DEERFIELD INN
Deerfield, Massachusetts

Located just a few minutes' stroll from historic Deerfield with its twelve beautifully restored and furnished museum houses, this inn, which was built in 1884 and restored a few years ago after a partial fire, carefully blends the charm and history of the past with present-day comforts and services. The inn is located on a mile-long street lined with graceful trees and historic 18th- and 19th-century houses, the scene of an Indian raid 300 years ago.

The inn contains twenty-three well-decorated guest bedrooms and a full dining room service, as well as a coffee shop.

A distinguished collection of early American furniture, silver, textiles, ceramics, and household objects is on view in Deerfield's museum houses, and there is a research library and an active education program dedicated to the history and culture of Deerfield and the Connecticut Valley.

Deerfield is the home of Deerfield Academy, Bement School, and the Eaglebrook School. Amherst College, Hampshire College, and the University of Massachusetts are located in Amherst just ten miles away, and Smith College in Northampton and Mount Holyoke College in South Hadley are also within an easy driving distance.

The village of Old Deerfield, which is a National Historic Site, is one of the most satisfying adventures into America's past, and the inn at Deerfield is a fitting complement to this environment.

DEERFIELD INN, The Street, Deerfield, Ma. 01342; 413-774-5587. A 23-bedroom inn (all private baths) air conditioned throughout, located in a historically preserved area just a few minutes from Amherst, Northampton, and Greenfield, Mass. Open year-round. Breakfast, lunch, and dinner are served every day. Conveniently located for all of the southern Vermont and western Massachusetts cultural, recreational, and historic activities. Paul Burns, Innkeeper.

Directions: From I-91 Exit 24 at So. Deerfield and follow Rte. 5 north to signs for Historic Deerfield.

For Lodging rates, see Index.

ELLING'S GUEST HOUSE
Great Barrington, Massachusetts

High on a rise above Route 23, just outside the bustling little town of Great Barrington, sits a beautiful, mid-18th century home amidst a spacious sloping lawn and stately trees.

From the little parking area, one walks around to the far side of the house and follows the stepping stones onto a pleasant veranda with wicker furniture.

A small room with a fireplace serves as both reception and living room, and a staircase leads to the second floor where there are six roomy bedrooms. Decorated with wallpapers in small floral patterns and criss-crossed, ruffled glass curtains, all the guests rooms are neat and clean with solid, comfortable-looking double or twin beds. The well-kept bathrooms look immaculately clean; two bedrooms have private baths, and two baths are shared among four bedrooms. There is also a little cottage under the trees a few steps from the house.

A continental breakfast of fruit or juice, homemade muffins or bread, and coffee or tea is set out on a tray in an alcove beside the stairs, and guests may take it to their rooms, or sit in the living room in front of the fireplace or on the veranda overlooking the lawn, garden, and Berkshire hills.

ELLING'S GUEST HOUSE, R.D. 3, Box 6 (Rte. 23), Great Barrington, MA 01230; 413-528-4103. A 6-guestroom (2 private, 2 shared baths) bed-and-breakfast home on Rte. 23, the main route into the Berkshires from NYC. Continental breakfast included in room rate. Open year-round; 2-night minimum stay required on weekends in summer. Accessible to all Berkshire attractions. No pets. No credit cards. Jo and Ray Elling, Proprietors.

Directions: Coming north on Rte. 23, beyond So. Egremont (3 mi.), look for sign on left. From the east, take Rte. 7 through Stockbridge and past main shopping district of Great Barrington. Turn right on Rte. 23, look for sign on right, approx. ½ mi.

For B&B rates, see Index.

THE FEDERAL HOUSE INN
South Lee, Massachusetts

In the very few years since they opened their restaurant at the Federal House Inn, Robin Slocum and Kenneth Almgren have achieved an enviable reputation for having one of the top restaurants in the Berkshires. Kenneth, who trained with the great Swiss chef Ans Benderer, has become known for his light, but masterful, touch with his menu of fourteen entrées and fourteen appetizers.

The three intimate dining rooms have a pristine quality, with their white walls, white tablecloths, lacy white curtains, and fresh cut flowers. One room is distinguished by an elegant black marble fireplace, another has a crystal chandelier, while the third has a charming French candelabra of brushed brass leaves intertwined with pink porcelain roses.

The Federal House Inn is an early 19th-century red brick building with beautiful white columns set back from the street and surrounded by large pine and copper beech trees. The bedrooms are roomy and are simply, but comfortably, furnished with bright and cheerful wallpapers and comforters and some antiques. All have private bathrooms and air conditioning. Robin notes that one room is graced with her great-great grandfather's sleigh bed.

Breakfast, included with the room charge, is served in the sunny dining room in summer and in the front dining room with a cheery fire in the winter. The fare is virtually unlimited, with fresh fruit, fresh-squeezed juice, eggs, kippers, Canadian bacon, sausage, potatoes—red flannel hash, french toast, and, of course, coffee.

THE FEDERAL HOUSE INN, Route 102, South Lee, Ma. 01260; 413-243-1824. A 7-bedroom inn (all private baths) in a quiet Berkshire community adjacent to the village of Stockbridge. Open for lodgings year-round. Summer weekends, 3-day minimum. Top-rated restaurant closed Tues. during off-season. Near all of the historic, cultural, and natural attractions of the Berkshires—Tanglewood, Berkshire Theatre Festival, Jacob's Pillow, Shakespeare & Company, Norman Rockwell Museum. Backroading, tennis, golf, swimming, boating, downhill and xc skiing nearby. Not suitable for children. No pets. Robin Slocum and Kenneth Almgren, Innkeepers.

Directions: From NYC take Taconic Pkwy. north to Rte. 23 east to Rte. 7 north to Stockbridge. Bear right on Rte. 102 east, about 1½ mi. Inn is on left. From Boston, take Mass. Tpke. west to Exit 2 in Lee; follow Rte. 102 west for 3 mi. to inn on right.

For B&B rates, see Index.

500 SOUTH MAIN STREET
Great Barrington, Massachusetts

The handsome, dark-haired young man put down his paint brush and, with his two friendly dogs, came over to greet me. It was early June, and all sorts of redecoration and sprucing-up were going on at 500 South Main Street. Robert Hafey was painting outside shutters, a front parlor was being converted into an antique shop that will feature country and primitive pieces, and various other projects were proceeding apace.

As Robert ushered me into the kitchen, an antique sign hanging over the crowded counter caught my eye: "Athol, Mass.—Steam Baths." Somehow it reflected the atmosphere of this pleasant, circa 1820, B&B—casual, easy-going, with amusing little surprises.

The bedrooms are simply but comfortably furnished; four are air conditioned and two have a particularly light and airy feeling.

Breakfast is served in the cozy dining room around a table that seats fourteen. There are all sorts of interesting and decorative pieces in the room, including two beautiful antique quilts used as wall hangings.

Robert, who has owned a restaurant, is very flexible on breakfasts—he'll do eggs any way, possibly hash-browned potatoes, stewed tomatoes, creamed chipped beef on toast, or blueberry pancakes, along with fresh fruit and juices, muffins, toast, and coffee or tea. He is also willing to do dinners if arrangements are made in advance.

500 SOUTH MAIN STREET, Great Barrington, MA 01230; 413-528-9673. A 7-guestroom (1 private and 2 shared baths) in-town guest house in the southern part of the Berkshire hills of western Massachusetts. Breakfast included in room rate. Open year-round. Dinners available by reservation. Two-night minimum stay required on weekends during the summer and foliage season. Tanglewood, Jacob's Pillow, Butternut Ski area, Berkshire Theater Festival, as well as many other recreational, cultural, and historic attractions nearby. No pets. No credit cards. Robert and Mary Hafey, Daniel Beck, Innkeepers.

Directions: From the south, after reaching Hillsdale, New York, take Rte. 23 east approx. 15 mi. At the junction with Rte. 7, turn right and look for 500 So. Main (Rte. 7) on the right. From the east, exit Mass. Turnpike at Lee and take Rte. 102 west approx. 5 mi. to Rte. 7. Continue south on Rte. 7 approx. 9 mi. thru Gt. Barrington shopping district, past junction with Rte. 23 to 500 So. Main on the right.

For B&B rates, see Index.

THE GLOUCESTER TRAVELER
Gloucester, Massachusetts

The Gloucester Traveler is situated on a wooded hilltop on the Old Carriage Road and it is particularly distinguished by its landscaped grounds, old stone walls, colorful gardens, and peace and quiet.

The main building of this establishment resembles many New England inns, as does the low-ceilinged breakfast room. It is the former estate of a well-known character actress, Jessie Ralph, who appeared in many films 35 or 40 years ago. I remember her very well, particularly in a movie with Gary Cooper.

The atmosphere is something like an idealized movie set. There are very tall evergreen trees with groups of cottages spaced far enough apart for privacy. Everything has been constructed around a rather massive rock formation which is left over from the glacial era. There are quite a few footpaths among the considerable acres which lead to several little dales and quiet places. A swimming pool is most welcome on warm days.

The accommodations are built of knotty pine and some have fireplaces.

Breakfast is served several months of the year at an additional cost of about four dollars, and consists of coffee, juice, homemade muffins, scrambled eggs and cheese, baked ham, and cold cereal.

The Gloucester Traveler, which is best described as a motor inn, has all the advantages of being close to the Cape Ann beaches and the even greater advantage of being away from the sometimes numerous people who seek them out.

THE GLOUCESTER TRAVELER MOTOR INN, 612 Essex Ave., Gloucester, Ma. 01930; 617-283-2502. A 25-bedroom secluded motor inn situated in a quiet, wooded area just a few minutes from the Cape Ann beaches. Efficiency units available. Open year-round. Breakfast at additional cost served from mid-June to mid-September. All of the North Shore and Cape Ann attractions available. Swimming pool and lawn games on grounds. Frank Kiley, Proprietor.

Directions: From Boston take Rte. 1 north to 128 north. Turn off at Exit 14 and drive toward Essex 1 mi. on Rte. 133. The Gloucester Traveler is on the left side, up the hill through the trees.

For Lodging rates, see Index.

GRAY MANOR
Gloucester, Massachusetts

Gloucester, like Rockport, Essex, and Manchester, is on Cape Ann which has 25 miles of coastline including America's oldest and most historic fishing port, 6 scenic harbors, 24 coves, and over 20 sandy beaches. Inland lie quiet, picturesque towns and dense woodlands, many of which have been set aside as public preserves.

Gray Manor is in a residential area of Gloucester on a rather quiet street. For a number of years it was, like many other Gloucester buildings, a private home. About nineteen years ago Mrs. Madeline Gray decided to take in a few roomers, and it's been a most pleasant experience for her and the Gray Manor guests ever since.

During the height of the summer season rooms of any kind are at a premium in Gloucester, and Mrs. Gray's rather modest place is a great joy with air conditioning, and the decorations and furnishings in each lodging room in carefully coordinated decorator colors. There are also six efficiencies which have stoves and refrigerators and all the utensils that you'll need. Shopping is done at the local supermarket. Mrs. Gray has a gas-fired barbecue in the backyard, as well as a large patio, for her guests' convenience. She does not serve breakfast and maintains that Charlie's Restaurant can do a much better job than she can.

Another great advantage here is that it is about a three-minute walk down the hill to a really white sandy beach that has a sort of hometown feeling about it and is a little less "touristy" than some of the others.

GRAY MANOR, 14 Atlantic Rd., Gloucester, Ma. 01930; 617-283-5409. Three private rooms and six efficiencies. Some rooms have a deck. Open May 15 to Oct. 31. Within two-minute walking distance of an excellent beach and convenient drive to several others. Near Beauport Museum and other Cape Ann attractions. Deep-sea fishing and whale-watching. No pets. No credit cards. Please telephone in advance to avoid disappointment. Mrs. Madeline Gray, Proprietor.

Directions: From Boston follow Rtes. 1 and 128 north to Gloucester. At rotary go half around to second rotary, half around that rotary down the hill to a set of lights and follow through to a second set. Then take a left on Bass Ave. and continue past Charlie's Place. Take the first road on the right, which is Atlantic Rd., and a left at the top of the hill. Gray Manor is on the corner of Atlantic Rd. and Beach Road, parking on the side.

For Lodging rates, see Index.

HARGOOD HOUSE
Provincetown, Massachusetts

Provincetown, located on the tip of Cape Cod, is a very popular place to visit in all seasons, but travelers waiting until after arriving to book rooms might well find themselves disappointed or perhaps forced to take rooms in one of the more congested sections of the town.

It is most rewarding to have advance reservations at Hargood House, right on the water's edge in Provincetown's quiet east end, just a short walk to the center of town. There are seventeen apartments in four carefully restored Cape Cod houses, all with private entrances, and most with private decks and patios. Three of the buildings surround a spacious lawn and garden area facing the harbor beach.

It was featured in several pages of *House Beautiful's Remodeling Guide* with stunning photographs showing truly spectacular decor and design.

High-season accommodations are available for a minimum of one week. During the off-season, two-night accommodations are available. Incidentally, Hargood House is totally full with a waiting list from Memorial Day until September, and nearly full in May and October.

HARGOOD HOUSE, 493 Commercial St., Provincetown, Ma. 02657; 617-487-1324. A waterfront apartment house with 17 apartments, all with kitchen facilities and private baths. Open year-round. No meals served. Garden and private beach on grounds. Convenient to all of the Provincetown and outer Cape historical, cultural, and recreational attractions. Advance permission required for pets. No credit cards. Robert Harrison and Harold Goodstein, Proprietors.

Directions: Take the first Provincetown exit from Rte. 6 and turn right on Commercial St.

For Lodging rates, see Index.

HAUS ANDRÉAS
Lee, Massachusetts

As a pleasant resort area with beautiful mountains, rushing streams, placid lakes, and delightfully cool evenings in midsummer, the Berkshires were discovered by affluent Bostonians in the 19th century. They built mansions which they called "cottages."

Some of the atmosphere of the "cottages" has been preserved at Haus Andréas, an impressive house with extensive grounds, where Queen Wilhelmina and Princess Juliana of the Netherlands summered in 1942.

An elegant and stylish country guest house, it has broad lawns for croquet and badminton, as well as tennis courts and a heated swimming pool. The living room has a frequently played piano, a welcome fireplace, stacks of classical stereo records, and shelves of books.

Three of the six generous-sized bedrooms have their own fireplaces. All have a view of the grounds, forest, and the Berkshire hills leading up the Tyringham Valley.

The proprietors are Lilliane and Gerhard Schmid. Gerhard is from Vienna and has gained an international reputation as the chef and owner of the Gateways Inn in nearby Lenox.

The continental breakfast features fresh, warm, homemade danish pastry, english muffins, or toast, with juice and coffee, and is served in the very pleasant dining room with a view overlooking the grounds.

A policy of required minimum stays is in effect for the various seasons and holidays; inquiries should be made in advance.

HAUS ANDREAS, Stockbridge Rd., Lee, Ma. 01238; 413-243-3298. A 6-room country guest house located in the quiet outskirts of a Berkshire village. Open year-round. Tennis, heated pool, croquet and badminton on grounds. Tanglewood, Jacob's Pillow, and the Berkshire Theatre Festival nearby. Unsuitable for children under ten. No pets. Lilliane and Gerhard Schmid, Proprietors.

Directions: From NYC via Taconic Pkwy. and Rte. 23 to Rte. 7, north through Stockbridge. Bear left at fire station, continue on Rte. 7 for 8/10 mi. Turn right on Stockbridge Rd. (unmarked) and go 1.9 mi. to Haus Andreas on the right. From Boston follow Mass. Tpke. to Lee Exit 2. Go north on Rte. 20 for 1 mi. to Stockbridge Rd. Go 1 mi. to Haus Andreas (on the left), which is beyond the Greenock Country Club.

For B&B rates, see Index.

THE HAWTHORNE INN
Concord, Massachusetts

A convenient distance from Boston, the town of Concord is unique in all of America because it has three famous periods in its history. The first began more than 300 years ago with the early Puritans. The second took place when Concord was the scene of the first battle of the war of the Revolution, and finally, during the 19th century, it was the home of Emerson, Alcott, Thoreau, and Hawthorne, the great authors of the period known as the "Flowering of New England."

I find it difficult to imagine a more appropriate place to stay for a night or two in Concord than the Hawthorne Inn, which has very good-sized bedrooms, beds with pleasant patchwork quilts, braided treads on the staircase, and dozens of little extras and fascinating surprises.

The house was originally a private residence built around 1870 and is almost certain to have been Nathaniel Hawthorne's property at one time. It has been redecorated with a great deal of care by innkeeper Gregory Burch, who, in many cases, used his own paintings and pieces which he felt fit into the everchanging moods of Concord.

Gregory says, "Our continental breakfast features home-baked goods, including raspberry muffins and fruit breads. The berries are grown right here at the inn. There's always fresh fruit and a special blend of coffee and herb teas. People enjoy sitting around our little dining room table in the morning."

THE HAWTHORNE INN, 462 Lexington Road, Concord, Ma. 01742; 617-369-5610. A 5-room bed-and-breakfast village inn approximately 19 mi. from Boston. Breakfast to houseguests is the only meal served. Closed Jan. and Feb. Within walking distance of all of the historic and literary points of interest in Concord. Limited facilities for young children, but ideal for young people who have an appreciation for history and literature. No pets. No credit cards. Gregory Burch, Marilyn Mudry, Innkeepers.

Directions: From Rte. 128 (the beltway around Boston) use exit 2A (Lexington Rd.). Travel west 4½ mi. Hawthorne Inn is on the south side (left) across from the Hawthorne House. Available by public transportation from Boston.

For B&B rates, see Index.

HISTORY HOUSE
Topsfield, Massachusetts

History House is an old yellow clapboard home that dates back more than a century. Originally an inn where the Boston-to-Newburyport stagecoach made its stop to change horses, it is set on a little knoll in a grove of maples.

One of the entrances is through a very warm kitchen leading into the low-ceilinged first floor.

Guests can enjoy the very pleasant sitting room, and occasionally Mrs. Pedersen has entertainment.

There are six bedrooms, including some corner rooms with views in two directions. I found spool beds, beautiful brass double beds, George Washington bedspreads, and many antiques.

Two enjoyable features are the summer porch and the swimming pool.

Mrs. Pedersen was very enthusiastic about the advantages of the Ipswich River Wildlife Sanctuary with its 2500 acres and fifteen miles of hiking trails, which are also used for skiing and snowshoeing. There are also many country markets, museums, historical sites, and beaches.

The full New England breakfast features homemade muffins, freshly prepared fruits and juice and coffee, and is included in the room rate.

With its location just thirty minutes from Boston and the country atmosphere, History House is an ideal place to stay to visit that part of Massachusetts.

HISTORY HOUSE, 78 High St., Topsfield, Ma. 01983; 617-887-2626. A 6-bedroom bed-and-breakfast inn in a pleasant north shore village. Breakfast only meal served. Open from April 15 to October 30. Conveniently located to visit the natural, historical, and recreational attractions in the area. Swimming pool on grounds. No credit cards. No pets. Mrs. Marjorie Pedersen, Innkeeper.

Directions: From Boston take Rte. 95 or U.S. 1. High St. in Topsfield is just off the village green. History House is on the corner of Rte. 1 and Rte. 97; the driveway is on Rte. 1.

For B&B rates, see Index.

THE INN AT STOCKBRIDGE
Stockbridge, Massachusetts

I'm personally quite familiar with The Inn at Stockbridge. Many years ago it was rented for the summer by some good friends of mine and I enjoyed pleasant evenings on the porch watching the sun go down and listening to the sounds of birds at eventide. On brisk evenings, my host always lit a fire in the fireplace, and the low ceiling, many books, and comfortable furniture encouraged us to much good conversation.

The scene is exactly the same today, except that Lee and Don Weitz have found a way to extend to many guests the warmth and hospitality of this big, lovely, old white house with the Grecian pillars and wonderful large rooms.

There are seven bedrooms, some unusually large, and five-and-a-half baths. These have all been very comfortably furnished and all have splendid views of the Berkshire Hills.

Some guests might find that lazing by the pool in summer or cross-country skiing on the inn grounds in winter is as much as they care to do; others will find that the Berkshires offer a wide variety of choices for recreation and entertainment.

The gourmet breakfast that might include a soufflé or even eggs Benedict is served in the dining room or on the porch. The meal is graciously served with cloth napkins, bone china, and silver accessories.

THE INN AT STOCKBRIDGE (formerly The Norris Putnam House), Rte. 7, Stockbridge, Ma. 01262; 413-298-3337. A 7-room country house (some shared baths) about 1 mi. north of the center of Stockbridge. Open year-round. Lodgings include a full breakfast. Convenient to all of the Berkshire cultural and recreational attractions. A summer swimming pool and xc skiing on the grounds. No pets. No credit cards. Lee and Don Weitz, Innkeepers.

Directions: From New York City: take any of the main highways north to Stockbridge. Look for small sign on the right-hand side of Rte. 7 after passing under the Massachusetts Turnpike 1 mi. north of Stockbridge. From Mass. Turnpike: exit at Lee, take Rte. 102 to Stockbridge and turn right on Rte. 7 going north for 1 mile as above.

For B&B rates, see Index.

THE INN ON COVE HILL
Rockport, Massachusetts

Pirate treasure may have been used to build the Caleb Norwood, Jr., mansion that is now the Inn on Cove Hill. Of course, that was in 1791. However, the story of the father who died poor, but whose sons were suddenly wealthy, still lingers. Happily for those seeking the richness of comfort plus historic tradition, the three-story Federal home is a B&B, painstakingly restored and decorated with family antiques and Laura Ashley prints.

The location is perfect for those who would be in the center of artistic Rockport. Motif Number One is only steps away, and Bearskin Neck with its shops and galleries is just beyond. The view from the inn deck is enough to drive anyone to camera, if not to sketch pad or canvas and brushes. Good restaurants are within immediate walking distance; Old Garden Beach is a stroll.

In summer breakfast is served under umbrellas in the daisy garden. In winter, trays are brought to the bedrooms. Either way, the china is English bone and the muffins fresh and home-baked.

The eleven bedrooms are both cozy and lavish with handmade quilts and afghans. Each has a small TV set and comfortable chairs. Downstairs there is a guest living room with especially choice antique furniture and plenty of books.

Marjorie and John Pratt are world travelers as well as downhome New Englanders. This is reflected in their eclectic collection of art work, as well as the care they take of their guests.

THE INN ON COVE HILL, 37 Mt. Pleasant St., Rockport, MA 01966; 6l7-546-2701. An 11-guestroom (eight with private baths) bed-and-breakfast inn in the center of Rockport, walking distance to everything. Breakfast is the only meal served, but many restaurants are nearby. Closed November to mid- February. No pets. No children under 10. No credit cards. Marjorie and John Pratt, Innkeepers.

Directions: As an alternative to driving, guests can arrive by train from Boston and will be picked up at Rockport Station. By road, follow Rte. 128 (Boston's inner beltway) to its northern end, then Rte. 127 to 127A. Once in Rockport Center, 127A takes a right, becoming Mt. Pleasant St.; the inn is on your left.

For B&B rates, see Index.

INNISFREE OF DENNISPORT
Dennisport, Cape Cod, Massachusetts

There is something about Innisfree of Dennisport that is completely identifiable: It is Irish.

The innkeepers, Mary Elizabeth McGee and Virginia O'Brien, are about as comely a pair of colleens as you'll find this side of Innisfree, Ireland. They told me that they had visited Innisfree twice and they both liked Irish poetry, especially Yeats. There is a line from one of his poems, *Isle of Innisfree*, that reads, " . . . I will arise and go now, and go to Innisfree . . . and I shall have some peace there . . . " As they explained, they chose the name for the inn hoping that whoever came would have some peace and rest from the cares of the world.

As far as I could determine, not only would the visitor have peace and rest, but a great deal of good fun, as well. Innisfree is Irish through and through, including many of the furnishings, decorations, and the like, and even an Irish dog, whose name is Kelly O'Brien. A small sign in Gaelic reads, *Cead mile Failte,* which means "a hundred thousand welcomes."

The sixteen bedrooms, including seven in a small dwelling next door, are all furnished in a Cape Cod-Irish way and seemed quite comfortable.

The Irish experience includes Virginia's delicious Irish soda bread with orange marmalade from Dublin and delightful currant scones, both of which are part of the continental breakfast included in the room rate.

The inn's location at mid-Cape makes it convenient for all of the many attractions, not the least of which are the warm waters of Nantucket Sound just a few steps away.

For future guests' information, Innisfree is pronounced *Innish-free.*

INNISFREE OF DENNISPORT, 32 Inman Rd., Dennisport, Ma. 02639; 617-394-5356. A 16-bedroom (4 private baths) inn with an Irish flair located on Nantucket Sound on Cape Cod. Continental breakfast included in room rate. Open Memorial Day and through Columbus Day. M.E. McGee and V.C. O'Brien, Innkeepers.

Directions: Take Exit 9 from Rte. 6 (Mid-Cape Hwy.), follow Rte. 134 south and turn left on Lower County Rd. and right on Inman Road in Dennisport.

For B&B rates, see Index.

LA MAISON DU POTHIER
Pittsfield, Massachusetts

On a quiet, tree-shaded street, lined with similar solidly built, comfortably proportioned homes, La Maison du Pothier, a red brick Georgian house with a green-tiled roof, offers bed-and-breakfast hospitality in the center of Massachusetts' well-loved Berkshires.

Built in 1912 by a prominent Pittsfield family, this graciously laid-out home has spacious rooms trimmed with polished mahogany moldings, beamed ceilings, oak floors, and original fittings such as brass gas lamps, light fixtures, and crystal doorknobs. Fireplaces in the living and dining rooms are lit in cool weather. Each of the large, airy bedrooms is pleasantly furnished and has its own tiled bath; two of the bedrooms have working fireplaces.

Joyce and Bob Pothier establish an easy atmosphere with a cheerful and attractive breakfast setting in the dining room. Joyce always has fresh flowers around and sets the tables with quilted placemats, charming handpainted French dishes, and her own silverware. Bob specializes in delicious fruit combinations like peaches and cream, melon and berries, and other fresh fruit in season. Joyce bakes corn muffins, honey muffins, or banana bread, and there are also fruit juices, coffee and tea, and, when desired, yogurt or bagels and lox.

Joyce is a fount of information on all the attractions available in and around this historically and culturally rich area, and enjoys advising her guests on good places to eat.

LA MAISON DU POTHIER, 187 Bartlett Ave., Pittsfield, Ma. 01201; 413-447-7231. A 3-bedroom (private baths) Georgian home within walking distance of downtown Pittsfield and historic sites. Open May 15 to Nov. 1 and during ski season on weekends. Continental breakfast included in room rate. Tanglewood, Jacob's Pillow, Williamstown and Berkshire Theatre Festivals, Hancock Shaker Village, South Mountain Chamber Music Concerts, Norman Rockwell Museum, Arrowhead (home of Herman Melville), all within an easy drive. Walking tours of historic sites, backroading, swimming, boating, downhill and xc skiing nearby. Crib and baby-sitting available with advance notice. Prefer no smoking. No pets. No credit cards. Joyce and Bob Pothier, Hosts.

Directions: From Mass. Tpke (I-90): Take Exit 2 at Lee and turn right onto Rte. 20 west which joins Rte. 7 north. Continue to Pittsfield and the rotary at Park Square (approx. 8 mi.). Continue east from the rotary for 2 blocks, past the courthouse and the Berkshire Atheneum, to Bartlett Ave. Turn right and proceed 4 blocks to 187 Bartlett Ave.

For B&B rates, see Index.

THE LION'S HEAD INN
West Harwich, Cape Cod, Massachusetts

Speaking of the Lion's Head Inn, the innkeeper-in-residence on the particular day of my visit, said, "It's a romantic inn with a sense of history." A well-turned phrase if ever I heard one.

Here's a bed-and-breakfast inn that makes the most of its quiet location and historic past. The rooms all have significant names and antiques to match. For instance, in the Morning Room the Cape Cod sunlight and antiques provide the guests with a pleasant countryside feeling, and the Map Room, which was once used as a study for the original owner, sea captain Thomas L. Snow, has maps showing the oceans of the world. Captain Snow's Suite has two rooms and an adjoining bath.

The house was built in the early 1800s as what is known locally as a "Cape half-house." It's been enlarged several times over the years and has a sort of rambling feeling now.

One of the more pleasant aspects is a social hour in which the innkeepers introduce incoming guests, and plans are made by all concerned for a special Cape Cod dinner. Many guests enjoy a quiet evening of entertainment with games such as backgammon, chess, and so forth, in the living room. In one corner there is a jigsaw puzzle of a line drawing of the inn and a list of the times that some people have taken to put it together. The best time so far was nine minutes; perhaps one of the readers of this book can do it in less.

THE LION'S HEAD INN, 186 Belmont Rd., West Harwich, Cape Cod, Ma. 02671; 617-432-7766. A 5-room inn on a quiet street in a south shore village on Cape Cod. Cottages which can accommodate children available in the summer. A full breakfast is the only meal served. Near all of the Cape Cod attractions, including beaches, biking, museums, and antiquing. No credit cards. No pets. Laurie and Djordje Soc, Innkeepers.

Directions: From Rte. 6 take Exit 9 (Dennis) to the right and go about ½ mi. to stoplight. Turn left (this is marked West Harwich). Continue on this road (Upper County Road). This will converge with Rte. 28 on the line between Dennis and Harwich. Go two blocks on Rte. 28; look for Belmont Rd., on the right at the gas station. Houses on Belmont are numbered.

For B&B rates, see Index.

MERRELL TAVERN INN
South Lee, Massachusetts

The Merrell Tavern Inn, built in 1794, is an excellent example of a historic building that is being both preserved and granted a new lease on life as a bed-and-breakfast inn.

With the assistance and guidance of the Society for the Preservation of New England Antiquities (SPNEA), the new owners of the inn, Charles and Faith Reynolds, have done a remarkable job of preserving the Federalist atmosphere of this former stop on the Boston-Albany stagecoach run. In recognition of their restoration of the 188-year-old inn, the Massachusetts Historical Commission has presented them with the 1982 Preservation Award.

The red brick exterior with first- and second-floor porches has remained unmarred by the passing years, and in repainting and installing new plumbing and wiring, the Reynoldses were careful to maintain the house's architectural and visual integrity.

Fabrics and original paint colors have been duplicated wherever possible, and the Reynoldses have supplemented their own collection of antiques with additional circa-1800 pieces. In addition to the four bedrooms created from the third-floor ballroom (quite a customary feature in early inns) there are five bedrooms on the first and second floors with views either of the main road passing through the village of South Lee or of the Housatonic River in the rear.

A picture in *Historic Preservation* shows Faith Reynolds serving breakfast in the original barroom where perhaps the only remaining circular Colonial bar in America is still intact, even to the little till drawer. The original grain-painted woodwork is protected by an easement.

MERRELL TAVERN INN, Main St., Rte. 102, South Lee, Ma. 01260; 413-243-1794. A 9-bedroom (most with private baths) beautifully preserved and restored historic tavern in a quiet Berkshire village. Lodgings include a full country breakfast; no other meals served. Open every day except Christmas Eve and Christmas Day. Holiday weekends, 2-night minimum stay; July, Aug., 3-night weekend minimum stay. Within a convenient distance of all of the Berkshire cultural, natural, and recreational activities including Berkshire Theater Festival, Tanglewood, and Shakespeare and Company. No pets. Charles and Faith Reynolds, Innkeepers.

Directions: South Lee is on Rte. 102, midway between Lee and Stockbridge.

For B&B rates, see Index.

THE MORGAN HOUSE
Lee, Massachusetts

Lee, Massachusetts, is a bustling, independent-minded community located near the point where the Massachusetts Turnpike, running east and west, intersects with Route 7, one of the principal north-south roads to and from New York City.

The Morgan House has an impressive record of continuous hospitality since 1853 when it was established as a stagecoach inn. Horace Greeley, Buffalo Bill Cody, Robert E. Lee, President Ulysses S. Grant, and George Bernard Shaw all wrote their names in the register, and many of these pages are now used to paper the small comfortable lobby of this village inn. You can see them for yourself.

The inn is a three-storied, clapboard building with a second-floor gallery that is a very pleasant place to enjoy breakfast or take some refreshments at any time of the day.

Today the innkeeping tradition is being well-preserved by Beth and Bill Orford, an enthusiastic young couple who have infused this venerable old hostelry with some of their youthful zest and vigor. They have completely redecorated all of the twelve lodging rooms.

The luncheon and evening meals feature such New England fare as prime ribs of beef and New England duckling, and are served in the cozy low-ceilinged dining room. A semi-full breakfast is offered to houseguests with hot or cold cereal, fresh fruit, homebaked breads, sweet rolls, juice, coffee, and boiling water in which you may cook your own morning eggs.

THE MORGAN HOUSE, Main Street, Lee, Ma. 01238; 413-243-0181. A 12-room village inn (1 private, 4 shared baths). Open every day including holidays. Closed Tuesday, except during the high tourist season. Near all of the Berkshire attractions including Tanglewood, Jacob's Pillow Dance Festival, The Berkshire Theater Festival, South Mountain Chamber Music Concerts, the Norman Rockwell Museum, Chesterwood, Hancock Shaker Village, and Berkshire Garden Center. Swimming, boating, canoeing, horseback riding, Alpine and cross-country skiing nearby. No pets. Beth and Bill Orford, Innkeepers.

Directions: From Massachusetts Turnpike: Lee is Exit 2. From Rte. 7: follow Rte. 102 from Stockbridge to Lee.

For B&B rates, see Index.

MORRILL PLACE
Newburyport, Massachusetts

Newburyport is one of the delightful surprises of New England. Unfortunately, many travelers headed north from Boston on I-95 see little or nothing of it as they push on towards New Hampshire, Maine, and the Canadian Maritime Provinces. This as-yet-unspoiled small city on the banks of the Merrimac River has a very delightfully restored waterfront area as well as the Parker River National Wildlife Refuge, The Custom House Maritime Museum, and a long street that has a truly impressive collection of early 19th-century private homes. One of these is Morrill Place, a most delightful opportunity to enjoy a night's lodging in the elegant surroundings of bygone days.

There are ten guest rooms, all furnished in period antiques and many with working fireplaces. Guests are conducted on house tours by the attractive innkeeper, Rose Ann Hunter, frequently accompanied by her young daughter Kristen and Monroe, the cat, who is reputed to be the real owner.

The feature of the entrance hallway is a double-hung staircase with six-inch risers. Rose Ann explains to her guests that this was built at the time when women wore hoop skirts.

The continental breakfasts, which are taken in the library in front of a good fire during the colder weather and on the outer porch in the summer, consist of tasty baked goods which are aided and abetted by juice and lots of coffee.

There are two bed-and-breakfast inns in Newburyport, the other being the Windsor House. When filled, each unhesitatingly recommends the other.

MORRILL PLACE, 209 High St., Newburyport, Ma. 01950; 617-462-2808. A 10-room guest house on one of Newburyport's beautiful residential avenues. Most rooms share bath with one other room. Lodgings include continental breakfast, only meal offered. Open every day in the year. Within a very convenient distance of all of the Newburyport historical and cultural attractions, and Plum Island Wildlife Refuge. Other recreational facilities nearby. Rose Ann Hunter, Innkeeper.

Directions: From Boston follow I-95 north and take Historic Newburyport exit and follow Rte. 113. This becomes High St. Follow it for about 2 miles. Inn is on right-hand side at corner of Johnson and High St. From Maine: Exit I-95 for Historic Newburyport and follow above directions.

For B&B rates, see Index.

MOSTLY HALL
Falmouth, Massachusetts

Although Mostly Hall was built in 1849 by a Yankee ship captain for his New Orleans bride, there is an English country house feeling to the place. It may be the beautifully restored and maintained front garden with its rolling lawn and dogwood. Few Cape Cod houses are set so majestically back from the road.

Ginny Austin sends her guests off each morning with a full breakfast, too, though it is a good deal more imaginative than standard English fare. Ginny's french toast stuffed with cream cheese and walnuts and topped with an apricot-orange sauce so inspired one guest he has put it on the menu of his own restaurant.

There is much to do in this corner of the Cape: warm water beaches, a four-mile ocean bike path, and the ferries to Martha's Vineyard and Nantucket Islands (wonderful day trips, if not longer). Mostly Hall is right on the historic village green with the shops, galleries, and summer theater of Falmouth close at hand. Of course, you can also spend the day playing croquet, reading, or visiting with other guests on the veranda of Mostly Hall.

There are five room with private baths, plus two with shared bath, all furnished with antiques and country pieces and many personal touches.

MOSTLY HALL, 27 Main St., Falmouth, MA 02540; 617-548-3786. A 7-guestroom inn (5 with private bath) on the village green in Falmouth, Cape Cod. Approx. 90 min. from Boston, Newport, or Provincetown. Open year-round. Full breakfast included in rate. No other meals served. Located in a historic and scenic area convenient to Woods Hole and ferries to Nantucket and Martha's Vineyard. No children under 16. No pets. No credit cards. Jim and Ginny Austin, Innkeepers.

Directions: As you approach the Cape, follow signs that say Cape Cod and the Islands to Hwy. 28. Mostly Hall is 14 mi. from Bourne Bridge. Turn left on 28-S; Mostly Hall is 4th house on the right. Off-street parking in rear.

For B&B rates, see Index.

NAUSET HOUSE INN
East Orleans, Massachusetts

The Nauset House Inn on Cape Cod is almost three-quarters of the way to Provincetown and within a short walk of Nauset Beach, which has some of the best surf in New England. A building of some gratifying antiquity, it is small enough for everyone to become quite friendly. The bedrooms are in the main house and the carriage house.

The new owners of the Nauset House are Albert and Diane Johnson, who have brought many new touches to this old inn, including several examples of stained glass, as well as some stenciling done by their daughter, Cindy.

Furnishings in the inn are a most intriguing mixture of antiques with some contemporary touches providing an interesting contrast. There's also a marked involvement in various crafts, as well.

It is obvious that Diane Johnson is very fond of flowers, because they are found in profusion in every bedroom and public room in the inn.

Every late afternoon, guests gather on the patio, in the fascinating glass greenhouse, or in the living room to enjoy hors d'oeuvres and refreshments. This is the time when newcomers are introduced.

On warm mornings, a full breakfast can be enjoyed on the apple-tree-shaded terrace; on chilly mornings, everyone repairs to the brick-floored dining room where there is a crackling fire.

Early risers can stroll through the grounds into the glass conservatory where coffee is available until breakfast time, when different types of omelets or french toast with maple syrup are served. Breakfast is not included in the room rate.

NAUSET HOUSE INN, P.O. Box 446, Nauset Beach Rd., East Orleans, Cape Cod. Mass. 02643; 617-255-2195. A 14-room country inn 90 mi. from Boston, 27 mi. from Hyannis. Breakfast (not included in room rate) served to inn guests only. No other meals served. Some rooms with shared bath. Open daily from Mar. 31 to Oct. 31. Within walking distance of Nauset Beach. Riding and bicycles nearby. No children under 12. No pets. Albert and Diane Johnson, Innkeepers.

Directions: From the Mid-Cape Hwy. (Rte. 6), take Exit 12. Bear right to first traffic light. Follow signs for Nauset Beach. Inn is located ¼ mi. before beach on Nauset Beach Rd.

For Lodging rates, see Index.

NORTHFIELD COUNTRY HOUSE
Northfield, Massachusetts

Brass beds, down comforters, bedroom fireplaces, individually decorated guest rooms filled with antiques, and the innkeeper's handwoven baskets and herb wreaths characterize this restored English manor house in one of the most attractive villages in New England.

The center of the inn is a great, beautiful living room with overhead beams and a gorgeous stone fireplace There are three commodious couches grouped around the fireplace.

In addition to being in an ideal location for cross-country and downhill skiing as well as for touring the beautiful western Massachusetts, Vermont, and New Hampshire countryside, the Northfield Country House is located just a few minutes from Northfield Mt. Hermon School and within a short distance of five major colleges in western Massachusetts, including Amherst, Smith, Mt. Holyoke, and Hampshire colleges, and the University of Massachusetts.

A typical Scandinavian breakfast begins with meusli—oatmeal, cream, nuts, coconut, fruit, with whipped cream on the top. Janice Gamache also offers something homemade every morning including hot cornbread, popovers or muffins, and then it's time to start on the bacon and eggs, blueberry pancakes, omelets, or whatever. It's a full country breakfast.

If you're traveling on I-91, get off at Northfield and spend a night (or even several) here. It's really a pleasure.

NORTHFIELD COUNTRY HOUSE, School St., Northfield, Ma. 01360; 413-498-2692. A 7-bedroom restored country house in the rolling Connecticut River Valley a few mi. south of the N.H. line. Open year-round, except closed Thanksgiving, New Year's Eve, 1st week of Jan., and 1st 2 wks. in Aug. Room includes full breakfast. Dinner served to houseguests and others by advance reservation. Tennis, swimming, xc skiing on grounds. Antique shops, flea markets, auctions, boating, fishing, golf, Old Deerfield Village, Mohawk Trail, and marvelous backroading nearby. Not suitable for children under 12. No pets. No credit cards. The Gamache Family, Innkeepers.

Directions: From I-91 use Exit 28A, follow Rte. 10 north to Northfield Center. Turn left toward Keene. Continue through main street of town and turn right on School St. (at firehouse). Go 9/10th of mi., crossing one blacktop country road and turn right at inn sign.

For B&B rates, see Index.

THE OLD INN ON THE GREEN
New Marlborough, Massachusetts

New Marlborough is located in an unusually beguiling part of the Berkshires, and this inn is situated on a village green around which are several very venerable 18th- and early 19th-century homes, some with Palladian windows and others with pillars and pilasters. The church with the white steeple serenely oversees the scene which is highly paintable and photographable.

Writing about this tiny inn which was already 100 years old in 1869, a travel writer of the day commented: "Pleasantly situated in the hilltown of New Marlborough, travelers will find here comforts for both man and beast. Summer boarders will find the society good, the air pure, trout brooks near, the surrounding scenery magnificent, and everything provided for their accommodation and comfort."

I can well imagine that the most frequent reaction of guests walking for the first time into the kitchen of this old inn is one of complete delight. The chances are that some goodies in the bake-oven are enveloping the room with divine aromas.

There are five bedrooms sharing two baths and everything has undergone a complete refurbishing.

One of the innkeepers, Leslie Miller, is an expert baker and has been putting her professional baking ovens to good use.

Besides the really authentic antique feeling of this inn, one of the most enticing features is the continental breakfast. There are always croissants and another type of coffee cake from Leslie's oven.

On Friday and Saturday evenings, a prix-fixe dinner is offered (by reservation only) in the newly restored tavern room, at the harvest table in the dining room, and in the private parlor.

THE OLD INN ON THE GREEN, Star Rte. 70, New Marlborough, Massachusetts 01230; 413-229-7924. A 5-room (shared baths) 18th-century tavern well-preserved and restored on green in a secluded Berkshire village. Very convenient for all of the Berkshire summer and winter recreational and cultural activities including Tanglewood, Berkshire Theater Festival, and Jacob's Pillow. Downhill and cross-country skiing. No pets. No credit cards. Open all year. Leslie Miller and Bradford Wagstaff, Innkeepers.

Directions: From the Taconic Parkway (en route from New York) use Exit 230. Follow Rte. 23 east through Great Barrington toward Monterey. Branch off on Rte. 57 and continue 5.7 mi. uphill to the New Marlborough Village Green. It is a large white building with an upper gallery.

For B&B rates, see Index.

THE OLD MANSE INN
Brewster, Cape Cod, Massachusetts

In my search for appropriate bed-and-breakfast accommodations on Cape Cod, I was delighted to find a few that were open year-round. Such is the case with The Old Manse Inn, on the north shore of the Cape in the very pleasant village of Brewster.

The white clapboard building is set off by towering trees, many varieties of flowers, and a pleasant garden table with an umbrella. Some people were just coming back from a swim and sun bathing on the beach, which is one of the things you do here in July and August. In other seasons you also go to the beach, but to walk rather than swim.

I sat with innkeeper Sugar Manchester in the typical New England living room. As she regaled me with some extremely amusing stories about innkeeping, two cats waited by the door to be petted, as she told me, by each and every guest.

This is the Manchesters' home, and there are tennis rackets, hockey equipment, a dart board, and other signs that there are young people in the house. Of interest to guests is the fact that cold things may be kept in the refrigerator.

There are patchwork quilts and flowery New England wallpaper in the bedrooms. Some have very attractive non-working fireplaces. The living room fireplace is used in winter and on cool spring and fall nights.

A breakfast featuring warm muffins, juice, cereal with fresh fruit, and coffee, tea, hot chocolate, or decaffeinated is served at the long dining table where guests sit and chat. Evening meals are also available by reservation.

Among the collection of good watercolors and American primitives there is a small sign with the aphorism, "Mingle with the Beautiful, the Famous, and the Polished."

THE OLD MANSE INN, Route 6A, 1861 Main St., Brewster, Ma. 02631; 617-896-3149. A 9-bedroom (private baths) inn in a picturesque Cape Cod village. Open year-round. Breakfast is included in the cost of the room. Dinner also served. Conveniently located for all of the Cape Cod historic, recreational, and cultural attractions. No pets. Sugar and Doug Manchester, Innkeepers.

Directions: Take Exit 9 from Rte. 6 and follow to the intersection of 6A. Turn right to Brewster.

For B&B rates, see Index.

ONE CENTRE STREET
Yarmouth Port, Massachusetts

An old Colonial home seems an appropriate stopping place along the Old King's Highway (Route 6A) of Cape Cod. Yarmouth Port is just about midway, too, and two of the best restaurants on the Cape are within walking distance of the One Centre Street Inn.

Barbara Mutchler agrees that the neighborhood's gourmet standards contribute to the very special breakfasts she serves her guests. In addition to a select fresh fruit compote, there may be fresh apple cake, pineapple cake, or a similar homebaked delight. Her omelets come in countless variations. Since many guests are sent by local residents, arrangements may be made to invite their friends to breakfast for a modest charge.

The rooms are light and airy. The inn supplies bikes for rides down the street to Grays Beach or just around town. On the occasional rainy day, there is a pleasant fire and lots of good books. For a family holiday, it would be hard to beat either the guest quarters or the location. Antique and crafts shops are nearby, as well as the village historical sites. Yarmouth Port also has an enormous used book store, quaranteed to keep any True Reader entranced for days. At the same time, you are only minutes away from the faster-paced south shore of the Cape.

Returning visitors to the Cape may remember when the inn was under former management as Greywillow.

ONE CENTRE STREET INN, One Centre St. and Old King's Hwy. (Rte. 6A), Yarmouth Port, MA 02675; 617-362-8910. A 5-guestroom (3 rooms with private baths) located on the quiet north side of Cape Cod. Open year-round. Breakfast is the only meal served, but it is full and special. Menus on hand for the many fine restaurants nearby. Barbara and Donald Mutchler, Jack Williams, Proprietors.

Directions: Coming on the Cape across Sagamore Bridge, go about 16 mi. on Rte. 6 (mid-Cape Hwy.) to Exit 7. Turn right at the end of the exit ramp and proceed on Willow St. to Rte. 6A. Turn right again and continue approx. 1½ mi. Inn is on your left at the corner of Centre St.

For B&B rates, see Index.

PARSON HUBBARD HOUSE
Shelburne Centre, Massachusetts

The Mohawk Trail (Route 2) began as an Indian path centuries ago and runs the sixty-three-mile distance between Petersburg, New York, and Orange, Massachusetts. It is one of the most scenic highways in the East and is particularly popular during the fall foliage season when every accommodation has been reserved for months in advance.

Happy, indeed, is the traveler who in any season finds accommodations with Jeanne and Richard Bole at the Parson Hubbard House, a beautiful white clapboard house with a slate roof, built in 1774. The white plaster walls, blue overhead beams, and twelve-over-twelve windows, as well as the four gorgeous maples on the front lawn, set the atmosphere. Richard and Jeanne provide an accompanying spirit of hospitality and enthusiasm which rounds out the whole experience.

There are two rooms with double beds and one room with a twin bed. They share one bath. These are augmented by most cordial sitting rooms and a Keeping Room that is the pride and joy of the house.

Jeanne's breakfasts include fresh raspberries and blueberries from the garden, baked apples done on the woodstove, truly wonderful pancakes served with maple syrup from the trees surrounding the house, and many other irresistible offerings.

By the way, the town of Shelburne Falls has the famous Bridge of Flowers, and the entire area abounds in beautiful scenic views. The Parson Hubbard House is a mere half-mile from Route 2—but so-o-o pastoral.

PARSON HUBBARD HOUSE, Old Village Rd., Shelburne Centre, Ma. 01370; 413-625-9730. A 3-bedroom (shared bath) guest home located in the original parsonage high atop a hill, just a few minutes from Rte. 2 (the Mohawk Trail). Breakfast is only meal served. Open spring, summer, and fall. Located a short distance from historic Old Deerfield, the 5-college area, and in the summer, the Mohawk Trail Concerts. Please, no smoking preferred. No credit cards. No pets. Mr. and Mrs. Richard Bole, Proprietors.

Directions: Traveling west on Rte. 2, turn right at Little Mohawk Rd., and continue for ¼ mi. to Old Village Rd. (first right). Turn right; 4th house on left.

For B&B rates, see Index.

PISTACHIO COVE
Lakeville, Massachusetts

Here is a pleasant bed-and-breakfast place just one mile from Route 140, and only a few miles from I-195 or I-95. Set at the end of a winding driveway in a two-acre pine grove with extensive lake frontage, the house is a contemporary building with barnboard siding. The furnishings reveal a flair for decorating in the bright, homey interior.

Dana Lapolla offers her guests a warm welcome with refreshments appropriate to the season, to be enjoyed on the porch in the summer or in front of a cheery fire in the winter.

The immaculate bedrooms are outfitted with all manner of conveniences for the comfort of her guests—electric blankets, backrests, alarm clocks, intercoms, telephones, radios and color TVs with earphones, and adjustable tables for snacking or reading.

Dana's breakfasts are exceptionally hearty with eggs or quiche, a variety of sausages and ham, homemade coffeecake, or fruit compote topped with homegrown blueberries.

All holidays are celebrated with a passion with special foods and decorations. The private beach offers swimming, boating, and fishing in the summer, and skating and ice boating in the winter. A state park is just twelve miles away.

As if that isn't enough, Dana also has a private kennel where a guest may keep a pet. Pistachio Cove is listed with Pineapple Hospitality, a New England reservation service.

PISTACHIO COVE, Lakeville, Ma. (Mailing address: Box 456, East Freetown, Ma. 02717); 617-763-2383. (Also listed with Pineapple Hospitality,,617-990-1696 or 997-9952.) A 4-bedroom home with 230-ft. lake frontage on Long Pond, approx. 1 mi. from Rte. 140; 45 mi. from Boston and 10 mi. from New Bedford. Open 365 days a year. Exceptionally hearty breakfast included in room rate. Dinner may be arranged by special request. Private beach affords swimming, boating, fishing, water-skiing, and winter ice sports. Freetown State Park 12 mi. Dana Lapolla, Hostess.

Directions: From New York City, take I-95 north to I-195 east to Rte. 140 north. Take Exit 9 (County Rd.-Long Pond) and turn right, continuing on County Rd. for just over 1 mi. to black mailbox on left marked "Dana's" (in hot pink). Follow driveway approx. 500 ft. to Pistachio Cove. From Boston, take I-93 (Southeast Expwy.) to Rte. 24 to Rte. 140 south. Take Exit 9 (County Rd.-Long Pond) and turn left, continuing on County Rd. as above.

For B&B rates, see Index.

THE QUEEN ANNE INN
Chatham, Cape Cod, Massachusetts

Chatham is one of the lovely villages on Cape Cod. From its shore myriad little fingers of land run out, making a coastline of blue inlets and crystal creeks. Sometimes it is like a fairy sea, shrouded in mists or jeweled in sunshine. The land itself has been torn by glacial action into exquisite patterns that change with different shades of light.

The Queen Anne Inn has a history dating to 1840 when it was built by a prominent Outer Cape sea captain as a wedding present for his daughter. It has had a number of different careers, but in the summer of 1978 it was completely restored and renovated and, where possible, much of the public areas and thirty guest rooms retain the original furnishings.

A continental breakfast is served in the gaily decorated breakfast room or on the porch overlooking the lawn in the rear. It includes a choice of juice, toast, or English muffins, or homemade blueberry, cranberry, apple, or raisin muffins, and coffee, tea, or hot chocolate.

I would suggest that one of the best times to visit the Queen Anne, are the months of June or September or October, for the Cape is a very popular place during midsummer.

THE QUEEN ANNE INN, 70 Queen Anne Rd., Chatham, Mass. 02633; 617-945-0394. A 30-room village inn on Cape Cod on the picturesque south shore. Full American, modified American, or European plans. Open Easter thru Thanksgiving. Breakfast, dinner, Sunday brunch, and Tuesday clambake served to travelers. Near all of the Cape's scenic, cultural, and historical attractions. Water skiing, deep-sea fishing, sailing, bicycles, backroading, beach walking nearby. No recreational facilities for children on grounds. Nicole and Guenther Weinkopf, Innkeepers.

Directions: From Boston: Take Rte. 3 south to Sagamore Bridge crossing Cape Cod Canal. Continue on Rte. 6 to Exit 11; take Rte. 137 south to Rte. 28, turn left. This is Chatham's Main Street. Turn right into Queen Anne Rd. From New York: Take I-95 north to Providence, R.I.; I-195 to Wareham, and Rte. 6 to Sagamore Bridge (see directions above).

For B&B rates, see Index.

THE RALPH WALDO EMERSON
Rockport, Massachusetts

Massachusetts' north shore is a most interesting combination of history and recreation. The small towns each have facts and legends in their past that bear retelling.

The Cape Ann section includes Gloucester, Essex, Manchester, and Rockport, and sea fever dominates these communities with their sun-bathed beaches, exciting rock formations, and casual disarrangement of fishing shacks and old homes.

Rockport has a fetching harbor and winding streets and a great number of year-round artists and craftsmen. The Rockport Art Association exhibits all year.

The Ralph Waldo Emerson is located in Pigeon Cove in Rockport and is owned by the Wemyss family who are also the proprietors of the Yankee Clipper. It is a traditional north shore hotel and an expansive view of the water may be enjoyed while rocking on the board front porch.

There is also a swimming pool, a most popular year-round sauna, as well as the opportunity to stroll the streets of this quiet seaside town.

The bedrooms are of a seaside-resort nature, reminiscent of the turn of the century.

RALPH WALDO EMERSON, 1 Cathedral Ave., Rockport, Mass. 01966; 617-546-6321. A 36-room oceanside inn, 40 mi. from Boston. Modified American and European plans. Breakfast and dinner served daily from July 1 to Labor Day; bed and breakfast only during remainder of the year. Closed Nov. thru mid-May; open weekends in April and early May. Pool, sauna, and whirlpool bath on grounds. Tennis, golf nearby. Courtesy car. No pets. Gary Wemyss, Innkeeper.

Directions: Take I-95 to Rte. 128 to 127 (Gloucester). Proceed 6 mi. on Rte. 127 to Rockport and continue to Pigeon Cove.

For B&B rates, see Index.

RIVER BEND FARM
Williamstown, Massachusetts

"Home is the sailor, home from the sea..." could be the song sung by David and Judy Loomis when they return to their 1770 Georgian bed-and-breakfast farmhouse after one of their year-long schooner trips 'round the world. David is a schooner captain and Judy is an able sailor, and every so often they set out from their quiet lives in Williamstown for adventure on the high seas.

But the rest of the time, says David, they enjoy working on the continuing restoration of their center-chimney Colonial home, built by Col. Benjamin Simonds, and used as a staging area for the militiamen who went to fight the British at the Battle of Bennington.

The Keeping Room has extra-wide paneled pine walls and a huge, old brick fireplace, where the crane holds a blackened iron kettle, old iron ladles, tongs, and such. This is the setting for breakfasts of fruit or juice, homemade breads and muffins, honey from the Loomis beehives, homemade jams, fresh milk from a neighbor's cow, and coffee or tea. Two rockers in front of the fireplace and the simple lines of authentic early Colonial furnishings lend an air of peace and tranquility to this history- laden house, which is listed in the National Register of Historic Places.

Downstairs is a large bedroom with a double bed, a crocheted bedspread, braided rug, Colonial candelabra, and another large working fireplace. The downstairs bathroom is most Colonial.

Up the twisty stairs, tucked away in various nooks and crannies, are four more simple bedrooms furnished in "early attic" with double or single beds, and another bathroom with a tub, in which, David says, "some guests like to have a good soak."

RIVER BEND FARM, 643 Simonds Rd. (Rte. 7), Williamstown, MA 01267; 413-458-5504 or 458-3121. A 5-guestroom (2 shared baths) 1770 farmhouse in a quiet, classic college town in the northern Berkshire hills. Continental breakfast included in room rate. Closed from Thanksgiving to April 1. Williamstown Theatre Festival, museums, college cultural events, Bennington, Vt, shops and antiquing nearby. Well-behaved children accepted. No pets. No credit cards. Smoking not encouraged in guestrooms. Dave and Judy Loomis, Proprietors.

Directions: Going north, Rte. 7 makes a left turn at intersection with Rte. 2 in Williamstown. Continue north on Rte. 7 for 1 mi. House is just beyond bridge on left. Coming from the east on Rte. 2, turn right onto Rte. 7 in Williamstown.

For B&B rates, see Index.

ROCKY SHORES
Rockport, Massachusetts

Low stone walls, a broad green lawn, a porch that invites rocking and conversation, and an excellent ocean view looking out towards Thatcher Island, to the only twin lighthouses on the Atlantic coast, are some of the hallmarks of this summertime bed-and-breakfast inn on Cape Ann.

Innkeepers Renate and Gunther Kostka have put much of themselves into this inn, and the furnishings and decorations of the living room, dining room, and bedrooms attest to their special attention and quiet good taste.

In addition to water-view bedrooms in the main house, there are several housekeeping cottages scattered throughout the property.

There's much to do for guests of all ages, including the use of several beaches, tennis courts, beach walking, and all of the interesting sights to be found in the village.

A full breakfast, which includes freshly made muffins, popovers, and cakes, is served each morning. Please make advance reservations for stays during July and August. Cape Ann is particularly pleasant during June, September, and October.

ROCKY SHORES, Eden Rd. Rockport, Ma. 01966; 617-546-2823. A waterside inn with 9 rooms and 12 housekeeping cottages. Open from Easter to the end of Oct. Breakfast is the only meal served. Conveniently located to enjoy all of the Cape Ann cultural, recreational, and historical attractions. Beach walking, swimming, sailing, tennis nearby. Excellent beaches. No pets. Renate and Gunther Kostka, Innkeepers.

Directions: From downtown Rockport, go south on Rte. 127A (South St.) 1½ mi. to Eden Rd. Turn left onto Eden Rd. for ½ mi. along ocean to Rocky Shores.

For B&B rates, see Index.

THE SALEM INN
Salem, Massachusetts

Although Salem was founded only six years after the Mayflower arrived at Plymouth and was of great importance in the seafaring history of the Colonies, it is best known today for seven month in 1692 when it was the center of witch hysteria. There are preserved and reconstructed relics of this period, but save time for the Peabody Museum with its memorabilia of the China Trade days, for Nathanial Hawthorne's House of the Seven Gables, and for exploring the maritime historical sites.

The Salem Inn has been at the center of town for 150 years, though only recently transformed into a bed-and-breakfast inn. For most of its existence, it was three separate townhouses, a fact which is reflected in its interior differences today.

There are nineteen rooms, including two suites, eleven fireplaces, and nine small kitchens. Since many of the rooms are quite large, cribs and rollaways may be brought in to accommodate a family. All rooms are equipped with telephone and color television.

A continental breakfast of juice, a variety of pastries, and coffee or tea is served in a sunny breakfast room on the first floor. This and the large brick patio serve as gathering places for guests during those rare moments when they are not out seeing the sights of Salem and surrounding communities.

Much is within easy walking distance of the inn. The Witch House is on the opposite corner; Chestnut Street with its beautiful Colonial homes is a block away; the museums are a five-minute stroll.

THE SALEM INN, 7 Summer St., Salem, MA 01970; 617-741-0680. A 19-guestroom (all private baths) inn in the center of Salem. Open all year. Breakfast is the only meal served. Very convenient for sightseeing, restaurants, shopping. Parking on street and in nearby municipal lot. Air conditioned. Cribs and rollaways available. No pets. Diane Pabich, Innkeeper.

Directions: The Salem Inn is located on Rte. 114 (Summer St.) at the corner of Essex. Take the Rte. 114 exit from either Hwy. 128 (Boston Beltway) to Hwy. 1 and follow signs to Salem.

For B&B rates, see Index.

SEACREST MANOR
Rockport, Massachusetts

The flag of Bermuda was flying with the American flag over the Yankee Brahmin mansion one sunny May morning. It turned out to be just one more way the innkeepers were signaling welcome to Bermudian guests, a nice gesture, though not surprising. There is a stately home atmosphere of appropriate greeting for all who stop at Seacrest Manor. With its highly polished furniture and paneled walls, this is not Colonial Rockport, but early 20th-century North Shore coupled with English country house, a tribute to living well.

Two acres of gardens and woodland, afternoon tea by the fire, and a library full of books almost make the delights of the area superfluous. Almost, but not quite. The views from the sundeck are too appealing—on a clear day you can see Maine.

Breakfast is the only full meal served, and it is an event. Fresh fruit cup, eggs and bacon are supplemented with such house specialties as blueberry-buttermilk pancakes, Irish oatmeal with dates, and corn fritters. However reluctant to leave the charming breakfast room with its garden view, even the most dedicated sightseer can last the morning on such fare.

"Decidedly small, intentionally quiet" is the motto of Seacrest. For the unwinding guests, this is the right idea.

SEACREST MANOR, 131 Marmion Way, Rockport, MA 01966; 617-546-2211. An 8-guestroom (4 with private bath; 2 of these with private entrace to deck as well) inn in a residential section of Rockport. Open year-round except Jan. Full breakfast and afternoon tea included in rate. No other meals served. Located in a historic and scenic area approximately one hour from Boston. No children under 16. No pets. No credit cards. Leighton T. Saville and Dwight B. MacCormack, Jr., Hosts.

Directions: From the end of Rte. 128 (Boston's inner beltway) take Rte. 127A not quite 5 mi. to Rockport. Marmion Way is on your right.

For B&B rates, see Index.

SEEKONK PINES INN
Great Barrington, Massachusetts

Here's a lovely home that was once a country estate and before that, a large working farm dating back to the 1830s. It sits on four acres of lawn, gardens, and wild-flower meadows in an area of the Berkshires that the Indians called "the place of the Seekonk" which is the Indian word for wild goose.

The atmosphere could best be described as rambling and friendly. Rooms with both private and semi-private baths are available with a continental breakfast of fresh homemade muffins with homemade jam and coffee or tea. There is a larger, optional, full-country breakfast available as well. The specialty of the house is pancakes made from scratch.

The bedrooms are decorated with antiques and old quilts. In the winter guests are invited to relax in the large living room with a raised hearth, or to soak up the sun by a welcome swimming pool in the summer.

The hosts, Linda and Chris Best, both of whom are musicians, are also avid gardeners and the fresh produce that they carefully nurture is available to their guests at farmstand prices. Imagine taking fresh corn home with you!

An engaging feature of the house is a collection of watercolors by Linda Best. They enhance the living room, dining room, and the bedrooms.

Seekonk Pines Inn is located within a pleasant drive of Tanglewood, Jacob's Pillow, and the Berkshire Theatre Festival. It is also just a few moments from two major alpine ski areas and cross-country skiing is at their doorstep. Bicycles are available along with friendly advice on scenic bike routes and hiking trails in the area.

SEEKONK PINES INN, Box 29AA, RD 1, Route 23, Great Barrington, Ma. 01230; 413-528-4192. A 7-bedroom guest home set among the pines in a beautiful meadowland. Two miles west of Great Barrington. Most bedrooms have shared baths. Breakfast is the only meal served. Open year-round. Swimming pool and pleasant walking paths on the grounds. Conveniently located for all the cultural, natural, and recreational attractions of the Berkshires. No pets. No credit cards. Linda and Christian Best, Hosts.

Directions: Seekonk Pines is located on the north side of Rte. 23, two miles west of Great Barrington.

For B&B rates, see Index.

1777 GREYLOCK HOUSE
Lee, Massachusetts

When I first moved to the Berkshires I lived across the road from this house for about three years. Historically it is known as the oldest building in Lee, although in the years since 1777 the original structure has been somewhat disguised by Victorian additions and embellishments.

It originally belonged to one of the earliest settlers in Lee, the Bassett family, and I was often a guest of Nancy and Hurlbut Bassett's. We spent many pleasant winter evenings in front of the fireplace in the low-ceilinged beamed living room, and enjoyed sitting in rocking chairs on the sideporch in the summer.

The house is in a very pleasant parklike atmosphere with a circular drive leading up to the sideporch.

Today it is an inviting bed-and-breakfast home with a suite of bedrooms on the first and second floors. All of the rooms are very comfortably and appropriately furnished.

It's open year-round, which is an advantage for summertime visitors headed for nearby Jacob's Pillow or Tanglewood, as well as for winter skiers during Christmas and Washington's Birthday week. There is even a very convenient room to store skis and boots so they are not carried in over the lovely polished hardwood floors.

On the day of my visit, Walt Parry was making bread for the continental breakfast the next morning. He explained that he had for many years been the owner of a restaurant in Lee.

Having enjoyed many pleasant times in this historic house, it gives me a great deal of pleasure to be able to recommend it as a good bed-and-breakfast accommodation in the Berkshires.

1777 GREYLOCK HOUSE, 58 Greylock St., Lee, Ma. 01238; 413-243-1717. A 5-bedroom bed-and-breakfast home on an extremely quiet street in Lee. Most rooms have shared baths. Open year-round. A continental breakfast is the only meal served; however, there are many restaurants nearby. Conveniently located to enjoy all of the cultural, recreational, and natural attractions of the Berkshires. No pets. No credit cards. Terry and Walter Parry, Hosts.

Directions: I would suggest that upon arriving in the town of Lee, the traveler telephone the 1777 Greylock House for expert directions.

For B&B rates, see Index.

STAVELEIGH HOUSE
Sheffield, Massachusetts

"The house named itself," Marion declared, as Dorothy pointed out the name carved in the corner fireplace. Sure enough, in Olde English lettering there was the name "Staveleigh" in bas-relief in the painted oak mantel framed with Welsh tiles. Incontrovertible evidence.

Marion Whitman and Dorothy Marosy welcome their guests into a spacious, open entrance area dominated by a handsome staircase. A sitting room is on the right with the famous fireplace, and on the left is a large dining room with a generous dining table covered with a lace tablecloth. Their furnishings are drawn from family pieces, auctions, and flea markets.

Both Marion and Dorothy like to cook, and their breakfasts are legendary. They'll make just about anything, and often have puffy pancakes, crêpes, cheese stratas, various breakfast meats, homemade muffins. "...or whatever...on rainy days, we go on a baking spree," Marion laughed.

Up the handsome staircase to a wide landing, decorated with one of the handmade quilts from Marion's family collection and a window seat covered with more handmade quilted cushions.

The extra-wide floorboards in the bedrooms are painted to match the color scheme of the room. The blue room with pretty white antique wicker furniture from Dorothy's family has its own bath. All of the five bedrooms are nicely decorated, and have good mattresses and reading lamps, which "we think are very important," Marion declared. "And we always have fresh flowers in every guest room," Dorothy added.

A very homey, comfortable place, indeed.

STAVELEIGH HOUSE, Main St. (Rte.7), Sheffield, MA 01257; 413-229-2129. A 5-guestroom (1 private, 2 shared baths) comfortable B&B at the southern tip of the Sheffield village green in the southern Berkshires. Breakfast and afternoon tea included in room rate. Open all year except Thanksgiving Day and from Christmas to New Year's Day. Within an easy drive of all Berkshire attractions and a few miles from Connecticut border towns of Canaan, Salisbury, and Lakeville. No pets. No credit cards. Marion Whitman and Dorothy Marosy, Proprietors.

Directions: From the south, take Rte. 23 out of Hillsdale, N.Y., to Rte. 7. Turn right, approx. 5 mi. to Sheffield. From the east, take the Mass. Tpke. to Lee exit and Rte. 102. Stay on Rte. 102 to Rte. 7 south; continue through Great Barrington to Sheffield.

For B&B rates, see Index.

THE SUMMER HOUSE
Sandwich, Massachusetts

Before arriving at the door of the Summer House, I had already admired it in the pages of *Country Living Magazine*. If you are in love with preserving and restoring old houses or just thinking of redecorating your own home, you owe yourself a stay at the Summer House to see what color and a gift for style can do.

Pamela Hunt did it all herself, too—from the puffy, white balloon curtains to the bold, oversized black-and-white checks on the breakfast room floor. Do ask to see the "before" pictures, and plan on taking lots of notes.

The Summer House is located on the Old Main Street of Sandwich, a few steps from Yesteryears Doll Museum and Dexter's Grist Mill at Shawme Pond. Seventeenth- and eighteenth-century houses and antique shops line the quiet street. Close at hand are Thornton Burgess Birthplace and Museum, Heritage Plantation, and the Sandwich Glass Museum. There are public tennis courts, and you may rent bikes for a trip along the path of the Cape Cod Canal.

Flowers from Pamela's garden fill the house, and she is collecting period rose bushes for an antique rose garden, as much in keeping with the 1835 house as the original woodwork and hardware.

A continental breakfast of fresh fruit, home-baked pastries, and a variety of teas and coffee is served. Sugar-, salt-, and caffeine-free diets are accommodated.

True to its name, the Summer House is only open May through October. Reserve in advance for this charmer.

THE SUMMER HOUSE, P.O. Box 341, Old Main St., Sandwich, Cape Cod, MA 02563; 617-888-4991. A 4-guestroom (2 baths) guest house in the center of old Sandwich. Continental breakfast the only meal served, but menus are available for the many fine area restaurants. Open May through Oct. No children under 14. No pets. Pamela Hunt, Owner.

Directions: Take Exit 2 off the mid-Cape Hwy. (Rte. 6) to Rte. 130. Turn left to Sandwich Village 1.3 mi. and bear right onto Old Main St. for .2 mi. to the Summer House.

For B&B rates, see Index.

THE TERN INN
West Harwich, Cape Cod, Massachusetts

Here are a few quotations from Jane Myers, describing the Tern Inn, which she and her husband, Bill, are keeping in West Harwich on Cape Cod's southern shore.

"My husband and I are among the lucky dreamers who realized our ambition when we purchased a lovely old inn on Nantucket Sound. We have renovated and refurbished it in keeping with its nearly 200-year vintage. The riff-cut wide pine floors are gleaming and the fifteen windows of the living room are sparkling; the guest rooms are fresh and bright. The daily challenge is to decide which of the muffin and hot bread recipes will become the favorite, and eventually our specialty.

"Our antiques and handmade pieces of furniture have found their proper home. But the ultimate treasure has been the fascinating variety of guests who have come our way."

After my visit, I feel there is nothing more to add, unless it be to mention the blueberry waffles, french toast, and Vermont maple syrup frequently included in the full breakfast. The inn, located about halfway out to the end of the Cape, is less than a half-mile from the beach and there is a very convenient and enjoyable bicycle trail that was formerly the old railroad right-of-way, now black-topped and running for seventeen miles from Dennis to the National Seashore.

For families with children, there are fully equipped various-sized cottages and efficiencies on the grounds, available for late spring, summer, and fall vacations.

The Tern Inn is bascially open year-round, except for a few weeks in the middle of winter. Better phone ahead to make sure.

THE TERN INN, 91 Chase St., West Harwich, Cape Cod, Ma. 02671; 617-432-3714. A 4-bedroom bed-and-breakfast home (private and semi-private baths) on a quiet street in a south shore village. Cottages also available. Open year-round. Full breakfast is served to inn guests. Most convenient to all of the Cape Cod natural and cultural attractions. Bill and Jane Myers, Innkeepers.

Directions: Follow Route 6 (Mid-Cape Hwy.) to Route 134 (Exit 9). Turn right on Rte. 134 and follow to Rte. 28. Turn left and follow for approx. 2.3 mi. Turn right on either River Road or Chase Street. Both lead to inn.

For B&B rates, see Index.

THE TURNING POINT
Great Barrington, Massachusetts

In earlier editions we featured a poem by a guest of the Turning Point, who referred to the breakfasts as "food worth a song." I agree. "Natural" and "creative" are the words for Turning Point breakfasts—hot cereals are made from soy, oats, rye, and wheat flakes; maple syrup is used as sweetening. There are always fresh-baked muffins or a breakfast cake. Shirley does the baking; Irving does the cooking, and he might make a frittata with asparagus just picked from the garden. Along with regular coffee and teas, there is grain coffee and a selection of herb teas, and of course, all kinds of fresh fruit and juices.

Perched on the corner of moderately-busy Route 23 and quiet Lake Buel Road, both of which lead into the bucolic woodland settings of the Southern Berkshires, the Turning Point is a short drive from the untouched country villages of Tyringham, Monterey, New Marlborough, Mill River, and Sandisfield.

The Yosts offer their guests conviviality and comfort with a cozy sitting room, where, over the Rumford fireplace, can be seen the faint antique lettering, "E. Pixley," undoubtedly the owner of the Pixley Tavern in the mid-1800s. The dining/living room has a baby grand piano and a conversational arrangement of a comfortable sofa and chairs, along with a beautiful dining table made from 200-year-old chestnut, found in the walls of the inn. This, of course, is where those incomparable breakfasts are served, under a hanging Tiffany lamp.

Bedrooms are all furnished differently; some are wallpapered, some have walls painted in Colonial colors; most have oriental scatter rugs—they all have a pleasantly harmonious feeling.

The poem probably said it all better: "...warm hearts and good beds for the night...."

THE TURNING POINT, Rte. 23 and Lake Buel Rd., RD2 Box 140, Great Barrington, MA 01230; 413-528-4777. A 7-guestroom (1 private, 3 shared baths) bed-and-breakfast inn in the Berkshires. Breakfast only meal served. Open year-round. Butternut Basin Ski Area, Beartown Mtn. xc ski trails, and Tanglewood nearby. Two-night minimum during summer and holiday weekends. Well-behaved children welcome. No pets. No credit cards. Please, no smoking. Irv and Shirley Yost, Innkeepers.

Directions: From Great Barrington, proceed east on Rte. 23 to the first crossroad after Butternut Ski Area. The Turning Point is on Rte. 23 at the corner of Lake Buel Rd. and Monument Valley Rd.

For B&B rates, see Index.

THE VICTORIAN
Whitinsville, Massachusetts

Although Route 146 doesn't look very impressive on a map, to those of us who have to make the journey between Worcester and Providence frequently, it is the handiest and most direct way. The town of Whitinsville (which is not far from Uxbridge) involves a slight side trip and is well worth it for the overnight or even longer stay at The Victorian.

This is an imposing mansion that sits regally above the road on a grassy slope. There is rich wood paneling everywhere and appropriate, somewhat massive, Victorian furniture.

Some of the eight bedrooms have walk-in closets, and one has a dressing room with full-length mirrors mounted on the mahogany doors. Little "extras" at the Victorian include apples in the guests' rooms, turn-down service, and hot mulled wine.

It isn't necessary to look elsewhere for dinner because the Victorian is well-known in the area for its delicious entrées.

A continental breakfast of juice, rolls, and coffee is included in the price of the room. For an additional charge a full breakfast is available, including eggs Benedict, various kinds of omelets, and fruit crêpes. Breakfast can be taken in the library, dining room, the porch overlooking the garden, or if one is romantically inclined, in bed.

THE VICTORIAN, 583 Linwood Ave., Whitinsville, Ma. 01588; 617-234-2500. An 8-room Victorian mansion in a quiet town 15 mi. from Worcester, Ma. and 40 mi. from Narragansett Bay in R.I. European plan. Dinner served to travelers daily except Mondays. Open on Sun. at 5 p.m. Overnight guests receive continental breakfast. Lawn games, ice skating, fishing on grounds. Golf and tennis nearby. Pets accepted. Orin and Martha Flint, Innkeepers.

Directions: From Providence, follow Rte. 146 north and take the Uxbridge exit. From the traffic light in Uxbridge, proceed north on Rte. 122 approximately 1½ mi. to Linwood Ave. (there will be a sign on the corner saying "Whitinsville—Left"). Bear left here. The inn is a few hundred yards around the corner. From Worcester, follow Rte. 146 south to the Whitinsville-Purgatory Chasm exit. Proceed into Whitinsville and keep right at the set of traffic lights onto Linwood Ave. The inn is on the left at the other end of Linwood Ave.—about 1½ mi.

For B&B rates, see Index.

THE VILLAGE INN
Lenox, Massachusetts

Located on Route 7, running north and south from New York to the Canadian border, the village of Lenox, settled in 1767, has thrived through several different historic and social epochs.

During one of these periods, the American Revolution, the Village Inn came into being and has operated for many years as an inn and a haven, first for Colonial travelers and then for visitors to Lenox during its famous "resort period."

Today, the area attracts music lovers, sports and nature lovers, as well as those who enjoy a stay in an inn atmosphere.

The guest rooms have an authentic New England flavor, and the low-ceilinged dining room with lovely paintings on the walls is usually abuzz with breakfast guests each morning.

This breakfast can be anything from a bowl of cereal and a muffin to Belgian waffles, bacon and eggs, omelets, pancakes, or fresh fruit with yogurt. Delicious Sunday brunches and afternoon English teas are added pleasant offerings. Dinner is served Friday, Saturday, and Sunday nights.

Please take note that lodgings do not include breakfast, although breakfast is available daily, and also that the lower rates (see Index) are not offered from July 1 to Labor Day or on holidays or during the foliage season.

The Village Tavern is open nightly except Monday and offers light fare and libations and live entertainment on weekends.

THE VILLAGE INN, Church St., Lenox, Mass. 01240; 413-637-0020. A 27-room inn in a bustling Berkshire town 4 mi. from Stockbridge, 8 mi. from Pittsfield, and 1 mi. from Tanglewood. Breakfast and afternoon tea served daily to travelers. Open every day of the year. Lenox is located in the heart of the Berkshires with many historical, cultural, and recreational features. Swimming in pleasant nearby lakes. All seasonal sports including xc and downhill skiing available nearby. No pets. Cliff Rudisill and Ray Wilson, Innkeepers.

Directions: After approaching Lenox on Rte. 7, one of the principal north-south routes in New England, exit onto Rte. 7A to reach the village center and Church Street. When approaching from the Mass. Tpke. (Exit 2) follow Rte. 20W about 4 mi. and turn left onto Rte. 183 to center of town.

For Lodging rates, see Index.

WALKER HOUSE
Lenox, Massachusetts

Here's a B&B inn that lovingly embraces classical music—in fact, even the rooms are named for great composers. The newly-arrived guest might be greeted with the rich, sonorous sounds of Telemann or Prokofiev, and from the impressive record collection and the unusual paintings on display it is obvious that Peggy and Richard Houdek certainly are lovers of the arts.

This classical Federal building was built in 1804 and is located in the center of Lenox within a very pleasant walk of the front gates of Tanglewood, where the Boston Symphony holds forth each summer.

The spacious bedrooms are decorated in styles and color schemes befitting the composers for whom they were named. All have private baths. There is a parlor of considerable size whose walls are lined with bookcases and which boasts a working fireplace and a piano. There are many cozy corners and a veranda just made to enjoy reading, conversation, and listening to music.

There are seven other working fireplaces, including one in the dining room and in five of the guest bedrooms. The entire house is furnished with antiques.

One of the pleasant surprises for newlyweds is a complimentary bottle of champagne with caviar and crackers.

The newest addition to the Walker House is a small shop located on one side of the inn featuring interesting and beautiful Mexican imports including brocaded dresses, natural color shirts for men, and serapes which are very good for snuggling into on chilly evenings at Tanglewood.

A most generous continental breakfast leading off with fresh juice, fresh fruit, hot croissants, blueberry muffins, and freshly ground coffee can be taken in the dining room or on the veranda in the summer.

WALKER HOUSE, 74 Walker Street, Lenox, Massachusetts 01240; 413-637-1271. An 8-room village inn in the Berkshires located within two blocks of the center of Lenox. Complimentary bicycles are available and croquet and badminton on the grounds. Tennis, swimming, downhill and cross-country skiing, and exceptional backroading in the area. Just a few moments from Tanglewood, the Berkshire Theater Festival and other Berkshire attractions. Afternoon tea also served. Open every day in the year. Peggy and Richard Houdek, Innkeepers.

Directions: Please see the general directions to the Berkshires.

For B&B rates, see Index.

THE WEATHERVANE INN
South Egremont, Massachusetts

The Weathervane Inn is a small cluster of buildings set off the highway, with sections dating back to 1785. It is located in the lovely little village of South Egremont in the Berkshires, where there are many pre-1800 houses and a graceful church. Replete with wide-board floors, beautiful moldings, and an original fireplace that served as a heating and cooking unit with a beehive oven, the inn has a comfortable, warm atmosphere.

In addition to a large, pleasant reception room, there is a living room with a color TV, for which innkeepers Anne and Vince Murphy are building a video tape collection. Still another gathering room has a little pub corner and a grouping of sofa and chairs in front of the fireplace.

The cheery dining room with its many windows, and tables covered with white tablecloths under gay red overcloths, brightens the morning for breakfasting guests. Anne's breakfasts feature among other things blueberry pancakes, french toast, sausage, bacon, and eggs in any style, including a marvelous Brie omelet.

The eight attractively furnished country-inn bedrooms come in all sizes and shapes, and each offers something different. They are prettily decorated with quilted pictures, dried-flower arrangements, ball-fringe curtains, and, more practically, with reading lamps, books, magazines, and electric blankets.

A swimming pool offers a cooling respite on hot summer days, and there is no end of things to do in and around the Berkshires during summer and winter.

THE WEATHERVANE INN, Rte. 23, South Egremont, MA 01258; 413-528-9580. An 8-bedroom village inn in the Berkshire foothills. Modified American plan daily in summer and Thurs. thru Sun. in winter. Breakfast served to houseguests. Open year-round. Swimming pool on grounds. Golf, tennis, bicycling, backroading, hiking, horseback riding, fishing, downhill and xc skiing nearby. Tanglewood, Jacob's Pillow, Berkshire Playhouse, Norman Rockwell Museum, and great antique shops all nearby. No pets. Vincent, Anne, and Patricia Murphy, Innkeepers.

Directions: From New York City follow Sawmill River Pkwy. to Taconic Pkwy. to Rte. 23 east. South Egremont and the inn are about 2 mi. past the Catamount Ski area.

For B&B rates, see Index.

THE WEBB-BIGELOW PLACE
Weston, Massachusetts

In 1827, a prosperous time for the young and growing nation, Alpheus Bigelow Jr., built a handsome home right on the Boston Post Road. Caring owners since have added to its charm, until today the preserved Federal period house, surrounded by lawns and flowers, is more a picture than ever, as well as a perfect example of a great B&B bonus, the historic property open to guests.

I reminded Jane Webb of the strangers who used to come to her door claiming ancestral connections just to have a look inside. "Even now I want people to telephone first," she laughed.

The Webb-Bigelow Place is set on three acres in Weston's National Registered Historic District, adjacent to an 800-acre town forest great for hiking or cross-country skiing. There is off-street parking on the circular driveway and a swimming pool on the grounds. In addition to being a short drive away from Walden Pond, Concord, and Lexington, Weston has interesting remnants of its Colonial past and some of the most beautiful residential streets in Massachusetts. Sudbury's Wayside Inn is just down the road a few miles.

This is a particularly prime location for visiting area colleges: Wellesley, Brandeis, and Regis are ten minutes away; Harvard, Radcliffe, M.I.T., and Boston College, half an hour.

There are three large guest bedrooms on the second floor, each with working fireplaces and one with twin beds. Two have a connecting bath, which makes a particularly nice arrangement for a family. Guests have their own comfortable living room downstairs with fireplace, TV, and plenty of good books. The house is furnished with antiques.

A full breakfast is the only meal served, but there are many restaurants nearby, including the original Red Coach, within walking distance.

THE WEBB-BIGELOW PLACE, 863 Boston Post Rd., Weston, MA 02193; 617-899-2444. A 3-guestroom, 2-bath B&B, 15 mi. from Boston. Breakfast only. Open year around. Sightseeing, antiquing, hiking, x-country, golf, nearby. Own swimming pool. Prefer non-smokers. Jane and Bob Webb, Hosts.

Directions: From Massachusetts Turnpike (I-90) take Exit 15, drive north on Rte. 128 (I-95) one exit (Exit 49). Drive west on Rte. 20 for 3.2 mi. House is on Weston-Wayland line, north side of Rte. 20, enclosed by stockade fence. Enter by driving through the gateway.

For B&B rates, see Index.

WESTMINSTER VILLAGE INN
Westminster, Massachusetts

Approaching Westminster Village Inn on Route 2, one could have the impression that it is a motel. However, rest assured, it is a most attractive non-motel motel.

Accommodations are in a series of relatively recently built buildings resembling an Early American style. Each of the thirty-one dwellings is in a different Colonial color and no two of them are alike. There are some with gambrel roofs; some contain two or three sets of lodgings; all are in a woodland setting that is further enhanced by a welcome swimming pool. All the rooms have a very pleasant atmosphere, and are furnished with reproductions of Early American furniture. My room had a fireplace and was extremely attractive.

An à la carte breakfast, not included in the price of the lodgings, is served every morning, and a simple dinner is served Monday through Thursday. Guests at the inn receive a discount at the nearby famous Old Mill Restaurant, which is also under the same proprietorship.

Westminister is located between Fitchburg, Leominster, and Gardner, and is on the extension of the famous Mohawk Trail, which was used by the Indians for centuries before the arrival of the American tourist. The Westminister Village Inn and the Old Mill will prove a most pleasant surprise.

WESTMINSTER VILLAGE INN, Route 2, Westminster, Ma. 01479; 617-874-5911. A 31-bedroom cluster of Early American-style lodgings tastefully situated in a grove of trees on the south side of Route 2. Continental breakfast not included in room price. Other meals offered at inn and also at the Old Mill Restaurant nearby. Open every day except Christmas. Swimming pool on grounds. Convenient for golf, tennis, and the Mt. Wachusett Theater nearby. The Fosters, Proprietors.

Directions: Westminster Village Inn is just east of Westminster on Rte. 2. It is 50 mi. west of Boston.

For Lodging rates, see Index.

WINDAMAR HOUSE
Provincetown, Massachusetts

I had almost despaired of finding some good, quiet accommodations in Provincetown, which has grown substantially in many respects since my early visits a number of years ago.

Furthermore, I almost missed Windamar House at the quiet east end which, along with Hargood House, provides excellent accommodations. Both are somewhat removed from the frequently frantic core of the downtown area.

A very discreet sign provides an appropriately low-key introduction to the double white house with narrow white clapboards and black shutters, a brick walk, and a beautiful garden in the rear.

The interior is equally fetching and the owner obviously has excellent decorating sensibilities, as is evidenced by the furnishings and adornments throughout the house and the harmonizing tones of brown, beige, and white in the hallways, ald a matching Afghan named Geraldine.

Bedrooms are distinctively decorated with fine antiques and paintings, with views of Cape Cod Bay in the front and the garden in the rear.

I confess I'm unable to do proper justice to the Windamar House with this limited space, but may I suggest that you write for a descriptive and absolutely truthful brochure.

The Windamar is more than I had hoped to find in Provincetown.

WINDAMAR HOUSE, 568 Commercial St., Provincetown, Ma. 02657; 617-487-0599. A Cape Cod home with 6 bedrooms sharing three baths and two apartments with kitchen conveniences located at the tranquil east end of Provincetown. Open year-round. Continental breakfast is included in the price of the room. Quite convenient for a stroll to the center of the village and also for swimming and sunbathing on the beach, sport fishing, dune taxi rides, tennis, golf, riding, sailing, and bicycling. No pets. No credit cards. Pickup service to and from the airport is also included. Bette Adams, Proprietor.

Directions: Follow Rte. 6 to the very end of Cape Cod and turn left at the first Provincetown exit. Turn right on Commercial St. (one-way) and look for Windamar House on the right.

For B&B rates, see Index.

WINDSOR HOUSE
Newburyport, Massachusetts

The Windsor House in Newburyport was built in 1796 as both a residence and a ship's chandlery. The kitchen was the original shipping and receiving room and there's a series of trapdoors which open up to the fourth story of the house where the original hoist wheel is located.

The brick wall of the fireplace separates the warehouse sections from the living section. The posts and beams throughout the entire house were built by ships' carpenters, the same men who built the clipper ships. There are six guest rooms of which three have their own private bathrooms. The other three share one bathroom.

Guests all gather around the long table in the high-ceilinged kitchen to enjoy a full English breakfast consisting of homemade breads, eggs cooked with fresh herbs from the Windsor House garden, meat, or fish. The wild beach plum and rose hip jellies are delectable and the coffee has been specially blended to meet the innkeepers' own taste. A Festival breakfast includes 18th-century dishes like Rink Tum Tiddy and Nantucket Souffle.

WINDSOR HOUSE, 38 Federal Street, Newburyport, Ma. 01950; 617-462-3778. A 6-room inn located in the restored section of Newburyport. Open year-round. Breakfast served to all guests; dinner by 3-day minimum advance reservation. Three miles from Plum Island and the Parker River Nat'l. Wildlife Refuge in the Merrimack River Valley. A short walk from the restored 19th-century retail area, restaurants, and museums. Also nearby: deep sea fishing, swimming, art galleries, antique shops, family ski area, horseback riding, and year-round theater. Some trundle beds available for children; no cribs or playpens. Parents must provide for infant care. Small dogs welcome. Can meet bus or planes at local airport. Judith Crumb, Innkeeper.

Directions: From Boston and Maine: From I-95 use exit to Rte. 113, turn right onto High St. (Rte. 1A) and proceed three miles to Federal St., turn left. Inn on left across from Old South Church (Rte. 1A is scenic drive from either Boston or New Hampshire).

For B&B rates, see Index.

YANKEE CLIPPER
Rockport, Massachusetts

Easily included as part of a New England seacoast odyssey, is Rockport, Massachusetts, on Cape Ann, an artists' colony for over 40 years. Some of the most important painters have either visited or lived in Rockport. Now it attracts all kinds of creative people, including photographers, writers, and craftsmen, as well as artists.

The town is filled with fetching little houses with beguiling roof lines, inviting gardens, and winding, elm-shaded streets.

The Yankee Clipper, which sits right on the water's edge, overlooking the sea, consists of three buildings. The first, perched on the rocks, is the original building where the dining area is located and where there are many large bedrooms with a sea view.

A few paces away there is the Quarterdeck, where some of the rooms enjoy an unobstructed view of the ocean and gardens. The third is called the Bulfinch House and is noted particularly for its architectural beauty. It is of Colonial Greek design, named for its designer, who also created the Boston State House.

In the Bulfinch House from May to November, B&B guests enjoy the benefits of a full American-plan breakfast that frequently includes delicious blueberry pancakes, homemade jams, and fresh fruit. It is served in the dining room or on the porch, where a view of the water through the trees may be enjoyed. A continental breakfast only is served from November 1 to April 1 in the main inn.

YANKEE CLIPPER, Rockport, Mass. 01966; 617-546-3407. An intimate 26-room inn on the sea, 40 mi. from Boston. Continental breakfast only. Nov. 1 to April 1. Modified American plan from May 15 to July 1 and Sept. 5 to Nov. 1. Breakfast and dinner served daily May 15 to Oct. 31. Lunch served during July and August. Ocean view, shoreline walks, many antique shops and other stores nearby. No pets. Fred and Lydia Wemyss, Barbara and Bob Ellis, Innkeepers.

Directions: Take I-95 to Rte. 128 to 127 (Gloucester). Proceed 6 mi. on Rte. 127 to Rockport and continue to Pigeon Cove.

For B&B rates, see Index.

THE NATIONAL HOUSE
Marshall, Michigan

The town of Marshall, Michigan, on I-69 contains some of the finest examples of Victorian architecture in North America. A great many of the buildings and homes have been added to the State of Michigan Historic Sites and to the National Register. Visits should include a tour of the town which takes in at least 40 historic and beautiful buildings. One of the most impressive of these is the National House Inn.

The building was opened in 1835 and is probably the oldest remaining hotel building in Michigan. In subsequent years it became a windmill, and then a wagon factory, and the restoration uncovered a solid, beautiful structure of the original brick, as well as the irreplaceable woodwork.

Each bedroom has its own ambience and there are colorful comforters, old trunks, marble top tables, bureaus, dried flower arrangements, electric lamps that are reproductions of gas lamps, candle sconces with reflectors, little corner sofas, unusual door-knobs, and special attention is given to the linens. The bedroom windows overlook either the residential part of town, or a beautiful fountain in the town center park.

The dining room at the National House is so attractive that even hurrying breakfasters frequently stay on for hours. The continental offering includes homemade things like bran muffins, bundt cake, blueberry muffins, and nut breads. English muffins are served with a wide variety of delicious homemade jams.

THE NATIONAL HOUSE INN, 102 South Parkview, Marshall, Mi. 49068; 616-781-7374. An elegantly restored 16-room Victorian-period village inn. Marshall is the finest example of 19th-century architecture in the Midwest. It has 15 State Historic Sites and 6 National Register Sites. European plan includes continental breakfast. No other meals served. Open year-round. Closed Christmas Eve and Christmas Day. Tennis, golf, swimming, boating, xc skiing nearby. Mike and Beth McCarthy, Innkeepers.

Directions: From I-69 exit at Michigan Ave. in Marshall and go straight 1 mi. to inn. From I-94 use Exit 110, follow old 27 south 1 mi. to inn.

For B&B rates, see Index.

ROSEMONT INN
Douglas, Michigan

Oddly enough, the vacationing possibilities of the Saugatuck-Douglas area of Michigan were discovered by a pleasure party of Chicagoans. The host was Stephen A. Morrison, one of the first settlers of the village, and the highlight of their vacation was being serenaded by the Saugatuck Silver Coronet Band. The year was 1880, the inauguration of this part of Michigan as a vacation spot.

Through the years many thousands have followed the little group, enjoying the bounties of nature and the relaxing pleasures. The town had grown originally as a result of the lumber business, but when the timber supply was exhausted, fruit became the big business, and today, the climate, the beauty of the countryside, and the friendly atmosphere have made it into a popular holiday region.

The Rosemont, a Queen Anne Victorian building originally built in 1886 as a tourist inn, has retained much of its original country feeling. The screened porch with hanging plants is a delightful spot on which to enjoy the cooling lake breeze. In addition to the waters of Lake Michigan, innkeepers Ric and Cathy Gillette have a heated pool on the grounds, which are shaded with big maples.

There are fourteen bedrooms with Victorian furnishings, spool and canopy beds, and many different kinds of quilts. All have private baths, Most have fireplaces and views of the lake through the trees.

THE ROSEMONT INN, 83 Lake Shore Drive, P.O. Box 541, Douglas, Mi. 49406; 616-857-2637. A fourteen-bedroom lakeside bed-and-breakfast inn in a pleasant residential section of Douglas. Continental breakfast the only meal served. Open all year. Swimming pool on grounds. Conveniently located for all of the many recreational advantages of the area. No pets. Ric and Cathy Gillette, Innkeepers.

Directions: Just south of Saugatuck off I-196. Head toward lake and Lake Shore Dr.

For B&B rates, see Index.

STAFFORD'S BAY VIEW INN
Petoskey, Michigan

These "American Style" accommodations include a great many restored and preserved Victorian mansions. Stafford's Bay View Inn, located in the well-known Bay View section of Petoskey, is a prime example. It is vintage gingerbread at some of its very best.

Bay View is a summer resort community which has grown up around a program of music, drama, art, and religious lectures and services. The early residents built Victorian homes which are scattered throughout Bay View today, and the programs are still going on.

The furnishings in the parlors and bedrooms of this inn reflect the changing periods of its history. It's sort of like visiting great-grandmother's house.

The full breakfast, included in the room rate, features hot inn-baked rolls, served as you are seated in the bustling, cheerful dining room, followed by your selection of tempting entrées.

STAFFORD'S BAY VIEW INN, Box 3, Petoskey, Mich. 49770; 616-347-2771. A 23-room resort-inn on Little Traverse Bay in the Bay View section of Petoskey. Breakfast, lunch, and dinner served daily to travelers. Open daily mid-May through October, Christmas week, and long weekends during the winter sports season. Lake swimming and xc skiing on grounds. Golf, boating, fishing, hiking, and Alpine skiing nearby. Pickup service provided from Pellston Airport on request. Stafford and Janice Smith, Judy Honor, Innkeepers.

Directions: From Detroit: take Gaylord Exit from I-75 and follow Mich. Rte. 32 to Rte. 131, north to Petoskey. From Chicago: use U.S. 131 north to Petoskey.

For B&B rates, see Index.

WICKWOOD INN
Saugatuck, Michigan

Saugatuck, just a few miles south of Holland, is on the eastern shore of Lake Michigan. It reminds the visitor of a New England coastal village with its many sailboat masts, tall shade trees, and attractive Victorian homes.

Residents of Michigan and Chicago have long known that the wide sandy beaches of Lake Michigan provide excellent vacation and holiday fare for everyone, with fishing, swimming, golfing, tennis, and other warm weather activities. Winter is also popular with cross-country skiing.

Oddly enough, I learned that the Wickwood Inn was inspired by one of my favorite London hotels—Dukes. Sue and Stub Louis, in converting this very attractive building to ten bedrooms with private baths, succeeded in saving some of the most desirable original features.

The library, which is reminiscent of an English gentleman's club, is all in mahogany with a high gloss finish. Passing through the french doors at the end of the living room, guests step down into the sunken garden room with its brick floor, cedar walls, vaulted, beamed ceiling, shuttered windows, and trees and flowering plants everywhere.

The bedrooms, each of which is distinctively furnished, have dressers, armoires, nightstands, and settees made of pine, walnut, and cherry. They are models for inn sleeping quarters.

Continental breakfast, including fresh-squeezed orange juice and hot homemade coffee cake awaits each guest. At teatime, hors d'oeuvres are offered.

There is a final touch. The association with Dukes is further enhanced by a London taxicab, which is available for limited livery service.

WICKWOOD INN, 510 Butler St., Saugatuck, Mi. 49453; 616-857-1097. A handsomely decorated 10-bedroom bed-and-breakfast inn (fully air conditioned) situated in one of Michigan's most attractive resort villages on the shore of Lake Michigan. Open year-round. Two-night minimum stay on weekends during summer. Continental breakfast is only meal served. Most conveniently located for all of the recreational advantages of the area. No children. No pets. Sue and Stub Louis, Innkeepers.

Directions: Saugatuck is located just off I-196. From the south, take Exit 36. From the north, take Exit 41.

For B&B rates, see Index.

LOWELL INN
Stillwater, Minnesota

The Lowell Inn, on the banks of the St. Croix River in Stillwater, Minnesota, is another example of "American style"; this time it is an inn whose facade somewhat resembles George Washington's home in Mt. Vernon, Virginia.

In many ways the origins and style of this inn are pure American. This saga begins in the 1920s with two young people, Arthur Palmer and his wife Nelle, who had met and married while working in vaudeville in the Midwest. The idea of becoming innkeepers occurred to them, and now many years later there is a third generation of Palmers, including Arthur Palmer, Jr. and his wife Maureen and their large family of innkeeping children at the Lowell Inn.

There are 22 bedrooms, each of them very tastefully and elegantly furnished and appointed. There are three dining rooms in the inn, each with its own decorative theme and one of them has a five-course fixed-priced dinner that includes a main course of beef fondue.

In addition to the continental breakfast that comes with the room, the Lowell Inn has a country breakfast platter that features fresh orange juice, breakfast meats, scrambled eggs, and Lowell Inn sweet-and-sour pancakes. This bounteous repast is available at a special price for houseguests, and is particularly appropriate for guests who are going to spend a pleasant day out-of-doors in the north country.

THE LOWELL INN, 102 N. Second St., Stillwater, Minn. 55082; 612-439-1100. A 22-room village inn 18 mi. from St. Paul, near all the cultural attractions of the Twin Cities. European plan. Lunch and dinner served daily except Christmas Eve and Christmas Day. Open year-round. No pets. Canoeing, tennis, hiking, skiing, and swimming nearby, including 4 ski resorts within 15 mi. Arthur and Maureen Palmer, Innkeepers.

Directions: Stillwater is on the St. Croix River at the junction of Minn. 95 (north and south) and Minn. 36 (east and west). It is 7 mi. north of I-94 on Hwy. 95.

For B&B rates, see Index.

NICOLLET ISLAND INN
Minneapolis, Minnesota

So you are headed for Mineapolis/St. Paul and you are tired of conventional accommodations and no surprises! Here's a great surprise—a bed-and-breakfast inn on an island close to the heart of Minneapolis; a three-story limestone building, formerly the home of the Island Sash and Door Company.

Both inside and out, the building has a marvelous scrubbed look. The decorative theme is reminiscent of late Victorian and each of the twenty-four guest rooms has an armoire with a television set discreetly hidden inside, a writing desk, comfortable wing-backed chairs, framed antique graphics, old-fashioned comforters and—wonder of wonders—fresh flowers every day. Many of the rooms overlook the Mississippi River, while others afford a view of the downtown Minneapolis skyline. Guest rooms are in three sizes, reflected in the ascending range of rates, and your stay includes a welcoming beverage on arrival, turn-down service, a bedtime chocolate, a complimentary continental breakfast, and a choice of morning newspapers, including the *Minneapolis Star Tribune, the Wall Street Journal* or the *New York Times.*

Overnight guests and the public can enjoy breakfast, lunch, and dinner in the dining room near a giant stone fireplace or in the four-seasons glassed-in porch facing the Mississippi River. The evening fare is best described as "Americana."

The Nicollet Island Inn, on the National Register of Historic Places, is a wonderful example of what imaginative designing can do with 19th-century mill and factory buildings.

NICOLLET ISLAND INN, 95 Merriam, Nicollet Island, Minneapolis, Mn. 55401; 612-623-7741. A 24-bedroom (private baths) contemporary inn on Nicollet Island in downtown Minneapolis. Open every day in the year. Breakfast, lunch, and dinner served daily. Room rate includes complimentary breakfast. Within a very convenient distance of all of the downtown Minneapolis business, shopping, and recreational attractions. Airport limousine service and free parking. Beth Ferrell, Innkeeper-Proprietor.

Directions: If arriving by air take limousine service. By auto, easily accessible from either downtown or the northeast via the Hennepin Avenue Bridge.

For B&B rates, see Index.

SCHUMACHER'S NEW PRAGUE HOTEL
New Prague, Minnesota

If you happen to reside in, or be passing through, the Minneapolis area, a visit to Schumacher's will prove to be a very pleasant and delicious surprise.

The New Prague Hotel was built in 1898, and John Schumacher has recently renovated the downstairs lobby to its original design, refinishing all the original maple hardwood floors and the hotel desk.

All twelve of the lodging rooms, which are named for the months of the year, are authentically hand-painted by the Bavarian folk artist, Pipka. Each room is furnished in a very unique fashion including such accessories as lamps, curtains, pictures, goosedown pillows and comforters. The 100% cotton bedding and tablecloths have been imported from Germany, Czechoslovakia, and Austria. The beds, wardrobes, trunks, and chairs are patterned from authentic German furniture and are custom-made.

It would really be a pity not to take advantage of the fact that John Schumacher is well known in the Twin City area for his wonderful dinners—so I hope that all B&B guests will be pleasantly advised. The menu has approximately 55 main dishes, most of them from central Europe and many of them have Czechoslovakian and German names.

A full Czechoslovakian breakfast is served in the sunny dining room consisting of fresh-squeezed orange juice, two scrambled eggs, sliced fried dumplings, Czech sausage, homemade kolacky, which is Czechoslovakian sweet roll, and tea or freshly ground coffee.

SCHUMACHER'S NEW PRAGUE HOTEL, 212 West Main St., New Prague, Mn. 56071; 612-758-2133. (Metro line: 612-445-7285.) A 12-room Czechoslovakian and German inn located in a small country town approximately 35 mi. south of Minneapolis and St. Paul in the verdant Minnesota countryside. European plan. Breakfast, lunch, and dinner served to travelers all year except three days at Christmas. Good bicycling and backroading nearby; also xc skiing, tennis, and golf. No entertainment available to amuse children. No pets. John Schumacher, Innkeeper.

Directions: From Minneapolis, take Rte. 494 west to Rte. 169 south to Jordan exit. Turn south on Rte. 21 for 9 mi. to New Prague. Turn left to Main St. at the stop sign, and the hotel is in the second block on the right.

For B&B rates, see Index.

ST. GEMME BEAUVAIS
Ste. Genevieve, Missouri

Interstate 55 sweeps down from the north through St. Louis and then roughly follows the course of the Mississippi River through Missouri into Arkansas and Tennessee and continues to New Orleans. A little over an hour south of St. Louis lies the village of Ste. Genevieve.

Ste. Genevieve is a living historic community and not an artificially created "tourist attraction." Most of the 18th- and 19th-century structures are still occupied as homes and businesses, and maintained with pride by their owners as living entities. Their original appearance can be enjoyed from the outside by visitors even when such buildings are not opened for tours.

Visitors are indeed fortunate to be able to spend a night and enjoy a splendid breakfast at the Inn St. Gemme Beauvais which has been associated with the same family for many years. Mr. and Mrs. Norbert Donze have made the old home into an old-fashioned inn with large comfortable bedrooms and such new-fashioned things as private baths, air conditioning, and telephones.

The dining room has beautiful walnut ladderback chairs, Belgian lace curtains, a marble fireplace, fine china, and graceful stemware. The bedrooms have a collection of many kinds of Victorian antiques, including marble-topped bureaus, high-backed beds, and old-fashioned flowered wallpaper. There are eight different suites in the inn and each has at least two rooms; most have two double beds.

Breakfast has a definite French style with ham-filled crêpes made with a special sauce, spiced or chilled fruit, orange juice, blueberry muffins, and lots of good hot coffee.

Take a moment to leave the interstate and spend an overnight visit at this fascinating, beautifully preserved reminder of America's heritage along the Mississippi.

ST. GEMME BEAUVAIS, 78 N. Main St., Ste. Genevieve, Mo. 63670; 314-883-5744. An 8-room village inn about 1½ hrs. from St. Louis. Modified American plan includes breakfast only. Breakfast served daily. Lunch served Mon. thru Sat. Open year-round. Closed Thanksgiving and Christmas Day. Golf, hunting, and fishing nearby. No pets. Frankye and Boats Donze, Innkeepers.

Directions: From St. Louis, south on I-55 to Hwy. 32. Exit east on 32 to Hwy. 61 to the Ste. Genevieve exit.

For B&B rates, see Index.

THE BEAL HOUSE INN
Littleton, New Hampshire

The Beal House Inn has been a New Hampshire landmark since 1833 and a famous White Mountain inn for over forty years. It is a classic white two-story Federal building with green trim and is rather prim and proper but with a touch of humor—something like an elderly maiden aunt slipping you a wink on the sly.

This touch of humor is particularly evident in the most cheerful interior, and starts in the parlor where there are all kinds of knick-knacks, a large woven portrait of the Beal House and a number of stereoscopic views of the White Mountains. I understand that these viewers used to be made in Littleton during the 19th century. The first thing I learned was that most of the beautiful antiques in all of the public rooms and bedrooms are an extension of the very attractive antique shop which occupies a considerable portion of the dining room where the hefty White Mountain breakfasts are served.

There are flowered wallpapers, many delightful decorations, brass beds, and canopied, four-poster, and spool beds in the guest rooms. These are connected by funny little staircases (I saw a Raggedy Ann doll perched on one step) and twisty passageways. The whole atmosphere conveys the feeling of a visit to a New England of the past.

The breakfast menu is posted on the wall of the dining room and includes fresh fruit, fruit juices, scrambled eggs with your choice of ham, bacon, or sausage, or waffles with the same choices, and the house specialty, fresh hot popovers.

On the many clear days which are prevalent in this part of New Hampshire, there is a view from Littleton of the famous Presidential Range with its glorious peaks that seem to march clear up to the heavens. I was there on a late winter afternoon when all of them were glowing domes in the brilliant afternoon sunshine.

THE BEAL HOUSE INN, 247 West Main St., Littleton, N.H. 03561; 603-444-2661. A 14-room (9 with private baths) village inn located on the edge of New Hampshire's White Mountains. Open year-round. Breakfast served every day except Wed. Christmas and Thanksgiving celebrations. The Old Man of The Mountains, Franconia Notch State Park, downhill skiing and xc skiing all within a short distance. This is the highly scenic portion of New Hampshire. Doug and Brenda Clickenger, Innkeepers.

Directions: From I-93 take Exit 41 into town and turn left (west) on Main St. The inn is on the right on the western edge of Littleton.

For Lodging rates, see Index.

THE CAMPTON INN
Campton Village, New Hampshire

Campton is at the western end of the Waterville Valley, one of the great ski areas, not only of New Hampshire, but of the Northeast. The Campton Inn is on a quiet street on Route 175 and just about two minutes from I-93. This is the great north-south traffic artery spanning the length of New Hampshire, and it is the main way to get to the White Mountains.

The building is an old farmhouse, considerably rehabilitated in recent years. One of the main features is a very efficient and handsome wood stove that heats more than half of the house from its location in the rather spacious front parlor.

Furnishings in both the public rooms and the bedrooms are, for the most part, a mixture of antique and country, but there is a rather warm, comfortable, old-fashioned feeling about this house, which extends through many periods of decorative design.

Breakfast is served in the dining room and, when weather permits, on a pleasant outdoor terrace. The full country breakfast changes each morning.

During the snow time, both cross-country and alpine skiers find their way to Waterville Valley, but this pleasant old-home B&B would be an excellent place to stop during other seasons as well.

THE CAMPTON INN, P.O. Box 282, Rte. 175, Campton Village, NH 03223; 603-726-4449. A 10-guestroom (1 private bath; others share baths) bed-and-breakfast inn. Breakfast is the only meal served; however, advance reservations can be made for dinner. Open all year. Most convenient for skiing at Waterville Valley and White Mountains. Cross-country trails nearby. Children welcome. No pets. Arlene and Bill Roberts, Innkeepers.

Directions: Take Exit 28 from I-93 north, turn east and follow the signs for Rte. 175. Turn left and proceed 1/2 mi. Inn is on the left.

For B&B rates, see Index.

CHENEY HOUSE
Ashland, New Hampshire

If you're going to be traveling on I-93 up through the middle of New Hampshire to the White Mountains, it would serve your aesthetic sensibilities well to plan a stopover at this little gem of a Victorian house that has been turned into a very tidy bed-and-breakfast inn by Mike and Daryl Mooney. I first met Mike when he was on the front desk at the Whitehall Inn in Camden in 1972. Now he has what so many country inn staff members desire most—his own inn.

I toured the house admiring the extremely well-furnished bedrooms with such fetching touches as old patchwork quilts. Everything has been beautifully preserved or restored, including the floors and staircase. Then the three of us sat on the back porch enjoying a cup of tea and I could see a farmer working in the fields on a pleasant sunny day in June.

Waterville Valley Ski Area is just 25 minutes away and guests receive passes to a small sandy beach on Little Squam Lake.

Breakfast could be popover pancakes with eggs, or muffins, or a pastry. It can be taken out on the back porch on sunny days.

The houses and the atmosphere of this area are vestiges of earlier, happier days that have all but disappeared. I imagine that it would be very nice here at twilight, and during foliage time it would be marvelous.

CHENEY HOUSE, P.O. Box 683, Ashland, N.H. 03217; 603-968-7968. An elegant 3-bedroom bed-and-breakfast inn in the Lake and White Mt. region of New Hampshire. Breakfast the only meal served. Open every day from Memorial Day through foliage season. Public tennis courts within walking distance; sandy beach rights on Little Squam Lake, 1 mi. Conveniently located for all the recreational, natural, and historical attractions of central New Hampshire. No pets. No credit cards. Mike and Daryl Mooney, Innkeepers.

Directions: Take Exit 24 from I-93 (Ashland) and turn left after Ashland Insurance building into Highland St. The inn is the 10th house on the right-hand side. You can't miss it because it is the most imposing structure on the street.

For B&B rates, see Index.

COLBY HILL INN
Henniker, New Hampshire

Route 202 used to be the most popular way to get from some of the eastern urban centers to the heart of New England in New Hampshire and Maine. Today it's easier (but less intriguing) to follow I-89 and then follow Route 202 to Henniker and the Colby Hill Inn.

Henniker is the home of New England College, and B&B guests at the inn quite frequently are likely to find members of the faculty or parents of visiting or prospective students also enjoying themselves here.

The ceilings are low, the walls are hung with oil paintings and prints, and the furnishings are country antiques. A grandfather clock ticks away in one corner.

Lodging rooms are typical of country New England; many have candlewick bedspreads, hooked rugs, old bowl-and-pitcher sets, and some of them have shared bathrooms.

The inn has a delightful swimming pool sheltered by an ell formed by two huge barns. I can personally attest to the fact that it is most welcome on hot days.

Homemade sourdough pancakes head the breakfast menu, which also has eggs that were probably gathered just a few moments after dawn. Dinner is also offered every night but Monday.

As you can see by the list of recreational and cultural attractions, the Colby Hill Inn offers a delightful prospect for an overnight stay or even longer.

COLBY HILL INN, Henniker, N.H. 03242; 603-428-3281. A 12-room inn on the outskirts of a New Hampshire college town. European plan. Two rooms with shared baths. Breakfast served to house-guests only. Dinner served to travelers Tuesdays through Sunday, except Thanksgiving, Christmas, and New Year's Day. Open year-round. Swimming pool on grounds. Tennis and xc skiing one short block; alpine skiing 3 mi., golf, canoeing, hiking, bicycling, and fishing nearby. No children under 6. No pets. The Glover Family, Innkeepers.

Directions: From I-89, take Exit 5 and follow Rte. 202 to Henniker. From I-91, take Exit 3 and follow Rte. 9 through Keene and Hillsborough to Henniker. Turn right at blinking light in the center of town. At the Oaks, W. Main St., ½ mile west of town center.

For B&B rates, see Index.

THE CORNER HOUSE INN
Center Sandwich, New Hampshire

Center Sandwich is one of those intriguing New Hampshire villages that one stumbles onto rather than drives to. It's one that particularly appeals to me because of the lovely collection of New England houses, churches, general stores, and excellent craft center.

Oddly enough, I have been stopping off to visit the Corner House Inn briefly for several years. It's on one of my regular routes in search of inns and B&Bs.

This time I was very pleasantly surprised by some significant changes that had been made at the inn, and I was impressed by its cheerful and homelike air. The old barn had been converted into an additional dining room and the atmosphere seemed rather contemporary and fresh.

I found lots of green plants, comfortable furniture, a downstairs parlor, an old spinning wheel and flax, antiques, and near-antique furniture.

The breakfast is full-size with a set main dish, either omelets or french toast or pancakes, and so forth. It is served in the very pleasant dining room within the inn itself.

Lunch and dinner are also served.

THE CORNER HOUSE INN, Jct. Routes 109 and 113, Center Sandwich, N.H. 03227; 603-284-6219. A 4-bedroom village inn (1 private bath and 3 rooms share 1 bath). Breakfast served only to houseguests, lunch and dinner served to the public. Open year-round. Closed Christmas and Thanksgiving for lunch and dinner. Excellent stopover or place to stay for more than one night to use as a center for touring the New Hampshire lakes and nearby mountains. Don Brown and Jane Kroeger, Proprietors.

Directions: From I-93 use Exit 24, follow Rte. 3 to Holderness and Rte. 113 to Center Sandwich.

For B&B rates, see Index.

CRAB APPLE INN
Plymouth, New Hampshire

Set in the midst of some very attractive lawns and gardens with an intimate view of the surrounding mountains, the Crab Apple Inn is an 1835 brick building of preeminently Federal design, beside a small brook. It is located in the beautiful Baker River Valley at the gateway to the White Mountain region.

Guests are quite likely to be greeted by a friendly toy poodle named Thora, who accompanies everyone on a tour of the four guest rooms, two of which have private baths.

Janene Davis, the innkeeper, is a most attractive woman, and her interests, as reflected by an extensive library, include photography, travel, art, and literature.

The bedrooms, as indeed the entire house, have beautifully finished wide pine floors and great care has been taken to furnish them with appropriate beds and other furniture. The wallpaper is definitely "New England."

A typical breakfast, taken either alfresco on the brick patio, or in the dining room, might be fruit juice, fresh fruit, an herb and cheese omelet, blueberry or zucchini nut muffins, and coffee or tea.

The inn's location near Holderness School and Plymouth State College is quite convenient for parents of prospective students. The area, close to mountains, rivers, and lakes, offers infinite possibilities for all kinds of recreational activities.

CRAB APPLE INN, RFD 2, Box 200B, West Plymouth, NH 03264; 603-536-4476. A 4-guestroom bed-and-breakfast village inn, 4 mi. west of Plymouth and just a few miles off I-93. Open all year. A full breakfast is included in the room rate. Conveniently located as a touring center for the New Hampshire Lake District or the White Mountains with rivers and ski areas. Local antique and crafts shops nearby. No credit cards. Janene Davis, Innkeeper.

Directions: From I-93 take Exit 26; go 4½ mi. west on Rte. 25. The inn is on the left-hand side.

For B&B rates, see Index.

DANA PLACE INN
Jackson, New Hampshire

The Dana Place Inn just a few miles south of Mt. Washington has been welcoming guests since the late 1880s. Originally a farm, many of the old apple trees are still in evidence around the property. Like so many New England dwellings, it has seen many additions, with buildings snuggled up against each other. The large white house, which is now the main inn, was originally called "Ferncliff Cottage." It was built by Ontwin and Safroni Dana to accommodate summer guests, many of them on their way to or from an overnight excursion to the summit of Mt. Washington.

Located in the heart of the White Mountains and surrounded by thousands of acres of national forest the inn offers opportunities for avid climbers and day-hikers alike. The crystal-clear Ellis River offers a challenge for the trout fisherman, and a dip in one of its deep pools is always refreshing.

Breakfast at the Dana Place is served in a pleasantly sunny dining room with large sliding glass doors overlooking the gardens. In winter one can glimpse a view of Mt. Washington from this room. At almost any time of the year breakfast guests are entertained by the many varieties of birds that visit the feeding station just outside. A full country breakfast featuring homemade muffins and cranberry pancakes is served in season to houseguests and travelers daily.

DANA PLACE INN, Route 16, Pinkham Notch, P.O. Box LB, Jackson, N.H. 03846; 603-383-6822. A 14-room inn, 5 miles from Jackson, N.H. in the heart of the White Mountains. Rates include lodging and full breakfasts. Lunches served on winter weekends only. Dinners served to travelers daily from mid-June to late Oct. and from mid-Dec. to mid-April. Closed Thanksgiving Day. Two tennis courts, hot spa, natural pool, trout fishing, xc skiing, birdwatching, on grounds. Hiking trails, 5 golf courses, downhill skiing nearby. Malcolm and Betty Jennings, Innkeepers.

Directions: Follow Rte. 16, 5 miles north of Jackson Village toward Pinkham Notch.

For B&B rates, see Index.

DEXTER'S INN
Sunapee, New Hampshire

Dexter's Inn, high on top of the hill overlooking Lake Sunapee, is a place where there is some activity for almost everybody to enjoy. Many guests stay for quite a few days and even a couple of weeks at a time. The principal activity in the summer is tennis, so everyone should be advised to bring the right equipment.

The lodging rooms place the accent on bright and gay colors in wallpaper, curtains, and bedspreads. The rooms of the main house are reached by using the funny little hallways that zigzag around wings.

It's possible to stay at Dexter's under the European plan which includes the B&B rates below in June and September only. At other times, it is under the modified American plan including breakfast and dinner.

Guests can enjoy the full New Hampshire breakfast in bed or in the dining room. Frank Simpson boasts that there are always hot blueberry muffins every day as well as fruit, a full range of cereals, pancakes or french toast, or eggs. The aroma of the sausage and bacon brings guests to breakfast early every morning.

DEXTER'S INN AND TENNIS CLUB, Box R, Stagecoach Rd., Sunapee, N.H. 03782; 603-763-5571. A 17-room country inn in the western New Hampshire mountain and lake district. Mod. American plan; European plan available in June and Sept. only. Breakfast, lunch, and dinner served to travelers by advance reservation; closed for lunch and dinner on Tues. during July and Aug. Lunches served only July, Aug. Open from early May to mid-October. Three tennis courts, pool, croquet, shuffleboard, 12½ mi. of hiking trails on grounds. Limited activities for children under 12. Pets allowed in Annex only. No credit cards. Frank and Shirley Simpson, Innkeepers.

Directions: From North & East: use Exit 12 or 12A, I-89. Continue west on Rte. 11, 6 mi.-just ½ mi. past Sunapee to a sign at Winn Hill Rd. Turn left up hill and after 1 mi. bear right on Stagecoach Rd. From west: use Exit 8, I-91, follow Rte. 103 east into N.H.-through Newport ½ mi. past Junction with Rte. 11. Look for sign at "Young Hill Rd." and go 1½ mi. to Stagecoach Rd.

For B&B rates, see Index.

FOLLANSBEE INN
North Sutton, New Hampshire

Interstate 89 is a pleasant and practical way of going to northern Vermont, eastern New Hampshire, and even on to Montreal. A late afternoon start from Boston via I-93 will get the traveler to Exit 10 at North Sutton in time for a very pleasant dinner and comfortable overnight lodgings at the Follansbee Inn in North Sutton.

The village is on Route 114 which runs between Henniker and New London, and is enhanced by the presence of beautiful Kezar Lake.

Larry and Joan Wadman have been working very hard during the past few years to put this building and all of the country-hotel-style bedrooms into very good shape. Cleanliness is certainly one of the watchwords.

Several of the individually furnished rooms have good views of the lake, which at the time of my visit was covered with snow and good for cross-country skiing. Joan pointed out that there were many combinations of double and single beds in each of the bedrooms. One bedroom had a bath with a great old tub that was certainly big enough for two and there are several connecting rooms that are handy for people traveling with children.

Incidentally the inn is a very convenient place to stop if you're bringing children up for interviews at Colby-Sawyer College in New London or Proctor Academy in Andover.

On the fixed-price breakfast there is an assortment of juices, eggs, bacon or sausage, pancakes or french toast. These are served in a very pleasant dining room with bright, cheerful colors. Breakfast is not included in the cost of accommodations.

FOLLANSBEE INN, North Sutton, New Hampshire 03260; 603-927-4221. A 23-room country inn located on the shores of Kezar Lake in central New Hampshire located in one of the scenic resort areas of the state. Private baths are available with second-floor rooms and shared baths with third-floor rooms. Closed two weeks in November and again in April. Dinner not served Monday nights. Hiking, back-roading, cross-country and downhill skiing nearby. Breakfast and dinner available. No pets. Larry and Joan Wadman, Innkeepers.

Directions: Take Exit 10 from I-89 and follow North Road to Rte. 114. Turn right and the inn is behind the church in North Sutton. From I-91 exit at Ascutney, Vt., follow Rte. 103 to Rte. 11, east to Rte. 114 and then south to North Sutton.

For B&B rates, see Index.

HAVERHILL INN
Haverhill, New Hampshire

I'm constantly amazed at the discrimination and taste reflected in some of the really handsome homes of the region built by the men and women who came to the Connecticut River Valley 150 years or more ago. On Route 10 beginning at Lyme, there are a series of villages that have an enchanting early-19th-century American character. In Orford, for example, there are the famous "ridge homes" built between 1773 and 1839 by the professional and business men of the town. Some of them are Bulfinch-style houses built around 1815, designed by Asher Benjamin, who was an associate of the famous Boston architect, Bulfinch.

Continuing north on Route 10, the towns are Piermont and Haverhill, where I found the attractive proprietors Stephen Campbell and Katharine DeBoer. Steve is a computer consultant and a tremendous man in height and accomplishment; although somewhat more diminutively fashioned, Katharine is an extremely gifted concert soprano.

Their beautiful, white 1810 home is set in its own grove of trees off the highway, and immediately impresses the visitor with its warmth and hospitality.

There are four bedrooms of unusual size with period furnishings, working fireplaces, and ample bathrooms. The views are of the meadows and forests nearby.

Conversation around the breakfast table is bound to include the unusual group of antique shops both on the New Hampshire and Vermont side of the Connecticut River, and many guests are interested in the extensive backroading available in both states.

One of the nicest trips is to go north on New Hampshire's Route 10 to Woodsville; then cross over to what becomes Route 5 south on the Vermont side, and continue south, crossing back over on the bridge at Thetford.

HAVERHILL INN, Box 95, Rte. 10, Haverhill, N.H. 03765; 603-989-5961. A 4-bedroom, elegant, early-19th-century home now offering bed and breakfast. Open year-round. Equally convenient to both New Hampshire and Vermont for exceptional backroading and located near many communities for outdoor recreation. Stephen Campbell and Katharine DeBoer, Proprietors.

Directions: From I-91, suggest getting off at Hanover and following Rte. 10 north.

For B&B rates, see Index.

HICKORY STICK FARM
Laconia, New Hampshire

I have been visiting Hickory Stick Farm for many years, not only to enjoy the company of the innkeepers, Scott and Mary Roeder, but also to savor the house specialty—roast duckling. The birds are roasted at low temperatures for eight hours and then refrigerated. As orders are received, they are placed in a very hot oven for fifteen to twenty minutes, which produces a golden brown bird with crisp, delicious skin.

The entrance to this old converted farmhouse is through a lovely old-fashioned door leading into a beamed, low-ceilinged room with a brick fireplace. The floors are of brick or stone, and there are antique and gift items scattered about in several rooms preceding the entrance to the restaurant. Mary Roeder's stenciling on some of the walls is after the manner of Moses Eaton, Jr., who used to travel around southern New Hampshire in the early 1880s as a journeyman stencil artist.

Scott and Mary very recently have made arrangements to provide two attractive guest rooms in the inn. These will be available during the restaurant's entire summer season, and also during the remainder of the year, except when Scott and Mary are on short vacations. Breakfast is also provided.

HICKORY STICK FARM, R.F.D. #2, Laconia, N.H. 03246; 603-524-3333. A hilltop country restaurant 4 mi. from Laconia in the lake country of New Hampshire. Two attractive lodging rooms with breakfast available most of the year. Restaurant open from Memorial Day to Columbus Day. Dinners served from 5:30 to 9 P.M. Sunday dinner served all day from noon to 8 P.M. Extended hours during fall foliage season—call ahead. When closed, dinner available to houseguests by prior arrangement. The Shaker Village in Canterbury is nearby, as well as the Belknap recreational area and other New Hampshire attractions. Scott and Mary Roeder, Innkeepers.

Directions: Use Exit 20 from I-93. Follow Rte. 3 toward Laconia approx. 5 mi. over bridge over Lake Winnisquam. A short distance past this bridge, turn right on Union Road immediately past Double Decker, a drive-in restaurant, and follow Hickory Stick signs 1½ mi. into the woods. If you do not turn onto any dirt roads, you are on the right track. From Laconia, go south on Rtes. 3 & 11 (do not take Rte. 106) and turn left on Union Road (about ½ mile past the Belknap Mall) and follow signs.

For B&B rates, see Index.

INDIAN SHUTTERS INN
North Charlestown, New Hampshire

Let's assume you're driving north on Interstate 91 and the shadows are beginning to lengthen and the pangs of hunger are beginning to assert themselves. The scenery is unquestionably beautiful, but it is time to stop for the night and you don't want to get too far off the main highway. At Springfield, Vermont, leave the Interstate, drive east and go over the tollbridge at Charlestown, make a sharp left on Lover's Lane, join Route 12, and look for the Indian Shutters Inn on the right-hand side on the way to Claremont.

Just for openers, the history of the Indian Shutters Inn begins on April 4th, 1780 when Elijah Parker picked up his hand-wrought shovel and removed the first piece of earth from the land granted to his father by the King of England. From then on it's been one interesting development after another up to the present day.

Today it is being carefully restored and preserved by another individual who always wanted to have a country inn—Bud Elliot.

The size of the parking lot indicates that it has certainly gained favor as a good place to have lunch and dinner, and Bud tells me that their reputation for good food is spreading throughout New England.

At the moment there are four large bedrooms, each overlooking the meadows and fields and all furnished in a comfortable country-inn style. There are also accommodations in cabins.

Most guests are conducted on an extensive tour of the building which might well include an inspection of the great high-ceilinged cellar and its brick floor. It was a stop on the underground railway during the American Civil War. Bud is also prepared to expound on the handful of men who held off at least 1,500 Indians at a nearby fort during the French and Indian War in 1745.

A full breakfast, although not included in the room rate, is available and is served in the family dining room and features, among other things, delicious sticky buns.

INDIAN SHUTTERS INN, Route 12, North Charlestown, New Hampshire 03603; 603-826-4445. A 4-room (shared baths) historic inn located between Charlestown and Claremont just a few moments from the Connecticut River near St. Gaudens. Open every day except Christmas Eve. Lunch and dinner also served. Swimming, boating, golf, tennis, alpine and xc skiing, hang-gliding nearby. No pets. Bud and Roseanne Elliot, Innkeepers.

Directions: Leave I-91 at Exit 7. Take Rte. 11 east, cross bridge and proceed north on Rte. 12. Inn is on east side of the road.

For Lodging rates, see Index.

THE INN AT CHRISTIAN SHORE
Portsmouth, New Hampshire

A journey along the New England seacoast in search of America's past should by all means include a stop at Portsmouth, New Hampshire, if for no other reason than to visit Strawbery Banke (sic). This is a maritime community museum preserving some of the early homes of Portsmouth and named for a profusion of wild berries found on the shores by the first settlers. Strawbery Banke evokes the way of life of sea captains, coopers, stage drivers, maritime tradesmen and merchants.

Four homes are authentically restored and furnished in different time periods showing the changes in life-style and architectural fashions. A total of 35 buildings stand within the 10-acre area, making this one of the few urban outdoor museums of its kind.

The Inn at Christian Shore, a restored Federal house built around 1800, provides the overnight visitor with an ideal ambience for visiting Strawbery Banke. Just a few years ago it was almost a total disaster, but the three innkeepers began the rewarding task of painstakingly restoring it. I believe "cozy" would be one of the first words that comes to my mind. All of the five bedrooms have been furnished with a mixture of antiques, reproductions, and decorations as close to the Federal style as possible. There are several fireplaces, including one in the sitting room, where the atmosphere is most agreeable to make new friends. The guests are frequently shown photographs of the building while it was being restored.

Breakfast, served in the low-ceilinged dining room, always begins with fresh fruit in season, including melon or grapefruit served with honey, and there are sweet breads, all types of eggs, steak or pork tenderloin, home fries, various types of breakfast vegetables and freshly ground coffee.

THE INN AT CHRISTIAN SHORE, 5 Northwest St., Portsmouth, N.H. 03801; 603-431-6770. A 5-bedroom (some shared baths) guest accommodation located in a history-laden city in the southeast corner of New Hampshire. Breakfast is the only meal served, but there are several well-known restaurants within a short distance. Open every day. Strawbery Banke, Theater-by-the-Sea, and the Young Fine Arts Galleries nearby. Charles E. Litchfield, Louis G. Sochia, and Thomas J. Towey, Proprietors.

Directions: From Boston take Exit 5 from I-95 to Portsmouth rotary circle. Follow Rte. 1 north to Maplewood Ave. Exit ramp to downtown Portsmouth. The inn is the sixth house on the left headed toward downtown. Sign in front—parking behind building.

For B&B rates, see Index.

THE INN AT CROTCHED MOUNTAIN
Francestown, New Hampshire

During the 1920s and '30s before the construction of the various Interstate highways, when taking an automobile for more than one night was called "touring," U.S. Route 202 was one of the most popular roads for traveling through New England.

The New Hampshire portion includes a very pleasant journey through the Mount Monadnock region and a slight detour at Bennington will bring the traveler to Francestown and The Inn at Crotched Mountain.

The inn is situated in a 150-year-old, ivy-covered colonial building 1,300 feet above sea level.

If nothing else, I can assure the reader that the view from this inn is well worth a side trip. It is enjoyed from a great many lodging rooms, as well as from the dining room, living room, terrace, and swimming pool.

Although the full breakfast is served in the dining room, guests may take their plates to the patio on sunny mornings and enjoy a beautiful view of truly inspiring mountains. Besides the usual offerings of eggs and bacon, there are particularly tasty french toast and eggs Benedict.

THE INN AT CROTCHED MOUNTAIN, Mountain Rd., Francestown, N.H. 03043; 603-588-6840. A 14-room mountain inn (5 rooms with private baths) in southern New Hampshire 15 mi. from Peterborough. Within a short distance of the Sharon Arts Center, American State Festival, Peterborough Players, Crotched Mtn. ski areas. European plan. Open from Memorial Day to Oct. 31; from Thanksgiving to the end of the ski season. Breakfast and dinner available to travelers in summer; breakfast or dinner, during winter and fall (telephone for reservations and exact schedule). Closed Easter. Swimming pool, tennis courts, volleyball on grounds. Golf, skiing, hill walking, and backroading in the gorgeous Monadnock region nearby. No credit cards. Rose and John Perry, Innkeepers.

Directions: From Boston: follow Rte. 3 north to 101A to Milford. Then Rte. 13 to New Boston and Rte. 136 to Francestown. Follow Rte. 47 2½ mi. and turn left on Mountain Road. Inn is 1 mi. on right. From New York/Hartford: I-91 north to Rte. 10 at Northfield to Keene, N.H. Follow 101 east to Peterborough, Rte. 202 north to Bennington, Rte. 47 to Mountain Rd. (approx. 4½ mi.); turn right on Mountain Rd. Inn is 1 mi. on right.

For B&B rates, see Index.

THE INN AT DANBURY
Danbury, New Hampshire

I had a hard time finding Danbury on the map of New Hampshire, although it's not really that far from I-93. It's just a little distance north of New London.

In the middle of several different New Hampshire resort areas, Danbury is east of Lake Winnipesaukee and not far from Newfound Lake and Lake Sunapee. Even at that, the town is off the beaten path and not heavily traveled.

The Inn at Danbury was originally a house built around 1850. There were about six of these houses built along the road in the village at that time, but this one apparently went far out by putting porches on the second floor.

The inn has two different types of lodging rooms; five rooms are traditional farmhouse bedrooms with an interesting assortment of auction-sale kinds of beds, bureaus, tables, and so forth. The other type of accommodation is three dormitories where up to twenty people can be confortably accommodated.

Guests come to the Inn at Danbury in the wintertime for good downhill and cross-country skiing. It's a reasonable drive to several areas. In the summer the main activity is bicycling, and the inn's services include a bike shop, rental bikes, instruction, and guides. Also there is hiking, mountain climbing, fishing, boating, swimming, craft shows, and antiques.

Breakfast is a real Yankee feast that includes home fries, french toast, pancakes, eggs any style, country sausage, bacon, toast, and as the innkeepers assured me, "You can have any and all of these that you like."

There's nothing pretentious about the Inn at Danbury, and it certainly impressed me as a very comfortable, friendly place.

THE INN AT DANBURY, Route 104, Danbury, New Hampshire 03230; 603-768-3318. A 5-room inn with additional dormitory space to accommodate 20 people, located in the resort section of central New Hampshire near several downhill and cross-country ski areas. Closed Nov., April, and most of May. Full breakfast included with lodgings. The evening meal also offered. Bike shop, rental bikes, instruction and guides available. No pets. No credit cards. George and Joan Issa, Innkeepers.

Directions: From I-93 take Exit 17 and follow Rte. 4 west to Rte. 104. Inn is ½ mile beyond junction in the center of Danbury.

For B&B rates, see Index.

THE JOHN HANCOCK INN
Hancock, New Hampshire

Travelers who are fond of fleetingly sampling New England's charms will find the John Hancock Inn a most pleasant diversion during the portion of their trip that includes the Monadnock region of southern New Hampshire.

The village of Hancock, which is accessible by several gentle "roller coaster" roads, has a handsome village green, a resident gazebo, and an ancient church and town hall. The houses are of early and mid-19th-century vintage and the tree-shaded streets seem almost too good to be true.

Although the John Hancock Inn was named for the famous signer of the Declaration of Independence, Mr. Hancock never visited it himself. It is the oldest continuously-operating village inn in New Hamphsire.

The Early American decor features primitive paintings, braided rugs, and a multitude of authentic antiques. The wide floorboards, fireplaces, and the very beams that have held this building together since 1789, are still much in evidence.

The John Hancock is well-known for the Mural Room, which has murals created in the 19th century by Rufus Porter, depicting scenes of the nearby countryside.

An à la carte breakfast offers a wide choice of fruits, juices, eggs, griddle cakes, and coffee.

Interesting diversions abound in the area, with crafts shops, summer theater, music concerts, and contra dancing.

THE JOHN HANCOCK INN, Hancock, N.H. 03449; 603-525-3318. A 10-room village inn on Rtes. 123 and 137, 9 mi. north of Peterborough. In the middle of the Monadnock Region of southern N.H. European plan. Breakfast, lunch, and dinner served daily to travelers. Closed Christmas Day and one week in spring and fall. All kinds of cultural events throughout the year. Antiquing, swimming, hiking, alpine and xc skiing nearby. Glynn and Pat Wells, Innkeepers.

Directions: From Keene, take either Rte. 101 east to Dublin and Rte. 137 north to Hancock or Rte. 9 north to Rte. 123 and east to Hancock. From Nashua, take 101A and 101 to Peterborough. Proceed north on Rtes. 202 and 123 to Hancock.

For Lodging rates, see Index.

LOVETT'S BY LAFAYETTE BROOK
Franconia, New Hampshire

Franconia, New Hampshire, off I-93, is a place that is held in reverence by lovers of downhill skiing in North America. It was to this area that some of the great early European ski instructors migrated a number of years ago, and here that American downhill skiing really had its beginning.

Lovett's by Lafayette Brook, to use the full name, was one of the earliest ski resorts, although the main house actually dates back to 1784.

Many of the guests have been returning for years, their fathers and mothers having come before them. In many ways, it's like a club.

Besides skiing, other seasons in Franconia have many delights which include antiquing, summer theater, horse shows, flower shows, auctions, and country fairs. The ski lifts are also run during the summer and autumn, providing the guests with spectacular views of the great White Mountains.

The full breakfast served at Lovett's before continuing a journey, or on a winter's morning before some skiing on Cannon Mountain, or in the summer for a day of rest, relaxation, and backroading, is a real White Mountain experience. Besides all types of juices and hot porridge served with maple syrup or brown sugar, if desired, there's a choice of roast beef hash with a poached egg, shirred eggs with fresh mushrooms, fried cornmeal mush, shirred eggs with eggplant, sour cream cheddar cheese omelet, and four different kinds (including parsnip) of pancakes. Breakfasts are an additional $5.00 each.

LOVETT'S BY LAFAYETTE BROOK, Profile Rd., Franconia, N.H. 03580; 603-823-7761. A 32-room country inn in New Hampshire's White Mountains. Modified American plan omits lunch, although box lunches are available. Breakfast and dinner served by reservation to travelers. Open daily between July 1 and Oct. 11 and Dec. 26 and April 1. No pets. Two swimming pools, xc skiing, badminton, lawn sports on grounds. Golf, tennis, alpine skiing, trout fishing, hiking nearby. Mr. and Mrs. Charles J. Lovett, Jr., Innkeepers.

Directions: 2½ mi. south of Franconia on N.H. 18 business loop, at junction of N.H. 141 and I-93 South Franconia exit. 2¾ mi. north of junction of U.S. 3 and 18.

For Lodging rates, see Index.

THE LYME INN
Lyme, New Hampshire

New Hampshire and Vermont *are* different although I'm not certain I can explain why. I would suggest that the traveler on I-91 leave this splendid highway and take Route 5 in Vermont going in one direction and on the way back use Route 10 in New Hampshire. Both are equally stimulating, and it's possible to see how the architectural modes in the two states have different qualities.

The Lyme Inn rests at the end of a long New England common on Route 10, just ten miles from Hanover, New Hampshire, the home of Dartmouth College.

The ten rooms with private baths and five with shared baths have poster beds, hooked rugs, hand-stitched quilts, wide pine floorboards, stenciled wallpaper, wing chairs, and all types of beautiful antiques. There is no entertainment provided for young children.

The spacious front entranceway, which is used as a summer porch, has a most impressive collection of white wicker furniture.

The main dishes on the dinner menu include lamb chops, hunter-style veal, Wiener schnitzel, and hassenpfeffer.

A full breakfast is included in the cost of the room, and might feature fried or scrambled eggs or french toast, along with fruit juices, fresh fruit in season, blueberry muffins, and coffee.

Even for one night, be sure to reserve well in advance.

LYME INN, on the Common, Lyme, N.H. 03768; 603-795-2222. A 15-room village inn, 10 mi. north of Hanover on N.H. Rte. 10. Breakfast included in rates. Open year-round. Some rooms with shared baths. Breakfast and dinner served daily to travelers, except dinner on Tuesdays. Closed three weeks following Thanksgiving and three weeks in late spring. Convenient to all Dartmouth College activities, including Hopkins Center, with music, dance, drama, painting, and sculpture. Alpine and xc skiing, fishing, hiking, canoeing, tennis, and golf nearby. No children under 8. No pets. Fred and Judy Siemons, Innkeepers.

Directions: From I-91, take Exit 14 and follow Rte. 113A east to Vermont Rte. 5. Proceed south 50 yards to a left turn, then travel 2 mi. to inn.

For B&B rates, see Index.

MOOSE MOUNTAIN LODGE
Etna, New Hampshire

Moose Mountain Lodge is really one of a kind. Built in the late 1930s, mostly of logs and stones gathered from the surrounding forests and fields, the lodge perches high on the western side of Moose Mountain. The broad porch extending across the entire front of the house has views of the rolling New Hampshire countryside and of famed Vermont peaks in the far distance.

The atmosphere is indeed rustic, with twelve real "up-country" bedrooms, enhanced by colorful quilts, bunk beds, and many, many flowers.

Bed and breakfast is available during the summer and fall only. During the winter, Moose Mountain Lodge is well known as a cross-country ski center, and a full American plan is in effect, including breakfast, lunch, and dinner.

The summer months find guests hiking, swimming, canoeing on the Connecticut River, visiting Dartmouth and Hanover, and sitting on the porch, watching the birds.

The fall foliage season weekends are almost always entirely booked; however, Tuesdays, Wednesdays, and Thursdays are wonderful times to take a vacation for a few days, and the early New Hampshire fall starts about the last weekend of September.

Moose Mountain Lodge is also part of a Connecticut River "canoeing-inn-to-inn" summer program.

MOOSE MOUNTAIN LODGE, Etna, NH 03750; 603- 643-3529. A 12-guestroom (5 shared baths) rustic lodge a few miles from Hanover, New Hampshire. Closed April and May, and from Nov. 15 through Dec. 26. Bed and breakfast available only during summer and fall. Winter rates include breakfast, lunch, and dinner served only to houseguests. Many wonderful New Hampshire and Green Mountain attractions, recreational, and cultural advantages nearby. No pets. No credit cards. Peter and Kay Shumway, Innkeepers.

Directions: If arriving for the first time, stop in Etna at Landers Restaurant or the Etna Store and telephone for directions.

For B&B rates, see Index.

THE PASQUANEY INN
Newfound Lake, Bridgewater, New Hampsire

Although the Pasquaney Inn would be an excellent place for a stopover for travelers between southern and northern New England and Canada, the blandishments to remain for extra days are bountiful.

For one thing, it sits on a little knoll overlooking Newfound Lake, and the temptation is very strong during the warm weather to just plunk one's self in a rocking chair on the front porch and watch the waterskiers and sailboats on the lake and the clouds rolling by overhead.

Bedrooms in this old lakeside New Hampshire hotel are indeed a flashback to earlier days. I found an assortment of rooms with queen-sized and double beds, flowered wallpaper, braided rugs, and upper New Hampshire country furniture. Everything looked spic-and-span.

The Pasquaney is a great place for people traveling with children because of the fabulous recreation barn, which is wonderful for rainy days. It has two shuffleboard courts, a basketball backboard with plenty of height for kids to play "one on one," and more—ping-pong tables, movies, games, and a place for parties as well.

There is also a little shop in the barn where you can buy fishing equipment, life preservers, and waterskis for more fun on Newfound Lake.

Dinners are also offered in the dining room with such main dishes as chicken cordon bleu, shrimp Pasquaney, prime ribs, trout amandine, and roast leg of lamb. All the breads and pastries are homemade.

Breakfast, not included in the cost of the room, is from an à la carte menu.

I warned you at the start that the Pasquaney Inn had many attractions that makes it much more than a bed-and-breakfast stop.

THE PASQUANEY INN, Newfound Lake, Bridgewater, N.H. (Mailing address: Star Rte. 1, Box 1066, Bristol, N.H. 03222); 603-744-2712. A 28-room resort inn (some with shared baths). Open from mid-May to mid-Oct.; Christmas Day to April 1. Modified American and European plans. Breakfast and dinner served (breakfast not included in room rate). Swimming, boating, tennis, golf, bicycling, antiquing. Especially suitable for children of all ages. No pets. The Zimmer Family, Innkeepers.

Directions: From I-93 use Exit 23, drive 5 mi. west on Rte. 104 to Bristol; north 5 mi. on Rte. 3A.

For Lodging rates, see Index.

PHILBROOK FARM INN
Shelburne, New Hampshire

Philbrook Farm Inn, within sight of Route 2, is the personification of New Hampshire. It is filled with New Hampshire prints, paintings, and photographs, some of them really irreplaceable. There are many, many books about New Hampshire, and many have been written by former guests.

There is a great tradition of "taking in guests" at this venerable White Mountain farm. It all started many years ago and Connie Leger and Nancy Philbrook are the fourth generation of Philbrooks carrying on the family tradition.

"Many of our guests have been coming back for so many years they know the kitchen almost as well as we do," said Connie, "and they love to come down and peel the potatoes or cut the beans and shell the peas and just sit and visit."

The guest rooms are farmhouse in nature and always immaculate.

Breakfast, with the morning sun lighting up the fields and mountains, is served in the old-fashioned dining room with the highly polished wood floors. There is a choice of fruit juice, hot or cold cereal, a choice of eggs and bacon, and toast made from homemade bread. On Sunday morning there are homemade fish balls and cornbread, as well—a real farm breakfast.

PHILBROOK FARM INN, North Rd., Shelburne, N.H. 03581; 603-466-3831. A 20-room country inn in the White Mountains of northeastern N.H., 6 mi. from Gorham and just west of the Maine/N.H. line. American & mod. American plans available. Open May 1st to October 31st; December 26th to April 1st. Closed Thanksgiving, Christmas. Pets allowed only during summer season in cottages. Shuffleboard, horseshoes, badminton, ping-pong, croquet, pool table, hiking trails, xc skiing, snowshoeing trails on grounds. Swimming, golf, hiking, backroading, bird watching nearby. No credit cards. Nancy C. Philbrook & Constance P. Leger, Innkeepers.

Directions: The inn is just off U.S. Rte. 2 in Shelburne. Look for inn direction sign and turn at North Rd., cross R.R. tracks and river, turn right at crossroad, and the inn is down the road apiece.

For B&B rates, see Index.

PINKHAM NOTCH CAMP
Gorham, New Hampshire

Here is bed-and-breakfast quite unlike anything I have discovered previously. The Pinkham Notch Camp is a world apart. The only skyscrapers in this neighborhood are the peaks of the White Mountains; the only distraction is the roaring of Glen Ellis Falls and Crystal Cascades; the only glaring light, that of the sunrise over Wildcat Ridge.

The camp is located eight miles north of Jackson on Route 16, just two and a half miles below the timber line. It is in the heart of the White Mountain National Forest at the base of Mount Washington and a short distance from Tuckerman's Ravine, the Alpine Gardens, and countless other scenic attractions.

The motto here is "Latchstring always out." There are accommodations for up to 107 people in two-, three-, and four-bunk rooms, with showers and bathrooms on each floor. As for meals, there is all you can eat at breakfast and dinner—all homemade and served family-style at long tables.

Here, the primary entertainment is the outdoors, with a network of hiking trails, back-country ski and snowshoeing trails, and there is a helpful staff for information and advice.

The camp is at the apex of the Appalachian Mountain Club Hut System, which maintains eight back-country huts along the Applachian Trail at intervals of one-day hikes.

If this has whetted your appetite for a different kind of bed-and-breakfast experience, I suggest that you write or call for further information. You might even want to join the Appalachian Mountain Club, 5 Joy Street, Boston, Massachusetts 02108 (617-523-0636)—members enjoy reduced rates.

By the way, you don't have to be a hiker or a skier to enjoy the camp accommodations. You can arrive and depart by car and just sit and bask in the sun without ever setting foot on a trail.

PINKHAM NOTCH CAMP (Appalachian Mountain Club), Route 16, Box 298, Gorham, N.H. 03581; 603-466-2727. A splendid mountain camp facility in the heart of the White Mountains. Breakfast, trail lunches, and dinner served daily to guests and public. Lodging rate includes breakfast. Various packages available. Open all year. Unlimited opportunities for hiking and skiing. Variety of evening events presented. Wonderful for families. No pets. No credit cards; personal checks accepted.

Directions: Route 16 runs north and south in New Hampshire. Pinkham Notch Camp is just a few miles above North Conway.

For B&B rates, see Index.

PLEASANT LAKE INN
New London, New Hampshire

If you have one or more active children in the car and the day is beginning to wane, the chances are that you'll be very happy if you've made reservations at the Pleasant Lake Inn, just a few minutes from Interstate 89 in New London.

Furthermore, the kids can be accommodated in a bunk room on the third floor, while you get a good night's sleep in a separate room.

All of the bedrooms have a very light and airy country resort feeling and many of them overlook the lawn and the lake.

This inn began as a farm in the mid-1700s and has been operating as an inn for a little over a hundred years. There's a good chance that there will always be an innkeeper within earshot because there are four of them here and they all seem to share equal responsibilities. Jerry and Branin Jaggard are brothers and Sue and Linda are their wives, so the chances are that the person greeting you at the front door is an innkeeper.

Both dinner and breakfast are served at very brightly covered tables in the pleasant, low-ceilinged dining room overlooking the lake. Linda told me that when they bought the place all the woodwork in the dining room and lounge was apple green, and I noted that it was now a very pleasant gold-beige.

Each morning a hearty country à la carte breakfast is served, and besides the usual offerings I noted that english muffins or bagels were served with cream cheese. Canadian bacon is also on the menu.

Parents or students on the "interview trail" will find that besides Colby-Sawyer in New London there are several other prep schools nearby.

PLEASANT LAKE INN, North Pleasant St., New London, N.H. 03257; 603-526-6271. A 16-room country inn overlooking one of New Hampshire's picturesque lakes. Some rooms have shared baths. Closed from March 22 for 2 or 3 weeks and also the week before and including Thanksgiving Day. À la carte breakfast offered. Lake swimming, paddle tennis and shuffleboard on grounds. Three golf courses, xc and downhill skiing, and backroading nearby. Mt. Sunapee, King Ridge, and Ragged Mountain ski areas within a few minutes' drive. No pets. The Jaggard Family, Innkeepers.

Directions: From I-89 (Exits 11 or 12) proceed toward the middle of New London to the Shell gas station and turn on North Pleasant St. Drive 1½ miles and the inn is on the left.

For Lodging rates, see Index.

SOUTHWORTH'S BED & BREAKFAST
Sugar Hill, New Hampshire

Sugar Hill, New Hampshire, is indeed an exceptional town for several reasons. First, because of its really idyllic location high in the mountains in northern New Hampshire on Route 117 between Franconia and Lisbon. And its residents have always been known for being singularly independent, a fact that was vividly borne out when the village broke off from Lisbon a few years ago to become a separate community.

Perhaps this is just the right atmosphere for David Southworth and his wife, Amy, as attractive a young couple as you will find anywhere, who moved here from Pittsburgh a few years ago to start a whole new lifestyle. David is self-employed nearby and Amy pretty much takes care of their trim little New Hampshire farmhouse during the daytime.

The house, a white clapboard with green shutters and a few added dormers, is located across the road from the Sugar Hill Meeting House and Sweet Pea Farm. At the time of my visit, almost the entire house had been redecorated, including the parlors and the three bedrooms which share one bath. The rooms are all done in a country fashion with pleasant, bright colors.

In addition to their collection of memorabilia, Amy and David have equipped a TV and game room with a variety of games and loads of books for on-the-premises entertainment.

Sugar Hill is within just a few minutes of Cannon Mountain Ski Area and there is plenty of cross-country skiing in the area, as well as a 9-hole golf course. It is a convenient, attractive place to stay in any season.

SOUTHWORTH'S BED & BREAKFAST, Route 117, Sugar Hill, N.H. 03585; 603-823-5344. A 3-bedroom, trim bed-and-breakfast home high in the mountains of northern New Hampshire. Homestyle accommodations with shared bath; continental breakfast included in room rate. Open all year. Convenient for all mountain attractions, including hiking, skiing, boating, fishing, tennis, and golf. Bruce and Judy Southworth, Owners; David and Amy Southworth, Proprietors.

Directions: From I-93 take Franconia exit, follow Rte. 117 to Sugar Hill. From I-91 take Wells River, Vt. exit; continue on Rte. 302 to a point above Lisbon and turn right on Rte. 117 to Sugar Hill.

For B&B rates, see Index.

STAFFORD'S IN THE FIELD
Chocorua, New Hampshire

Stafford's in the Field is that highly sought-after inn "at the end of the road." It's like being in a very big farmhouse, and all of the parlors, the lodging rooms, and the dining room have a wonderful 19th-century farmhouse feeling.

It's fun to sit on the porch and look out over the fields to the woods beyond. There are deer, rabbits, foxes, and game birds sharing this wonderful country, and once in awhile someone sees a small bear.

Mt. Chocorua is just a few miles away and only a short distance farther are the great peaks of the White Mountains where there is good fun and recreation in both summer and winter.

Although this inn has a special B&B rate available to our readers, I would suggest that when making reservations arrangements should be made also to enjoy dinner, because Ramona Stafford is a true gourmet cook and perhaps the traveler will be lucky enough to be there on an evening when spare ribs cooked in maple syrup are on the menu.

A full breakfast is served, usually including blueberry pancakes made with maple syrup from trees on the property. At various times there are apple muffins, Mexican specialties, omelets, baked apples, fritters, and other unusual treats. The orange juice is always freshly squeezed. On warm mornings breakfast is served under the maples in the garden.

STAFFORD'S IN THE FIELD, Chocorua, N.H. 03817; 603-323-7766. A 12-room resort-inn with cottages, 17 mi. south of North Conway. Some rooms in inn with shared baths. Modified American plan at inn omits lunch. B&B rate available. Open all year. Bicycles, tennis, and xc skiing on the grounds. Summer theater, square dancing, golf, swimming, hiking, riding, and fishing nearby. No pets. The Stafford Family, Innkeepers.

Directions: Follow N.H. Rte. 16 north to Chocorua Village, then turn left onto Rte. 113 and travel 1 mi. west to inn. Or, from Rte. 93 take Exit 23 and travel east on Rtes. 104 and 25 to Rte. 16. Proceed north on Rte. 16 to Chocorua Village, turn left onto Rte. 113 and travel 1 mi. west to inn.

For B&B rates, see Index.

WOODSTOCK INN
North Woodstock, New Hampshire

So you are between New York and Canada on Route I-93 and it's getting a little late in the afternoon—time to think about some nice cozy place to stay overnight and a hefty breakfast in the morning.

Isn't it interesting that you happen to be within telephoning distance of the Woodstock Inn?

Snuggled on the lower slopes of the White Mountains, this 100-year-old-Victorian home has now been fully restored by its chef and owner, Scott Rice, and his wife, Eileen. Each room is comfortably furnished in a Victorian style with twins and double beds, and is especially convenient for families. This is old-style country hospitality and the baths are down the hall. Across the street, in a 120-year-old building, are twelve additional rooms, all with private baths.

One of the most interesting features of this little inn is the glassed-in porch with additional tables for breakfast and dinner. The chairs are old movie-house seats—this is the first time I have ever seen them used for this purpose. The atmosphere is enhanced with many hanging plants.

Dinner, an eight-course meal, is served six nights a week.

Because Woodstock is near several ski areas, as well as the spectacular White Mountain scenery, innkeeper Rice has provided many additional package plans, but all of the rates include breakfast, which is served to the public until noon.

WOODSTOCK INN, P.O. Box 278, Main St., North Woodstock, NH 03262; 603-745-3951. A 6-guestroom in-town inn, all with shared baths. Open all year. Breakfast included in room rate. Conveniently located for all of the White Mountain attractions, including Franconia Notch, Kancamagus Highway, Crawford Notch, Loon Mt. Gondola, Cannon Mtn., and Waterville Valley. Not suitable for very young children. No pets. Scott and Eileen Rice, Innkeepers.

Directions: Leave I-93 at Loon Mt. exit (Rte. 112), North Woodstock. It is just a short distance west on Rte. 3.

For B&B rates, see Index.

COLLIGAN'S STOCKTON INN
Stockton, New Jersey

The beautiful Delaware River valley, north of Philadelphia, separates New Jersey and Pennsylvania in about as beautiful and fascinating a way as could be imagined. The area is rich in history, dating even before Washington's famous crossing of the Delaware during the Revolutionary War. Later on, canals were built on each side of the river and many small river towns grew up around the resulting profitable trade.

One such town is Stockton, New Jersey, and one of the earliest continuing accommodations has been on the site of the present-day Stockton Inn, which dates back about a hundred and fifty years.

The stone walls of the inn have a wonderful weathered look, and the mansard roof indicates the Victorian addition in later years.

This is the inn made famous during the thirties by the Rodgers and Hart melody, "There's a Small Hotel," and the famous wishing well is still very much in evidence.

Although today's Stockton Inn is better known as a restaurant serving an international cuisine, there are a few bedrooms and suites with fireplaces available for overnight-and-longer guests. A continental breakfast of fruit juice, cheese, sweet roll, and coffee or tea is offered with the room rate.

COLLIGAN'S STOCKTON INN, Route 29, Stockton, N.J. 08559; 609-397-1250. A traditional inn located in a Delaware River village. Lunch and dinner served every day. Continental breakfast included in room rate. Open all year except Christmas Day. All of the scenic and cultural attractions of nearby Bucks County, Pa., and New Jersey are within a very short distance. No pets. Todd and Penny Drucquer, Innkeepers.

Directions: From New York City: Take New Jersey Turnpike south to Exit 10, then follow I-287 north of Somerville, exiting to Rte. 22 west. Go 2½ miles and then take Rte. 202 south, past Flemington to the Delaware River. Use the last exit in New Jersey marked "Rte. 29, Lambertville and Stockton." Go 3 miles north on 29 to Stockton. From Philadelphia: Follow I-95 north to the Delaware River. Cross the Delaware to the first exit in New Jersey marked "29 Trenton/Lambertville." Follow 29 north through Lambertville, approximately 17 miles to Stockton.

For B&B rates, see Index.

CONOVER'S BAY HEAD INN
Bay Head, New Jersey

I visited Bay Head for the first time a number of years ago and I enjoyed an overnight visit with Carl and Beverly Conover at Conover's Bay Head Inn which is just one block from the beach. It is a three-story typical Jersey coast home with a very pleasant front porch overlooking the main street, as well as second-floor porches on the front and rear. A carriage house in the rear is available from September 15 to June 1.

It's obvious that the innkeepers have had a lot of fun visiting antique and tag sales, because the twelve lodging rooms are all furnished with some interesting pieces, and also boast matching spreads and ruffled pillows. Beverly's mother crochets the wash-clothes and she also does the dress scarfs and doilies in bright colors.

Breakfast is taken in the dining room or on the porch. The oranges used for the freshly squeezed juice have probably been sent north from Florida by Beverly's parents, and breakfast also includes such tempting offerings as bran muffins, blueberry-corn muffins, carrot muffins, Hungarian nut crescents, fruit kuchen, and coffee cake. Carl pitches in and, for an additional charge, will make bacon and eggs during the season, although they are included in the room rate from October to end of April.

CONOVER'S BAY HEAD INN, 646 Main Ave., Bay Head, New Jersey 08742; 201-892-4664. A 12-room inn in a conservative town on the New Jersey coast. (Some shared baths.) Continental breakfast included in room rate during the season; full breakfast in off-season. Croquet, paddleball, and horseshoes on the grounds; swimming, sailing, fishing, tennis, golf, and racquet sports nearby. Open February 15 to December 15. Closed Christmas and New Years. No pets. Beverly and Carl Conover, Innkeepers.

Directions: Take Exit 98 off Garden State Parkway to Rte. 34 to Rte. 35 south. Follow signs to Pt. Pleasant Beach. Bay Head is the next town. Rte. 35 is Main Ave. in Bay Head. From Philadelphia, take Rte. 195 to Rte. 34, and then 35 south. By rail: take the North Jersey Coast Line from Penn Station and arrangements can be made to be picked up at the Bay Head Station.

For B&B rates, see Index.

THE KENILWORTH
Spring Lake, New Jersey

This is very much like a little British seaside resort hotel except that it is far superior to many I've seen cheek-by-jowl in places like Brighton and Hastings.

To add to the English flavor, I was shown about by the manager, Ivy Mason, who is herself from England.

Located on Ocean Avenue, the Kenilworth is just a few steps across the road from the Spring Lake boardwalk and a private sandy beach.

The 25 bedrooms, a few of which have private baths, have a seaside-resort atmosphere with 19th-century furniture. It's all very pleasant and homey.

One of the rooms overlooks the famous Spring Lake private croquet club where enthusiasts from all over the world come to play in tournaments.

A generous continental breakfast is the only meal served and it includes all kinds of fresh fruits, cereals, bagels, danish, and doughnuts.

Spring Lake is a community where many people have lovely summer homes and have been able to exist in harmony with very pleasant and conservative guest houses and small hotels. If I lived in New York City I would certainly come here on many pleasant winter weekends to bundle up and walk on the beaches and boardwalk, and to get the smell of the salt air and enjoy the lovely atmosphere and quiet. Of course it's very popular in the summer.

THE KENILWORTH, 1505 Ocean Ave., Spring Lake, N.J. 07762; 201-449-5327. A 25-bedroom (8 with private baths) Victorian ocean-front seaside hotel located in a conservative resort community on the northern New Jersey coast. Open year-round. Breakfast is the only meal served, but boxed lunches are available with notice. Private beach. Convenient to all resort activities. No pets. No credit cards. Ron and Ivy Mason, Proprietors.

Directions: Leave Garden State Parkway at Exit 98 and proceed to Rtes. 34 and 524. Follow Rte. 524 to Ocean Ave. and turn right.

For B&B rates, see Index.

THE MAINSTAY INN
Cape May, New Jersey

Cape May, along with Marshall, Michigan, enjoys the distinction of being one of the best preserved and restored Victorian communities in North America. The tree-shaded streets of the historic district contain marvelous Greek Revival, Gothic, Queen Anne, Italianate, and Mansard architecture, often with several styles combined. It is a composite picture of Victorian dignity and elegance, southern charm and hospitality, and a scattering of colonial simplicity.

One of the most handsome examples is The Mainstay, a lovely guest house kept by Tom and Sue Carroll, who are among the leaders in the effort to keep Cape May a place "set apart."

The house has had a most interesting history since it was built in 1872 as an elegant gambling club. It was sold in 1898 to a sedate Philadelphia family who added the back wing and entertained some of the great and near-great of Philadelphia society during the many years that followed.

Today, the dining room, living room, and all the lodging rooms contain an outstanding collection of Victorian antiques. They are the subject of much "oohing and ahing" on the daily house tour.

From mid-June to mid-September, a full breakfast is served in the formal dining room with homemade dishes, such as strawberry crêpes, quiches, and soufflés. In midsummer a lighter breakfast, consisting of fruit juices, cereal, coffee, tea, and homemade coffee cakes, is served on the broad porch.

THE MAINSTAY INN, 635 Columbia Avenue, Cape May, N.J. 08204; 609-884-8690. A 12-bedroom inn in a well-preserved Victorian village one block from the ocean. Breakfast served to houseguests. Open every day April thru Oct. Boating, swimming, fishing, bicycles, riding, golf, tennis, and hiking nearby. Not suitable for small children. No pets. No credit cards; personal checks accepted. Tom and Sue Carroll, Innkeepers.

Directions: From Philadelphia take the Walt Whitman Bridge to the Atlantic City Expy. Follow the Atlantic City Expy. to exit for Garden State Pkwy., south. Go south on the Pkwy. which ends in Cape May. The Pkwy. becomes Lafayetts St.; turn left at first light onto Madison. Proceed 3 blocks and turn right onto Columbia. Proceed 3 blocks to inn on right side.

For B&B rates, see Index.

THE NORMANDY INN
Spring Lake, New Jersey

The Normandy is located in the residential north section of Spring Lake, a town that proudly proclaims its Irish heritage. The inn is within one block of the bathing beach, pavilion, and pool. There's a large front porch where you may wish to relax and read the newspapers or a good book, and the bedrooms are larger than usual and air conditioned.

It's a many-layered Victorian house built in 1888 and cited by the Spring Lake centennial committee.

The new owner-innkeepers, Michael and Susan Ingino, are in the process of capturing that Victorian feeling with period furnishings. There is a nine-foot gold leaf oval mirror in the side parlor and an eight-foot walnut bed in one of the guest rooms. Throughout the inn there are many antique clocks that Michael has collected over the years.

A hearty Irish breakfast is served in the dining room, and there is a little closed-in porch with a refrigerator for guests to use. There are many fine restaurants nearby for dinner.

THE NORMANDY INN, 21 Tuttle Ave., Spring Lake, N.J. 07762; 201-449-7172. A 17-bedroom Victorian inn in a quiet community on the north Jersey seacoast. All but three rooms have private baths. Open year-round. A full breakfast is included with the price of the room. Located ½ block from ocean and boardwalk. Convenient to all of the Jersey coast recreational and entertainment activities. No credit cards. Michael and Susan Ingino and daughter, Beth, Innkeepers.

Directions: From Garden State Pkwy. take Exit 98 and follow Rte. 34 to first circle. Go ¾ of the way around the circle to Rte. 524 and follow this to the ocean. Turn right on Ocean Ave. one block and right again on Tuttle.

For B&B rates, see Index.

THE WOOLVERTON INN
Stockton, New Jersey

The Woolverton Inn is an elegant stone manor house set amidst formal gardens and stately trees just a few minutes from the Delaware River in the rather conservative village of Stockton, New Jersey, across the river from Bucks County, Pennsylvania.

It's an unusual blend of both 18th- and 19th-century architecture, having been built in 1793 and later remodeled by Maurice Woolverton, whose family held the property from 1850 to 1939.

In 1972 the property was purchased by George and Ann Hackl who decided to turn it into an inn.

Each of the ten bedrooms has been furnished with most tasteful antiques and each one expresses an early-American individuality. The master suite has a canopy bed.

Guests enjoy homebaking for breakfast and afternoon tea, which, by the way, is a very welcome break after a day spent exploring nearby Bucks County and the Delaware River Valley or perhaps walking along the river towpath.

THE WOOLVERTON INN, R.D. 3, Box 233-A, Stockton, New Jersey 08559; 609-397-0802. A 10-room pastorally-oriented inn on the east side of the Delaware River within just a few moments of historic Bucks County, Pa. Open year-round. Breakfast is the only meal offered on a regular basis and is included in the price of the rooms. Bocci and croquet on grounds. Swimming, tubing, canoeing, tennis, golf, and wonderful history-laden back roads including visits to Washington's Crossing nearby. No pets. Gary Wheeler, Innkeeper.

Directions: From New York City: Take New Jersey Turnpike south to Exit 10, then follow I-287 north of Somerville, exiting to Rte. 22 west. Go 2½ miles and then take Rte. 202 south, past Flemington to the Delaware River. Use the last exit in New Jersey marked "Rte. 29, Lambertville and Stockton." Go 3 miles north on 29 to Stockton and turn right on Rte. 523, up hill ¼ of a mile to a sharp left-hand turn—the inn sign. The inn is the second driveway on the right. From Philadelphia: Follow I-95 north to the Delaware River. Cross the Delaware to the first exit in New Jersey marked "29 Trenton/Lambertville." Follow 29 north through Lambertville, approximately 17 miles to Stockton.

For B&B rates, see Index.

GRANT CORNER INN
Santa Fe, New Mexico

When news of the extraordinary breakfasts served guests at the Grant Corner Inn began to circulate in Santa Fe, a curious thing happened. Outsiders asked if they could come too. Please. So now, with a day's notice, you can breakfast here in front of the fire or on the veranda, depending on the season, even if you're not lucky enough to cadge a bedroom for the night.

New Mexican favorites (huevos rancheros; green chile crêpes) are offered with such house specialties as spinach omelet, cherry blintzes, Dutch Babies, and stuffed french toast. On Valentine's Day, the french toast is heart-shaped, but any day, the juice is fresh-squeezed; the coffee fresh-ground; the breads and jams homemade.

Although no other meals are served, the Walters will put together an elegant picnic lunch to accompany you on day trips to the backlands of this enchanting region. In-town, you can leave your car in the off-street parking area and walk to a dozen fine restaurants, as well as the shops and museums of the Plaza— heart of Santa Fe.

Louise and Pat Walter rescued the spacious old townhouse from oblivion and put their considerable designer talents together to produce a real charmer. No two guest rooms are alike, but all are handsomely decorated with antiques, and there are fresh flowers throughout the house year around. The portrait smiling approval from the mantel is of Jack Stewart, founder of Arizona's famed Camelback Inn and Louise's father.

GRANT CORNER INN, 122 Grant Avenue, Santa Fe, NM 87501; 505-983-6678. A 9-guest room (five with private baths) bed-and-breakfast inn in downtown Santa Fe. Breakfast only meal regularly served. Open year around. Sightseeing, restaurants, shopping nearby. Louise and Pat Walter, Innkeepers.

Directions: From I-25 to St. Francis, drive west. Turn right on Alameda, left on Guadalupe, right on Johnson. Inn is on corner of Johnson and Grant with own parking lot on left side of Johnson.

For B&B rates, see Index.

THE PLAZA HOTEL
Las Vegas, New Mexico

Don't confuse this Las Vegas with the Nevada version. Las Vegas, New Mexico, is older, smaller; infinitely less commercial and more historic. The Plaza Hotel has led the way in the historic rehabilitation of the Old Town section, where once the desperados of the Old West made this the roughest, toughest town in a rough, tough region. Shades of Doc Holliday, Billy the Kid, Big Nose Kate!

After the West was won, the Plaza Hotel became the location for many silent films; following that, the hotbed of New Mexico politics. The hotel is now a wonderful example of the best in historic preservation and rehabilitation with handsome period furnishings. Even the old plaza, at its doorstep, has been taken back to the late 1800s and restored.

The fine dining room has made the hotel so popular with local ranchers, guests should made reservations for dinner when they reserve their rooms. It is open for breakfast, lunch, and Sunday brunch, as well as the evening meal.

The Plaza is on the National Register of Historic Places, and the town has nine designated Historical Districts. You can visit the Teddy Roosevelt Roughrider Museum (there were more roughriders from New Mexico than any other state), tour the back country, and even see the wagon ruts left by the users of the old Santa Fe Trail, just outside of town.

THE PLAZA HOTEL, 230 on the Old Town Plaza, Las Vegas, NM 87701; 505-425-3591. A 38-guestroom inn (all private baths) on the old plaza in a historic town 60 mi. east of Santa Fe. Open all year. Breakfast is not included, but a Plaza Special of two eggs, hash browns, and biscuits is only $1.25. Excellent full-service dining room. Arrangements made for tours to nearby historic sites such as Fort Union, as well as genuine ranch round-ups. Children under 12 are free. Facilities for the disabled. Katherine and Wid Slick; Lonnie and Dana Lucero, Proprietors.

Directions: Exit from I-25 at the University Exit (Exit 345), turn left over the hwy. and follow the Plaza Hotel signs to Plaza/Bridge. The Plaza Hotel is on the northwest corner of the plaza. Coming from Taos on Hwy. 3, continue into town. Turn right at the intersection of 7th St. and National, and follow signs. Las Vegas, NM, is a stop for AMTRAK Chicago-Albuquerque, so convenient for a stopover by train as well as automobile.

For Lodging rates, see Index.

PRESTON HOUSE
Santa Fe, New Mexico

Poet Peggy Pond Church used to play "Sardines" in Preston House with the children of early owners. "A Queen Ann-style house has lots of wonderful hiding places," she reminisces.

It also has leaded glass windows, a red plush window seat on the landing, and many distinctive architectural features that have been enhanced by the deft restoration and original paintings of present owner, artist/designer Signe Bergman. The hundred-year-old home, much a part of Santa Fe's Anglo history, has a carefully selected library to put you right in the mood to learn more. Yet its garden setting is an easy walk to the far older Plaza and the far newer galleries, shops, and restaurants. Centuries overlap in Santa Fe.

Preston House opened in 1981 as Santa Fe's first contemporary B&B, achieving instant reputation in a distinct departure from the big tourist/convention-oriented hotels. With only five rooms, it is always booked well ahead.

Breakfast, served in the sunny dining room overlooking the garden, is basically continental with American-style variety: assorted fresh fruits, fresh-squeezed juice, home-baked goodies like maple-bran muffins and fresh apple cake, a selection of teas and very good coffee. On cool mornings, a fire burns briskly in the corner fireplace.

Two of the bedrooms also have fireplaces, and one will accommodate three guests. Preston House combines pleasant informality with late-nineteenth-century grace. Easy to see where even a famous poet would remember every corner.

PRESTON HOUSE, 106 Faithway St., Santa Fe, NM 87501; 505-982-3465. A 5-guestroom (3 with private baths) bed-and-breakfast inn 3 blocks from the Plaza. Breakfast only. Open year around with advance reservations necessary. Restaurants, sightseeing, galleries, shopping nearby. Children under 15 not encouraged. No pets. Signe Bergman, Owner.

Directions: From Albuquerque take I-25, Old Pecos Trail exit. Turn right on the Paseo de Peralta, right on Palace, and left on Faithway. Since the Plaza is the central point in Santa Fe, you might just aim for that, then follow Palace St., 3 blocks east to Faithway. Preston House is on your right, end of the street.

For B&B rates, see Index.

ADELPHI HOTEL
Saratoga Springs, New York

Walking through the lobby of the Adelphi Hotel feels like stepping through a time warp into the Gilded Age. The dark, rich woods, ornate mirrors, antique paintings, potted palms, and over-stuffed sofas, settees, and chairs re-create the ambience of Saratoga's heyday.

Sheila Parkert and Gregg Siefker fell in love with the defunct 1877 hotel the first time they saw its dilapidated three-story Italianate facade. Now, several years and countless hours of hard work later, the hotel stands as a lone and stunning example of the grand hotels that once proliferated in this legendary town.

All of its three stories of rooms reflect Sheila's and Gregg's attention to the minutest of details and to the Victorian theme, with elegant draperies, fabric wall coverings, period paintings and photographs.

A continental breakfast can be taken in bed, in the second-floor sitting room, or outside terrace. There is a delightful courtyard where luncheons and light suppers are served, as well as an impressive dining room where dinner is available in July and August. Sometimes there are impromptu late-night concerts, when a few members of the New York City Ballet orchestra gather on the raised platform in one corner of the dining room and play a little chamber music.

Today, with the Saratoga Performing Arts Center, the famed Saratoga racetrack, and the state-run mineral baths, this area teems with activity during the summer months, and, of course, during the fall foliage season.

ADELPHI HOTEL, 365 Broadway, Saratoga Springs, N.Y. 12866; 518-587-4688. A 20-bedroom (all private baths) elegant Victorian hotel in the center of town. Open May 1 to Nov. 1. Continental breakfast included in room rate. Lunch and dinner served to the public during July and August only. Saratoga Performing Arts Center (summer home of New York City Ballet and Philadelphia Symphony Orchestra), Saratoga Raceway, harness racing, Saratoga State Park with mineral springs and baths, tennis, swimming, golf, antiquing, backroading nearby. Sheila Parkert and Gregg Siefker, Innkeepers.

Directions: From I-87, take Exit 13N. Continue 3 mi. to downtown district. Hotel is on the left.

For B&B rates, see Index.

ASA RANSOM HOUSE
Clarence, New York

With goggles in position, and eyes straight ahead, travelers speeding across the New York State Thruway will never see Clarence, New York, more's the pity. This is the oldest town in the Erie County and the first settler was a young silversmith by the name of Asa Ransom who had been plying his trade in the fur trading posts on the shores of Lake Erie.

Today Mr. Ransom would be very surprised to know that his two-story log cabin, which served as a hostelry, would still be commemorated by the Asa Ransom House which is a very handsome place indeed, well-known to people who live in the vicinity for its excellent meals, and already sought after by the road-wise bed-and-breakfast traveler.

There are four totally different bedrooms, each with a name to suit its own personality. All have been delightfully furnished by innkeepers Bob and Judy Lenz.

The full breakfast served in the dining room is featured by a special breakfast pie which is a deep casserole containing smoked corned beef and potatoes, and topped with scrambled eggs and melted cheese. If that isn't quite enough, there are freshly made muffins and lots of fresh fruit.

Please note that the Asa Ransom House is closed Friday and Saturday because of religious beliefs of Bob and Judy. The inn is open on Sundays.

ASA RANSOM HOUSE, Rte. 5, Clarence, N.Y. 14031; 716-759-2315. A 4-room village inn approximately 15 mi. from Buffalo near the Albright Knox Art Gallery, the Studio Arena Theatre, the Art Park, Lancaster Opera House, and Niagara Falls. European plan. Dinner served Mon. through Thurs. 4 to 8:30 p.m.; Sun., 12 to 8 p.m. Jackets required. Lunch is available on Wed. only. Closed Fri. and Sat. Tennis, golf, fishing, swimming nearby. Limited amusement for children under 12. No pets. No credit cards. Bob and Judy Lenz, Innkeepers.

Directions: From the New York Thruway traveling west, use Exit 48A-Pembrook. Turn right to Rte. 5 and proceed 11 mi. to Clarence. Traveling east on the N.Y. Thruway, use Exit 49; turn left on Rte. 78, go 1 mi. to Rte. 5, turn right and continue 5¼ mi. Coming from the east via Rte. 20, just east of Lancaster, N.Y., turn right on Ransom Rd., go to end and turn left.

For B&B rates, see Index.

BAKER'S BED AND BREAKFAST
Stone Ridge, New York

Many a snug little bed-and-breakfast establishment, shunning the continental breakfast, turns in exactly the opposite direction and serves a sumptuous many-course morning meal that is reminiscent of the full English breakfasts served in the Cotswolds and the Lake Country of England. Such a place is Baker's Bed and Breakfast, where a frittata or puffy Finnish oven pancakes with maple syrup are more likely to be the rule than the exception, and shirred eggs with a snappy cheddar accompaniment might also be augmented by delicious, thin strips of sauteed vension. I particularly remember the super-delicious rolls.

However, there's more to Baker's than merely breakfast. There's a wonderful atmosphere of intellectual curiosity and involvement not only with all of the arts—music, dance, paintings, sculpture, and crafts—but also a definite affinity with nature and its many moods and offerings.

An interesting sidelight is a hot tub in a solar greenhouse attached to the dining room. For those of our readers in the East who have never had the pleasure of sinking luxuriously into this West Coast innovation, perhaps Baker's would be a good place to start.

There are five bedrooms sharing two baths, and the decor reflects an interest both Fran Sutherland and her husband, Doug Baker, have in the many varieties of both American and English furniture.

BAKER'S BED AND BREAKFAST, R.D. 2, Box 80, Stone Ridge, N.Y. 12484; 914-687-9795. A 5-bedroom 1780 stone farmhouse (2 baths) in Ulster County's Rondout Valley, with views of the Shawangunk Mtns. Open year-round. Full breakfast with lodgings. De Puy Canal House restaurant, antique shops, Delaware and Hudson Canal Museum, Woodstock art colony, Lakes Mohonk and Minnewaska minutes away. Birding, bicycling, hiking, fishing, tennis, golf, xc and downhill skiing nearby. No children under 12, except Sun. to Thurs. Smoking permitted beside the fire or on the porch. No pets. No credit cards. Fran Sutherland and Doug Baker, Proprietors.

Directions: Leave the New York State Thruway at Exit 18 and follow Rte. 299 to Rte. 32, turning right and continuing to Rte. 213. Proaeed west throueh High Falls and turn left on Rte. 209. Take the second left to Old Kings Highway; Baker's is on the right.

For B&B rates, see Index.

THE BALSAM HOUSE
Chestertown, New York

The best way really to enjoy all the many recreational and culinary delights of the Balsam House is to spend two or three days; however, if you are traveling the Northway (I-87) between Montreal and New York City, and the day is getting longer and you're a little weary of the miles, turn off for about twelve miles into the beauty of the Adirondacks and the Balsam House. Here, you can enjoy a very pleasant evening, a comfortable bed, and a sumptuous continental breakfast at this newly refurbished and renovated Victorian hotel.

The Balsam House sits among the evergreens on a knoll above the private and clear, sparkling waters of the Friends Lake. Dominating the building is a central tower with a mansard roof flanked by two gables. It is a type of architecture that is often seen on Prince Edward Island.

The front porch has handsome wicker chairs, and stepping into the lobby is like a visit into the late nineteenth century. As is the case with many buildings of that vintage, there are numerous nooks and crannies and recessed windows. The beds have grandmother spreads, feather pillows, and each of the twenty bedrooms has a private bath.

If you're arriving at dinnertime, the country French cuisine created by the Swiss chef will be a very pleasant surprise, indeed, and there may be a little entertainment afterward as well.

I suspect that the other recreational blandishments, including fishing, white-water rafting, hiking, canoeing, horseback riding, bicycling, golf, and the like, will delay your return to the main road, but I'm also certain you will agree it was well worth it.

THE BALSAM HOUSE, Chestertown, N.Y. 12817; 518-494-2828 or 494-4431. An elegant 20-room resort inn in the Adirondack Mountains, just a short distance from I-87. Open all year. Lodging rates include a generous full breakfast. Dinner is also served. Canoeing, sailing, rowboating, fishing, and lawn games on the grounds. Hiking, white-water rafting, tennis, horseback riding, bicycling, golf, hunting, and other joys of the Adirondacks are easily accessible. Frank Ellis, Innkeeper.

Directions: From I-87, take Exit 23 (Warrensburg) to Rte. 9 north. Proceed approx. 4 mi. to Rte. 28 (veer left) and continue for exactly 3 mi. to Potterbrook Rd. Turn right for 4 mi. to the Balsam House.

For B&B rates, see Index.

THE BARTLETT HOUSE INN
Greenport, Long Island, New York

The permanent residents of outer Long Island's north fork will probably insist that there is something special about their little part of the world. "Our villages are different from those on the south fork," is one person's opinion. "I think we are more natural; there is a little less hoopla over here, and there is just as much to do off- as on-season, but it is always rather quiet."

I'm sure those are some of the reasons why John and Linda Sabatino decided to convert this very attractive old-fashioned Victorian house in Greenport into a bed-and-breakfast accommodation.

Throughout the house are evidences of John's real love of wood and woodworking. The well-preserved original embellishments of this house, including the parquet flooring, must have appealed to him immediately, and he has augmented them with his own touches.

The inn is located in a residential portion of Greenport, which is, by the way, the ferry terminus for the trip to Shelter Island, and just a few minutes away from Orient Point, where the ferry leaves for New England.

The bedrooms remind me of my aunt's house back in Elmira, New York. One has a private bath and the others have large, shared bathrooms. The house used to be a convent and was empty for eight or ten years. One of the features in the living room is the carved Corinthian columns.

The continental breakfast is served in the dining room and Linda is especially careful to keep a supply of as much fresh fruit as possible, with which she makes simple cobblers from time to time. Both Linda and John are walking encyclopedias of information on all of the amusements and recreation on the north fork.

THE BARTLETT HOUSE INN, 503 Front St., Greenport, L.I., N.Y. 11944; 516-477-0371. A 6-bedroom (private and shared baths) bed-and-breakfast home in the Greenport residential area. Open all year. Conveniently located for all eastern Long Island recreational attractions. Near Orient Point ferry terminal for trips to New England. Linda and John Sabatino, Proprietors.

Directions: From New York take exit on L.I. Expy. Greenport is the principal village on the Long Island north fork.

For B&B rates, see Index.

BASSETT HOUSE
Long Island, East Hampton, New York

For as long as I can remember, "the Hamptons" have been a sought-after holiday objective for many people who live in the New York City area. On the outer end of Long Island's South Fork, the Hamptons offer much to discover, including miles of ocean, sound, harbor, and pond. An endless variety of natural beauty coupled with cultural sophistication make the Hamptons an area of stimulating contrasts. Pine, oak, and hickory forests with generous amounts of laurel, blackberry, and dogwood make it a wonderful place for bird watchers. East Hampton also has excellent summer theater and many galleries.

Michael Bassett's Bassett House fits right in with the eclectic mood of the Hamptons. It is furnished in what he calls "early American yard sale," and there are several very interesting pieces scattered around, including railroad semaphores, lots of campy photographs, paintings, and prints—and everything is carefully placed in a way that contributes to a relaxed atmosphere and so that it doesn't overwhelm the viewer.

Most of the bedrooms are quite large and interestingly furnished.

A full breakfast is served, and Michael will also do a special dinner if you are in the mood.

BASSETT HOUSE, 128 Montauk Highway (Box 1426), East Hampton, L.I., N.Y. 11937; 516-324-6127. A 12-bedroom (7 baths) tidy little inn on the western end of East Hampton. Open all year; 3-night minimum stay only on weekends late June, July, and August. Most convenient for all of the outer Long Island recreational and cultural attractions. Michael Bassett, Innkeeper.

Directions: The inn is located 1.5 miles west of the center of East Hampton village on Rte. 27 (Montauk Highway).

For B&B rates, see Index.

BEEKMAN ARMS
Rhinebeck, New York

The Beekman Arms shares the reputation of being the oldest continuously operating inn in America with Longfellow's Wayside Inn in South Sudbury, Massachusetts. It is located in Rhinebeck, New York, deep in the beautiful Hudson River Valley and is most convenient for some of the exciting attractions in the Rip Van Winkle area. The inn is an American landmark and began life as a fort built to withstand attacks from unfriendly Indians.

During the Revolution, George Washington and his staff enjoyed the inn hospitality, and later Franklin Roosevelt, who lived close by at Hyde Park, wound up every campaign for both governor and president with an informal talk from the porch.

It is fitting that an inn with such historical integrity should also have a guest house connected with it that is one of the architectural jewels of the Hudson Valley. It was designed and built by Alexander Jackson Davis for the first owner, Henry Delamater in 1844. The house has been in an excellent state of preservation and remains one of the few early examples of American Gothic residences still in existence. It is reputed to be the first batten-and-board home to be built in the United States.

The seven bedrooms in this early Victorian mansion have been furnished with taste and care and with particular attention to authentic detail.

A simple continental breakfast is offered at the Delamater House; however, a full à la carte breakfast, including omelets of all kinds, eggs Benedict, and croissants, are featured at the Beekman Arms.

Bookings for Delamater House, as well as for the inn itself, are arranged directly through the Beekman Arms.

BEEKMAN ARMS, Rhinebeck, N.Y. 12572; 914-876-7077. A 13-room village inn with an adjacent 7-room guest house, 1 mi. from Amtrak Station at Rhinecliff. Breakfast, lunch, and dinner served to travelers daily. Open year-round. Short drive to F.D.R. Library and Home in Hyde Park, Vanderbilt mansion, World War I Aerodrome. European plan. Golf, tennis, swimming nearby. No amusements for young children. Charles LaForge, Innkeeper.

Directions: From N.Y. Thruway, take Exit 19, cross Rhinecliff Bridge and pick up Rte. 199 south to Rte. 9. Proceed south on Rte. 9 to middle of village. From Taconic Pkwy. exit at Rhinebeck and follow Rte. 199 west 11 mi. to Rte. 308 into village.

For Lodging rates, see Index.

BIRD AND BOTTLE INN
Garrison, New York

Bed and breakfast in an inn that probably played host to Benedict Arnold and other shadowy figures of the American Revolution? Yes, but only between Sunday and Thursday. See the Index for special rates at this time.

The Bird and Bottle goes back to the mid-1700s, when it was a stagecoach stop on the New York to Albany route. Its nearness to West Point undoubtedly made it a meeting place for many plots and counterplots.

Today, the Colonial atmosphere of narrow clapboards, low ceilings, and rich paneling is preserved and enhanced with such beautiful decorations as period wallpapers, pewter, old paintings, duck decoys, and many wooden accessories.

Canopied or four-poster beds and woodburning fireplaces carry the Colonial theme into the bedrooms, all of which have private bathrooms.

Lunch and dinner are served daily, and Sunday brunch is served year-round. So the culinary delights may persuade the bed-and-breakfast guest to stay even longer.

Breakfast is selected before retiring from a menu that includes all kinds of fruit juices, eggs, sausage, and imported jams and jellies. French toast with syrup or honey is one of their specialties.

BIRD AND BOTTLE INN, Garrison, N.Y. 10524; 914-424-3000. A 4-bedroom country inn, rich in antiquity, located on Rte. 9, a few miles north of Peekskill, N.Y. Open year-round. B&B rates available Sun. thru Thurs. Lunch and dinner served daily. Sunday brunch served year-round. A short distance from Boscobel Restoration, U.S. Military Academy at West Point, and Sleepy Hollow Restorations. Ira Boyar, Innkeeper.

Directions: From NYC: cross George Washington Bridge and follow Palisades Pkwy. north to Bear Mtn. Bridge. Cross bridge and travel on Rte. 9D north 4½ mi. to Rte. 403. Proceed on Rte. 403 to Rte. 9, then north 4 mi. to inn. From I-84, take Exit 13 and follow Rte. 9 south for 8 mi.

For B&B rates, see Index.

THE BOWDITCH HOUSE
Shelter Island, New York

Shelter Island is really a place set apart. It lies between the north and south fork of Long Island with Peconic Bay to the west and Gardner's Bay to the east. Although it is only two hours east of New York City, it has many of the characteristics of a New England fishing village. I'm told that one of the most attractive things about Shelter Island is its slow and easy pace.

The island has been carefully zoned to protect residential areas and it has activities for both seashore and country. One of the most interesting areas is the "The Heights," famous for its Gothic Revival architecture and gingerbread houses.

In such an atmosphere, the Bowditch House, run by James and Nora Furey, is very much in place. I think it could best be described as "homey." There are nine bedrooms sharing the two baths.

Breakfast is served in a pleasant dining room with three dining tables, white walls, cottage curtains, and matching wallpaper. There is a most agreeable, casual atmosphere about the entire house, and it is a pleasant alternative to a larger inn or a lodge.

The Bowditch House was mentioned in July 1982 *Good Housekeeping*, and also in an article about Shelter Island in *Gourmet* magazine in the August 1982 edition.

The Inn is a very short walk to the harbor, facing the north fork. Breakfast is the only meal served, but there are restaurants on the island with which the Fureys are well acquainted.

THE BOWDITCH HOUSE, Route 114, Shelter Island, N.Y. 11965; 516-749-0075. (Winter: 516-887-1898.) A 9-bedroom bed-and-breakfast home (2 shared baths). Open Memorial Day and weekends until school is out; then every day until Labor Day; then weekends until end of Oct. There is a 2-night minimum stay for weekends and 3-night minimum for holidays. Many outdoor activities easily accessible, including golf, fishing, tennis, bicycling, and the beach. James and Nora Furey, Proprietors.

Directions: Shelter Island is reached by car or train to Greenport (north fork). The ferry at the terminus on Shelter Island is just 1 mi. from the Bowditch House on Rte. 114.

For B&B rates, see Index.

CAPTAIN SCHOONMAKER'S BED AND BREAKFAST
High Falls, New York

It may come as a surprise that this section of New York's Catskill and near-Catskill mountains has so much Revolutionary War history. Washington's headquarters were in nearby Newburgh, and there are beautiful old stone buildings, built even before the break with the mother country—many have been declared historic places.

Such an award has been made to Captain Schoonmaker's, built by an officer in Washington's army in 1760 and, according to the citation, "fortified and used as a place of refuge during the war." With a front wall of hand-planed boards, which is typical of Hudson Valley Huguenot dwellings ("best face forward"), the remaining three sides are finished in stone.

Sam and Julia Krieg are the hosts at this cheery and restful accommodation. There are many different levels and several different combinations of beds and baths in the main building and in the renovated barn. There are more bedrooms in a recently acquired historical landmark building, which once housed the lock-tender for Lock #17 on the Delaware-Hudson Canal.

Because breakfast is included in the lodging tariff, it might be well to note that many different surprises are offered in addition to a cheese-dill souffle—or scallion cheese quiche, bacon, scrapple, sausage, and freshly baked bread, still warm from the oven. There are such extras as apricot strudel and, at the time of my visit, a walnut-apple-and-raisin confection.

Julia explained that Captain Schoonmaker's does not offer dinner because the area is replete with restaurants. "We provide menus and are happy to telephone with our guests' reservations, if it will help," she added.

CAPTAIN SCHOONMAKER'S BED AND BREAKFAST, R.D. 2, Box 37, High Falls, N.Y. 12440; 914-687-7946. A 12-bedroom (6 baths) bed-and-breakfast inn located in a snug old farmhouse and renovated barn. Open all year. Breakfast is the only meal served. Golf, tennis, swimming, hiking, tubing, horseback riding, and fascinating back-roading nearby. The facilities are a bit confining for small children. No pets. No credit cards. Sam and Julia Krieg, Hosts.

Directions: From the New York State Thruway (I-87) take exit 18 (New Paltz) and drive west on Rte. 299. Turn right on Rte. 32 in New Paltz, then left on Rte. 213 thru Rosendale to High Falls.

For B&B rates, see Index.

CEDAR HILL INN
Ghent, New York

There's much more to this inn than I can possibly include on a single page. For one thing, the traveler-in-a-hurry would never even suspect that this modernized farmhouse on a dirt road was just a short distance from the Taconic Parkway or Route 9H. It is well worth a short side-trip to remain overnight or for several days.

Situated on twenty acres of rolling countryside, it has a swimming pool, an all-weather tennis court, a badminton court, marvelous walks through the fields and woods, good cross-country ski trails, and exceptional backroading.

Accommodations are in different types of bedrooms, both in the main house and in an adjacent outbuilding. Everything is linked together by very warm living rooms with big fireplaces, a baby grand piano, and books galore.

A full breakfast is included in the cost of accommodations; however, other meals are also offered. Breakfast usually includes fresh fruit, homemade muffins or coffee cake, blueberry pancakes, french toast with maple syrup, bacon and eggs, and homemade granola.

CEDAR HILL INN, Ghent, N.Y. 12075; 518-392-3923. An 8-bedroom rural farmhouse converted into a small country inn. Open year-round. Tennis court, lawn games, xc ski trails, badminton, swimming pool on grounds. Two ski areas, Tanglewood, summer theaters, and other natural and cultural events nearby. No pets. Mark and Marie-Claire Wadden, Innkeepers.

Directions: Take Harlemville Rd. Exit from Taconic Pkwy., turn west and go 1½ miles. At fork, bear left on Tice Hill Rd.

For B&B rates, see Index.

CHRISTMAN'S WINDHAM HOUSE
Windham, New York

I've lost track of the number of times that I've traveled on Route 23 in the northern Catskills and passed this extremely attractive Greek Revival building. However, until last spring it was closed each time I passed it.

This time I stopped and to my most pleasant surprise discovered that it was operated by Stanley and Roberta Christman, the aunt and uncle of Laura and Barbara Stevens, innkeepers at the Greenville Arms. I've also met Roberta's mother who has been a hotel keeper in the Catskills probably longer than anyone else.

Roberta says of the Windham House, "We have had many people coming back for years and years. We will not necessarily have many rooms available in the high season, around July and August, but in June or September we will be happy to accommodate the overnight traveler and provide dinner."

The original house was built in 1805 and at one time was a drovers' inn. It is the oldest continuously operating inn on the mountaintop. Last year it was included in the Greene County Historical Society's tour of old Windham homes.

Pasture and woodlot accommodate a two-mile hiking trail, and a renovated loft in the barn furnishes even more recreation. Swimming and tennis facilities are also available.

Fertile fields, once a part of the prosperous farm, have been converted into a full-sized nine-hole golf course that borders the Batavia Kill and is adjacent to one of the mountains for which the Catskills are famous.

Breakfast includes pancakes or french toast with maple syrup made right from the trees on the property, among other things. Lunch and dinner are also offered.

CHRISTMAN'S WINDHAM HOUSE, Windham, N.Y. 12496; 518-734-4230. A 38-bedroom 19th-century Greek Revival inn in the northern Catskill Mtns. Open from May 25 to Oct. 14, and Dec. 15 to April 1. Breakfast included with lodgings; lunch and dinner available. Swimming, tennis, 9-hole golf course, 2-mi. nature trail, pond for boating on grounds. Recreation room with pool table, ping-pong, etc. Windham ski area, horseback riding, backroading nearby. No pets. Stanley and Roberta Christman, Innkeepers.

Directions: From N.Y. Thruway take Exit 21. Turn west on Rte. 23 and continue to Windham.

For B&B rates, see Index.

82 VERMONT TERRACE
Tuckahoe, New York

Finally, at last, a bed-and-breakfast home ideally situated for the New York visitor who arrives by car, but does not want to deal with the hassle and frustration of New York City traffic!

Eighty-two Vermont Terrace is about a three-minute walk from the Crestwood Railroad Station and the trains that whizz into Grand Central in less than thirty minutes. They run approximately every half-hour all day, and less frequently, but consistently, until late in the evening. You could be entertained in New York and still catch the last train back. Baseball fans will be interested to know that Yankee Stadium in the Bronx is only twenty minutes away.

The area is residential to say the least, and Gloria Bantz and her husband, Norman, make you feel like a guest in their home. All of the Bantz children grew up leaving five bedrooms with three shared baths available, and so Norman and Gloria sensibly decided to bring the world to 82 Vermont Terrace. From conversations I had with their guests, they have been most successful.

Norman Bantz's full and copious breakfasts are highlighted by honey made right on the porch outside the big living room. Bees are kept in hives and guests always find them very interesting. They never bother anybody, and Norman entertains the guests with explanations about the care and feeding of bees. He's a master beekeeper.

Even if 82 Vermont Terrace was not wonderfully convenient for a thirty-minute commute to New York City, I would resoundingly extol its virtues. Others have, so be sure to make your reservations early.

82 VERMONT TERRACE, Tuckahoe, N.Y. 10707; 914-779-6411. A 5-bedroom bed-and-breakfast home (3 shared baths) within 30 min. by commuter train from Grand Central Station, New York City. A full breakfast is the only meal served, but there are good restaurants nearby. Also conveniently located for visits to Sarah Lawrence and Concordia Colleges and the Montefiore Hospital. Yankee Stadium nearby. No pets. Norman and Gloria Bantz, Proprietors.

Directions: This is not hard to find, but since it is accessible from all directions, please telephone the Bantzes for individual instructions.

For B&B rates, see Index.

THE FRIENDS LAKE INN
Chestertown, New York

Innkeepers Sharon and Greg Taylor explain that this once famous mountain hostelery was standing empty and forgotten when they found it.

These two ambitious young people are particularly well-suited to innkeeping because they're both quite capable of making major and minor repairs to the inn. They worked together on the considerable major rehabilitation and they also share the duties of the kitchen as well.

I was particularly impressed with the bright bedrooms overlooking the lake. They were furnished with gay wallpaper and typical Adirondack country-inn furniture, some of which had been gathered from older inns that had gone out of existence on Friends Lake. Sharon pointed out that one of the quilts belonged to her great grandmother.

Guests at the inn in the wintertime ski Gore Mountain or enjoy many miles of cross-country skiing. At other seasons there's rafting on the Hudson, climbing the nearby peaks, enjoying summer water sports on the lake, and especially long, quiet walks in the mountains.

There are fourteen bedrooms, some with lake views and some with shared bathrooms. The veranda across the front of the inn has a splendid view of the Adirondack scenery.

Although many of the guests will be staying under the modified American plan, bed-and-breakfast guests will also be welcome, and a hearty North Country breakfast is included in the room rate.

Besides a definite "back country" atmosphere at Friends Lake Inn, there's a feeling of youthful expectancy and optimism that radiates from both of the young, attractive innkeepers.

THE FRIENDS LAKE INN, Friends Lake Road, Chestertown, NY 12817; 518-494-4251. A 14-guestroom restored mountain inn (6 private baths) in the heart of the Adirondacks. Modified American plan; B&B rate available. Dinner served. Open most of the days of the year, but check ahead in late spring. All of the area's historic, natural, and cultural activities are within a convenient drive. No pets. No credit cards. Sharon and Greg Taylor, Innkeepers.

Directions: From the south: take Exit 23 from I-87. Go north 4 mi. on Rte. 9 to Rte. 28. Follow Rte. 28 to the Glen, 5 mi. Just before the Glen, turn right on Friends Lake Rd. The inn is 4 mi. ahead on the left. If you have any problems just ask someone. Everyone knows the Friends Lake Inn.

For B&B rates, see Index.

GARNET HILL LODGE
North River, New York

Garnet Hill Lodge is a rustic resort high in the Adirondack Mountains on 13th Lake, and is centered around the Log House which was built in 1936.

Lodgings are in individual bedrooms, very clean and neat; about half have private bathrooms.

There's a great deal of recreation and outdoor activity at Garnet Hill Lodge in all seasons of the year. In the wintertime the snow frequently is up to the roof of the porch. This encourages a great deal of cross-country skiing, snowshoeing, and downhill skiing nearby.

In summertime there is sailing, canoeing, fishing, swimming, backroading, and wonder walks in the woods where beaver, deer, hares, loons, blue herons, foxes, weasels, and raccoons share the sylvian confines.

Garnet Hill Lodge guests are served an Adirondack Mountain breakfast, which offers a choice of just about everything imaginable, including home-baked breads. The morning view from the dining room and porch is splendid.

For the traveler passing through the Adirondacks, Garnet Hill Lodge would make an excellent overnight stop. Fortunately, a most enticing dinner is also served.

GARNET HILL LODGE, 13th Lake Road, North River, N.Y. 12856; 518-251-2821. A 15-room rustic resort-inn high in the Adirondacks, 32 mi. from Warrensburg. Open year-round. Mod. American and European plans available. Breakfast, lunch, and dinner served to transients. Swimming, boating, hiking, fishing, and xc skiing on grounds. Downhill skiing, long-distance hikes, and beautiful Adirondack drives nearby. The area has many museums, arts and crafts centers, and historical points. No pets. No credit cards. Taxi service provided to bus stop 30 mi. away. George and Mary Heim, Innkeepers.

Directions: From the Northway (I-87) take Exit 23 and follow Rtes. 9 and 28 north 4 mi. Take left fork (Rte. 28) 22 mi. to North River. Take second left (13th Lake Road) 5 mi. to Lodge. For more explicit directions, write for brochure.

For B&B rates, see Index.

GILL HOUSE INN
Henderson Harbor, New York

After visiting the Gill House Inn on the eastern shore of Lake Ontario, I discovered that most of my notes dealt with the excellent lunch I had enjoyed, particularly the freshly caught perch fried in Gill House batter. It is one of several traditions at this old 1813 inn; another of which is chicken and biscuits on Sunday.

With the extensive luncheon and dinner menu, plus all of the recreational advantages at lakeside, I would see it as a place to stay for several nights.

Fishing is certainly one of the main diversions, and bass, steelhead, and brown trout, along with several other of the finny denizens offer the greatest sport. Fishing guides can be arranged at the inn, and watery excursions are taken to nearby islands where box lunches or shore dinners supplied by the inn can be enjoyed in pleasant solitude.

One of the most difficult things I've had to do this past year was to leave the sun-drenched Gill House Inn instead of going for a swim or a sail. It was mid-July and the weather was ideal.

GILL HOUSE INN, Henderson Harbor, N.Y. 13651; 315-938-5013. A 12-bedroom lakeside inn on the eastern shore of Lake Ontario, south of Watertown, New York. All private baths. Breakfast, lunch and dinner served daily. Open from April 1 to Oct. 30. Waterside recreational facilities available. David and Leah McCrea, Innkeepers.

Directions: From I-81 take Exit 40 (Ellisberg). Continue west to Rte. 3, turn right and continue on to Henderson Harbor. Gill House is through the village, on the lakeside. It is easily identifiable by an outdoor reproduction of a sailboat with a mainsail and a jib.

For Lodging rates, see Index.

THE GOULD
Seneca Falls, New York

For many years I have strongly recommended Route 20 as an alternate east-west route in New York State. It passes through some of the most verdant farm country in North America and the region is blessed with a rich history and many pleasant diversions for the traveler.

One of the more interesting communities is Seneca Falls, famed as the birthplace of women's suffrage—the First Women's Rights Convention was held there in 1848. Two of America's leading suffragettes, Elizabeth Cady Stanton and Amelia Bloomer lived there, and it is the home of the newly created, "National Women's Hall of Fame," currently honoring women of the past and present for their contributions to the arts, athletics, education, government, the humanities, philanthropy, and science.

For years there wasn't a place to stay in Seneca Falls, but now Mr. and Mrs. George Souhan have opened the Gould, on the corner of State Street and Route 20.

The entrance is through a revolving door. To the right is a formal dining room and on the left is the local pub. There's lots of decorative glass, still another low-ceilinged, less-formal dining room with some original paintings.

There are five suites and two bedrooms and baths available for accommodations. Furnishings are a blend of textured woods, contemporary wall-hangings, Picasso posters, rather gaily colored pillows, and a contemporary feeling that belies the basic exterior of the Gould. There are telephones, cable TV, and air conditioning. Continental breakfast is provided at an additional nominal charge.

I was delighted to find the Gould, and I'm quite enthusiastic about the opportunity it provides the pleasure and business traveler for overnight or longer stays in this quiet, conservative, western New York village.

THE GOULD, 108 Fall St., Seneca Falls, NY 13148; 315-568-5801. A small restored hotel with 5 suites and 2 guestrooms (private baths). Open year-round. Breakfast is available at an additional cost. Lunch and dinner served throughout the week. Dining room closed Christmas Day and 4th of July. Very convenient for drives in the wine country and visits to many of the Finger Lakes. Just a few miles from the New York State Thruway. Not suitable for children under 12. Mr. and Mrs. George Souhan, Innkeepers.

Directions: Seneca Falls is between Auburn and Buffalo on Rte. 20.

For rates, see Index.

GREENVILLE ARMS
Greenville, New York

The Greenville Arms is located in the foothills of the northern Catskill Mountains and has been operated by the Stevens family for thirty years. It is a Victorian country home, with several interesting porches, cupolas, gables, and hidden corners. The grounds are well shaded with tall trees and beautifully landscaped with bushes and shrubs. The atmosphere here can best be described as homey and inviting.

Across the stream behind the main building, there is a large, beautiful lawn with a swimming pool, swings, and lawn games. The inn's carriage house, with nine bedrooms and a spacious living room, overlooks the pool area. During the summer, horses graze in a nearby pasture.

The inn is open spring, summer, and fall with trout fishing, hiking, bicycling, golf, tennis, horseback riding, antiquing, and country auctions nearby. Its location in the Hudson River Valley provides the perfect opportunity to explore a region rich in history and in natural beauty.

Guests who enjoy walnut and strawberry pancakes with locally made maple syrup, eggs Benedict, or special omelets are in for a real treat.

GREENVILLE ARMS, Greenville, NY 12083; 518- 966-5219. A 20-guestroom Victorian country inn in the foothills of the northern Catskill Mountains, 25 mi. south of Albany, 120 mi. north of New York City. Modified American or bed-and-breakfast rates available mid-April through mid-Nov. Children are welcome. Pets accommodated in nearby kennels. No credit cards. Laura and Barbara Stevens, Innkeepers.

Directions: Exit NY Thrwy. at 21B (Coxsackie-New Baltimore). Turn left on 9W south 2 mi. to traffic light. Turn right on Rte. 81W 13 mi. to Greenville. Turn left at traffic light. Inn is second house on right. Via Taconic Pkwy., exit at Ancram on Rte. 82W over Rip Van Winkle Bridge and follow Rte. 23 to Cairo. Turn right on 32N, 9 mi. to Greenville.

For B&B rates, see Index.

HILLSIDE BED & BREAKFAST
Cazenovia, New York

The central New York State Finger Lakes district is well known to New York State residents, but is always a surprise to people from out of state. This unusual geography was created by the melting of the glaciers many millions of years ago, leaving many lakes, some of which are extinct. The result is that driving east and west on Route 20, there is a kind of roller coaster effect going up to the top of a hill and down into a valley.

Hillside Bed and Breakfast is a Cape Cod style house, just off Route 92 and close to Route 20, the scenic route through New York State.

It is comfortably furnished in Early American antiques and is open for guests the year 'round. There are hiking trails, beautiful views of the rolling hills, and cross-country skiing out the back door. Downhill skiing is just ten minutes away.

Cazenovia Lake is three miles east with public access areas, and Hillside offers canoe rentals and wind-surfing lessons with advance notice.

Merilyn Hill, the hostess, is a graduate of the Culinary Institute of America and she owns and operates her own catering service.

There are two upstairs bedrooms, both neat as a pin, sharing one bath. One is a twin-bedded room with very pleasant white quilts and the other has a double bed with stenciling on the walls.

HILLSIDE BED & BREAKFAST, P.O. Box 47, Cazenovia, NY 13035; 315-655-3033 or 655-9881. A 2-guestroom (shared bath) most comfortable bed-and-breakfast home a few miles from Cazenovia, New York. Breakfast is included in the room rate and is the only meal served. Open year-round. Hiking trails, xc skiing on premises. Downhill skiing, tennis, lake swimming and other seasonal recreation nearby. No credit cards. No pets. Merilyn Hill, Hostess.

Directions: From Cazenovia go west on Rte. 20. At end of lake turn right to Rte. 92 north. Go 3.3 mi. and take left at Bethel Rd. Hillside Bed & Breakfast is first house on left.

For B&B rates, see Index.

HOUSE ON THE HILL
High Falls, New York

The Catskill Mountains as a resort and vacation area came into their own during the last part of the 19th century, although artists, as well as people fascinated with the outdoors, discovered it much earlier.

The area is quite extensive and offers year-round recreation, including skiing, swimming, golfing, fishing, and hunting. The Catskills have hosted and entertained visitors for generations, and of course are already a legend in their own time as the proving grounds for many of today's entertainers.

In that sense, High Falls, New York, in Ulster County is quite different from the Catskill image. Located on Route 213, going from Rosendale to Stone Ridge, on the banks of Roundout Creek and the Delaware and Hudson Canal, High Falls has a few stores, but nothing flashy. The well-known Depuy Canal House is here.

The House on the Hill fits right into this ambience, set back in its own little park of evergreens and maples. It's possible to sit on the front porch of an afternoon and watch the occasional car on the highway. Guests' bedrooms are on the second floor and feature some very handsome quilts that came from southern Illinois where Sharon Glassman grew up. There is one bathroom for four of the country-style bedrooms, and the fifth room has a private bath.

Shelly Glassman is in charge of breakfast, which features crêpes and different treatments of eggs, depending on Shelly's mood, and is served in the farmhouse dining room in a little glassed-in corner in summer, or in the rustic country kitchen with expansive seasonal views.

The spacious grounds also include a duck pond complete with ducks, as well as a badminton set and a barbecue for guests who like to do their own.

HOUSE ON THE HILL, Box 86, Route 213, High Falls, N.Y. 12440; 914-687-9627. A 5-bedroom guest house circa 1825 in the middle of a pleasant Hudson Valley hamlet. Five bedrooms share two baths. Open year-round for bed-and-breakfast from Thurs. night through Sun. night. Walk to antique shops, swimming, and gourmet dining at the Depuy Canal House and Top of the Falls restaurants. No credit cards. Sharon and Shelly Glassman, Innkeepers.

Directions: From New York State Thruway use Exit 18 (New Paltz). Turn left on 299 into New Paltz and right on 32 north to Rosendale, then left on 213 to High Falls.

For B&B rates, see Index.

LINCKLAEN HOUSE
Cazenovia, New York

Let's assume that the gentle reader is preparing to take his tenth or twelfth trip across central New York State between Albany and Rochester or Buffalo on the Thruway, a highway of considerable convenience, but hardly inspiring.

An alternate suggestion would be to follow Route 20 which runs parallel to the Thruway, but about ten miles to the south, and passes through some very attractive and appealing New York State towns and villages, including Cazenovia, right on the edge of the Finger Lakes District.

Here, the traveler will find the Lincklaen House, built in 1835 as a luxurious stopover for the travelers of the day, and named for the founder of Cazenovia.

The main floor has high ceilings with handsome geometrically carved moldings, painted wood panels, and impressive Williamsburg chandeliers. There are three huge fireplaces on the ground floor—the colonial source of winter heat.

Guest bedrooms are about as far from the conventional motel as one could imagine, and there is a wide variety of sizes and styles available on the second and third floors.

Arrival in the late afternoon is particularly fortuitous because houseguests are invited by the innkeeper, Helen Tobin, to be her guest at afternoon tea with some homemade cookies served in front of a blazing hearth.

The traveler may also enjoy dinner in the elegant dining room.

Breakfasts are served in a very sunny terrace room whose walls have been thoughtfully adorned with watercolors.

LINCKLAEN HOUSE, Cazenovia, N.Y. 13035; 315-655-3461. A 27-room village inn, 20 mi. east of Syracuse. European plan. Modified American plan upon request. Breakfast, lunch, afternoon tea, and dinner served to travelers daily. Open year-round. Near several state parks, the Erie Canal Museum and the Canal Trail. Tennis, golf, bicycles, alpine and xc skiing nearby. Helen Tobin, Innkeeper.

Directions: From west on N.Y. Thruway, take Exit 34A, follow Rte. 481 south, take Exit 3E and follow Rte. 92 east to Cazenovia. From east on N.Y. Thruway, take Exit 34 and follow Rte. 13 south to Cazenovia. From Rte. 81, take Exit 15 (LaFayette) and follow Rte. 20 east, 18 mi. to inn.

For B&B rates, see Index.

THE MERRILL MAGEE HOUSE
Warrensburg, New York

Although for years a well-kept secret shared only by a privileged few, the Adirondack Mountains in New York State are fast becoming the focus of many vacationers who are seeking out some of the few areas that have not been discovered.

Interstate 87 (the Northway) carries the expectant traveler deep into the heart of the Adirondacks, and Warrensburg, just above Lake George, is a small town that provides a view of some of the unique architectural features and folkways of this vast natural area.

Tucked behind a very high white picket fence, the Merrill Magee House, literally beside the bandstand in the middle of the village, is much the same today as a century ago. The house abounds with lovely antiques, original wallpapers, glowing fireplaces, and a most inviting atmosphere.

Luncheon and dinner are served here, and one of the Carrington children (there are six) is the chef.

There is a tiny, proper English pub connected with the inn, which is most appropriate because Mr. Carrington is English.

One of the most welcome surprises is a swimming pool in one corner of the parklike grounds.

THE MERRILL MAGEE HOUSE, at the Bandstand, 2 Hudson St., Warrensburg, NY 12885; 518-623-2449. A 3-guestroom village inn (sharing 1 bath) at the southern gateway to the Adirondacks. Breakfast included in room rate. Lunch and dinner served daily. Dining room open daily during July and Aug.; closed Mon. the rest of the year. Open year-round. Swimming pool on grounds. Convenient to all of the Adirondack area's natural and cultural attractions, including hiking, golf, boating, fishing, Saratoga Raceway, and major downhill and xc ski areas. No pets. The Carrington Family, Innkeepers.

Directions: From I-87 take Exit 23, proceed on Rte. 9 to middle of town. The inn is on the left.

For B&B rates, see Index.

THE MEWS
Cold Spring-On-Hudson, New York

The village of Cold Spring was a very small, sleepy village on the east bank of the Hudson until 1818 when the West Point Foundry opened and brought with it hundreds of new settlers from the Old World.

Through all the changing times, Cold Spring is unique among the Hudson River communities in having retained its fundamental character by adapting to the needs of the present while carefully preserving its heritage and way of life.

A walking tour booklet contains 28 points of interest that can be reached by walking from The Mews, which is a very stylish guest house located about two pleasant blocks from the bandstand.

The proprietor at The Mews is Jack Kelly, who has been a man of many careers and triumphs, and in many ways brings them all to fruition here in this very pleasant atmosphere.

At the time of my visit there were two bedrooms, each with its own bath. The front room is very *chic* and Mr. Kelly's eclectic tastes are demonstrated everywhere. The other bedroom is L-shaped with a working corner fireplace; the walls are papered in a paisley pattern with matching drapes.

The kitchen, where Jack himself prepares the full breakfasts, is done in beautifully selected, mellowed barn siding. There's a big oak table which invites second or third cups of coffee and lots of good conversation.

THE MEWS, 73 Main Street, Cold Spring-on-Hudson, N.Y. 10516; 914-265-3727. A 2-room bed-and-breakfast inn located in a very pleasant out-of-the-way Hudson River community, almost opposite West Point. Open every day in the year. Conveniently situated for visits to Boscobel Restoration, Manitoba Nature Conservatory, and the Putnam County Historical Society. Bear Mountain and Fahnestock ski areas and cross-country skiing nearby. Jack Kelly, Innkeeper.

Directions: From New York City, cross the George Washington Bridge, follow the Palisades Parkway in New Jersey across Bear Mountain Bridge and turn north on Rte. 9D to Cold Spring. From Albany: leave Taconic Parkway at Rte. 301 and follow it west to Cold Spring.

For B&B rates, see Index.

THE MILL-GARTH
Amagansett, New York

There really is a windmill at the Mill-Garth, although it is a smaller replica of the original one built in 1797 that was destroyed by fire.

This 19th-century farmhouse and surrounding five secluded cottages have been turned into homey, but sophisticated, accommodations. Just a short distance from the ocean, on a quiet country road, the bucolic setting is complete with spacious lawns, beautiful trees, ivy-covered fences, and many flowers.

All of the rooms are handsomely furnished, and each has its own fully equipped kitchen. The cottages have such names as the Dairy House, which has a studio living room with a skylight; the Gazebo, octagonally shaped, with a paneled living room and dining area; the Carriage House, with a fireplace and a studio living room that opens out on a private patio.

One of the vacation villages a little beyond the Hamptons on Long Island, Amagansett is most conveniently situated for fishing, boating, golfing, antiquing, and walking on the beaches.

I was delighted to discover that the Mill-Garth has an additional advantage: it is open all year, and this part of Long Island can be especially attractive during the spring and fall. In winter it is a perfect hideaway for a weekend. It is necessary to reserve minimum stays of seven days during July and August. I'd make reservations for those periods as early in the year as possible.

THE MILL-GARTH, Windmill Lane, Amagansett, L.I., N.Y. 11930; 516-267-3757. A splendid 11-apartment hideaway just north of Montauk Highway in one of outer Long Island's most historic villages. Each accommodation has its own kitchen. Open year-round. Very convenient for all of the outer Long Island cultural and recreational attractions. Burton and Wendy Van Deusen, Proprietors.

Directions: Turn left off Montauk Hwy. (Rte. 27) upon entering Amagansett. It is plainly marked.

For Lodging rates, see Index.

THE MILLHOF INN
Stephentown, New York

Travelers on Route 22 to upper N.Y. State have to digress only a few miles to stop here. The word "millhof" really means millhouse and this building which is located in Stephentown, New York right on the Massachusetts-New York State border, was actually used as a sawmill for many years.

Innkeepers Frank and Ronnie Tallet have made numerous alterations and additions, but the basic structure remains the same, and with its hand-carved and colorfully decorated railings and window shutters it is similar to many small *pensions* that I have visited, particularly in Germany's Black Forest.

The European Alpine theme extends throughout the inn and particularly to the lodging rooms, each of which is individually decorated and furnished with plants, books, and magazines.

Additional enticement at the Millhof is its inviting swimming pool and the fact that there is hiking, skiing, backroading, and all of the famous Berkshire recreational attractions nearby, including the Tanglewood Music Festival each summer.

The Europa Dining Room or the Garden Deck, depending upon the weather, is where guests enjoy a full à la carte breakfast, including homemade jams, stoneground wheat cakes, omelets, and and other things from the garden in season.

THE MILLHOF INN, Route 43, Stephentown, N.Y. 12168; 518-733-5606. A 10-room central-European-style country inn. 14 mi. from Pittsfield, Mass., and 12 mi. from Williamstown, Mass., on the NY/Mass. border. European plan. (Breakfast not included in room rate.) In wintertime, breakfast is served every morning, and dinner is served on the weekends and during holiday weeks by reservation; breakfast and lunch are served daily during the summer to guests only. Open every day from May 26 through March 31. Swimming pool on grounds. Hiking, skiing, backroading, and all of the famous Berkshire recreational and cultural attractions nearby. No pets. Frank and Ronnie Tallet, Innkeepers.

Directions: From New York: exit the Taconic Parkway on Rte. 295. Travel east to Rte. 22 north. Turn east at Stephentown on Rte. 43. The inn is one mile on the left. From Boston: exit Mass. Turnpike at New Lebanon. North on Rte. 22 to Rte. 43, etc.

For Lodging rates, see Index.

RAM'S HEAD INN
Shelter Island, New York

Situated at the far eastern end of Long Island, Shelter Island, when observed on the map, looks like a tasty morsel of lobster or fish about to be devoured by a crocodile. More recently, it's been discovered by the "B&B" crowd from the City who have found that it is very convenient to drive or take the train to Greenport on the north fork and enjoy a few days or a weekend while walking the beaches, playing tennis, and roaming through the town.

If walking the beaches is something that appeals to you, then it will be of interest to note that the Ram's Head Inn has 800 feet of its own beachfront and even has two 13-foot sloops and a rowboat for guests to enjoy.

This old center-hall Colonial is located away from "downtown Shelter Island," and there is a terrace, dining room, and lounge overlooking Coecles Harbor. Among the other amenities are a tennis court and most pleasant harbor. Many times, boats pull in at the moorings, which are on a first-come first-serve basis. Although no lunch service is provided, the evening meal is available.

The proprietors are Linda and James Eklund, who acquired the property a few years ago and slowly have been redecorating and reestablishing it. Located on Big Ram Island, which is negotiated by a very pleasant little causeway, the Ram's Head Inn is the only commercial property in the area.

RAM'S HEAD INN, Ram Island, Shelter Island, N.Y. 11965; 516-749-0811. A 17-bedroom conventional inn (4 are suites), private and semi-private baths. Continental breakfast included with room. Open early May to late Oct.; weekends only to mid-June. There is a 2-night minimum stay on weekends and 3-night minimum on holiday weekends. Tennis, sailing, and beach on grounds. Ocean and bay swimming; bicycles available nearby. Linda and James Eklund, Innkeepers.

Directions: Proceed to the north fork of Long Island's east end by car or train. Take ferry from Greenport to Shelter Island, then follow Rte. 114 south, past Mobil gas station. Make left turn on Winthrop Rd.; right turn on Cobbets Lane to dead end. Left turn, then first right over causeway to inn. Guests arriving by train can be picked up at ferry.

For B&B rates, see Index.

THE REDCOAT'S RETURN
Tannersville, New York

When Tom and Peggy Wright took over the Redcoat's Return in the fall of 1972 they converted it into an English country inn. Tom, originally from London, has not only been the chef, turning out prime ribs with Yorkshire pudding, poached fillet of sole, roast duck a l'orange, steak and kidney pie, but also the carpenter, enlarging rooms and adding bathrooms. "I would stop hammering and sawing," he said, "and run downstairs and check the sauce and test the roast."

The Redcoat's Return is in the center of the Catskill Game Reserve. There is a wealth of recreational activities available to the guests in every season of the year. Activities include hiking trails, golf, swimming, tennis, and horseback riding nearby. There's downhill skiing in Cortina Valley, Hunter Mountain Ski Bowl, and Windham Mountain.

There are twelve rooms, all of them with wash basins—and the changes have now provided private bathrooms for several more rooms.

There's no skimping on breakfast here—it starts off with fresh orange juice and several different choices including blueberry pancakes, french toast, and any style of eggs with bacon or sausage.

THE REDCOAT'S RETURN, Dale Lane, Elka Park, N.Y. 12427; 518-589-6379. A 12-room English inn approx. 4 mi. from Tannersville, N.Y., in the heart of the Catskill Mts. Within a short drive of several ski areas and state hiking trails. European plan. Lodgings include breakfast. Dinner served daily except Thursdays; no lunches served. Open from Memorial Day to Easter. Closed 3 wks. in Nov.; reopen for Thanksgiving and winter season. Please call for details. Hiking, nature walks, trout fishing, croquet, skiing, swimming, golf, ice skating, riding, tennis nearby. Tom and Peggy Wright, Innkeepers.

Directions: From N.Y. Thruway, going north, use Exit 20; going south, use Exit 21. Follow 23A to Tannersville; turn left at traffic light onto Country Road 16. Follow signs to Police Center, 4½ mi. Turn right on Dale Lane.

For B&B rates, see Index.

ROYCROFT INN
East Aurora, New York

It had been some years since my last visit to the Roycroft Inn, and as soon as I arrived on what is known as the Roycroft campus, I discovered many very pleasant surprises.

The Roycroft concept was actually the inspiration of Elbert Hubbard, writer, lecturer, innovator, philosopher, and author of *A Message to Garcia*. In 1895, Mr. Hubbard brought skilled artisans together at Roycroft. These "Roycrofters" became famous for their printing, book binding, leather crafts, text illumination, modeling, hand-wrought metal and furniture, and their products were sold worldwide until 1938 when Roycroft was closed.

The spirit behind the Roycroft renaissance is Kitty Turgeon, who has rekindled the entire Roycroft feeling, not only by restoring many of the crafts and artisans' shops, but also in the renewal of the Roycroft Inn.

It is in the inn that our interest lies at this time. Oriental rugs have been placed in the main dining rooms where snowy white linens cover the tables, accented by bright red napkins. Lovely centerpieces have been fashioned in the Roycroft shops and various other decorative features bear the traditional Roycroft symbol. Many of the handsome pieces of Roycroft furniture owned by people in the community have been returned to the inn, and much restoration has been done to beautify and preserve the elegant atmosphere.

All of this has been woven into the Roycroft Inn by Kitty and Robert Rust, who shares her great enthusiasm and love for things Roycroft.

There are seventeen bedrooms, some with shared baths; many with the distinctive Roycroft furniture, which has increased in value considerably during the past few years. A complimentary continental breakfast is served to inn guests. Luncheon and dinner are served every day.

ROYCROFT INN, East Aurora, NY 14052; 716-652-9030. A 17-guestroom (most with private baths) village inn. Continental breakfast is included with the room rate. Lunch and dinner served daily. Closed Christmas Eve. Convenient to enjoy all of the Roycroft arts and crafts including antiques, galleries, weavers shop, blacksmith shop, and a splendid Roycroft gift shop. No pets. Kitty Turgeon, Innkeeper.

Directions: Going west on the New York State Thruway, take the Benbrook exit. Go south on Rte. 77 to Rte. 20A (18 mi.). Turn west into the main street of East Aurora and proceed to the inn.

For B&B rates, see Index.

SEAFIELD HOUSE
Westhampton Beach, New York

If you have a trip to the outer end of Long Island in mind, may I suggest that you put off your excursion until after the summer season is over? The traffic in and out of the city can be absolutely murderous in midsummer, and restaurants and other attractions are unusually crowded.

It is only a coincidence that Seafield House, a bed and breakfast in Westhampton Beach, is open from September 15 until May 15. It is a beautiful home, lovingly preserved by Mrs. Elsie Collins, filled with her antiques and personal touches that include Victorian lounges, a caned rocker, hurricane lamps, an antique pine apothecary chest, Shaker benches, Chinese and English porcelain, and other eclectic furnishings harmonized to create the casual, country-inn atmosphere.

The three bedrooms are all attractively furnished and all have handmade coverlets and quilts. Most of the rooms have private baths.

Mrs. Collins' full breakfast includes homemade coffee cake and fresh-squeezed orange juice. When guests check in there is a glass of wine or a cup of hot tea or coffee waiting for them, and when they leave, they always get a little loaf of cranberry bread or a jar of jelly.

There is plenty to do in Westhampton during the off-season, including visiting museums, bird watching, beach walking, antiquing; and indoor tennis courts and Guerney's International health Spa are an hour away.

SEAFIELD HOUSE, 2 Seafield Lane, Westhampton Beach, N.Y. 11978; 516-288-1559. A 3-bedroom pleasant private home converted to bed-and-breakfast accommodations between Sept. 15 and May 15, when breakfast is the only meal offered. Swimming pool and tennis court on grounds and ample opportunity for outdoor recreation nearby. No credit cards. No pets. Mrs. Elsie Collins, Hostess.

Directions. From New York City take L.I. Expy. to Wm. Floyd Pkwy. and proceed to Rte. 27 and Sunrise Hwy. to Westhampton. Take a right turn to Six Corners (2nd traffic light) then make a left on Mill Rd. to end, which is Main St. Another left on Main St., and Seafield Lane is second street on right.

For B&B rates, see Index.

THE SEDGWICK INN
Berlin, New York

Those of us who live within a pleasant drive of the Sedgwick Inn think of it as an excellent place for lunch or dinner; however, the traveler on Route 22 is very pleasantly surprised to find that this inn also has some excellent bed-and-breakfast accommodations.

The inn is situated on twelve acres in the beautiful Taconic Valley on the western side of the Berkshire Mountains, and dates back to 1791 as a part of the Van Rensselaer land tract. Incidentally the indentures hang in the reception room of the Colonial main house.

The building has served as a stagecoach stop, a summer house for a prominent New York City family, and for many years was renowned in the area as the Ranch Tavern.

A part of this pleasant experience is the Antique Shop, housed in a beautiful one-room building designed in the neo- classic style of the early 19th century, dating back to 1834. An old carriage house has been converted into an art gallery where old prints, modern paintings, sculpture (including some by innkeeper, Edie Evans), and stained glass are on exhibit.

Breakfast, included in the room rate, is served on a glass enclosed dining porch facing an English garden.

The luncheon and dinner menus are short but appetizing. Three dinner entrées are offered, and the menu changes twice weekly, with such offerings as filet mignon, beef carbonnade, Yankee pot roast and sole Veronique. Area diners often speak glowingly of the soups and desserts.

THE SEDGWICK INN, Rte. 22, Berlin, NY 12022; 518-658-2334. A 5-guestroom (private baths) country inn almost midway between Tanglewood, Shaker Village, and Williamstown. European plan. Breakfast, lunch, and dinner served daily, except Mon. Open all year. Conveniently located to enjoy all of the recreational and cultural activities of the Berkshires. Motel accommodations also available. Bob and Edie Evans, Innkeepers.

Directions: The inn is located on Rte. 22 between Petersburg and Stephentown, New York.

For B&B rates, see Index.

THE 1770 HOUSE
East Hampton, Long Island, New York

East Hampton is one of the jewels of outer Long Island. Its sedate streets arched overhead with swaying trees and the beautiful colonial homes and well-ordered and fashionable shops have an ambience of their very own. The John Drew Theater, which is open for much of the year, is one of the oldest and most prestigious in the Northeast. One of the most enjoyable experiences is to visit during the winter months and dress warmly to walk the broad beaches and thrill to the surf.

My place to stay in East Hampton is the 1770 House, kept by Miriam and Sid Perle, along with their son, Adam, and wife Pat, and their daughter and son-in-law, Wendy and Burton Van Deusen.

The house has 18th-century origins and has served over the years as a general store, a dining hall for boys from the Clinton Academy next door, a private home, and a public inn. Today the wood-paneled library with its cozy fireplace offers a very pleasant meeting place for guests, and the six guest rooms are furnished with good antiques and have wide-plank floors and a homelike atmosphere.

By all means plan to arrive in time for dinner, but be certain that you've made a reservation. The menu features a complete meal with the exception of dessert, and main courses are a good showcase for Miriam's considerable talents. She conducted a cooking school for twelve years.

Continental breakfast has some of her homemade baked goods including biscuits, scones, coffee cakes, and brioches served in the dining room in the winter, and on the patio underneath the apple trees when the weather permits.

1770 HOUSE, 143 Main St., East Hampton, Long Island, N.Y. 11937; 516-324-1770. An elegant 7-room village inn near the eastern end of Long Island. Open all year. Dinner served Fri. thru Wed. in season; Fri. and Sat. off-season. Minimum stays of 3 and 4 days required in July and Aug. Convenient to many cultural and recreational diversions, including antiquing and backroading. Available by public transportation; consult innkeepers. Not comfortable for children under 14. No pets. The Perle Family, Innkeepers.

Directions: From New York City: take the Long Island Expressway to Exit 70, and then turn south to Rte. 27 East, which is the main street of East Hampton. The inn is located diagonally across the street from Guild Hall.

For B&B rates, see Index.

SHADOWBROOK FARM
Canaan, New York

The milk couldn't be anything but fresh with 130 registered Jerseys in the barn just down the hill. And farm breakfasts were never like Carol Benson's: Finnish or blueberry pancakes, french toast, sausage quiche, fruits in season, homemade strawberry or cranberry breads, blueberry, sunshine, bran muffins. "I enjoy doing breakfasts," Carol told me, "and I like my guests to feel well fed before I send them off for the day."

Well fed and well cared for are guests here in this sparkling, cozy little B&B. A living-dining area has two comfortable loveseats in front of a raised brick hearth with a Franklin stove, and a dining table beside a window overlooking a garden. The plants, bookcases, oriental rugs, shuttered windows, and other adornments create an interesting, lived-in feeling.

Three second-floor bedrooms are immaculate and bright with pretty wallpapers, double and twin beds with down comforters, country curtains, and on each bed special soap and a stack of nice, thick towels.

Opening the sliding glass door near the dining area, Carol led me out past a little brick patio with an umbrella-covered table and up a short incline to the swimming pool, where guests can enjoy a cooling splash or loll in the sun, soaking up the country air.

With 160 acres of rolling hills, woodland, and a brook, there's no end of nature walks in the summer and cross-country skiing in the winter, right from the back door.

SHADOWBROOK FARM, Rte. 5, Canaan, NY 12029; 518-794-9624. A 3-guestroom (shared bath) cozy, immaculate B&B in the rolling country of Lebanon Valley on the western edge of the Berkshires. Breakfast only meal served, but many restaurants nearby. Open year-round. Swimming pool, nature walks, xc skiing on grounds. MacHayden Theater, Old Chatham Shaker Museum, Empire State Plaza, SUNY campus in Albany, as well as all Berkshire attractions, and downhill ski areas within an easy drive. No pets. No credit cards. Advance reservations necessary. Carol and Tom Benson, Hosts.

Directions: From NYC, take the Taconic Pkwy. to Rte. 295 east. Turn left in Canaan at Columbia County Rte. 5, continue 3 mi. to Shadowbrook Farm on left. From the east, Mass. Tpke. to Rte. 22 north. Turn left at Rte. 295 west, turning right in Canaan at County Rte. 5, continue 3 mi.

For B&B rates, see Index.

THE SHERWOOD INN
Skaneateles, New York

Skaneateles, New York, located on Route 20 at the head of one of the Finger Lakes bearing the same name, is one of the beauty spots of New York State. The exceptionally pure water makes it ideal for all summer sports. On the Fourth of July and Labor Day weekend the scene is considerably enlivened by sailing regattas.

The Sherwood Inn overlooks the waters of the lake, and all but just a few of the fifteen bedrooms enjoy the inspiring view. The Honeymoon Suite is decorated in shades of blue, the pattern of the quilt on the four-poster canopied bed matches both the draperies and the wallpaper.

Breakfast is served in the cheerful lobby of the inn whose broad windows also overlook the ever-changing scene on the Lake. Besides the ever-present coffee pot, there is orange juice, hot homemade muffins and breads and a choice of breakfast beverages.

Travelers moving across New York State on the New York Thruway would do well to turn onto Route 20 and enjoy a restful evening and happy stay at the Sherwood Inn in Skaneateles.

THE SHERWOOD INN, 26 West Genesee St., Skaneateles, N.Y. 13152; 315-685-3405. A 15-room village inn on the shores of Lake Skaneateles in the Finger Lakes district of New York State. Continental breakfast included in room tariff. Lunch and dinner served daily to travelers. Open every day except Christmas. Tennis, swimming, golf, and indoor winter ice skating available nearby. Near Everson Museum, Barrow Art Gallery, and William Seward House. Francis Lee, Innkeeper.

Directions: From New York State Thruway use Weedsport exit and follow Rte. 34 south to Auburn (6 mi.). Turn east on Rte. 20, 7 mi. to Skaneateles. Inn is located in center of village.

For B&B rates, see Index.

SOUTH MEADOW FARM LODGE
Lake Placid, New York

If you're into cross-country skiing in the winter and lots of walking, hiking, backroading, reading, talking, eating, and general jollification in summer, then Betty and Harry Eldridge and their daughter Anne, their twin daughters Katie and Noni, and son Alan at the South Meadow Farm Lodge are certainly for you.

The first person I met was Alan and he couldn't have been more accommodating, showing me through their very fascinating home that is dominated by a common room with a cathedral ceiling, soaring windows, and a huge fireplace. Some of the bedrooms are located in a loft underneath the rafters of this most impressive room, and there are curtains between them, but no walls. There are two conventional bedrooms also available.

There are lots of windows, and throughout the house there's a wonderful feeling for textures and gay colors. It's the kind of house in which two people make it possible for their four children to be alert and tuned in to the world of ideas. There is a loom in one corner, a piano, stacks of games in another, magazines of all kinds, at least three cats, and much more.

Olympic cross-country ski trails cross the farm and they are excellent for skiers, runners, and walkers. Harry, an enthusiastic licensed Adirondack guide,is available for treks into the High Peaks region.

The full farm breakfast is included in the price of the lodging. Dinner is also available, and it is whatever the family is having.

SOUTH MEADOW FARM LODGE, Cascade Rd., Lake Placid, N.Y. 12946; 518-523-9369. A 5-bedroom contemporary farm-lodge in the Adirondacks with Olympic cross-country ski trails crossing the property. Shared bath. Open year-round. Closed Christmas. Full breakfast included with lodgings. Family-style dinner available. Within minutes of Cascade Mt. and Marcy Mt. trails; ½ mi. east of Olympic bobsled and luge runs. Excellent cross-country skiing, snowshoeing, hiking, nature walks, running, swimming on grounds and nearby. Betty and Harry Eldridge, Lodgekeepers.

Directions from N.Y.C.—Leave Northway (I-87) at Exit 30 and follow signs to Lake Placid. (Rte. 73.) 7 miles west of Keene, look for pale blue sign on left for South Meadow Farm Lodge and follow signs and dirt road. The lodge, a gray contemporary building, is visible from the turn.

For B&B rates, see Index.

SPRINGSIDE INN
Auburn, New York

One of the most pleasant journeys in New York State is along Route 20, which runs between Albany and Buffalo, and one of the places to stop on the "B&B route" is the Springside Inn in Auburn, New York, at the head of Owasco Lake, one of the prettiest of the Finger Lakes.

This area is rich in entertainment and recreation of all kinds in all seasons. Fall foliage is reflected in the crystal waters of the lake and there is a variety of scenic roads and picturesque vantage points. Waterfalls, State parks, historical homes, and much history is woven into the fabric of nature's backdrop.

Each of the lodging rooms at the Springside Inn is decorated to give a different feeling. One is in shades of pink with a pink bedspread and matching curtains. A friendly rocking chair is in the front window overlooking the lake. Another room has twin beds, Victorian furniture, and lamps with red bows. A room on the top floor is done in shades of beige and yellow with formal valances at the window, a Tiffany-type lamp, hooked rugs, and twin beds.

Although the inn has attractive B&B rates, it is especially well known in the area as an excellent restaurant.

The porch and lounge, each of which shares a view of the placid pond in front of the inn, also provide an ideal setting for the continental breakfast, which might be homemade blueberry, apple, or zucchini muffins and assorted fruits. Breakfast is on a "help yourself" basis.

SPRINGSIDE INN, 41 West Lake Rd., Auburn, N.Y. 13021; 315-252-7247, A 7-room country inn, 1 mi. south of Auburn with a view of Owasco Lake. In the heart of the historical Finger Lakes. Lodgings include continental breakfast. Some rooms with shared bath. Open every day, except Christmas. Kitchen closed Memorial Day, July 4, and Labor Day. Boating, swimming, bicycles, golf, riding, alpine and xc skiing nearby. Bill Dove and Family, Innkeepers.

Directions: From N.Y. Thruway, take Exit 40 and follow Rte. 34 south through downtown Auburn to Rte. 38. Follow Rte. 38 south to traffic circle at lake and take 2nd exit right at West Shore of Oswasco Lake. Drive ¼ mi. to inn.

For B&B rates, see Index.

THE STAGECOACH INN
Lake Placid, New York

Here's a bed-and-breakfast inn whose owners have a show-business background. Peter Moreau is a playwright, actor, director, and producer. His wife Sherry is an actress. The inn is a fitting dramatic setting for two such interesting and vibrant people.

The only remaining Adirondack Mountain landmark from the romantic stagecoach days of the 19th century, the inn's dramatic cathedral-ceilinged living room, with its impressive fireplaces and posts and beams in yellow Adirondack birch, is furnished with interesting pieces that obviously belong.

The bedrooms have a wonderful "out of the woods" feeling and are extremely warm and comfortable. There are books everywhere and inviting rocking chairs on the broad front porch where one could read for hours.

Some very interesting and well-known guests have stayed at the inn, particularly during the 19th century, including the famed Adirondack photographer Seneca Ray Stoddard who spoke glowingly of his stay at the "North Elba Hotel," which was the name of the inn in those days. It was also a summer retreat for Chancellor James R. Day of Syracuse University.

Richard Henry Dana, the author of *Two Years Before The Mast* and *How We Met John Brown* also used the inn as a base when he visited the Adirondacks.

Visitors here can use the inn as a hub and enjoy the entire Adirondack State Park which embraces an area almost as large as the state of Vermont and has 46 mountain peaks over 4,000 feet high. Peter is well qualified to advise the novice hiker and walker about the many day-trips, including a visit to the various sites which were used in the recent Winter Olympics.

THE STAGECOACH INN, Old Military Rd., Lake Placid, N.Y. 12946; 518-523-9474. A 7-bedroom historic Adirondack inn (4 bedrooms share 2 baths). Open year-round. Conveniently located to enjoy all of the considerable recreational attractions in the Adirondack Mtns., including swimming, tennis, indoor ice skating, golf, hiking, walking, downhill and xc skiing. No credit cards. H. Peter Moreau, Innkeeper.

Directions: From the Northway follow Rte. 73 past the Olympic ski jumps and look for Old Military Rd. on the left.

For B&B rates, see Index.

SWISS HUTTE
Hillsdale, New York

This continental-type inn in a hidden Berkshire Valley on the New York-Massachusetts line is an ideal distance for leaving New York City late in the afternoon and arriving in time for dinner.

There are two kinds of accommodations available. One is in the main inn where there are country inn-type rooms. The other fifteen rooms are in chalet-type motel units, each with its own balcony and excellent view of the Catamount Ski Area which is literally a five-iron shot across the valley.

To those of us who live in this area, the Swiss Hutte is best known for its food. Both lunch and dinner are leisurely affairs with individually prepared dishes. The accent is on French cuisine.

Guests enjoy an à la carte breakfast of freshly squeezed orange juice, berries in season, homebaked bread and rolls, and various types of pancakes, eggs, bacon, ham, and sausage served on the porch, which has an intimate view of the meadows and mountains.

SWISS HUTTE, Hillsdale, N.Y. 12529; 518-325-3333. A 21-room Alpine country inn overlooking Catamount Ski Area, 6 mi. from Gt. Barrington, Mass. Modified American plan omits lunch. Breakfast, lunch, and dinner served to travelers daily. Closed month of April and from Nov. 15 to Dec. 15. Pool, tennis, putting green, Alpine and xc skiing on grounds. Tom and Linda Breen, Innkeepers.

Directions: From Boston, travel on Mass. Tpke. and take Exit 2. Follow Rte. 102 to Rte. 7. Proceed on Rte. 7 to Rte. 23. From New York City, follow Taconic Pkwy. and Rte. 23. From Albany, follow N.Y. Thruway and Taconic Pkwy. Inn is 10 mi. east of Pkwy. on Rte. 23.

For Lodging rates, see Index.

THREE VILLAGE INN
Stony Brook, Long Island, New York

The Three Village Inn is located in one of the most interesting and well-preserved towns in Long Island about sixty miles from New York City. It is only a few minutes from the SUNY campus (State University of New York) and is in the residential area of a very quiet, conservative, but unstuffy, community.

The building itself has a most interesting history. It was built during colonial times by an old Long Island family, and has green shutters and gay geraniums. Ivy climbs the narrow white clapboards and nearby trees.

Lodging rooms are located in the main building of the inn and in several attractive cottages that face the Stony Brook Yacht Club and a marina. This is a wonderful place to walk around, particularly after dark when the boats are quiet and gently rocking on the placid water.

The breakfast menu (not included in the lodging rates) has the usual eggs, bacon, sausage, ham, and so forth, as well as hot or cold cereals, muffins, and breakfast pastry. It is served in the dining room overlooking the water.

Incidentally, the Long Island railroad has a stop at Stony Brook and is just a pleasant walk to the front door of the Three Village Inn.

THREE VILLAGE INN, 150 Main St., Stony Brook, L.I., N.Y. 11790; 516-751-0555. A 13-room village inn with 19 adjacent cottage/motel accommodations, 5 mi. from Port Jefferson, N.Y., on Long Island's historic north shore. Near the museums of Stony Brook. European plan. Lunch and dinner served to travelers daily. Closed Christmas. Golf, swimming, and boating nearby. Accessible to the handicapped. No pets. Nelson, Whitney, and Monda Roberts, Innkeepers.

Directions: From L.I. Expressway, take Exit 62 and travel north on Nichols Rd. to Rte. 25A. Turn left on Rte. 25A and proceed to 2nd light. Turn right onto Main St., and travel straight ahead to inn. Available from New England via L.I. ferries from Bridgeport during the summer. Ferry reservations advisable. (N.Y.: 516-473-0286. Conn.: 203-367-8571.)

For Lodging rates, see Index.

THE WHITE INN
Fredonia, New York

Fredonia is a bustling little town, usually connected with nearby Dunkirk, a port on Lake Erie. It has a very pleasant town square with benches and trees and also a gazebo. Fredonia is the site of one of the several branches of the University of the State of New York, where many cultural and sporting events are open to the public.

Fredonia is basically a Victorian town, and slowly but surely the businesses on the main street are removing their modern facades and allowing the pure Victorian architecture underneath to shine forth. Part of the town is listed in the National Register of Historic Places.

Certainly the restoration of the White Inn is proving most beneficial to travelers and townsfolk alike.

The first thing I observed was a hundred-foot-long veranda on the front, shaded by two ancient maple trees planted in 1821 by one Squire White, for whom the inn has been named.

The inn is certainly the center of town activity. The two owners, David Palmer and David Bryant, philosophy teachers at the Fredonia State University, have put a great deal of time, effort, and money into this first-class renovation. David Palmer's wife, Nancy, who has a degree in art history from the University of North Carolina, is the decorator.

The bedrooms are light and airy and probably larger than average.

Incidentally, the White Inn was one of the charter members of the Duncan Hines organization many years ago, and today three dining rooms provide a congenial setting for all meals. Lunch and dinner are served seven days a week and hotel guests receive a complimentary breakfast.

The White Inn, just a few minutes from the New York State Thruway, will make an excellent overnight or even longer stay on the far reaches of western New York State.

THE WHITE INN, 52 East Main St., Scenic Rte. 20, Fredonia, NY 14063; 716-672-2103. A 20-guestroom village inn (all private baths) on the main street in Fredonia. Open every day, all year. Quite convenient for visits to nearby Chautauqua and other western New York State cultural and recreational attractions. No pets. David Palmer and David Bryant, Innkeepers.

Directions: From New York State Thwy. take Exit 59, follow Rte. 60 to Rte. 20; turn right to the inn.

For B&B rates, see Index.

THE BAIRD HOUSE
Mars Hill, North Carolina

This bed-and-breakfast inn has so many attractive features that I'm not quite sure what to mention first.

Supposing we start with breakfast. While we were rocking on the front porch overlooking a part of the campus of Mars Hill College, innkeeper Jeanne Hoffman explained that breakfast is sausage balls, apple fritters, orange juice, and coffee. It is served in the dining room, kitchen, or on the back terrace.

She was enthusiastic about the Southern Appalachia Repertory Theater, just a short distance away. They have a playwrights' conference here once a year and select a play for a world premiere. One play a year is on an Appalachian theme and the others are Broadway hits. During the summer it is a state theater, and during the remainder of the year the college drama department presents plays.

There are six guest rooms furnished and decorated in the traditional manner with poster beds and usable fireplaces. An inviting parlor provides the opportunity to visit with either Jeanne or her assistant innkeeper, Elizabeth Narron.

I'm delighted that Jeanne Hoffman wrote me a letter and that eventually I found my way to Mars Hill. Although it's the only place to stay in town, it would be a credit to any community.

BAIRD HOUSE, 121 Main St., Mars Hill, NC 28754; 704-689-5722 or 704-689-4542. A 6-guestroom (some shared baths) bed-and-breakfast accommodation in a quiet college town about 20 min. north of Asheville. Breakfast is included in the lodging rate and is the only meal served. Open year-round. Mars Hill is a convenient distance from Grandfather Mountain, Biltmore House and Gardens, the Appalachian Trail, the Great Smoky Mountains National Park, Mount Mitchell, and many other western North Carolina attractions. The area abounds in wonderful vacation opportunities. No credit cards. Jeanne Hoffman, Innkeeper.

Directions: Mars Hill is west of Rte. 19-23, which runs north out of Asheville. Turn towards town center and watch for sign to turn left for Baird House at the first light.

For B&B rates, see Index.

BLUE BOAR LODGE
Robbinsville, North Carolina

This is truly an unusual experience. Originally built as a hunting lodge, it is reached by a dirt road that runs for some distance alongside Lake Santeetlah. It is a small secluded hideaway nestled in a hollow of the Nantahala National Forest.

The bedrooms have pine-paneled walls and are very pleasant. Guests gather in the lobby and living room which is dominated by a huge fireplace and two boars' heads. There's a little trout pool almost within casting distance of the sideporch.

Mountain nights mean a crackling fire even in July and August, and guests relax among the rustic furnishings or catch up on their reading.

During the day they can swim or sun on the shores of beautiful Lake Santeetlah, boat or canoe along the 108 miles of shoreline and catch their own small- or large-mouth bass, walleye, panfish, muskie, or channel blue cat. There is also trout in the well-stocked pond where guests may catch their own dinner.

Both breakfast and dinner are included in the rates. Dinner is served at 6 P.M., and is one main entrée served family style, and breakfast is a full mountain breakfast.

BLUE BOAR LODGE, Joyce Kilmer Forest Road, Robbinsville, N.C. 28771; 704-479-8126. A 7-bedroom lodge in the woods high in the Great Smoky Mountains just a few minutes from the main entrance to Joyce Kilmer National Forest. Open April 1 to Mid-Oct. for summer guests, and mid-Oct. until just after Christmas for hunting only. Hunting, fishing, swimming, birdwatching, hiking, rafting, nature walks, and marveloous backroading in the Great Smokies. No pets. Ray and Kathy Wilson, Proprietors.

Directions: Follow Joyce Kilmer Forest Road ten miles from Robbinsville. Look for turn-off on right and follow signs on woods road.

For rates, see Index.

BUTTONWOOD INN
Franklin, North Carolina

The town of Franklin is surrounded by 420,000 acres of the Nantahala National Forest with such recreational opportunities as hiking, fishing, hunting, rafting, whitewater canoeing, horseback riding, and camping. There are also facilities for skiing, golfing, tennis, and other sports. The good people in Atlanta, Charlestown, and Savannah are well acquainted with this mountain area of North Carolina which is beautiful in all four seasons.

The Buttonwood is a small country inn with four guest rooms located next to the Franklin Golf Course.

The original residence was a small cottage built in the late 1920s between the 5th and 7th greens. A new wing retains the same rustic charm and now accommodates the inn's guests.

Dogwood and rhododendron bloom abundantly during the spring and a spacious lawn with a view of the mountains is enjoyed by the guests.

Completely surrounded by tall pines, the small and cozy Buttonwood will appeal to the person who prefers simplicity and natural rustic beauty. It provides comfortable lodgings for the overnight traveler and also for those wishing to make their stay longer. There is a cheerful apartment available by the week or month.

The Buttonwood was one of the most pleasant surprises that I have encountered in my search for B&B s.

BUTTONWOOD INN, 190 Georgia Rd., Franklin, N.C. 28734; 704-369-8985. A 4-bedroom (plus one suite) bed-and-breakfast home adjacent to the Franklin Golf Course. Continental breakfast only. Open year-round. Located in the beautiful Great Smoky region of western North Carolina with all the natural, cultural, and recreational advantages. No pets. No credit cards. Frank and Gerry Heenan, Proprietors.

Directions: From Dillard, Georgia, drive north to the outskirts of Franklin, N.C., on Rte. 441 (Business). Immediately look very sharply on the left for a very small sign saying Buttonwood Inn. If you pass the entrance to the Franklin Golf Course, you've gone too far.

For B&B rates, see Index.

HAVENSHIRE INN
Hendersonville, North Carolina

Driving between Hendersonville and Brevard, I saw a sign for the Havenshire Inn and turned off on a black-topped road that followed the course of a river through some very pleasant meadowlands. It felt longer than the posted two miles, but—ah well—it was the first week of June, the laurel was out in beautiful profusion, the sun was shining, and the birds were singing.

Now, in a verdant, rolling valley, I saw a large redwood-and-cedar house greatly resembling an English country manor—the Havenshire Inn. The curved road wound its way through lush lawns and I discovered that the front of the inn looked out over the valley of the French Broad River. There were many beautiful pine trees and a wonderful air of tranquility.

From my first glimpse, I felt this was going to be exceptional, and it was.

I walked onto an unusually large screened-in porch, where guests enjoy breakfast, and into a high-ceilinged center hallway with impressive chandeliers.

Each of the six guest rooms is handsomely furnished and enjoys lovely views of the grounds and countryside.

Kay Coppock was kind enough to lead me down the garden path just a few paces to Bowman's Bluff, overlooking the river, and of course it has a legend about an Indian maiden.

The wonderful sweeping lawns and the house itself are bordered by a brown rather than white, horse fence, behind which horses graze. They are quite friendly and enjoy being patted.

Havenshire Inn was an unexpected surprise for me, and I was delighted to find a bed and breakfast with such an unusual ambience and ample amusement and recreation nearby.

HAVENSHIRE INN, Rte. 4, Box 455, Cummings Rd., Hendersonville, NC 28739; 704-692-4097. A 6-guestroom (some shared baths) bed-and-breakfast inn on a handsome estate between Hendersonville and Brevard. Breakfast is the only meal served and is included in the room rate. Open April 1 thru Oct. 31. Conveniently situated to enjoy all of the many recreational, cultural, and historical attractions in the area, including the Brevard Music Festival and the Vanderbilt Mansion in Asheville. No facilities to amuse small children. Kay Coppock and Cindy Findley, Innkeepers.

Directions: Look for inn sign off Rte. 64 between Horseshoe Bend and Etowah; follow Rte. 4 a little over 2 mi. and look for inn on right.

For B&B rates, see Index.

HEMLOCK INN
Bryson City, North Carolina

Bryson City is in the heart of western North Carolina's Great Smoky Mountains, and it is also at the juncture of roads that lead in all directions. Asheville is just a short distance to the east, the towns of Brevard and Highlands are to the south, while the Nantahala Gorge, Topton, and Murphy are to the west.

At the Hemlock Inn everybody is introduced to everybody else. It's a place where you can fill the day with hikes in the woods or driving and sightseeing in the mountains. On the other hand, if you care to just sit and look at the scenery, read, or perhaps play a little shuffleboard or ping-pong, that's handy as well. It's a bird watcher's and botanist's heaven.

After an early morning cup of coffee on the terrace, everyone is summoned to breakfast at eight-thirty by the tolling of a bell and all stand behind the chairs which have been set around Lazy Susan tables while innkeeper John Shell asks the blessing.

Country milled grits, eggs with sausage, bacon, country ham, or corned beef hash are passed around and the meal is topped off with homemade biscuits and jellies.

If you want to have quiet days with serene drives through the mountains and not much traffic, May, early June, and September are good times to visit the Hemlock Inn.

HEMLOCK INN, Bryson City, N.C. 28713; 704-488-2885. A 25-room Smoky Mountain inn 4 mi. from Bryson City and 60 mi. from Asheville. Near Fontana Village, Cherokee, and Pisgah National Forest. Modified American plan omits lunch. Breakfast and dinner served to travelers by reservation only. Sunday dinner served at noontime. Open from early May to early November. Shuffleboard, skittles, ping-pong, hiking trails on grounds. Tubing, rafting, and tennis nearby. No pets. No credit cards. Ella Jo and John Shell, Innkeepers.

Directions: Located 1 mi. off Rte. 19 between Cherokee and Bryson City, N.C. Take paved road to top of mountain.

For B&B rates, see Index.

MOUNTAIN KEY LODGE
Pisgah Forest, North Carolina

For many, many years now, people who live in Atlanta, Savannah, Charleston, and Florida have known that western North Carolina, high in the Great Smoky Mountains, is one of the coolest places to visit in the summer. However, it is not only the cool breezes that entice visitors from warmer climes to this section of North Carolina, but also the many natural and cultural attractions for which the region is famous.

The Mountain Key Lodge is ideally situated to enjoy all of these advantages, including a pleasant proximity to the Brevard Music Festival each summer.

The house itself was built in the early 1860s out of wood, sand, and layered rock hauled from the mountainside behind the home-site. The furnishings are an interesting mix of Colonial and Victorian. Many of the pieces came from innkeeper Daniel Stewart's family, including a table made by his great-great- grandfather.

There are six guest rooms with various types of bath arrangements. All have been individually furnished and quite a few have handsome carved bedsteads.

Behind the inn is a trail that begins at the lodge and continues to climb toward one of the numerous waterfalls in the area. From the bridge overlooking the falls it's possible to follow the course of the stream as it meanders its way toward the French Broad River.

Breakfast consists of country ham, biscuits, apple sauce, or various other appetite appeasers such as bacon, pancakes, link sausage, and many varieties of fruits. Apples are from the inn's own trees, and grapes are from vines growing on the house.

MOUNTAIN KEY LODGE, 15 Seven Springs Rd., Pisgah Forest, NC 28768; 704-884-7400. A 6-guestroom (some private baths) bed-and-breakfast inn near Brevard and the Pisgah National Forest. Breakfast, the only meal served, is included in the room rate. Open April 1 to Oct. 31. Tennis court, a pleasant fishing pond, horseshoes and croquet on grounds. Key Falls Trail, waterfalls and recreational areas nearby. Daniel Stewart, Innkeeper.

Directions: From Brevard follow Rte. 276 toward Asheville. Bear to the right before Barry's Restaurant on Old Rte. 64. Continue on to the village of Pisgah Forest, ignoring the left-hand turn, and proceed over railroad tracks for another mile or so. Turn right at the sign marked Eagle's Nest Camp. It's the second turn after the bridge.

For B&B rates, see Index.

NU-WRAY INN
Burnsville, North Carolina

The Nu-Wray is known throughout the southern highlands as the inn where a bell rouses everyone at 8 A.M. and a similar tolling at 8:30 beckons all of the houseguests, and any other lucky people who happen to be passing through, for a fabulous breakfast.

Burnsville is in the heart of Yancey County, which contains the highest peak east of the Rockies. It's a mountainous country ranging in elevation from 1,700 to 6,300 feet.

At the Nu-Wray there are old-fashioned door keys and every guest returns his to the old-fashioned key rack in the lobby. There's a big fireplace at one end and many, many antiques of all kinds.

There are lodging rooms on the two upper floors of this village inn in the mountains, and all of them have remained unchanged during the many years that I've been visiting.

The full breakfast is enjoyed by all guests seated around wonderful long tables with white tablecloths. There are platters of scrambled eggs, steaming pancakes, warm syrup, country ham, grits, red-eye gravy, applesauce, hot biscuits, apple butter, great pots of honey, and tubs of fresh country butter. Everyone is introduced and soon there's lots of talking, laughing, joking, and perhaps the making of new friends.

Dinner is served in the same manner, with everybody sitting around the long tables and falling to with a will summoned by the bell.

THE NU-WRAY INN, Burnsville, N.C. 28714; 704-682-2329. A 35-room village inn on town square on Rte. 19E, 38 mi. north of Asheville. A few miles from Mt. Mitchell. European plan. Lodgings available year-round. Breakfast and dinner served every week-day to travelers. Noon dinner served on Sundays only. Dining room open daily mid-April to Dec. 1. Golf, swimming, hiking, and skiing nearby. Betty Wray Souders, Innkeeper.

Directions: From Asheville, go north on Rte. 19-23 for 18 miles, then continue on 19. Five miles from Burnsville, 19 becomes 19E. From the north via Bristol or Johnson City, Tenn., take Rte. 19-23 to Unicoi. Turn left on 107 to N.C. State Line. Take 226 and turn right on Rte. 197 at Red Hill to Burnsville.

For B&B rates, see Index.

THE ORCHARD INN
Saluda, North Carolina

I saw this inn during the final days of its rehabilitation and I can assure the reader that it promises to be nothing short of a spectacular mountain experience that is hard to beat, with a view overlooking the Warrior Mountain Range.

It was built early in the 1900s by the Southern Railway Company, providing railroad clerks and their families a summer mountain retreat until 1963. It has now been taken over and completely renovated by two very energetic and attractive young people, Ann and Ken Hough, who have created a minor miracle in getting it into such tiptop shape.

There's an 80-foot glassed-in porch across the front and many of the eight bedrooms and three cottages enjoy this matchless view.

Lunch and dinner are available to inn guests by reservation, as well as to travelers and the public. Gentlemen are requested to wear jackets at dinner.

THE ORCHARD INN, Box 725, Saluda, N.C. 28773; 704-749-5471. An 8-bedroom mountaintop (2500 feet) inn in western North Carolina. A short distance from Tryon. Open year-round. Breakfast included with room rate. Lunch and dinner available. Antiquing, hiking, wild flower collecting, birdwatching, and superb country roads abound. Pets in cottages only. No credit cards. Ann and Ken Hough, Innkeepers.

Directions: From Atlanta come north on I-85 to Hwy. 5. Inn is two miles off I-26. From Asheville take I-26 south.

For B&B rates, see Index.

RAGGED GARDEN INN
Blowing Rock, North Carolina

The full name of this very pleasant, in-town accommodation is the Ragged Garden Inn & Restaurant, and after I had a good chat with Joe Villani, I realized that his background, first at Sardi's in New York and then later at other restaurants of his own in Connecticut and Florida made cuisine a very important part of the popularity of the inn.

He explained that the menu is basically northern Italian, although there are also many continental and American dishes. Part of our conversation was in the kitchen, where he was making homemade fettucini.

An imposing porte cochere ushers the guest into this rather grand old house, built at the turn of the century. It is surrounded by roses, rhododendrons, and trees, and is centrally located, permitting guests to enjoy art galleries, boutiques, the parks and attractions of Blowing Rock.

There are five very pleasantly decorated guest rooms, available for overnight and longer stays.

Blowing Rock is the highest town in North Carolina at 4,200 feet,and derives its name from a blowing rock overhanging the Johns River Gorge. The sheer rock walls form a flume, and when the wind sweeps down, a strong force is created, and a light object will blow back each time it is tossed out into the gorge.

The Ragged Garden Inn is indeed a dream come true for Joe Villani and his wife, Joyce. They are very personable and considerate people, and the inn reflects a warm and welcoming atmosphere.

RAGGED GARDEN INN & RESTAURANT, Sunset Dr., P.O. Box 1927, Blowing Rock, NC 28605; 704-295-9703. A 5-guestroom inn (all private baths) in North Carolina's delightful mountain country. Room rate includes breakfast. Dinner served nightly except Sunday. Open mid-April. Closed Jan. 2. Conveniently located to enjoy the many recreational and cultural attractions in this area. Not suitable for young children. Joe and Joyce Villani, Innkeepers.

Directions: Ragged Garden Inn is located 1 block off Main St. in Blowing Rock.

For B&B rates, see Index.

THE RED ROCKER INN
Black Mountain, North Carolina

For the first-time visitor, western North Carolina is jam-packed with surprises. One of the best is the Red Rocker Inn in the town of Black Mountain at the entrance of the eastern Great Smoky Mountains. I learned about it through a letter from a former classmate at Bucknell University, Louise Brosius Hurd. She said, "The warm personality of the host, the special quality of the food, and the charm and imaginative decor of the bedrooms all add up to a unique and delightful experience—and I just feel your readers should be aware of it."

Louise, you were right, and Fred Eshleman who, incidentally, taught at the Muncy, Pennsylvania, high school (relatively near Bucknell) for ten years, explained that the bedrooms were decorated "with humor."

When he and his wife, Pat, first acquired the property, it had twenty-one bedrooms and one bath down the hall. In providing more bathrooms, they placed free-standing bathtubs in some of the bedrooms, cleverly concealed behind curtains. There are many other extremely clever touches, including the decorations in one bedroom that consist entirely of the awards won during Fred Eshleman's tenure as a teacher. A great, oversized red rocker sits on the front lawn.

Food, however, is one of the important features of the Red Rocker. I happened to be there during lunch hour, and the looks of anticipation on the part of the continuous stream of ladies and gentlemen was enough to convince me that I was on the right track. The evening meal is served family style with a changing menu every day.

It's worth noting that special modified American plan rates are in effect before and after the high season.

If you don't have a sense of humor before you visit the Red Rocker, you'll have one after you leave.

THE RED ROCKER INN, 136 N. Dougherty St., Black Mountain, NC 28711; 704-669-5991. An 18-guestroom (most with private baths) country inn in a small, relaxed mountain community. Open May 1 to Nov. 1, and Thanksgiving weekend. Breakfast not included in room rate. Conveniently located to enjoy the many cultural and recreational attractions in the area. Advance reservations suggested for evening meals. Pat and Fred Eshleman, Innkeepers.

Directions: Leave Rte. 40 at the Black Mountain Exit, 17 mi. east of Asheville. Come into town, turn left at the main intersection, go one block, turn right at Dougherty St. and look for inn.

For rates, see Index.

SNOWBIRD MOUNTAIN LODGE
Robbinsville, North Carolina

Snowbird Mountain Lodge is not strictly a bed-and-breakfast inn; however, because it is so delightfully remote and so high in the sky, overnight guests will undoubtedly wish to avail themselves of the opportunity to have lunch (or take a box lunch) and also stay for dinner. The rates quoted in the Index are for lodgings and three meals a day and there is no B&B rate.

The question naturally arises as to why Snowbird was included in this book. The answer is that we felt its truly unusual location—high in the Great Smoky Mountains of western North Carolina, in a natural bird sanctuary where at least 314 birds of the middle-Atlantic states have been sighted and an incredible number of mountain wild flowers have been observed—was something to be highly recommended.

On the terrace that almost hangs over Lake Santeetlah more than a thousand feet below, the mountain peaks seem, in this wonderful, rarefied air, almost close enough to touch, but actually are four to five thousand feet high.

All the roads leading to Robbinsville, North Carolina, traverse some really incredibly magnificent scenery particularly Route 19 from the east through the Nantahala Gorge.

SNOWBIRD MOUNTAIN LODGE, Joyce Kilmer Forest Rd., Robbinsville, NC 28771; 704-479-3433. A 22-guestroom inn on top of the Great Smokies, 12 mi. from Robbinsville. American plan (room and 3 meals). Open from end of April to early Nov. Lunch and dinner served to travelers by reservation only. Shuffleboard, table tennis, archery, croquet, horseshoes, badminton on grounds. Swimming, fishing, hiking, backroading nearby. For nature lovers. Not suitable for children under 12. No pets. The Rhudy Family, Innkeepers.

Directions: The inn is located at the western tip of North Carolina, 10 mi. west of Robbinsville. Approaching from the northeast or south take U.S. 19 and 129; from the northwest take U.S. 129, then follow signs to Joyce Kilmer Memorial Forest.

For rates, see Index.

WOMBLE INN
Brevard, North Carolina

In her book, *Music Festivals in North America* (Berkshire Traveller Press), author Carol Rabin says, "'The Summer Cultural Center of the South' is the proud claim of the Brevard Music Center. Nestled in the Smoky Mountains and the Pisgah National Forest in Transylvania County, thirty miles south of Asheville, is the little North Carolina community of Brevard. Most of the year the rural town is quiet and serene, but Brevard begins bustling in June when over 300 students and 125 faculty come to the Brevard Music Center."

She continues, "The main thrust of the center is on education and performance by young students who are enrolled in an intensive seven-week course, but much emphasis is placed on the festival performances as well. There are over forty-five different programs offered during the season, ranging from symphonic and chamber works to opera, light opera, choral works, and solo recitals."

Fortunate, indeed, are guests who can enjoy the hospitality of the Womble Inn during the festival season. It is a very pleasant red brick building with wrought iron decorations and a second-floor gallery facing Main Street.

The guest rooms and parlor are very homey in nature and most attractive. Some of the guest rooms have two double beds and some have singles. There are many family portraits of young people everywhere and, as one would imagine, a very good piano.

Although the Womble Inn is undoubtedly booked well in advance during the festival season from the first of July until mid-August, it is open every day all year. Breakfast is served in your room on a silver tray or in the dining room with a big picture window looking out over the residential area of the town, and guests often browse in the large, very clean kitchen.

WOMBLE INN, 301 Main St., Brevard, NC 28712; 704-884-4770. A 6-guestroom (all with private baths) bed-and-breakfast inn located in the beautiful Great Smoky Mountains of North Carolina. Open all year. Breakfast is the only meal served. Brevard Music Festival July 1 to mid-Aug. Immediately convenient to enjoy the many attractions of the Pisgah National Forest. Breakfast is the only meal served. No credit cards. Mrs. Beth Womble, Proprietress.

Directions: Once in Brevard you can't miss Main St., continue north and look for inn on left-hand side.

For B&B rates, see Index.

THE INN AT HONEY RUN
Millersburg, Ohio

Although the Inn at Honey Run is a contemporary country inn with all the most modern comforts and conveniences, it reflects, nonetheless, a respect and consideration for Holmes County's deep-rooted Amish culture. For example, in deference to local religious beliefs, alcoholic beverages are not allowed in public areas of the inn.

In the midst of about sixty acres of forest and pastureland, the multilevel building was designed and constructed by architect Julius Blum to harmonize with the wonderful contours and textures of the surrounding hills. Mr. Blum has brought the forest environment into the inn with his use of wood and stone and glass. Almost every bedroom has a feeling of being in the treetops.

The innkeeper and guiding spirit of the inn is Marjorie Stock, who insists on high standards in every area of the inn, from the kitchen to the immaculate bedrooms, and she has instilled a sense of pride in the inn staff, both Amish and non-Amish of all ages—all of whom seem to enjoy serving the guests.

In addition to offering bed-and-breakfast accommodations, the inn also serves lunch and dinner, and the food is special, with everything made from scratch.

There's much to do in the near area, including visits to the Wool Mill, cheese factory, and the quilt shops. A tour of the Amish community is most rewarding and provides further insight into the customs of these unusual people who came to this country in 1754 to escape religious persecution in Europe.

Your first overnight visit at the Inn at Honey Run, I'm sure, will inspire many longer ones.

THE INN AT HONEY RUN, 6920 County Road 203, Millersburg, Ohio 44654; 216-674-0011. A 25-bedroom country inn located in north-central Ohio's beautiful, rolling, wooded countryside. Open all year. Lunch and dinner served Mon. thru Sat. by reservation only. Sun. breakfast and lunch served to houseguests only. Breakfast is included in the overnight rate. Ample opportunities for recreation and backroading in Ohio's Amish country. Marjorie Stock, Innkeeper.

Directions: From Millersburg, proceed on E. Jackson St. (Rtes. 39 and 62) past Courthouse and gas station on right. At next corner turn left onto Rte. 241. At one mile the road goes down hill. At 1¾ mi. it crosses the bridge over Honey Run; turn right immediately around the small hill onto Rte. 203 (not well marked). After about 1½ mi. turn right at inn sign. (Watch out for the Amish horse-drawn buggies.)

For B&B rates, see Index.

THE WOOSTER INN
Wooster, Ohio

One of the best times to visit Ohio is in the early fall. The rolling countryside has beautiful tints and hues of autumn, the cornfields, in their own particular shade of beige, lie fallow, and the roads follow the contours of the land, with cattle peacefully grazing, and an occasional small village that gives one the unmistakable feeling of being in America's heartland.

In the middle of all this beautiful farming country is the bustling town of Wooster and the College of Wooster, a progressive co-educational institution that, among other things, is the proprietor of the Wooster Inn.

The inn, offering full services, reflects a great deal of the town-and-gown spirit with its furnishings and location right on the edge of the campus. In fact, it is possible to watch a soccer game out of one set of windows and enjoy the golf course through the others. During the college year the cultural events on the campus, such as lectures, music, plays, and art exhibits, are open to the public and, of course, the inn guests. There are also various athletic events providing an interesting diversion for the bed-and-breakfast traveler.

A full breakfast is included in the cost of the room.

THE WOOSTER INN, Wayne Avenue and Gasche Street, Wooster, Oh. 44691; 216-264-2341. A pleasant 14-bedroom inn on the campus of the College of Wooster, about 60 mi. southwest of Cleveland. Breakfast included in room rate. Breakfast, lunch, and dinner served every day. Convenient to all of the college cultural and athletic events. Golf and tennis nearby. Willy Bergmann, Innkeeper.

Directions: Wooster is the hub of a series of highways leading from all directions, including U.S. Rtes. 30 and 250, and State Rtes. 3, 585, and 83. Locate the college and then ask for directions to the inn.

For B&B rates, see Index.

CAMPUS COTTAGE
Eugene, Oregon

I drove about a hundred miles out of my way to visit Ursula at the Campus Cottage, and it was well worth it.

Ursula explained that the cottage was built in 1922 and purchased in 1981 especially for the purpose of establishing Eugene's first bed-and-breakfast place. All of the renovations retained the original mid-20s character. It is located just off the campus of the University of Oregon.

Ursula is an attractive, contemporary-minded woman whose many interests are reflected in the books and paintings in the house. Also, she obviously has a keen enthusiasm for interior decorating.

There are two bedrooms; one, "The Suite," is the original master bedroom with a queen-sized brass bed, a sitting room with a twin Jenny Lind bed, and a bathroom with a large bathtub/shower combination. The other is a cozy south-facing bedroom with a queen-sized oak bed and down-filled reading chair. The private bath has a cedar-lined shower.

A full breakfast is served in the living room in front of the fire and could include any of Ursula's repertoire of delicious egg dishes. There is a deck overlooking a small garden to the rear where breakfast may also be enjoyed.

Eugene is a pleasant university town, and if your travels take you there, I think you will enjoy the Campus Cottage.

CAMPUS COTTAGE, 1136 E. 19th Ave., Eugene, Or. 97403; 503-342-5346. A 2-bedroom tiny bed-and-breakfast inn just a few blocks from the Univ. of Oregon campus. Open year-round. Bicycles provided. Older children welcome. No pets. No credit cards. Ursula Bates, Proprietress.

Directions: From the south, leave I-5 at Exit 192 and proceed to Franklin Blvd. Ignore first turn to left, continue on Franklin Blvd., a few blocks; turn left at Univ. of Oregon sign and proceed down Agate St. (not marked) to 19th St., through the university grounds with the stadium on the right. Turn right on E. 19th and go 3½ blocks to inn, which is between two fraternity houses. From the north, leave I-5 at Exit 194; follow all Univ. of Oregon exit signs to Broadway. Turn right on Patterson; left on 19th Ave., and proceed 6½ blocks to the inn.

For B&B rates, see Index.

CHANTICLEER INN
Ashland, Oregon

For many years the main reason to go to Ashland was the Oregon Shakespearean Festival which, after modest beginnings, now presents the works of the Bard from as early as late February to the end of October. There are three different playing areas, including a beautiful outdoor theater, a 600-seat indoor stage, and a smaller, intimate theater as well. In addition to Shakespeare's plays, there are offerings by other playwrights and a program of classic films.

While I bow to no man in my admiration of the theater, I must say that the Chanticleer Inn, situated in a residential part of Ashland, now provides an even more enticing reason to visit this beautiful section of Oregon.

In a community that is rapidly gaining a reputation for bed-and-breakfast places, the Chanticleer stands out. It is the concept of Jim Beaver, a former reporter for NBC radio in San Francisco, and his wife, Nancy, a former personnel manager.

The first thing that impressed me was the friendly living room with an open-hearth fireplace that is often so welcome at the end of the day. There are shelves loaded with books and magazines, and an atmosphere that encourages good conversation, whether it be about the play or about a day skiing at Crater Lake.

Individually decorated bedrooms, all with their own baths, have queen-sized beds, and fluffy comforters.

The full breakfast could include cheese-baked eggs, fresh squeezed orange juice, blueberry muffins, and freshly ground coffee served in the attractive sunroom. The Chanticleer is an inn for all reasons.

CHANTICLEER INN, 120 Gresham St., Ashland, Or. 97520; 503-482-1919. A 6-bedroom bed-and-breakfast inn overlooking Bear Creek valley and Cascade foothills. Open every day all year. A short walk from the Oregon Shakespearean Festival, Lithia Park, and many shops and restaurants. Rogue River white water rafting and Mt. Ashland's ski slopes nearby. No credit cards. Jim and Nancy Beaver, Innkeepers.

Directions: Ashland is on Rte. 5, halfway between San Francisco and Portland. Gresham St. is in the center of town, running at right angles to the main street.

For B&B rates, see Index.

THE JOHNSON HOUSE
Florence, Oregon

Florence is one of the many interesting towns located on Highway 101 on Oregon's spectacular coast. The area abounds in rivers, lakes, sea fishing, beachcombing, bird watching, historical sites, viewpoints, and, of course, the presence of the mighty Pacific Ocean.

The Johnson House in Old Town Florence is an Italianate Victorian, circa 1892, and has been restored and furnished with fine original antiques and Early American prints. Periodic art exhibits are open to the public. The four bedrooms share three baths.

The Old Town section is being restored and has a wonderful 1925 movie house, the Harbor Theatre, a fine restaurant, a general store, and a 1905 mercantile building that is reputed to be one of the finest of its kind in Oregon. This area with its many lakes is a wintering place for swans, and it is a favorite spot for avid bird watchers.

Guest will enjoy the hearty breakfast that includes orange juice, a fruit plate, cheese, ham and eggs, homemade bread, and special, freshly ground coffee or tea.

The Johnson House would make a very pleasant overnight stop with, perhaps, a long morning or afternoon excursion to points of interest nearby.

THE JOHNSON HOUSE, 216 Maple St., P.O. Box 1892, Florence, OR 97439; 503-997-8000. A 4-guestroom (3 baths) bed-and-breakfast inn located in the historic section of Florence just a short distance from Rte. 101. Open all year. Full breakfast included in room rate. There is a wealth of Oregon coast natural attractions within easy distance. Jayne and Ronald Fraese, Proprietors.

*Directions: Coming north on Rte. 101 turn right after the bridge and follow briefly, turning left on Maple St. Comi
turn left onto Maple St.*

For B&B rates, see Index.

299

JUDGE TOUVELLE HOUSE
Jacksonville, Oregon

Judge Touvelle House is located one block off Main Street in the registered National Historic Landmark town of Jacksonville, Oregon. It is situated on a gentle rise on four acres of land, with stone walls and white post fences that enclose the large, beautiful old farmhouse, the connecting guest annex, and a three-story carriage house.

The house was built in 1856 and reconstructed in 1916 by Judge Touvelle and his bride, who had just migrated out West. The building features a wraparound outside porch enhanced by antique white wicker pieces. The only modern touches are a swimming pool and hot tub nestled among redwood and oak trees.

Referred to as the "museum by the side of the road," it is completely furnished with antiques in keeping with the elegant house. The guest rooms are furnished with marble-topped dressers and other beautiful walnut Victorian pieces. There is one guest room on the first floor that is ideal for disabled and older people; the remaining five bedrooms are on the second and third floors, and feature oriental rugs, Laura Ashley wallpapers, down comforters, a private balcony, and two nonworking fireplaces.

Breakfast, served on beautiful china with silver cutlery, features croissants or waffles or hot fruit strudel, as well as fresh fruit in season, and of course coffee or tea. Fresh raspberries and blackberries in cream are served in season.

JUDGE TOUVELLE HOUSE, 435 Oregon St., Jacksonville, OR 97530; 503-899-8223. A 6-guestroom (1 private bath) elegantly decorated Victorian home in a Historic Landmark town in southern Oregon. Open year-round. Continental breakfast included in room rate. The Peter Britt Musical Festival in July and Aug.; Shakespearean Festival in nearby Ashland, and many outdoor activities: hiking, fishing, rafting, downhill and cross- country skiing. No children. No pets. No credit cards. Verne and Tony Beebe, Innkeepers.

Directions: From Medford, take Rte. 238, which becomes California St. in Jacksonville. Proceed down California St. to Oregon St., turn right for 1 block. Judge Touvelle House is on the left near a historic cemetery.

For B&B rates, see Index.

LAKE CREEK LODGE
Sisters, Oregon

Travelers arriving at this little-publicized country-inn resort experience an almost immediate feeling of exhilaration. There are blue skies feathered with white clouds, crisp mountain breezes whispering among the tall ponderosa pines, while the sun provides a welcome warmth. There is a marvelous aroma of pine and cedar in the air.

The main lodge and a dozen cottages and houses are grouped around a small pond made by damming Lake Creek, a tributary of the beautiful Metolius River, which runs behind the grounds. A luxuriant lawn extends down to the waterfront. A walk behind the lodge and beside the creek reveals green meadows dotted with such wild flowers as buttercups, forget-me-nots and wild roses.

The smaller cottages have two bedrooms, a bath, and a refrigerator, while the knotty-pine-paneled houses include a kitchen, living room, two and three bedrooms, single and double bath, and a large, screened porch. Some have fireplaces.

Dinner at Lake Creek is a sociable event with guests gathered around the pine-plank tables. There is one entrée each night that might include salmon, barbecued steak, lamb, or country fried chicken. This fare is enhanced with homemade breads, crisp salads and enticing desserts, such as ice cream cake topped with chocolate sauce.

Breakfast is a hearty meal with piping hot fluffy pancakes, hot rolls, and a varied selections of eggs, cereal, and breakfast meats.

Fishing the Metolius River is a thrilling challenge for the avid fly angler. There is bait fishing on the lower Metolius and trolling and spin fishing on the crystal clear lakes nearby.

LAKE CREEK LODGE, Sisters, OR 97759; 503- 595-6331. A 15-cottage (all private baths) secluded resort-inn in Oregon's gorgeous high country. Open all year. Modified American plan only June 15 to Sept. 16. Dining room closed Sept. 17 to May 25; however cottages with kitchen facilities available. Two-night minimum stay and 3-night minimum on holidays. Fishing, xc skiing, volleyball, swimming, tennis, hiking, bicycling on grounds. Golf, horseback riding, downhill skiing, nearby. Glenna Grace, Manager.

Directions: From Bend, drive 32 mi. west on Rte. 20, exit at Camp Sherman, continue 3 mi. on Camp Sherman Rd. to inn sign on right. From Salem, drive 99 mi. on Rte. 20. Look for "Camp Sherman" turn-off and follow directions as above.

For Lodging rates, see Index.

MADISON INN
Corvallis, Oregon

Corvallis can best be described as a town of "trees and clouds, cleanliness and quiet." It has tree-lined streets, beautiful old homes, and pleasant riverside parks with lawns and flowers. Ivy and roses climb up some of the telephone poles, and students from nearby Oregon State University stroll on the promenade around the campus. Two blocks from the campus is the Madison Inn bed and breakfast, catering to visiting professors and families of students during college activities. The inn boasts seven hosts and hostesses; Kathryn Brandis and her six, almost-grown children.

This large, four-storied Victorian house was built in 1901 by a physician to house his medical practice along with his residence. Later, it was purchased by Kathryn's grandfather and has been in the family ever since, serving for many years as a fraternity house. Kathryn and her children, Shannon, Honore, Katy, Paige, Mathew, and Michael opened the house as a bed and breakfast in 1981, after she and her children had taken it down to the studs, then rebuilt, restored, and decorated it to its present beauty.

The decor throughout the house is a blending of deep blue and burnt orange. Beautiful area rugs grace the highly polished oak floors.

A beautiful, polished, solid oak stairway leads to the guest rooms on the second floor. Comfortable beds with colorful down quilts, scatter rugs, comfortable chairs, books, and flowers complete the picture.

Breakfast in the dining room may include strawberries picked fresh each morning, swedish pancakes with homemade maple or blueberry syrup, fresh juice, cheese strata or dutch babies (scones) with dates, real butter and homemade preserves.

MADISON INN, 660 Madison St., Corvallis, OR 97330; 503-757-1274. A 5-guestroom (1 private and 2 shared baths) Queen Anne Victorian B&B in a quiet college town 18 mi. west of I-5, about 60 mi. south of Portland. Breakfast included in room rate. Open year-round. Oregon State University campus and all the attendant cultural diversions nearby. Children welcome. No pets. Kathryn Brandis and Family, Innkeepers.

Directions: From Portland (north) take I-5 south to Albany (60 mi.) turn west on Hwy. 20 at Corvallis exit. Proceed 11 mi., cross bridge at entry to town, turn left on 2nd St.; proceed down 2nd St. to 7th and Madison—4-story, deep orange house on the left.

For B&B rates, see Index.

MARJON BED AND BREAKFAST INN
Leaburg, Oregon

The idyllic setting of Marjon Bed and Breakfast Inn is just 24 miles from Eugene, on the banks of one of the most beautiful and spectacular rivers in Oregon—the McKenzie. The inn is surrounded by nature's splendor: towering trees, crystal clear rivers, lush woodlands, and majestic mountains.

The inn nestles on the edge of the McKenzie River and from the beautiful living room, one looks past flowers, ferns, and trees to the river and beyond. The overall decor of this magnificent contemporary house is oriental; however, the master suite, with a 7' x 12' bed, is done in white French provincial furniture and overlooks both the river and a secluded Japanese garden. The second guest room, slightly smaller, is light and airy with oriental decor, and has a unique "fishbowl" shower that overlooks the river.

A full gourmet breakfast, included in the price of the room, featuring exotic juices, soufflés or omelets, fruit, and hot breads, can be eaten either in the dining room or on a covered terrace overlooking the river. Guests can relax or venture through two acres of grounds, where there are landscaped gardens and wooded riverside trails that wind through feathery ferns, azaleas, and rhododendrons, across a plank footbridge, past hidden seating areas, and down to a floating deck for an intimate view of the river.

Countess Margaret Olga Von Retzlaff Haas—otherwise known as Margie Haas—explained that she has set a goal. "I want the prestige of being known throughout the United States as having one of the most beautiful and elegant breakfast inns." She has plans to add four more rooms—what a beautiful and romantic inn....

MARJON BED AND BREAKFAST INN, 44975 Leaburg Dam Rd., Leaburg, OR 97489; 503-896-3145. A 2-guestroom beautiful, contemporary house on the bank of the spectacular McKenzie River 24 mi. from Eugene. Open every day, all year. Rates include a full breakfast. Drop-in arrivals welcome, but reservations are recommended. Trout fishing, rafting, and nature sightseeing on grounds. Golf, water and snow skiing, boating, guided raft trips, mountain climbing, and endless hiking trails nearby. Restaurants within short driving distance. No children. No pets. Margie Haas, Proprietress

Directions: From Eugene, Oregon, proceed east on Hwy. 126 for approx. 24 mi. Turn right on Leaburg Dam Rd., cross bridge, drive 1 mi. to inn on your left.

For B&B rates, see Index.

METOLIUS RIVER LODGES
Camp Sherman, Oregon

Located in the heart of the famous Metolius Recreation Area, this lodge offers the unique advantage of a setting on the banks of the cold, spring-fed, crystal clear waters of the Metolius River. Guests can fish for rainbow, brown brook and Dolly Varden trout just a few paces from the door.

The lodge offers a variety of accommodations, from sleeping rooms with refrigerators to fully equipped, two-bedroom housekeeping lodges, many with fireplaces. Rates include continental breakfast and firewood. During the summer season, barbecue kettles and charcoal are provided. The library on the grounds has a plentiful supply of books for adults and children, along with games and puzzles. A general store, laundromat, and post office are within a short walk.

The lodges are near several well-known mountains in the Cascade Range—Black Butte, Three Sisters, Mount Washington, and Mount Jefferson. The area is famous for downhill and cross- country skiing. Within a short distance horseback riding and golf (in season) can be enjoyed. Hiking trails begin just outside the door.

METOLIUS RIVER LODGES, P.O. Box 110, Camp Sherman, OR 97730; 503-595-6290. A mountain lodge with 12 accommodations (10 have kitchens) on the Metolius River in central Oregon, 38 mi. from Bend. Continental breakfast is included in room rate. Open every day, all year. Activities on grounds include fly fishing, hiking, photography, and bird watching. Downhill and xc skiing, horseback riding, and golf nearby. Pets allowed during spring, fall, and winter only. Pick-up at Redmond/Bend Airport can be arranged. Byron and Lee Beach, Proprietors.

Directions: From Bend, take Rte. 20 northwest for 32 mi., exit at the Camp Sherman-Metolius River Junction. Go 5.5 mi. to Camp Sherman store. The lodges are 100 yards upstream.

For rates, see Index.

THE MORICAL HOUSE
Ashland, Oregon

At the time of my first visit to the Morical House, the carpenters, road menders, and gardeners were all at work and Phyllis Morical was on the scene making sure that everything was going according to her plans. For instance, the paneling of the old staircase had been taken right down to the natural wood, and the effect in the Victorian atmosphere is splendid. The stained-glass windows and detailed woodwork, too, were receiving needed attention.

Each of the five guest rooms has been decorated in a turn-of-the-century motif with appropriate antiques and homemade comforters, and each has a private bath. All of the bedrooms have a view of the Cascade Mountains in the distance, as well as views of the lawns and adjacent gardens, which have over 100 varieties of colorful and fragrant trees, shrubs, and flowers.

A full breakfast, including fresh-baked goods, is served in the dining room or on the porch, and a light afternoon refreshment is a welcome touch.

The Morical House is a fifteen-minute walk to the theaters of Ashland's well-known Shakespeare Festival, which runs from the end of February through October.

Incidentally, things are very busy here during the height of the festival, between the first of June and the middle of September, and weekends, even in the spring and fall, are packed, so it is well to reserve in advance.

THE MORICAL HOUSE, 668 No. Main St., Ashland, Or. 97520; 503-482-2254. A 5-bedroom bed-and-breakfast inn located in scenic, south-central Oregon. Breakfast is the only meal served. Open year-round. Bent grass putting green on grounds. Conveniently located for guests to enjoy the many cultural, natural, and historical attractions nearby, including the Shakespeare Festival. Joe and Phyllis Morical, Innkeepers.

Directions: Ashland is in southern Oregon on Rte. 5. The Morical House is on Main Street, at the north end of the town.

For B&B rates, see Index.

PARADISE RANCH INN
Grants Pass, Oregon

I believe the biggest problem that the bed-and-breakfast visitor would have at Paradise Ranch Inn is staying for only one night. There is so much to do and see and enjoy that the temptation to cancel the rest of the trip would be enormous.

Paradise Ranch Inn, in the beautiful Rogue River Valley in southern Oregon, is a picturebook ranch with white fences, green meadows, neat barns, and marvelous vistas. Cattle, horses, chickens, and other farm animals complete the picture.

The proprietors, Mattie and Ollie Raymond, have that magic quality of hospitality and warmth that gives all the guests the feeling everybody has been friends for years and years. They give their guests the run of the ranch, including the lounge with a fireplace, books, ping-pong, and other entertainment.

The big time to get together is at Mattie's really staggering breakfasts served every morning. I might point out that bed-and-breakfast accommodations are available all year. Dinner is available with reservations.

Accommodations in sophisticated-rustic quarters have been created in barns and other outbuildings on the original ranch property. There are comfortable ranch-style furnishings, and full private baths.

If you are planning on remaining for just one night, let me suggest that you get there early in the afternoon to enjoy the wonderful atmosphere and maybe a game of tennis or horseshoes, and perhaps a swim in the heated pool or a relaxing soak in the hot tub.

For Route I-5 travelers between Portland and the Bay area, Paradise Ranch Inn is most conveniently situated for a stop.

PARADISE RANCH INN, 7000 Monument Dr., Grants Pass, Or. 97526; 503-479-4333. A splendid 14-bedroom ranch-inn nestled in the beautiful mountains of the Rogue River Valley. Open year-round. Full Amer. plan in summer; bed-and-breakfast available year-round. Heated swimming pool, tennis courts, fishing, surrey rides, hayrides, cattle roundup, square dancing, recreational barn and children-watching available on grounds. Spectacular Rogue River raft trips and all-day horseback riding nearby. Mattie and Ollie Raymond, Innkeepers.

Directions: From the Bay Area follow Rte. 101 north to Crescent City and then Rte. 199 to Grants Pass; turn north on Rte. 5 and exit at Merlin. Go under Rte. 5, turn right on Monument Mountain Drive for 2½ miles. Ranch is on left.

For B&B rates, see Index.

THE PRINGLE HOUSE
Oakland, Oregon

When the Pringle House opened its doors in April, 1984, it became the first approved bed and breakfast in Douglas County. A beautiful, two-story, Queen Anne-style Victorian house, it stands on a rise at the end of the main street in this registered National Historic village (population 850).

From the Pringle House sign, a cast iron relic from an Englishman's fireplace, to the Victorian gingerbread, painted in five colors, to the flower gardens, bird baths, and walkways, and, eventually, to the gazebo, this bed and breakfast is a picture out of the past.

Jim and Demay Pringle are the happy, caring innkeepers who accomplished this transformation almost single-handedly. The interior is decorated appropriately with antiques, wallpaper, chandeliers, stained glass windows, and oriental rugs on the polished floors.

The study betrays Jim's past. It contains a piano, record collections, books, and photographs on the wall depicting marching bands, and choirs under his direction. You guessed it, Jim has been a music teacher for almost thirty years.

The two guest rooms have been decorated with antique beds and bureaus, beautiful quilts, coordinated wallpaper, and oriental rugs. A hundred-year-old quilt on one bed is described by Jim as an anthology of feather stitching with hundreds of different stitch patterns. The "his and hers" bathroom is shared.

Bring a good appetite, as the continental breakfast is huge, offering fruit juice, coffee, tea, milk or hot chocolate, fresh baked breads or croissants, cheese, fruit in season with yogurt dressing or cream, crème caramel, or perhaps a ham and cheese quiche.

THE PRINGLE HOUSE, 114 N.E. 7th St., P.O. Box 578, Oakland, OR 97462; 503-459-5038. A 2-guestroom (shared bath)Victorian bed-and-breakfast inn 1 hr. south of Eugene in an National Historic Register village. Open all year. Historic walking tour, city museum, hiking, wildlife safari, backpacking, and fishing nearby. Older children only. No pets. No credit cards. Checks accepted with bank guarantee. Smoking in designated areas only. Demay and Jim Pringle, Innkeepers.

Directions: From Eugene going south, drive approx. 60 mi., to Exit 138, proceed 2 mi. to Oakland, continue up Locust St., the main street. The Pringle House is at the end of the street on corner of 7th and Locust. From Roseburg driving north, drive approx. 18 mi., to Exit 138, then proceed with instructions above.

For B&B rates, see Index.

SPINDRIFT
Bandon, Oregon

Ocean lovers will enjoy the breathtaking beauty of the Oregon coast at Spindrift bed and breakfast. This lovely home is perched on a bluff just forty feet above a long, sandy beach that is framed by massive offshore rock formations. Floor-to-ceiling windows and a large deck, with direct beach access, offer views of changing surf, sea animals, and glorious sunsets.

Hosts Don and Robbie Smith have given the house a pleasantly unique feeling with antiques (many from Don's grandparents) and books that hint of Don's many years as a librarian. Their bedroom contains one of Robbie's weaving looms. Don, who looks like a New England sea captain (he was born and reared in Maine) enjoys winemaking.

There are two guest rooms. The floor-to-ceiling corner window in the Seaview room is spectacular, with a panoramic view of the ocean. The room has a private bath, fireplace, and queen- sized bed with a down quilt. French doors open onto the deck and a ramp has been added for the disabled.

The second bedroom, the Surfsound, is smaller and does not have an ocean view, but is restful with twin beds and down quilts. The bath is shared.

Breakfasts at Spindrift are hearty, and include eggs cooked any way, breakfast meats, or even seafood in season, popovers, fresh fruit, and fresh-brewed coffee.

SPINDRIFT, 2990 Beach Loop Rd., Bandon, OR 97411; 503-347-2275. A 2-guestroom inn (1 private bath) by the sea, 25 mi. south of Coos Bay on the southern Oregon coast. Full breakfast included. Open every day all year. Fishing, crabbing, clamming, hiking, horseback riding, golfing nearby. Many interesting shops to explore—the famous Cranberry Sweets Manufacturing Co.; Bandon Cheddar Cheese factory. No pets. Smoking area provided. Don and Robbie Smith, Innkeepers.

Directions: From Roseburg, drive south on I-5. Exit at Rte. 19, proceed 3 mi. to Winston. Turn right at first light in Winston, following Rte. 42 to Coquille. Turn left at Coquille and on to Bandon. Continue south on Hwy. 101, past 11th St. traffic light for approx. 1 mi. Turn right (west) on Seabird Dr. to Beach Loop Rd.; turn right (north), and Spindrift is the 2nd house on the left. From Coos Bay, drive 25 mi. south on Coast Hwy. 101. After arriving in Bandon, continue on 101 and follow above directions.

For B&B rates, see Index.

STEAMBOAT INN
Idleyld Park, Oregon

Route 138 proceeds east out of Roseburg, Oregon, into the mountains, following the course of one of the famous wild rivers of Oregon, the Umpqua. The road points upwards almost immediately.

Here, up in this wonderful, wild country, I found Jim and Sharon Van Loan and the Steamboat Inn. Although it is on the road to Diamond and Crater lakes, and is a major east-west route to Highway 97, most people who find their way here for either overnight accommodations or dinner, or both, have heard about it in advance.

Originally, this inn attracted people who came for the steelhead fishing on the North Umpqua River. However, in recent years many non-fishermen and their families have discovered that this is a very exciting hideaway with an appeal for every member of the family. There's good swimming and backpacking and hiking trails. But most of all, there's a wonderful feeling of literally being embraced by nature.

Each of the eight accommodations has a breathtaking view of the river that is enhanced by a broad veranda. Nestled among the towering firs, the inn is about two hours by car from airports at Eugene or Medford.

One of the big attractions here is dinner. It is served each night of the summer about a half hour after dark and in the winter about seven o'clock. It is by reservation only and the cabin guests have automatic reservations. Sharon Van Loan's cold salmon with mustard sauce is one of the many different menu items, along with the homemade breads, that are changed each day. She relies on farmers' produce stands and people who bring fruits and vegetables from their gardens.

The Steamboat Inn is one of the most unusual places I have ever visited. You can stay for one night if you care to, but the temptation to remain on and on is very great.

STEAMBOAT INN, HC60, Box 36, Idleyld Park, Or. 97447; 503-496-3495 or 503-498-2411. An 8-room rustic riverside inn in one of Oregon's most spectacular nature areas. Open all year. Breakfast, lunch, and dinner served daily; breakfast is not included in the room rate. Dinner ½ hr. after sundown in summer, 7 P.M. in winter. Fishing, backpacking, and hiking in abundance. Sharon and Jim Van Loan, Innkeepers.

Directions: From Roseburg drive 38 mi. east on Rte. 138.

For Lodging rates, see Index.

WOLF CREEK TAVERN
Wolf Creek, Oregon

As in many cases, I just stumbled onto the Wolf Creek Tavern. I was driving north of Grants Pass on Highway 5, and saw a little sign at the exit saying that Wolf Creek Tavern was nearby. I proceeded with some misgivings, because I've turned off the road for many a tavern or inn sign to find it was a great disappointment. Not so in this case.

Wolf Creek Tavern has a very fascinating past, which has been most intelligently preserved by the Oregon State Parks and Recreation Division. Someone obviously saw the advantage of retaining such an architecturally interesting building, and furthermore, had the good sense to try to continue its useful function, which began as a stagecoach stop in 1873.

A brochure supplies some excellent historical material, and at the same time points out that the tavern's restoration renewed long-forgotten crafts and revealed fine workmanship and carpentry. Original wood-molding patterns, no longer available, had to be custom made. Wainscoting, doors, and window casings have a "hand-combed" finish which simulates red oak grain.

This is an excellent and thoughtful job of preserving the best of the past and, fortunately for travelers, this is a full-service inn serving breakfast, lunch, and dinner year around.

Reflecting the various historic periods of the inn, rather than one particular time, the bedrooms have been furnished in various modes. However, every effort, including the addition of individual bathrooms, has been made to make them much more comfortable then they were 100 years ago!

The innkeepers, Vernon and Donna Wiard, lease the tavern from the state and are preserving its historic integrity, as well as providing a warm and personal atmosphere.

WOLF CREEK TAVERN, P.O. Box 97, Wolf Creek, Or. 97497; 503-866-2474. An 8-bedroom, thoughtfully restored late 19th century stagestop, continuing its useful life today by offering sustenance and good beds year-round. Breakfast is not included in room rate. Closed Christmas and New Year's. Conveniently located to enjoy the beautiful scenery and recreational advantages of southern Oregon. No pets. Donna and Vernon Wiard, Innkeepers.

Directions: Wolf Creek is located off Exit 76 from I-5. Located south of Roseburg and north of Grants Pass.

For Lodging rates, see Index.

BARLEY SHEAF FARM
Holicong, Pennsylvania

Barley Sheaf Farm, in the heart of Bucks County was a part of the William Penn Land Grant and was originally built during the time that the Lenape indians lived in this area.

As is the case in many early Pennsylvania dwellings, there are actually two buildings: the original wooden dwelling built in 1740, and the stone house built probably between 1770 and 1800. Much of the feeling of colonial antiquity has been preserved by the original wide floor boards and beautifully crafted doorways and windows.

Apparently this has been a farm for most of its years, although there have been quite a few owners. The present proprietors, Don and Ann Mills and their family, were inspired to open a bed-and-breakfast inn by their trip to England, during which they stayed in several farm-type accommodations.

The house sits a pleasant distance from the road and is surrounded by fields and a wooded area. Of particular note is a gorgeous irreplaceable copper beech tree which is growing just outside the entrance to the house.

There are 10 bedrooms of ample size and all very tastefully furnished with colorful furniture, curtains, and bedspreads. Three of them have a shared bath. Some of these rooms as well as the breakfast and living rooms have some early American paintings.

A full farm breakfast is served on the sunporch, and almost everything is either raised or prepared right on the farm. The eggs are gathered every morning from the barn and the bees that buzz around the bushes and flowers make the honey. There's bacon or ham and homemade scrapple, as well as freshly baked breads and homemade jams.

BARLEY SHEAF FARM, Box 66, Holicong, Pa. 18928; 215-794-5104. A 10-room bed-and-breakfast inn, 8 mi. from Doylestown and New Hope, Pennsylvania. Near Delaware River, Bucks County Playhouse, George Washington's Crossing. Breakfast only meal served; bag lunches on request. Open March 1 thru weekend prior to Christmas. Croquet, badminton, swimming pool, farm animals on grounds. Tennis, boating, canoeing, and horseback riding nearby. Near all of the natural and historical attractions of Buck's County, Pennsylvania. Recommended for children over 8. No credit cards. Don and Ann Mills, Innkeepers.

For B&B rates, see Index.

CAMERON ESTATE INN
Mount Joy, Pennsylvania

Tucked away in the Pennsylvania farming country near Lancaster, this bed-and-breakfast stop has been designated by the Department of the Interior as a National Historic Landmark.

This mansion was built in 1805 and later became the country home of Simon Cameron, Lincoln's first secretary of war. He was also a four-time U.S. senator and ambassador to Russia.

Just four miles from Mt. Joy, the inn is set in a commodious grove of trees through which a well-stocked trout stream meanders.

There are oriental rugs and period furnishings in the parlor, dining rooms and generously sized bedrooms, some of which have canopy beds and quite a few of which have fireplaces.

The proprietors are Abe and Betty Groff of the internationally acclaimed Groff's Farm Restaurant, just a few miles away.

In addition to breakfast, which is offered as part of the B&B rates, dinner is also served with choices from an international menu.

CAMERON ESTATE INN, R.D. #1, Box 305, Donegal Springs Road, Mount Joy, Pa. 17752; 717-653-1773. An elegant 18-room (most with private baths) inn in a former mansion 4½ mi. from both Mount Joy and Elizabethtown. Continental breakfast included in rates. Lunch and dinner served Mon. thru Sat. Closed Christmas. Open all year. Convenient to all of the attractions in the Pennsylvania Dutch country including museums, art galleries, and theaters. Located halfway between Gettysburg and Valley Forge. Not recommended for young children. No pets. Abram and Betty Groff, Innkeepers.

Directions: Traveling west on the Pennsylvania Tpke. take Exit 21. Follow Rte. 222 S to Rte. 30 W to Rte. 283 W. Follow Rte. 283 W to Rte. 230 (the first Mount Joy exit). Follow Rte. 230 through Mount Joy to the fourth traffic light. Turn left onto Angle St. At first crossroads, turn right onto Donegal Springs Rd. Go to the stop sign. Turn left onto Colebrook Rd. Go just a short distance over a small bridge. Turn right, back onto Donegal Springs Rd. Follow signs to inn—about ½ mi. on the right.

For B&B rates, see Index.

DISCOVERIES BED & BREAKFAST
Sigel, Pennsylvania

This place really thrilled me. It is located in northwestern Pennsylvania, north of I-80, in the Cook Forest State Park area.

The house is a beautiful Victorian built in 1880, and this is an area where extra bedrooms are called "spare rooms." In addition to an immaculately clean and well-run B&B, there is also an antiques and crafts shop with the attractive extra feature of fruits and vegetables in season.

The owners are Bruce MacBeth and his wife, Pat. He is a college professor and she is a medical technologist. They have lived here for the past twenty-eight or more years, but now that their two older children are grown and away, they thought it would be fun to have a B&B, and it has worked out beautifully.

The house has three fireplaces and the bedrooms look like the spare rooms of 100 years ago. There are many white-painted cast iron beds and beautiful, carved antiques as well. I was particularly impressed with all of the many different kinds of quilts, which are also on sale in the crafts shop.

Vacationers and travelers coming to this part of the world, which abounds in so many recreational opportunities, will be glad to know that a full breakfast is served to the MacBeth guests. Among other things, there might be a cheese omelet served with home-cured bacon, hot muffins, fresh fruit, and coffee. This is served in the dining room with good china and silver.

"Discoveries" was indeed a great discovery for me. (I just couldn't resist saying that.)

DISCOVERIES BED & BREAKFAST, RD#1, Sigel, Pa. 15860; 814-752-2632. A 5-bedroom (sharing two baths) B&B located in the scenic Cook Forest and Clear Creek State Park area of north-western Pennsylvania. Breakfast is the only meal served. Open year-round. An excellent crafts and antiques shop adjoins. No credit cards. No pets. Bruce and Pat MacBeth, Proprietors.

Directions: Discoveries is located on Rte. 36, 2½ mi. north of Sigel. From I-80 use Exit 13 and follow Rte. 36 north.

For B&B rates, see Index.

EVERMAY-ON-THE-DELAWARE
Erwinna, Pennsylvania

At Evermay-on-the Delaware overnight guests enjoy not only a breakfast included with the price of the rooms, but *afternoon tea* as well!

The inn is situated right on the picturesque Delaware River in the upper section of Bucks County, Pennsylvania, and the earliest part of the building dates to 1700. It took on new life as a hotel from 1871 to 1930, and during that time many prominent people enjoyed its hospitality, including the famous theatrical Barrymore family.

Today it has been beautifully restored by Ron Strouse and Fred Cresson. Each of the bedrooms has views of either the Delaware or the rolling fields at the rear of the inn, and has been furnished with carefully chosen antiques. All have a very romantic atmosphere.

The public rooms and the dining room all have been painstakingly restored to create a 19th-century feeling.

Afternoon tea can be taken on the back porch or in the warm and gracious parlor. The breakfast dining room is at the back of the inn, overlooking the fields and low hills and is enhanced by Victorian stained-glass windows.

A prix fixe dinner, usually five courses with a choice of two or three entrées, is also offered at Evermany. There is one sitting at 7:30 P.M.

EVERMAY-ON-THE-DELAWARE, Erwinna, Pa. 18920; 215-294-9100. A 16-bedroom riverside inn in upper Bucks County. Breakfast and afternoon tea included in the room tariff. Box lunches available for houseguests. Dinner served Fri. Sat., Sun., and holidays at 7:30 P.M. by reservation. Convenient to all the Bucks County natural and historical attractions including handsome mansions, museums, and historical sites. Xc skiing, backroading, and canoeing nearby. No amusements for small children. No pets. Ron Strouse and Fred Cresson, Innkeepers.

Directions: From New York City: take Rte. 22 to Clinton; Rte. 31 to Flemington; Rte. 12 to Frenchtown. Cross river and turn south on Rte. 32 for 2 mi. From Philadelphia: follow I-95 north to Yardley exit and Rte. 32 north to Erwinna. There are several other routes also.

For B&B rates, see Index.

FAIRFIELD INN & GUEST HOUSE
Fairfield, Pennsylvania

Gettysburg is one of the great tourist objectives in North America, and deservedly so, although I have personally taken the tour of the battlefield with mixed emotions.

Be that as it may, the whole trip can be an adventure, although there are quite a few commercial intrusions; namely, motels, restaurants, and souvenir stores, named after some of the principal field commanders.

Fortunately it's possible to avoid the hurly-burly of downtown Gettysburg by staying overnight at either Hickory Bridge Farm, which I have mentioned elsewhere, or the Fairfield Inn, whose history long antedates the summer of 1863.

It was originally the plantation home of Squire William Miller who settled in Fairfield in 1755. In those days the highway was known as the "Great Road" from York to Hagerstown and the inn was a stagecoach stop as well as a drovers' tavern. It has been in continuous operation since 1823.

In 1980, the enterprising owner of the inn, David Thomas, completed restoration of another of the first homes of Fairfield, which for many years has been known as the Cunningham House. During the War Between the States the house was used as a hospital for wounded officers and it has been said that a ghost of one of them may still be in residence.

This guest house has been painstakingly furnished, mostly with antiques. There are four bedrooms in all. Some of them look out over the village street scene, and others in the rear look out at the beautiful mountains.

Overnight guests may cross the village street to the main inn where luncheon and dinner are served every day except major holidays and Sundays. It's a country breakfast, for sure, served à la carte in the dining room featuring Adams County country ham, freshly baked biscuits, and honey from local beehives. Just the sort of fortifying needed to sustain one for a tour of the historic environs.

FAIRFIELD INN & GUEST HOUSE, Main St., Fairfield, Pa. 17320; 717-642-5410. A country restaurant near Gettysburg with 4 lodging rooms available. Breakfast, lunch, and dinner served daily. Closed on major holidays, Sundays, and first week in Sept. and Feb. Dinner reservations advised. Nearby region is rich in history, including Gettysburg Battlefield. No pets. David W. Thomas, Innkeeper.

Directions: Fairfield is 8 mi. west of Gettysburg on Rte. 116.

For Lodging rates, see Index.

HICKORY BRIDGE FARM
Orrtanna, Pennsylvania

American history buffs are really in luck when they visit the Gettysburg Battlefield National Park because they have a choice of at least two places in which to enjoy overnight accommodations that are a sufficient distance from the inevitable crowds that always flock to this great American shrine.

One of them is the Hickory Bridge Farm in Orrtanna, which is hidden away back in the foothills to the west of Gettysburg.

The building is a 19th-century farmhouse furnished with period furniture including beds with lovely old quilts, beautiful old chests, braided rugs, antique dolls, and marble-topped bureaus.

Additional bedrooms are to be found just a short distance away in two cottages in the woods reached by a footpath that follows the brook.

The entire bucolic atmosphere is enhanced by a bass pond and a rustic bridge leading to a gentle island woodland, which makes a beautiful sight for guests enjoying breakfast on the outer deck of the farmhouse.

Adding to this atmosphere is a collection of turn-of-the-century farm machinery that was put back into working order by one of the farm neighbors with the help of the Hammett sons.

The farm restaurant is located in the barn across from the farmhouse. Farm-style dinners are served to guests and travelers on Saturday evening.

A full breakfast is served by innkeeper Nancy Jean Hammett and her daughter Mary Lynn in the dining room. In the summer breakfast is just perfect on the sunny porch overlooking the creek.

HICKORY BRIDGE FARM INN, Orrtanna, Pa. 17353; 717-642-5261. A 7-room country inn on a farm 3 mi. from Fairfield and 8 mi. from Gettysburg. Open year-round. A deposit required. A 2-night minimum stay on weekends, May 1 to Oct. 31. Full breakfast included in room rate. Near Gettysburg Battlefield Natl. Park, Caledonia State Park, and Totem Pole Playhouse. Hiking, biking, fishing, hunting, and country store museum on grounds. Golf, swimming available nearby. The Hammett Family, Innkeepers.

Directions: From Gettysburg take Rte. 116 west to Fairfield and follow signs 3 mi. north to Orrtanna.

For B&B rates, see Index.

THE INN AT STARLIGHT LAKE
Starlight, Pennsylvania

The casual tourer in northeast Pennsylvania or the traveler using Route 17 to cross New York State by way of Binghamton, Corning, Olean, and Jamestown will find that the short side trip from Hancock, New York, to Starlight, Pennsylvania, will reward him with a night's lodging at the Inn at Starlight Lake.

As the name implies, the inn is located beside a lake of pure, clear spring water and it is surrounded by many acres of untouched forest and farmland meadows.

The main house provides seventeen comfortable rooms, ten cottage rooms, and a three-bedroom family house, all open year-round. Boarding for pets can be arranged at a nearby kennel.

This pleasant informal atmosphere could be a welcome change for travelers with children because there are plenty of diversions next to the lake and in the game room for young people of all ages. In fact Jack and Judy McMahon have children of their own and the inn is their home.

Because this inn is slightly off the beaten path, it is a good idea to plan to take the evening meal as well.

The sunny dining room with views of the lake is the scene of the full American breakfast, which includes homemade breads, coffee cakes, raised-dough waffles, blueberry pancakes, and always fresh-ground coffee!

THE INN AT STARLIGHT LAKE, Starlight, Pa. 18461; 717-798-2519. A 30-room resort-inn located 5 mi. from Hancock, N.Y. Modified American plan. Breakfast, lunch, dinner served daily. Closed between April 1 and 15. Swimming, boating, canoeing, sailing, fishing, hunting, tennis, hiking, bicycling, xc skiing, and lawn sports on grounds. Canoeing, hunting, fishing, golfing nearby. No pets. Judy and Jack McMahon, Innkeepers.

Directions: From N.Y. Rte. 17, exit at Hancock, N.Y. Take Rte. 191S over Delaware River to Rte. 370. Turn right, proceed 3½ mi. turn right, 1 mi. to inn. From I-81, take exit 62 and go east on Rte. 107. Turn left on Rte. 247 to Forest City. Turn left on Rte. 171, go 10 mi. to Rte. 370. Turn right, proceed 12 mi. Turn left, 1 mi. to inn.

For B&B rates, see Index.

MAPLE LANE FARM
Paradise, Pennsylvania

I can assure those among our readers who have never visited the Pennsylvania Dutch country, that they are in for a most unusual experience. The wonderful farms, so clean and neat, operated very frequently by the Amish people, and the engaging little towns and villages provide a backroading experience that has remained unchanged for over a hundred years in many cases.

In the heart of this country, I found The Maple Lane Farm which is just outside of Strasburg, Pennsylvania.

Marion and Edwin Rohrer have been taking in guests for seventeen years, and one of the very attractive features about this guest house is the fact that it's across the road from the original old farm which is constructed of beautifully mellowed Pennsylvania stone. Mr. and Mrs. Rohrer are delighted to have their guests visit the farm and the barn and watch the milking or take a hike in the woods. Children can even wade in the brook. There's a forty-mile view at the top of the hill.

The guest house itself is a colonial-style brick building which was built relatively recently and all of the bedrooms are very pleasantly furnished with Pennsylvania antiques, framed needlework, and some exceptionally fine quilts.

A very pleasant parlor has been set aside especially for the use of the guests.

Morning coffee is provided and there are excellent restaurants nearby for full breakfasts.

Most guests find Mrs. Rohrer's collection of covered boxes a very interesting hobby.

MAPLE LANE FARM, 505 Paradise Lane, Paradise, Pa. 17562; 717-687-7479. A 4-room farm guest house (2 with private baths) located just a short distance from Strasburg. Open all year. Within a short distance of many area attractions including the Strasburg Railroad. No credit cards. Mr. & Mrs. Edwin Rohrer, Proprietors.

Directions: Turn south on Rte. 896 off Rte. 30. Proceed to Strasburg. Turn left on Rte. 896 at traffic light and proceed 1½ mi. out of town and turn at sign for Timberline Lodge which is Paradise Lane.

For Lodging rates, see Index.

OVERLOOK INN
Canadensis, Pennsylvania

The Overlook Inn is located high in the Poconos Mountains in northeastern Pennsylvania. The fragrant pine, blue spruce, and locust forests stretch out in all directions, and the cardinals, quail, and robins flit about in the rhododendron and mountain laurel.

All of the country inn bedrooms have baths and all have patchwork quilts and books and plants, adding immeasurably to the homey feeling. My favorite room is one that looks out over the high fields at the rear of the inn. It's such a quiet and peaceful place in the early morning.

In pleasant warm weather, the porch is an ideal place to enjoy the full breakfast. There are fresh orange juice, homemade muffins, Danish and other breakfast pastries, fruit-filled pancakes, Welsh rarebit, Pennsylvania scrapple, and homemade sausage. It's hard to leave breakfast because almost everybody starts interesting conversations.

Travelers to and from New England on I-84 can take the "Promised Land" Exit (Route 390) and be at the inn in a very short time for a pleasant overnight stay.

OVERLOOK INN, Dutch Hill Rd., Canadensis, Pa. 18325; 717-595-7519. A 20-room resort-inn in the heart of the Poconos, 15 mi. from Stroudsburg, Pa. Mod. American plan. Breakfast and dinner served to travelers. Open every day of the year. Pool, shuffleboard, bocci, hiking on grounds; golf, tennis, alpine slide, ice skating, downhill and xc skiing, indoor tennis, antiquing, backroading, summer theater nearby. No children under 12. No pets. Bob and Lolly Tupper, Innkeepers.

Directions: From the north (New England, New York State, and Canada) use I-84 and take Rte. 390 south through "Promised Land" about 12 mi. to traffic light in Canadensis. Make right-hand turn on Rte. 447 north—go 1/3 mi. to first right-hand turn (Dutch Hill Road). Inn is 1½ mi. up hill. Look for new sign on right. From New York City, take George Washington Bridge to I-80 west. Turn off at Pennsylvania Exit 52. Follow Rte. 447 north straight through Canadensis traffic light. Turn right on Dutch Hill Road as above.

For B&B rates, see Index.

PUMP HOUSE INN
Canadensis, Pennsylvania

In spite of the jokes and references about heart-shaped beds and bathtubs furnished by certain resorts catering to honeymooners or romantic weekenders, most of the Poconos is a rather conservative, sedate, and natural area which has been a vacation objective for some of Philadelphia's and New York's most discriminating families.

In this book I am happy to point out three Pocono country inns that also provide bed-and-breakfast accommodations. One of them is the Pump House Inn in Canadensis.

Although it has established a more than ten-year reputation as an excellent restaurant, fortunately, the Drucquer Family has also provided five extremely comfortable lodging rooms furnished with typical country inn furniture and decorations.

A continental breakfast of juice, fruit, cheese, hot biscuits, and coffee is offered at a freshly laid table with gleaming white linen.

Every effort should be made to arrive in time for dinner (please reserve), which offers three different types of dining. One menu presents the French cuisine that has made the Pump House nationally famous. It is set with crystal goblets, fresh flowers, and starched linens.

THE PUMP HOUSE INN, Canadensis, Pa. 18325; 717-595-7501. A 5-room country inn high in the Poconos, 1½ mi. north of Canadensis village and 16 mi. northeast of Stroudsburg. European plan. Sophisticated country dining. Dinner served to travelers daily. Open every day in summer. Closed Mon. in spring and fall, and Mon. and Tues. in winter. Closed Christmas and New Year's Day. Bicycles and golf nearby. The Drucquer Family, Owners; H. Todd Drucquer, Innkeeper.

Directions: From the north, follow I-84 to Rte. 390 south. Inn is located 13 mi. south on Rte. 390. From the south, follow I-80 west to Exit 52. Follow Rte. 447 north 20 mi. to Canadensis. At light, turn right, 390 north. Inn is 1½ mi. north from light.

For B&B rates, see Index.

1740 HOUSE
Lumberville, Pennsylvania

Bucks County, Pennsylvania, is rich in history. It is here that Washington's army made its famous crossing of the Delaware River, and the Battlefields of Trenton and the encampment of Valley Forge are both nearby. It's possible to stay in Bucks County for two or three days just to follow the historically oriented back-road tours.

The 1740 House is located on the Delaware River just a few miles from New Hope, Pennsylvania. It is conservative and quiet.

Weekend reservations must include two nights; usually these are booked well in advance. Dinner is served between 7:00 and 7:30 P.M. in a small dining room overlooking the canal and river, and it is necessary for everyone—even houseguests—to have advance reservations.

Guest rooms are located in the main house and also in several outbuildings along the canal side. All are furnished with exceptional care and taste.

All the rooms have terraces or balconies with lovely views of the tree-lined and sometimes ivy-covered embankment sloping down to the river. There is a pleasantly furnished cozy living room and a welcome swimming pool for the warm weather.

Harry Nessler refers to the morning meal as a buffet breakfast, with orange juice, coffee, cold cereal, scrambled eggs, danish, croissants, english muffins, jam, and homemade bread.

1740 HOUSE, River Rd., Lumberville, Pa. 18933; 215-297-5661. A 24-room riverside inn, 6½ mi. north of New Hope, in the heart of historic Bucks County. Lodgings include breakfast which is served to houseguests daily; dinner served daily except Sundays by reservation only. Open year-round. Pool and boating on grounds. golf and tennis nearby. Harry Nessler, Innkeeper.

Directions: From N.Y.C., travel south on N.J. Tpke., and take Exit 10. Follow Rte. 287 north to another Exit 10. Proceed west on Rte. 22 to Flemington, then Rte. 202 south over Delaware Toll Bridge. After an immediate right U-turn onto Rte. 32N, drive 5 mi. to inn. From Pa. Tpke., exit at Willow Grove and proceed north on Rte. 611 to Rte. 202. Follow Rte. 202 north to Rte. 32 and turn north to inn. From Phila., take I-95 to Yardley-New Hope Exit, follow 32N through New Hope and 7 miles to inn.

For B&B rates, see Index.

SHENANGO INN
Sharon, Pennsylvania

Have you ever driven across Pennsylvania and Ohio on I-80? It seems like miles and miles of concrete, and what you really need is a good break—a pleasant dinner, perhaps a dip in a swimming pool, a quiet night's respite to make the rest of the journey even better than tolerable.

The Shenango Inn in Sharon, Pennsylvania, true to the spirit of this book, offers bed and breakfast in a way that is most welcome.

The atmosphere is "Williamsburgian," with a stately four-story building located far away from the traffic noise, literally in the middle of a residential section. It has a sweeping driveway to the front door and there is a good possibility that a bellman in a Colonial costume will be there to help with the bags. The swimming pool and jacuzzi are barely visible behind a screen of roses.

This eighteenth-century decor is continued in the reception area and in many of the bedrooms.

After a bath or a swim, a pleasant dinner, and a quiet night's rest, the topper comes in the morning when your continental breakfast is delivered to your room along with the morning newspaper.

If you'd care to stay over for another day, there's a secluded 320-acre park just one block away, providing jogging, bicycling, tennis, cross-country skiing, and a golf course at no charge.

SHENANGO INN, 1330 Kimberly Rd., Sharon, Pa. 16146; 412-981-5000. A 70-room, full-service inn located in a very quiet residential district about 12 min. from I-80. Continental breakfast included in room rate. Breakfast, lunch, dinner served daily. Open all year. Exercise room, swimming pool, jacuzzi on grounds. Racquet ball, golf course, bicycling, jogging, tennis, xc skiing nearby. Jim and Donna Winner, Innkeepers.

Directions: From I-80, take Exit 1 north. Go north on Rte. 60 to Rte. 18 north to Sharon. Take the second turn-off for Rte. 62. Turn left, proceed about 2 mi. and look for inn sign on right. (Inn is 5 mi. from I-80.)

For B&B rates, see Index.

SOCIETY HILL HOTEL
Philadelphia, Pennsylvania

Typifying the term "urban inn," the Society Hill Hotel is located on Third and Chestnut Streets in the midst of Independence National Historical Park, the federal development that sparked the revitalization of Society Hill and the old section of the city. These areas today have become an attraction to over three million visitors per year.

Known affectionately as "Philadelphia's smallest hotel," the Society Hill Hotel is within two blocks of Independence Hall, Franklin Court, Penn's Landing, and is diagonally across the street from the Federal Visitors Center.

The twelve guest rooms have been decorated with brass double beds, beautiful antiques, and fresh-cut flowers, and six of them are two-room suites.

The restaurant, designed in light woods, stained glass and greenery, contributes to the congenial and casual atmosphere, and the huge windows give patrons a spectacular view of the park.

The breakfast served in each room is fresh-squeezed juice, coffee or tea, and warm croissants or coffee cake with butter and jam. A Sunday brunch is offered in the restaurant and includes Belgian waffles, eggs Benedict, and steak and eggs.

Bed-and-breakfast has arrived in Philadelphia in a manner that even Benjamin Franklin would applaud.

SOCIETY HILL HOTEL AND RESTAURANT, Third & Chestnut Sts., Philadelphia, Pa. 19106; 215-925-1394 (restaurant 925-1919). A 12-bedroom urban hotel in the heart of Philadelphia. Air conditioning, color TV, and private baths. A continental breakfast is served in the room every morning. Open year-round. Within walking distance of many of the important cultural, recreational, and historic attractions of the Old City. Kate W. Carnwath, Innkeeper.

Directions: From the New Jersey Tpke. take Exit 4 and Rtes. 30 & 38 across the Ben Franklin Bridge and turn left on 6th St. to Chestnut. Turn left to Third and Chestnut.

For B&B rates, see Index.

SPRING HOUSE
Airville, Pennsylvania

Thanks to my Stockbridge friend Mark Swann, the Spring House at Muddy Creek Forks in York County is a real find—an 18th-century stone house in a historic pre-Revolutionary village.

Mark described the village to me, "It's much as it was a hundred years ago with clapboard mill buildings, a creamery, and a Gothic country store. It is reached by unpaved roads, and the now-unused railroad bed of the 'Ma and Pa' (Maryland and Pennsylvania) Railroad provides splendid hiking opportunities."

The Spring House, with a history as a tavern, is the dream-come-true for Ray Hearne who visited a number of B&Bs in England and conceived the idea of turning this beautiful old house into an inn. She restored it literally with her own hands, preserving the creaky floorboards, uncovering the stencils on some of the walls, and restoring the interior. Indoor plumbing and running water have been added, but the three guest bedrooms have been furnished with featherbeds from Ireland, and additional stenciling and murals in the old-time manner have been created by artist Peggy Kurtz.

The kitchen has an old pie safe, a jelly cupboard, and a coffee grinder, and among the time-to-time offerings on the full breakfast are scrapple, local sausage, or French pancakes with hand-picked, tree-ripened peaches, blackberries, or raspberries. Honey is provided from hives on the property and all the eggs come from local chickens. Breakfast is eaten in the dining room or on the front porch overlooking the sylvan scene.

SPRING HOUSE, Muddy Creek Forks, Airville, York County, Pa. 17302; 717-927-6906. A 3-bedroom country bed-and-breakfast experience some distance from the madding crowd. Open year-round, except for "1 month plus" during winter, and Christmas and New Year's. Breakfast is the only meal served, but prior arrangements can be made for dinner. Walking, swimming, fishing, canoeing, and swinging on the porch all readily available. Conveniently located for trips to all of the historical, recreational, and cultural attractions in the area, including 4 wineries. No pets. No credit cards. No smoking. Ray Constance Hearne, Innkeeper.

Directions: Because this is such a rural location, complete directions for arriving from all points of the compass would be well-nigh impossible and I suggest you call Ray Hearne. I'm certain she will put you on the right road.

For B&B rates, see Index.

STERLING INN
South Sterling, Pennsylvania

A few miles out of the way from I-84 and I-80, the Sterling Inn is on a back road in the Poconos. There is a very pleasant nine-hole putting green, a swimming area with a sandy beach, and a little pond with willow trees, which is sometimes home to a select group of ducks.

Lodgings are in several very attractive buildings in a parklike atmosphere. They are all beautifully situated with extremely pleasant rooms that have been colorfully decorated. All have private baths.

Breakfast at this inn in the woods is a Major Project beginning with a choice of fruit or juice and continuing on to hot or cold cereal, eggs any style and bacon or sausage; or homemade hot cakes, or blueberry hot cakes, or waffles, or french toast—all of them served with bacon or sausage. Every plate will have some fried potatoes or hash-browns, coffee cake, and, of course, lots of beverages.

Basically, this is an American plan resort inn, but a few B&B accommodations have been set aside for readers of this book. Please make reservations considerably ahead to avoid disappointment.

THE STERLING INN, Rte. 191, South Sterling, Pa. 18460; 717-676-3311 or 3338. (Toll-free from Conn., N.Y., N.J., Md., Del., Wash. D.C.: 800-523-8200.) A 60-room secluded country inn resort in the Pocono Mountains, 8 mi. from I-84 and 12 mi. from I-380. American plan. Reservation and check-in office closes at 10 P.M. Breakfast, lunch, and dinner served to travelers daily. Breakfast served 8-9 A.M.; lunch served 12:30-1:30 P.M.; dinner served at two seatings 6 P.M. and 7:30 P.M. Jackets required for dinner. Open year-round. Swimming, boating, 9-hole putting green, shuffleboard, all-weather tennis court, scenic hiking trails, all on grounds; also x-country ski trails, game room, tobogganing, sledding, ice skating. Golf courses and horseback riding nearby. Golf packages available. No pets. Ron and Mary Kay Logan, Innkeepers.

Directions: From I-80, follow I-380 to Rte. 940 to Mount Pocono. At light, cross Rte. 611 and proceed on Rte. 196 north to Rte. 423. Drive north on Rte. 423 to Rte. 191 and travel ½ mile north to inn. From I-84, follow Rte. 507 south through Greentown and Newfoundland. In Newfoundland, pick up Rte. 191 and travel 4 mi. south to inn.

For B&B rates, see Index.

TULPEHOCKEN MANOR INN AND PLANTATION
Myerstown, Pennsylvania

George Washington slept here not just once—but three times! The first time was to rest and hunt, and the next two times were to inspect the locks being constructed on the property for the Union Canal. He reputedly slept in the southeast room on the second floor. I might cautiously point out that that is just a portion of the history and tradition connected with this manor house-cum-inn-cum-plantation which, although it had fallen into considerable disrepair, was lovingly and expensively restored by innkeepers Esther Nissly and Jim Henry, starting over twenty years ago.

Every room is chock-full of antiques, quilts, woodwork, mirrors, and impressive beds, tables, bureaus, and armoires. Every bedroom has a history, and fortunately Esther and Jim have gone to a lot of trouble to track down as many of the original furnishings as possible, returning them to their original setting.

The estate consists of 150 acres, a working farm growing hay and corn for the Angus herd bred and raised on the plantation. There are geese on the trout stream and an off-limits 18-acre quarry lake. Except for the acreage that is farmed, much of the land is wild.

Also on the grounds are a smokehouse, a washhouse, a cider house filled with old tools and implements, a pond with ducks and geese, and a large lake. The remains of the Union Canal locks are also visible.

Jim points out that juice and sometimes coffee, is served to houseguests and there are several restaurants serving hearty Pennsylvania Dutch and country food within a short distance.

As I heard another guest on the house tour remark, "I still don't believe it."

TULPEHOCKEN MANOR INN AND PLANTATION, 650 W. Lincoln Ave., Myerstown, Pa. 17067; 717-866-4926 or 392-2311. A 13-bedroom restored manor house (shared baths) located in the picturesque Pennsylvania Dutch country. Open every day. Longer stays of varying lengths in the several additional houses on the estate may be arranged. Near the Middle Creek Wildlife Preserve. No pets. No credit cards. Jim Henry and Esther Nissly, Innkeepers.

Directions: From New York City follow Rte. 22 to Easton then take Rte. 78 south and pick up Rte. 501 to Rte. 422 and turn right. The Manor is located 2 mi. west of Rte. 501 and Myerstown on Rte. 422.

For Lodging rates, see Index.

WOODWARD INN
Woodward, Pennsylvania

Ah, central Pennsylvania! I spent several happy years in this area while attending Bucknell University in Lewisburg, so I am quite familiar with all of its many beauty spots.

One of the beauty spots is the little village of Woodward, the location of the Woodward Inn, which is kept by Mr. and Mrs. Raymond Schuckers.

The inn was built in 1814 by John Motz and the beautiful Pennsylvania stone walls have acquired the unmistakable patina of age. There are many trees and shrubs, adding so much to its home-like feeling.

Mrs. Schuckers's grandparents were the owners for many years, and the Pennsylvania and National Historical Societies have conferred membership upon it. It was a stagecoach stop in the 1800s, and one of its notable guests was Thomas A. Edison.

There are eight bedrooms: three with private baths and the others with running water.

The continental breakfast consists of a choice of juice, coffee or tea, homemade rolls, breads, and jelly.

Woodward is about halfway between State College and Lewisburg; in fact, I used to pass through it during my undergraduate days. There are two state parks nearby, two caves, and many walking trails. The beautiful Penns Creek, which is a fisherman's paradise, is also nearby. Incidentally, there are special rates for children.

WOODWARD INN, Woodward, Pa. 16882; 814-349-8118. An 8-bedroom (some shared baths) bed-and-breakfast home on Rte. 45, midway between State College and Lewisburg, Pa. A continental breakfast is the only meal served. Open all year. Convenient for many of the recreational, historical, and cultural attractions in area. Behaved pets and children welcome. Mr. and Mrs. Raymond Schuckers, Innkeepers.

Directions: Woodward is on Rte. 45 between Lewisburg and State College. From I-80 take your pick of the many mountain roads that lead south.

For B&B rates, see Index.

THE BRINLEY VICTORIAN INN
Newport, Rhode Island

There are so many wonderful, small touches of Victoriana in this handsome, two-house inn, guests quickly fall under the spell of authentic 19th-century charm. There is, for example, the parlor where even the books are chosen for their century-old popularity. As for the bedrooms, no two are alike. All is circa 1870.

Fresh flowers and collectible, miniature antique lamps appear throughout the house. There are mints on the pillows. It is not surprising that many choose the Brinley for Christmas and New Year holidays as well as the summer season. You are near the Newport Art Association and the boutiques and restaurants on and off Bellevue Avenue. It is only a ten-minute walk to the waterfront. You can even stroll to the mansions.

On your way to the magnificent cottages, you will pass the old Newport Casino, also on Bellevue Avenue. Once the most complete resort in America, it now houses the International Tennis Hall of Fame and the Tennis Museum. It's a great place to pick up a souvenir for your partners at home. There is also a pleasant restaurant serving both simple and full luncheons, and an evening meal as well.

The Brinley Victorian will put you in the right frame of mind for your meanderings. Included in the nightly rate is a continental-plus breakfast of juice, fruit, home-baked coffee cake, cheese, and coffee, tea, or milk. After that, most of Newport is within walking distance, and you are on your own.

THE BRINLEY VICTORIAN INN, 23 Brinley St., Newport, RI 02840; 401-849-7645. A 17-guestroom (7 with private baths) guest house centrally located on a quiet street. Breakfast is the only meal served. Open year-round. The Kay Street and Bellevue Avenue area offers sightseeing, restaurants, and shopping. Parking. Children over 12 accepted. No pets. Amy Weintraub and Edwina Sebest, Proprietors; Robert Matoes, Innkeeper.

Directions: Brinley St. is a one-way arc that can only be entered from Kay St. (across Kay St. it becomes Bull St.). The inn is on your right almost at the end of the block.

For B&B rates, see Index.

CAPTAIN SAMUEL RHODES GUEST HOUSE
Newport, Rhode Island

Colonial Newport is light years away from the mansions of the Gilded Age in the Bellevue Avenue section of the city. The area now known as Historic Point was where the sea captains lived during the Days of Sail and where the still-honored custom of hanging a pineapple on the door originated. When a ship returned, the captain spent the first days home with his family, then hung out a pineapple indicating it was appropriate for friends and neighbors to call.

Captain Rhodes, commander of the "Africa" and trader in rum and slaves, owned this house in 1740. It has been meticulously restored, and there is a large enclosed garden with comfortable outdoor furniture. Breakfast is a help-yourself affair with guests gathering around the table in the old Keeping Room or in the garden.

Upstairs there are three bedrooms. The Captain's Quarters, with private bath, dressing room, queen bed, and fireplace is naturally the most impressive. There are also two other period rooms that have individual charm and a shared bath.

This is a very relaxed sort of place. Pattie Murphy, who also owns and operates the Willows of Newport across the street, knows how to put the "guest" in guest house.

CAPTAIN SAMUEL RHODES GUEST HOUSE, 3 Willow St., Newport, RI 02840; 401-846-5486. A 3-guestroom (1 private bath) historic guest house in the old Historic Point section of Newport. Continental breakfast the only meal served. Menus and touring information at hand. Open year-round. Near downtown and waterfront restaurants and shops. Children over age 12 accepted. No pets. No credit cards. Pattie Murphy, Proprietor.

Directions: From Rte. 95, take Rte. 138 east to Newport. Cross Newport Bridge, downtown exit right at first traffic light onto Van Zandt Ave., proceed to waterfront. Turn left at Washington St., and go 7 blocks to Willow St., turn left and continue to 3 Willow St. From Rte. 24, take Rte. 114. Turn right on Coddington Hwy., and follow signs to Newport Bridge. Go right at traffic circle onto Third St. and turn left at Washington St. Continue 7 blocks to Willow St., as above.

For B&B rates, see Index.

ELLERY PARK HOUSE
Newport, Rhode Island

This is another B&B accommodation that can be booked only through Pineapple Hospitality (617-990-1696), a highly recommended New England B&B reservation service. I ask readers please not to contact the Ellery Park House directly.

This is an 1899 restored Victorian home located in historic Newport on a restored street within easy walking distance of the downtown shops and just four blocks from the picturesque wharves. It is situated in "the Point," a particularly historic section of Newport.

There are two bedrooms in this guest house and a continental breakfast is offered, including freshly made hot muffins or bread and homemade jam, juice, coffee, or tea. It is served in the dining room or on the outdoor patio in the spring or summer.

Newport, I need not add, is one of the most rewarding holiday experiences on the East Coast. Not only does it have the famous Newport mansions on Ocean Drive, but it is also the site of many museums and art galleries, restored colonial homes, the Touro Synagogue (the oldest in the United States), and the Tennis Hall of Fame.

ELLERY PARK HOUSE, Newport, R.I.; 617-990-1696 or 997-9952 (Pineapple Hospitality). A 2-bedroom guest house offering continental breakfast. Located just a few steps from downtown Newport. Open year-round. Breakfast the only meal served, although arrangements can be made for dinner in advance. No pets. No credit cards. Margo and Michael Waite, Proprietors.

Directions: Will be supplied by Pineapple Hospitality. However, it's not necessary to drive through the congested downtown area to get to the Ellery Park House.

For B&B rates, see Index.

INN AT CASTLE HILL
Newport, Rhode Island

Two of the places I've suggested in Newport are owned by the same innkeepers; one is the Inntowne, and the other is the Inn at Castle Hill, which presents quite a different aspect of Newport.

Actually antedating the famous Newport mansions, the Inn at Castle Hill is built on a point where Narragansett Bay joins the Atlantic Ocean, and many of the guest rooms, as well as the dining room, offer a full view of the ever-changing panorama of sea, sky, and water.

Lodgings are in the main mansion which has retained much of the original character and many of the original furnishings, including oriental rugs and hand-crafted oak and mahogany paneling. For many years the eminent American playwright Thornton Wilder was a regular guest. These lodgings are available year-round. There are other bayside cottages, beautifully furnished and roomy enough to accommodate three people comfortably, down near the water's edge and available during warmer weather. I might add that reservations for all of these accommodations should be made well in advance.

The cheerful Sunset Room is the scene of a very pleasant continental breakfast.

The regular visitors to Newport as well as the local residents speak glowingly of the dinners which are served every day except Sunday during the period from Easter to early December.

Newport is a very busy place during the height of the season and I suggest that it may be enjoyed to the fullest around the first of September and the first of June.

INN AT CASTLE HILL, Ocean Drive, Newport, R.I. 02840; 401-849-3800. A 10-bedroom mansion-inn on the edge of Narragansett Bay. European plan. Continental breakfast included in room tariff. No dinner served on Sun.; no lunch served on Mon. Dining room closed from early Dec. to Easter. Guest rooms open all winter. Lounge open winter weekends. Near the Newport mansions, Touro Synagogue, the Newport Casino, and National Lawn Tennis Hall of Fame, the Old Stone Mill, the Newport Historical Society House. Swimming, sailing, scuba diving, walking on grounds. Bicycles and guided tours of Newport nearby. No pets. Jens Thillemann, Manager; Paul McEnroe, Innkeeper.

Directions: After leaving Newport Bridge follow Bellevue Ave. which becomes Ocean Dr. Look for inn sign on left.

For B&B rates, see Index.

THE INNTOWNE
Newport, Rhode Island

It's mid-winter and you've either had it with skiing or else there's a shortage of snow and you're dying to get away for a short trip. May I respectfully suggest Newport, Rhode Island?

The Inntowne is a perfect complement to the rest of historic Newport. It is open twelve months of the year and is most convenient for visiting Bowen's Wharf with its many shops and boutiques, and furthermore, it's easy to drive around the Ocean Drive for a tour of the many mansions, some of which are open year-round, as is the Tennis Hall of Fame.

The Inntowne is owned and kept by Betty and Paul McEnroe, and the interior design, which is exceptionally attractive, has been created by Rodney and Ione Williams, who are also the innkeepers at the Inn at Sawmill Farm in Vermont.

Each room has been individually designed, reflecting Ione's really exquisite taste. The drapes, bedspreads, wallpapers, lamp-shades, and small touches have all been almost choreographed to create a beautiful decorator feeling. They are very bright and gay, just the kind of rooms that make you want to smile when you enter. All have air conditioning but no telephones or television.

The building is on Thames Street and one square from the waterfront area. It is one of the old Newport buildings that has been completely restored and at the same time has maintained the integrity of its colonial heritage. Stepping into the lobby is like entering a very tastefully decorated living room.

Although dinner is not served, Paul and Betty will be happy to make arrangements for the evening meal at the Inn at Castle Hill or at other excellent restaurants in the Newport area.

THE INNTOWNE, 6 Mary St., Newport, R.I. 02840; 401-846-9200. An elegant 20-room inn in the center of the city of Newport overlooking the harbor, serving continental breakfast only. Open every day. Convenient for all of the Newport historical and cultural attractions which are extremely numerous. No recreational facilities available; however, tennis and ocean swimming are nearby. Not adaptable for children of any age. No pets. Betty and Paul McEnroe, Innkeepers.

Directions: After crossing Newport bridge turn right at sign: "Historic Newport." Drive straight to Thames Street; Inntowne is on corner of Thames St. and Mary St., across from Brick Marketplace.

For B&B rates, see Index.

LARCHWOOD INN
Wakefield, Rhode Island

Rhode Island is a state of stone walls. They come in various heights, thicknesses, and condition of repair. Roads leading through the woods between the fields are most numerous for a state that is reputedly small, and often offer some interesting historical sites as well as beautiful homes.

There is much to see and do, but perhaps one of the most impressive things about Rhode Island is the south-shore beaches which are often favorably compared with others elsewhere in New England.

The Larchwood Inn is a large manor dating back to 1831. The interior has many Scottish touches, including quotations from Robert Burns and Sir Walter Scott, and photographs and prints of Scottish historical and literary figures. One of the dining rooms has wall paintings showing farms and seascapes of southern Rhode Island.

In addition to bedrooms at the main inn, accommodations now include splendid rooms at Holly House, located just across the street from the inn itself. The building is about 150 years old and all the furniture has been carefully selected to match the ambience of the manor.

The Larchwood is a full-service inn, offering breakfast, lunch and dinner. Bed-and-breakfast devotees will be very enthusiastic about the à la carte breakfast menu, which includes everything from a dish of seasonal fruit to steak and eggs.

Wakefield is on the western side of Narragansett Bay and is a few miles from the famous bridge that leads over the bay into Newport. It is a very pleasant holiday experience.

LARCHWOOD INN, 176 Main St., Wakefield, R.I. 02879; 401-783-5454. A 19-room village inn just 3 mi. from the famous southern R.I. beaches. Some rooms with shared bath. European plan. Breakfast, lunch, dinner served every day of the year. Swimming, boating, surfing, fishing, xc skiing, and bicycles nearby. Francis and Diann Browning, Innkeepers.

Directions: From Rte. 1, take Pond St. Exit and proceed ½ mi. directly to inn.

For Lodging rates, see Index.

PHOENIX INN
Narragansett, Rhode Island

There was no sign on the stone pillars at the Gibson Avenue entrance but, map in hand, I found the Phoenix. Roses were blooming, and a boat was parked casually on one side of the driveway. Was I in the right place? Happily, yes.

The impressive shingle mansion, designed by Stanford White in the late 1800s for the New York restaurateur Louis Sherry, was originally one of several houses ("cottages" in the local lexicon of understatement) in a family compound. When fire swept the others, this one rose from the ashes to become, in present life, a bed-and-breakfast country retreat.

Second-floor east and west wings each have two bedrooms and one bath; a smaller bedroom on the third floor has a private bath. Downstairs there is a large living room and the dining room where breakfast is served guests in a big way. Guests also enjoy the veranda.

Fresh fruit at breakfast is followed by eggs prepared in such creative forms as shrimp and avocado omelet or eggs Benedict. There may be cheese blintzes with strawberries; ham, bacon, or sausage. Fresh baked breads are as fragrant as the newly ground coffee. All this and Wedgewood too.

Narragansett Pier is undergoing a revitalization of the shops and restaurants, as well as the popular beach area, but such things are far removed in spirit, if not in distance. The beach is close by—a mile. Newport is approximately twenty minutes over the Jamestown (free) and Newport (toll) Bridges.

PHOENIX INN, 29 Gibson Ave., Narragansett, RI 02882; 401-783-1918. A 5-guestroom bed-and-breakfast home (1 private, 2 shared baths) in a pleasant, quiet neighborhood across Narragansett Bay from Jamestown Island and Newport. Full breakfast the only meal served. Open all year. Swimming, boating, surfing, fishing nearby. Children over age 10 preferred. Joyce and Dave Peterson, Proprietors.

Directions: From the north, follow the signs on Rte. 1 to the Pt. Judith exit, which puts you on So. Pier Rd. From the south, take the Narragansett exit. You will be on So. Pier Rd. Continue to Gibson Ave. and turn right. After Westmoreland St. watch on right for stone pillars directly opposite Earles Ct. Rd. Turn in. Follow driveway bearing to your left to Phoenix Inn.

For B&B rates, see Index.

THE QUEEN ANNE INN
Newport, Rhode Island

Peg McCabe's bed-and-breakfast inn is only two blocks from the waterfront and has its own off-street parking, two factors which in themselves make it remarkable. Much more, however, awaits those who stay in this Newport rose Victorian. The rooms are done with great style, and breakfast, whether served before the fireplace in the reception room or in the pretty garden, is a chance to visit with an international clientele. Many are returned visitors.

Of course Peg knows everything that is gong on in Newport (past and present) and can recommend restaurants in all price ranges. Breakfast, however, is the only meal served at the Queen Anne, and might consist of fresh fruit or Portuguese sweet bread with jams, and coffee or tea.

Clarke Street is a historic street usually discovered only on foot. You may find yourself going around in circles looking for its one-way access, but once there, you can leave your car and walk to all the downtown attractions.

If you turn right outside the door of the Queen Anne and walk to the end of the block you will be on Touro Street and near the Touro Synagogue, the oldest Jewish house of worship in North America (1763). It stands beside the Newport Historical Society, which houses priceless Townsend and Goddard furniture, as well as Rhode Island pewter and silver.

At the end of a day of walking and looking, it's especially nice to have a charmer like the Queen Anne Inn waiting.

THE QUEEN ANNE INN, 16 Clarke St., Newport, RI 02840; 401-846-5676. A 12-guestroom (7 shared baths) bed-and-breakfast inn in the heart of Newport. Open "almost all year." No pets. No credit cards. Private off-street parking. A 2-night stay is required during July and August and on weekends all year. No phone service between 11 P.M. and 8 P.M. Peg McCabe, Innkeeper.

Directions: Clarke is a one-way street one block long that can only be entered off Touro St., one block east of Thames St. The inn is on your left.

For B&B rates, see Index.

THE 1661 INN
Block Island, Rhode Island

Here's a good idea if you happen to be traveling on the New England coast: schedule an overnight trip to Block Island, off the coast of both Rhode Island and Connecticut. Ferries run year-round, and even during the winter there are two a day.

Fortunately there are excellent year-round accommodations at the 1661 Inn which is set apart from the rest of Block Island's little world on a height of land overlooking the sand dunes and the ocean.

The country-inn-type bedrooms are located in the original early 19th-century house, and in some very attractive new ocean-view rooms in the guest house that are particularly adaptable for off-season holidays. There are additional accommodations now in the Manisses, a recently restored and authentically furnished Victorian building.

From Memorial Day to Columbus Day, a full buffet breakfast is served, including a wide variety of fresh fruit juices, homemade muffins and breads, Rita's homemade preserves, scrambled or hard-boiled eggs, breakfast meats, especially prepared quiches, and daily hot seafood and poultry specialties. In the off-season, it's a mini-buffet that includes all of the above, except the hot specialties.

Caution: the 1661 Inn is fully booked during the height of the summer season, but a chance telephone call may be rewarded with a room made available by a last-minute cancellation. Other times can be fairly open.

THE 1661 INN, Spring St., Block Island, R.I. 02807; 401-466-2421 or 2063. A 25-room island inn off the coast of R.I. and Conn., in Block Island Sound; 11 private baths. Mod. AMerican and European plans. Open from Memorial Day thru Columbus Day weekend. Breakfast served to travelers daily. (Guest House open year-round; continental breakfast included in off-season rates.) Dinners are available at the Manisses in-season, and in town off-season. Lawn games on grounds. Bicycling, ocean swimming, sailing, snorkeling, diving, salt and fresh water fishing nearby. Block Island is known as one of the best bird observation areas on the Atlantic flyway. The Abrams Family, Innkeepers.

Directions: By ferry from Providence, Pt. Judith, and Newport R.I. and New London, Ct. Car reservations (401-789-3502) must be made in advance for ferry. By air from Newport, Westerly, and Providence, R.I., New London and Waterford, Ct., or by chartered plane. For air information and reservations: 401-596-2460.

For B&B rates, see Index.

SUNNYSIDE MANSION
(COMMODORE WM. EDGAR HOUSE)
Newport, Rhode Island

In 1886, Commodore Edgar of the New York Yacht Club finished his summer cottage in Newport. As Tomar Waldman points out, there have been sailors in residence ever since. Many of the guests come for the races or just to sail the blue Narragansett Bay waters, but even she and her husband chose Newport as their home because their boat was already moored in the harbor. "It was a matter of changing the direction of our commute," she says.

This elegant mansion was designed by famed architects McKim, Mead, and White. It has what may be the first sliding glass windows in America, a rare brass staircase, and a real yachtsman's front door with a ship's wheel set in it. The rooms and suites are done with eclectic taste and often themed to memorabilia from exotic places the Waldmans have visited. Some rooms have private balconies; some have kitchens. One even has a Steinway piano. There are many working fireplaces.

The shared-bath rooms are true bargains, and the third-floor shared-kitchen is a bonus for those who would like to skip eating out for a night or two. Lots of visiting goes on around that kitchen table.

Sunnyside is set well back from the road amid three acres of gardens, and the buffet breakfast is served on the veranda. You can walk to the beach, shops, restaurants, and the "other summer cottages" of this remarkable section of a remarkable town.

SUNNYSIDE MANSION, 25 Old Beach Rd., Newport, RI 02840; 401-849-3114. A 13-guestroom (6 private baths) mansion set on beautiful grounds between Bellevue Ave. and the beach in an exclusive section of Newport. Open May 1 to Nov. 1. Breakfast is the only meal served, but some rooms have private kitchens and there is a community kitchen as well. Near beach, mansions, restaurants, shopping. Pool room. Off-street parking. French spoken. No pets. Tomar and Paul Waldman, Proprietors.

Directions: Old Beach Rd. runs between Bellevue Ave. and Memorial Blvd. Sunnyside is on the south side of the street (your right if you are driving from Bellevue Ave.)

For B&B rates, see Index.

WAYSIDE
Newport, Rhode Island

Part of the fun in visiting the "cottages" of the very rich is imagining how it would be to spend the night in such opulence. Now if you have made reservations well in advance, you can turn into the circular driveway almost opposite the Elms and play Houseguest-for-a-Night-or-More at the Wayside.

Among those neighbors: The Elms is across the street; down the block is Chateau-súr-Mer, Rosecliff (where *The Great Gatsby* was filmed), Mrs. Astor's Beechwood, Marble House, and Belcourt Castle. The tour guides will tell you all about the scandals as well as the costs of living it up in the Gilded Age.

The Georgian-style, 1890s mansion has bedrooms so large they are sitting rooms as well; and fireplaces and marble bathrooms. Alas, the retinue of servants is gone, and you serve yourself a simple continental breakfast from a buffet in the lobby before starting out on foot to pay calls at the museum palaces of the neighbors.

After a day's walking, it's especially nice to be able to take a dip in the house swimming pool before heading out for dinner in one of the fine restaurants of Newport.

Oh yes, the servants' quarters are also available. Here you share the bath.

WAYSIDE, Bellevue Ave., Newport, RI 02840; 401-847-0302. An 8-guestroom (most with private baths) guest house on famous and fabulous Bellevue Avenue. Continental breakfast the only meal served. Open year-round. Swimming pool, ocean beach, mansions, restaurants, shops nearby. No pets. No credit cards. Off-street parking. Reservations should be made well in advance. Al and Dorothy Post, Proprietors

Directions: Bellevue Avenue is probably Newport's most famous street. As you drive towards Ocean Avenue, the Elms will be on your right. Watch for driveway on left marked "Wayside" (nothing so crass as house numbers in this neighborhood) and turn in.

For B&B rates, see Index.

THE WILLOWS OF NEWPORT
Newport, Rhode Island

These two adjoining townhouses in the oldest part of historic Newport were actually built 100 years apart, so when Pattie Murphy set out to restore them she left each in its own time. They are both, incidentally, on the National Register of Historic Places. Since Pattie is a True Believer in the theory that a vacation should be a fantasy, she has converted these rooms into dreamy period pieces: a Colonial Wedding Room and a Canopy Room in the 1740 house; a Victorian Wedding Room and French Quarters in the 1840 segment. The shared parlor is pink.

To keep the fantasy going, breakfast is served to guests in bed, using silver and bone china. In the evening, guests find mints on their pillows, their beds turned down, and the lights left on low. Some rooms have working fireplaces. Even your automobile gets special treatment at the Willows, as there are closed garages, as well as off-street parking next door.

Although bustling Newport is only a few minutes' walk away, this quiet and for the most part pre-Revolutionary enclave is worth a lot of wandering. Hunter House, pride of the Preservation Society, is down on the Battery, a five-minute walk.

Many of the restored houses here on "The Point" are labeled with the names of their original owners and the approximate dates of construction. Except for Hunter House, however, they are not open to the public. This is just one more reason (and not the least) you will enjoy being a genuine resident, if only for a few nights, in another place, another time. As Pattie says, "part of the fantasy."

THE WILLOWS OF NEWPORT, 8-10 Willow St., Newport, RI 02840; 401-846-5486. A 4-guestroom (all private baths) guest house in the Historic Point section of Newport. Open year-round. Breakfast-in-bed the only meal served. Close to all downtown and waterfront Newport activities. Garage parking next door. No children. No pets. No credit cards. Pattie Murphy, Proprietor.

Directions: From Rte. 95, take Rte. 138 east to Newport. Cross Newport Bridge, downtown exit right at first traffic light onto Van Zandt Ave., proceed to waterfront. Turn left at Washington St., and go 7 blocks to Willow St., turn left and continue to 8 Willow St. From Rte. 24, take Rte. 114. Turn right on Coddington Hwy. and follow signs to Newport Bridge. Go right at traffic circle onto Third St. and turn left at Washington St. Continue 7 blocks to Willow St., as above.

For B&B rates, see Index.

SWORDGATE INN
Charleston, South Carolina

Sometimes termed "America's most nostalgic city," Charleston is a place where you depart reluctantly, with the feeling of having left something behind. If I had to find one word to describe it, the word would be "genteel." It is civilized without being stuffy. Charleston's cobbled streets, old homes, splendid gardens, and sequestered byways are a delight. Its history spans centuries and can be found everywhere.

Among the beautiful restored and preserved dwellings in Charleston is the Swordgate Inn, whose own history will be lovingly recounted by innkeeper Walter Barton.

The six guest rooms are individually decorated with distinctive sheets, pillowcases, bedspreads, and ruffles. Two of the bedrooms have tester beds and another has a brass bed. Fresh fruit and flowers are placed in the guest rooms daily, and there is a newspaper at the door each morning. Five of the rooms are on the first floor of the old mansion; the sixth room on the third floor has a canopy bed and a view of the fascinating rooftops of the old city.

Many pleasant friendships start in the breakfast room where the guests fall to at the full breakfast of juice, beverages, a choice of sourdough or bran muffins, english muffins, delicious sweet rolls, a special recipe of Swordgate Inn grits and coddled eggs, or sausage balls, or hot apples. This would fortify anybody against a walking tour of Charleston.

The Spoleto Festival is held in Charleston during May and June each year with a real outpouring of music and art. Reservations at the Swordgate are made at least a year in advance. However, Charleston is enjoyable in any season.

SWORDGATE INN, 111 Tradd St., Charleston, S.C. 29401; 803-723-8518. A quiet 6-room elegant inn located in the center of an historic area of the city, amidst distinguished 18th and 19th century homes. Within walking and biking distance of most of Charleston's cultural and historic landmarks. Bicycles furnished without charge to guests. Lodgings include breakfast. No other meal served. Closed Christmas Eve and Christmas Day. Beaches, sailing, and fresh-water and deep-sea fishing nearby. Not suitable for children. No pets. Walter E. Barton, Innkeeper.

Directions: Take I-26 to Meeting St. South Exit. Turn right on Meeting St., 12 blocks to Broad St.; turn right on Broad, two blocks to Legare St. Turn left on Legare for one block; turn left on Tradd St. Look for small sign on right that says Swordgate Inn.

For B&B rates, see Index.

PARISH PATCH INN
Normandy, Tennessee

If you are traveling on Route 41-A or I-24, between Nashville and Chattanooga, I have some excellent news for you.

Just outside the small town of Normandy, I have discovered the Parish Patch Inn, right in the middle of a 750-acre working farm in southern Tennessee.

With waving fields of grain, a feed lot, and many cattle, the setting is unmistakably bucolic. However, there is a great deal more to be experienced than meets the eye.

The main house was built by Chuck Parish, who was, until his passing, the head of the largest manufacturer of baseballs and bats in the world. He built the house to entertain friends, guests, and people associated with the company.

The exterior is of board and batten construction quite in keeping with this part of Tennessee. The interior, which might be described as "elegant rustic," has a living room, library, and dining room with splendid cherry and walnut paneling. There are also two kitchens, a master bedroom with a balcony and two bathrooms, and three other double bedrooms also with bathrooms.

In the bedrooms, furniture, counterpanes, and comforters are all blended to create a marvelous feeling of relaxation and harmony. The living room, kitchens, and dining room all enjoy the views of the meadows and the orchard.

The overnight guest will be enticed to stay longer for the swimming, fishing, boating, canoeing, water skiing, picnicking, bicycling, and bird watching which abound on or near the actual inn property.

PARISH PATCH INN, Normandy, Tenn. 37360; 615-857-3441. An elegant bed-and-breakfast inn in the verdant Tennessee countryside. Breakfast is included in the room rate; evening meals are served to houseguests only with advance reservations. Open all year. Arrangements must be made in advance if an earlier than 2 P.M., later than 4 P.M. arrival is anticipated. Wide variety of recreation available (see above). Marty Ligon, Owner; Allen Kimbro, Innkeeper.

Directions: From Shelbyville continue south on 41-A for 7.2 mi. and look for a left turn at the sign for Normandy. From I-24, take Exit 97 (Beechgrove-Shelbyville-Hwy. 64 Exit). Take Hwy. 64 west to Wartrace. In Wartrace do not cross RR tracks. Pass shops and turn left at yellow light, up hill; bear right on Knob Creek Rd. Inn is 4 mi. from Wartrace.

For B&B rates, see Index.

RIVERHOUSE
Gatlinburg, Tennessee

Shortly after leaving Cherokee, North Carolina, U.S. 441 runs concurrently with the Shenandoah Parkway to Gatlinburg, Tennessee. It is a spectacular road, and because it is a parkway there are no billboard signs or commercial vehicles. However, at times the speed limit is 35 m.p.h. and there are few places to pass slower vehicles. There are several overlooks and many opportunities to gaze at this gorgeous scenery.

The Riverhouse in Gatlinburg is a rather fancy motor lodge featuring log-burning fireplaces and private balconies overlooking a mountain stream. All of the rooms are spacious with color TVs, direct-dial phones, refrigerators, and queen-sized beds.

A fire is built each day in the room fireplaces, and a continental breakfast, featuring freshly squeezed orange juice and delicious, fresh, homemade doughnuts, is brought to the rooms every morning.

Reservations are made a year in advance for the high and foliage seasons. January, February, and March are the only months where it is possible to walk in and enjoy an overnight reservation.

RIVERHOUSE MOTORLODGE, Box 690, River Rd., Gatlinburg, Tenn. 37738; 615-436-7821. A 44-bedroom (34 with fireplaces) motor hotel in a highly popular tourist area in the mountains of eastern Tennessee. Conveniently located for all of the cultural, recreational, and natural beauties of the area. No pets. Reservations advisable most months. Hugh Faust, Manager.

Directions: Gatlinburg is located at the junction of Rte. 73 and U.S. 441. The Riverhouse is one block from the west side of the main street.

For B&B rates, see Index.

BARROWS HOUSE
Dorset, Vermont

If you're traveling north or south on Route 7 in Vermont let me make a suggestion: a very pleasant variation, and still in the same basic direction, is to take Route 30 which begins in the south at Manchester and ends in the north at Middlebury. This would include a ride through some most pleasant Vermont villages such as Dorset, Pawlet, and the Mettowee Valley, past Lake St. Catherine to Poultney (the home of Green Mountain College), and north through Castleton, past Lake Bomoseen, and on to Hubbardton, Sudbury, and Cornwall. Part of the method in my madness is to suggest an overnight stop at Barrows House in Dorset, which is itself a jewel of a village.

The Barrows House is a traditional New England white clapboard building with black shutters, set considerably back from the main road of the village. It has a rather large English garden on the east side with many varieties of flowers including phlox, lilies, iris, tulips, and peonies. The entire setting is in a small park with elms, sugar maples, birches, locusts, and various evergreen trees.

One of the front parlors has a welcome fireplace and an entire wall of books. It's a comfortable place in which to relax in any season.

The bedrooms are replete with flowered wallpapers, country and antique furniture, and lots of books and magazines. There are all sizes and kinds of rooms available: some are in the several buildings clustered on the grounds; some are suites with sitting rooms; and all double rooms have private baths.

A full breakfast is served with the B&B rate, including small, light pancakes, either plain, apple, or blueberry, served with Vermont maple syrup; french toast made with homemade bread, eggs any style, and a variety of breads, homemade sourdough english muffins, fresh fruit and juices, and aromatic freshly brewed coffee and a variety of teas.

BARROWS HOUSE, Dorset Vt. 05251; 802-867-4455. A 29-room village inn on Rte. 30, 6 mi. north of Manchester, Vt. Modified American plan omits lunch. Breakfast and dinner served daily to travelers. Swimming pool, sauna, tennis courts, bicycles, xc skiing facilities, including rental equipment and instruction on grounds. Golf, tennis, trout fishing, and alpine skiing nearby. No credit cards. Charles and Marilyn Schubert, Innkeepers.

Directions: From Rte. 7 in Manchester, proceed 6 miles north on Rte. 30 to Dorset.

For B&B rates, see Index.

BIRCH HILL INN
Manchester, Vermont

Travelers on U.S. 7, one of the main north-south arteries in Vermont, or Route 30, a very interesting road that starts in Brattleboro and cuts across the state in a northwesterly direction, will be delighted to find Birch Hill Inn which is just a few moments away from where the two roads intersect in Manchester, Vermont.

It is a beautiful, private country home that has within recent years been converted into an intimate inn. The original part of the house was built in 1790 with harmonizing additions having been made since 1919, and today it is owned by Pat and Jim Lee who offer bed-and-breakfast accommodations, as well as lodgings on the modified American plan.

Bedrooms are characterized by country wallpaper, French prints, hunting prints by Paul Brown, and in two of the large bedrooms there are exposed beams.

A full breakfast is offered including eggs or pancakes served with either sausage or bacon, homemade muffins, and coffee.

Birch Hill has much to recommend it as a vacation accommodation with cross-country skiing, a private trout pond, and a swimming pool on the grounds. There are numerous golf and tennis facilities nearby and alpine skiing at several central Vermont areas.

Arrive in time for dinner, it's a real treat—but be sure to make reservations in advance.

BIRCH HILL INN, Box 346, West Rd., Manchester, Vt. 05254; 802-362-2761. A 5-bedroom (some shared baths) extremely comfortable country home-inn (a cozy cottage nearby) about 5 min. from downtown Manchester Center. Breakfast included in room rate. Dinner offered to houseguests by reservation only. Kitchen closed Weds. and some Suns. Open after Christmas to mid-April, and May to late Oct.; 2-night minimum preferred. Swimming pool, xc skiing, trout fishing, and walking trails on grounds. Alpine skiing at major areas, as well as tennis and golf nearby; great biking. No pets. No credit cards. Pat and Jim Lee, Innkeepers.

Directions: From New York City: Taconic Pkwy. to U.S. 22. Turn east from Rte. 22 at NY Rte. 7 to Bennington, Vt. Take Vt. Rte. 7 north to Exit 4 and follow Rte. 30 to Historic 7A. At Center (7A) take Rte. 30 north 2½ mi. to Manchester West Rd. Turn left and look for inn on left, ¾ mi. From Boston: Mass. Tpke. to I-91 to 2nd Brattleboro Exit and continue to Manchester on Rte. 30 to Center at Historic 7A. Go north on Rte. 30—following above directions from this point.

For B&B rates, see Index.

BROMLEY VIEW INN
Bondville, Vermont

Bromley View Inn is a small bed-and-breakfast inn—not elaborate, but clean, comfortable, and friendly. The twelve rooms have individually controlled heat, double beds, and private baths.

It is located high in the Green Mountain National Forest, close to nature and everything Vermont has to offer. In summer the mountain area is bustling with numerous activities from fishing or canoeing the famed Battenkill, hunting, tennis, golf, biking, hiking the Appalachian and Long trails, to summer theater, art galleries, antique shops, and of course a ride on the famous Bromley Alpine Slide.

For winter sports, it is within a short drive of three major ski areas, Bromley, Stratton, and Magic Mountain, and there are miles of ski touring trails to be found right outside the door.

There are two outstanding things about Bromley View Inn. The first is a fantastic view of Bromley Mountain Ski area from some of the bedrooms, the dining room, and the lounge. The other is the fact that the inn can boast of two fiberglass spas and a redwood hot tub. All three of them have Jacuzzi jets and are located in a separate area. Exercise equipment is also available.

The atmosphere of this inn is that of a very homey lodge and this informality makes it possible for the guests to mingle with each other quite freely. Children are most welcome.

A full breakfast is served every morning and this includes a choice of eggs, french toast, pancakes, sausage or bacon, and there are always homemade muffins and breads. In summer and foliage season, lunch is available, and dinners are served in ski season.

BROMLEY VIEW INN, Rte. 30, Bondville, VT 05340; 802-297-1459. A 12-guestroom (private baths) ski lodge-inn located on a mountain with a spectacular view of Bromley Mountain Ski area. A full breakfast is included in room rate. Open all year. Conveniently located for marvelous recreational, cultural, and scenic adventures in south-central Vermont. Three major ski areas; xc skiing nearby. Bick and Amy Atherton, Proprietors.

Directions: Rte. 30 cuts diagonally across southern Vermont. Bromley View Inn is located just a few miles from the junction of Rtes. 30 and 11.

For B&B rates, see Index.

CAMEL'S HUMP VIEW FARM
Moretown, Vermont

Camel's Hump is a 4,083-foot peak in the Green Mountains of Vermont, much praised by hikers who want above-treeline views for their efforts, and by photographers who see it as one of the state's most picturesque landmarks. This is the view to the west of Camel's Hump View Farm, a country inn with all the comfort and cheer you might expect in a friendly home.

The Mad River flows on the east side of the 1831 farmhouse, and there is a barnyard full of animals. Home-grown and homemade are the adjectives applied to all the good things that appear on the table here. In addition to a full country breakfast, included in the B&B rates, dinner is available (to guests only) at a modest charge.

Camel's Hump Farm is a member of the "Country Inns Along the Trail" that caters to hikers along an 80-mile section of Vermont's Long Trail. You don't have to be quite so ambitious—there are many short trails in the area where you can work up an appetite suitable for Wilma's hearty meals.

In the winter there is cross-country and downhill skiing. All year there is great sightseeing, and arts, crafts, and antique shopping in the villages. You are also near Montpelier, state capital of Vermont; Barre, with its granite quarries open to the public; and Burlington, with its famous Shelbourne Museum.

A variety of accommodations are included in the inn's eight rooms: double beds, twin beds, 4-bunk beds, all with shared baths and a family suite with private bath. There is a bright living room for guests and a dining room where meals are served family style, as well as porches, nooks and crannies. In short, a thoroughly delightful place.

CAMEL'S HUMP VIEW FARM, RFD #1, Rte. 100B, Moretown, VT 05660; 802-496-3614. An 8-guestroom (1 private, 4 shared baths) country inn in Mad River Valley, central Vermont. Full country breakfast included, plus evening meal on request to guests only. Convenient to hiking, skiing, swimming, fishing, shopping, and sightseeing. Member Country Inns Along the Trail. No smoking. No pets. Children over 10 preferred, though younger accommodated in suite. Wilma and Jerry Maynard, Proprietors.

Directions: From I-89, take Exit 9 (Middlesex) and Rte. 100B south. Camel's Hump View Farm will be on your left. From Rte. 100, watch for junction with 100B in Moretown as you drive north. You will now be going east, and the inn is on your right.

For B&B rates, see Index.

THE CAPT. HENRY CHASE HOUSE
Guilford, Vermont

Set in a rural, agricultural valley that seems to have been bypassed by time, this 1798 white clapboard farmhouse is a ful example of the best of Vermont country architecture.

Because it is really in the country and because there are horses, chickens, goats, and ducks, it is an excellent place for children. There are stables and horseback riding nearby. Guests may be greeted by "Gilly," short for Guilford, who is a combination of a French poodle and a retriever.

There is a handsome old fireplace in the main living room, as well as a spinet and lots of books. There are two separate bedrooms on the second floor sharing a bath; for a family traveling with children, there is also an additional small bedroom. It is all very homey.

In good weather breakfast is served on the terrace, screened in on three sides, and during cold weather, in a nice little dining room off the kitchen.

The cross-country skiing is so good in this area that Bill Koch, a silver medal winner in the 1980 Olympics, has trained in this valley. I should imagine that it would be absolutely glorious during the winter season.

In summer there is much to do in this section of Vermont and nearby New Hampshire, and it would be lovely to return to such a quiet, pleasant atmosphere. Be sure and call ahead.

THE CAPT. HENRY CHASE HOUSE, West Guilford Rd., Guilford, Vt. Mailing address: RFD#4, Box 282, West Brattleboro, Vt. 05301; 802-254-4114. A 2-bedroom (1 bath) bed-and-breakfast home—extra adjoining bedroom available. Open all year. Breakfast only meal served. Convenient for many southern Vermont and New Hampshire cultural, recreational and historic attractions. Closed Thanksgiving and Christmas. Patrick and Lorraine Ryan, Proprietors.

Directions: Use Exit 2 from I-91, go west on Rte. 9 toward Bennington; on the far side of West Brattleboro look for Greenleaf St. on the left next to Lou's Amoco. You are now exactly 6.5 mi. from the Capt. Henry Chase House. Stay on paved road until you notice a large house on the right across street from a barn at beginning of dirt road. Capt. Henry Chase House is next place on right, past Green River Rd.

For B&B rates, see Index.

CHESTER INN
Chester, Vermont

There are few interstate highways from which the traveler can enjoy such impressive scenery as I-91, which can be followed all the way from New York to Canada. I'd like to suggest that in planning this trip, the traveler on I-91 could digress for a few miles and make a very enjoyable overnight visit to the Chester Inn, located in one of central Vermont's unusual villages.

Chester has some very intriguing history and many 19th-century homes and buildings, including a striking group of stone houses at the eastern end.

The inn is on a long narrow village green and is characterized by an architectural soufflé that is only matched by some of the entrees on the evening menu.

First-time visitors are impressed with the very large lobby and living room. There is a big fireplace with several comfortable chairs and couches and an ever-changing assortment of original watercolors and oils add an even further distinction to the room.

Traveling families with children will be delighted to know that there's a wonderful, grassy play area to the rear of the inn, which includes a swimming pool and tennis courts. Babysitters can be obtained.

Breakfast features scrambled eggs, bacon, ham or sausage, homemade banana bread, hot and cold cereal, french toast with Vermont maple syrup, and fresh fruit in season.

CHESTER INN, Chester, Vt. 05143; 802-875-2444. A 30-room village inn on Rte. 11, 8 mi. from Springfield, Vt. Convenient to several Vt. ski areas. Lodgings include breakfast. Dinner served to travelers daily. Pool, tennis, and bicycles on grounds. Golf, riding, alpine and xc skiing nearby. No pets. Jeff and Sandi Hecht, Innkeepers.

Directions: From I-91 take Exit 6. Travel west on Rte. 103 to Rte. 11 and on to Chester.

For B&B rates, see Index.

COLONIAL GUEST HOUSE
Bennington, Vermont

Instead of my retelling it here, I think it would be more fun for visitors to Bennington to visit the Bennington Museum, which is absolutely splendid, and to stop at the Bennington Monument and learn for themselves about the truly significant place that Bennington enjoys in American history.

From the terrace of the Colonial Guest House there is an excellent view of the mountain and the imposing monolith of the monument. The museum and other recreational, natural, and cultural attractions are all nearby.

The Colonial Guest House is tidy and rather homey. The bedrooms are very pleasant and the bathrooms seemed unusually bright and shiny. One of the first rooms I saw had a candlewick bedspread and a bed with a canopy. Every room has a wash basin; some have air conditioning, and some have TV. The rates indicate that one room that sleeps four would be very convenient for traveling families.

A full breakfast is available for an additional charge, and arrangements for dinner can also be made.

COLONIAL GUEST HOUSE, Orchard Road, Bennington, Vt. 05201; 802-442-2263. A 5-bedroom guest house on the outskirts of Bennington. Open year-round except Christmas and Easter. Family-style meals served to guests with sufficient advance notice. Historical sites, art and craft galleries, antiques, horseback riding, bicycling, swimming, golf nearby. Within convenient driving distance of 12 major ski areas. No pets. No credit cards. Charles and Josephine Reis, Proprietors.

Directions: From Rte. 7, take Historic Rte. 7A north 2 mi. from town center. (Do not take new Rte. 7 Bypass.) Colonial Guest House is at the bottom of Harwood Hill.

For Lodging rates, see Index.

THE COLONIAL HOUSE
Weston, Vermont

Travelers will find the Colonial House ideal, not only because the village of Weston is one of the prettiest in Vermont, nor because they can walk out the door, put on their cross-country skis, and start off on 150 miles of trail, but also because of the food. The Nunnikhoven family believes in feeding quests well and often.

Hikers, bikers, and skiers will find hot cider, cheese, and crackers waiting in the big, comfortable living room. Tea and home-baked goodies are ready for the relax-by-the-fire crowd. There are memorable dinners prepared only for guests with such things as Savoury Soup and Burgundy Berry Pie. Breakfasts are nothing short of amazing: five kinds of hot cereal served with butter and maple syrup; eleven ingredients to combine at will in the omelets, fresh-baked breads, berry or fruit pancakes. "We don't need alarm clocks," John says. "The fragrance of Betty's early morning baking brings everyone downstairs on the double."

There are six simple rooms with shared baths in the old inn, and a modest motel wing with private baths adds facilities, if not atmosphere. Either way, you share the Nunnikhoven hospitality, which includes advice on the sights, shopping, and outdoor activities available; the schedule of the famous Weston Playhouse in summer. They can also put you in touch with local professional hiking and ski touring leaders and arrange inn-to-inn trail trips.

THE COLONIAL HOUSE, Rte. 100, Box 138RB, Weston, VT 05161; 802-824-6286. A 6-guestroom (2 baths) bed-and-breakfast inn (9 bedrooms with private baths in the motel) south of Weston village. Afternoon tea and/or cider included along with breakfast in the rate; dinners served only to guests. Open all year. Hiking and xc skiing at the door; downhill skiing nearby; all village amenities nearby, as well as the Weston Priory. No pets. Betty, John and David Nunnikhoven, Proprietors.

Directions: Take Exit 6 from Hwy. I-91, then Rtes. 103 and 11 to Rte. 100. Go north towards Weston. The Colonial House will be on your right 1½ mi. south of the village.

For B&B rates, see Index.

DARCROFT'S SCHOOLHOUSE
Wilmington, Vermont

When snow is on the ground this is one of the most popular areas in the Green Mountain state because there are several downhill ski areas, all within a very short distance, including Mt. Snow and Haystack.

Darcroft's Schoolhouse is about four miles north of the crossroads of Routes 9 and 100, and is located on the west side of Route 100. It is indeed a former schoolhouse of sturdy construction, and today its utilitarian lines serve the purpose of housing a very pleasant bed-and-breakfast guest house.

On the first floor where valley scholars had formerly learned their reading, writing, and arithmetic, guests enjoy a common room with a low-beamed ceiling and a raised-hearth fireplace that is big enough for everybody to gather around it and become acquainted. Upstairs there are two bedrooms and also a sort of informal dormitory arrangement that works out well if you're traveling with kids.

A continental breakfast is offered every morning to guests by proprietress Doris Meadowcroft, but guests also have kitchen privileges for preparing the evening meal, should that be desirable.

DARCROFT'S SCHOOLHOUSE, Wilmington, Vt. 05363; 802-464-2631. An 1837 one-room schoolhouse converted to a 2-bedroom and dormitory guest house on Rte. 100 just a few miles south of Mt. Snow. Open during the ski season (from the first snow until mud season) and from mid-April until late fall. Continental breakfast included with the price of the room and kitchen privileges offered for the evening meal. Convenient to major downhill ski areas and excellent xc skiing; also golf, tennis, swimming pool, antiquing, backroading, and walking. No pets. No credit cards. Doris Meadow-croft, Proprietress.

Directions: Drive 4 mi. north on Rte. 100 from the center of Wilmington and look for the sign on the left side of the road.

For B&B rates, see Index.

DEERHILL INN
West Dover, Vermont

Olé Retlev's letter said that there were, indeed, some major changes at Deerhill Inn. These were obvious to me as I drove up Route 100, turned up the hill and saw a complete change in the outside look of this inn. Where there was previously an alpine feeling, there is now a softer, more inviting style of New England architecture.

The new entrance and reception area has brick flooring and beautiful wallpaper in a bird pattern. Wall-to-wall carpeting and Scandinavian decorations arranged around a welcome fireplace enhance the new sitting room.

This fireplace theme continues on into a bright, new dining area with a raised hearth and a pair of wonderful, old-fashioned, long wooden skis on the wall.

The decor of the inn continues to be an interesting mix of colorful floral prints, antique furnishings, and soft pastel touches. The bedrooms are extremely bright and cheerful. Some look out over the swimming pool and tennis courts, and others look across the valley to the mowings beyond.

West Dover is dominated by the presence of Mt. Snow and other nearby ski areas, where extensive snowmaking assures a long season from early December well through Easter. Throughout the valley, miles of well-maintained, cross-country ski trails wind through tranquil pastures and woods. The other three seasons abound with pleasures that are to be found on winding country roads with covered bridges, at country auctions and fairs.

A full breakfast included in the room rate is served every morning.

DEERHILL INN, Box 387, Valley View Road, West Dover, VT 05356; 802-464-3100. A 17-guestroom (private baths) country inn in the scenic Mt. Snow area of southern Vermont. Modified American plan; B&B rates available on request. Open all year. Mt. Snow, Carinthia, and Haystack ski areas, all most convenient. Xc skiing nearby. Backroading, golf, and other outdoor recreational, cultural, and scenic attractions abound. Not suitable for children under 6. The Retlev Family, Innkeepers.

Directions: Deerhill Inn is located just off Rte. 100 in West Dover village. From the south, go past the church and post office and turn right at the antique store on the corner of Valley View Rd.

For B&B rates, see Index.

1811 HOUSE
Manchester Village, Vermont

It could be the home of a Colonial gentleman of means, surrounded with reminders of his English past. It could be, but it isn't. The 1811 House is an elegant bed-and-breakfast inn where guests may feel at home among the beautiful appointments—handsome American and English antique furnishings, oriental rugs, fine paintings, porcelains, and objets d'art.

Each of the thirteen bedrooms, all with private baths, has been given a distinctive treatment—three have working fireplaces, several have canopied or four-poster beds. The bedroom of an earlier owner, Mary Lincoln Isham, Lincoln's granddaughter, has a marble shower and a porch overlooking the Equinox golf course. Even the bathrooms are all different. Telephones and TV's are available for the rooms, if desired.

Mary and Jack Hirst go all out on the full English breakfast they offer. Beginning with fresh-squeezed orange juice and fresh fruit in season, the menu might have anything from eggs with bacon to kippers to chicken livers, accompanied by grilled tomatoes, mushrooms, sautéed apple rings, fried bread, and home fries. The huge eggs come (within a day of laying) from a local farm, and the jams come from Clearbrook Farm in Ohio.

I could go on about the authenticity and luxury of the period decor and furnishings, or describe the reproduction of an Early American tavern with its pewter mugs, horse brasses, and carriage lamps—but more important is Jack's comment that informality is the rule, and this is the kind of a place where guests can wander into the kitchen to make themselves a cup of tea, or kick off their shoes in the library and curl up with a good book.

1811 HOUSE, Manchester Village, Vt. 05254; 802-362-1811. A 13-bedroom beautifully restored Federal inn adjacent to the Equinox golf course in a bustling Vermont village. Full English breakfast included in the cost of the room. Open year-round. Golf, tennis, fishing, backroading, antiquing, biking, xc and downhill skiing nearby. Not suitable for children under 16. No pets. Mary and Jack Hirst, Innkeepers.

Directions: From New York City: Taconic Pkwy. to U.S. 22. Turn east from Rte. 22 to N.Y. Rte. 7 and continue to Bennington, Vt. In Bennington, take Vt. Historic Rte. 7A to Manchester Village. Inn is on the village green next to the Congregational Church.

For B&B rates, see Index.

THE GOVERNOR'S INN
Ludlow, Vermont

Although this handsomely restored and preserved Victorian mansion has bed-and-breakfast rates, it is in reality a village inn that also offers a modified American plan including dinner. Guests enjoy the magnificent hand-painted slate-and-mirrored fireplace and crackling fires on chilly winter nights, and the refreshing mountain breezes in summer. The view of Okemo Mountain from the living room is especially spectacular during the fall foliage season.

Fluffy comforters, large towels, and fragrant potpourri in each room make a stay even more enjoyable. One room is graced with a 100-year-old brass four-poster bed. Six of the rooms have private baths and two others share a bath.

After enjoying one of their six-course dinners, I'd suggest that B&B guests plan on arriving in time for the evening meal. Breakfast and dinner are served in the recently opened "country room," which sports a beautiful, antique Crawford wood stove.

Charlie and Deedy enjoy sharing the treasures they have collected in their world travels, and guests are likely to discover they are using a spoon from Cairo, Egypt, or a cup from France.

THE GOVERNOR'S INN, 86 Main St., Ludlow, Vt. 05149; 802-228-8830. An 8-bedroom village inn (2 rooms share a bath) in a bustling central Vermont town. Open year-round. B&B rates available. Modified American plan includes dinner. Conveniently located for many Vermont historical, recreational, and cultural attractions. Okemo Ski Area, 1 mi. distant; Stratton, Killington, Bromley, and others within 30 min.; also xc skiing, horseback riding, biking, golf, hiking, and antiquing abound. Charlie and Deedy Marble, Innkeepers.

Directions: From I-91, take Exit 6 and follow Rte. 103 to Ludlow.

For B&B rates, see Index.

GREEN MOUNTAIN TEA ROOM
South Wallingford, Vermont

Built in 1792, this historic house was originally a stagecoach stop and tavern on the old stage road from Bennington to Rutland. Here the driver would exchange his tired horses for fresh ones, and most likely have a convivial visit in the tavern to catch up on local gossip.

Herb and Peg Barker are the hosts these days, and offer five bedrooms to overnight guests. Three of the bedrooms were created out of the former upstairs ballroom and all have been furnished in an up-country Vermont manner.

A pleasant tradition at this guest house on Route 7 is afternoon tea, which includes fifteen varieties of tea in colorful individual pots, along with homemade desserts or Vermont cheese and crackers.

If you're staying overnight you'll be tempted to stay longer after you see the view of Otter Creek from the bedrooms in the back and learn that there's trout fishing, hiking, skiing, and Appalachian Trail walks nearby.

Breakfast and lunch are served here, all with homecooked flavor.

South Wallingford is on Route 7, the direct north-south road from southern New England to Canada, wending its way up the west side of Vermont.

GREEN MOUNTAIN TEA ROOM & GUEST HOUSE, South Wallingford, Vt. 05773; 802-446-2611. A 5-bedroom guest house in the valley of Otter Creek. Open year-round. Restaurant open 7:30 A.M.-4:00 P.M.; closed Mondays and Tuesdays. Breakfast, lunch, and afternoon tea served. Canoeing, fishing, swimming, picnicking on grounds. Backroading, skiing, antiquing, and other Vermont diversions nearby. No credit cards. Herb and Peg Barker, Proprietors.

Directions: South Wallingford is just a few moments south of Wallingford on Rte. 7.

For Lodging rates, see Index.

HILL FARM INN
Arlington, Vermont

U.S. 7, which starts in southern Connecticut and goes north through the Berkshires of Massachusetts and on up to the very top of Vermont, is one of the principal roads in the East that leads to vacation and holiday destinations.

In Arlington, Vermont, Historic Route 7A is particularly attractive, threading its way between Mt. Equinox on the west and undulating forest and farmland on the east. In Sunderland, just north of Arlington, there is a small sign directing the traveler to the right on a country road past the Union Church to Hill Farm Inn with its broad, pleasant porch and dairy farms and herd in the rear.

My grandmother didn't live in Vermont, but if she had, I wish it could have been in a house like this one, owned by George and Joanne Hardy. As you step inside, a welcome feeling pervades the light and airy dining room with its sturdy wood tables decorated with pots of African violets. I didn't have breakfast, but I can imagine what a cheerful and fortifying experience it must be with oatmeal or other cereals, eggs, bacon or sausage patties, toast and homemade jams, or perhaps George's french toast or pancakes with maple syrup. And it's all included with the room rate. You might decide to stay for one of Joanne's special dinners that includes vegetables from George's garden, homemade soups and breads and desserts, along with a hearty main dish.

The rooms are neat and comfortable, and a basket of apples and a jar of homemade jam welcome the newly-arrived guest. Two cheery back bedrooms with an adjoining bath, along with a four-bunk-bed room, made ideal family accommodations.

HILL FARM INN, R.R. 2, Box 2015, Arlington, Vt. 05250; 802-375-2269. A 6-bedroom farmhouse inn with 5 rooms in guest house (5 private baths). Open year-round. Modified American plan. B&B guests may make arrangements for dinner in advance, if desired. Convenient to all of the recreational, cultural, and natural attractions in the area. Pets allowed in cabins only. Please, no smoking in bedrooms. George and Joanne Hardy, Innkeepers.

Directions: Coming north, follow Historic Rte. 7A to Arlington, and about 3 mi. north, watch for signpost on the right. (The road is just beyond "Christmas Days.") Coming south on 7A, look for road on the left just beyond "Basketville."

For B&B rates, see Index.

HOBBY HILL
Newfane, Vermont

I'll be forever indebted to the postmistress at Williamsville, Vermont, for telling me about Hobby Hill. It is just the kind of place that will delight anyone who would like to spend a holiday in the Vermont Green Mountains in an old 1790 farmhouse.

Located behind the village on a dirt road high in the mountains with a view of Mt. Oregon, the highest point in the town of Newfane, the house is surrounded by sugar maples.

In addition to the main white clapboard building, there is a small, secluded stone house on the property with a beautiful big fireplace and a couch that opens up into a double bed to provide extra accommodations. This guest cottage has kitchen conveniences.

In the living room in the main house are all the things you ever wanted in your grandmother's home—knickknacks, deer antlers, guns and swords and old rifles, pictures of relatives, stacks of the *National Geographic*, and all kinds of books and magazines.

The bedrooms are just as old-fashioned and comfortable as the dining room and kitchen, and have several different combinations of beds. There are old quilts and views of the countryside.

Marion and Red Chaffee serve a full breakfast in the beautiful old-fashioned kitchen and they are as warmhearted as the big stove in the corner.

As Marion says, "We take care of a few guests at our convenience, because Red and I frequently do some traveling on our own. Please tell your readers that they must telephone ahead for reservations in order not to be disappointed as we are not here on a regular basis."

HOBBY HILL, Newfane, Vt. 05345; 802-365-4038. A snug 4-bedroom old Vermont farmhouse serving a full breakfast and providing warm hospitality. Breakfast the only meal served. Open occasionally. A guest cottage is available May to Nov. Conveniently located for good xc and downhill skiing, woodland walks, backroading, antiquing, and all the other delights of central Vermont in all seasons. No credit cards. Marion and Red Chaffee, Proprietors.

Directions: From the center of Newfane, follow the road behind the Court House, (Wardsboro Rd.) and take the first left at the end of the blacktop. There is a sign that says Hobby Hill. Continue on that, ever upwards through the woods.

For B&B rates, see Index.

THE HUGGING BEAR INN
Chester, Vermont

Of all the stories Georgette and Paul Thomas tell about the inn, my favorite concerns the little girl who carried twenty bears up to her room for a good night's sleeping, then returned them all to the Hugging Bear Shoppe before 9:00 A.M., the next morning. "Absolutely within our rules, such as they are," Georgette says.

None of this paltry "Three Bears plus Goldilocks" either. There are bears at the windows, bears on the beds, bears in the chairs and one that is a life-sized floor mattress by a New York artist. All the bears are available for hugging, and the ten percent discount in the shop for inn guests lasts a full month after departure. "So many people telephone a week later and say they simply *must* have that bear." The proprietors understand the feeling.

The inn is a delightful Victorian structure, built in 1850, and later embellished with a tower and bow windows (all the better for bears to peek from). Each of the six bedrooms is different, though each has its share of bears as well as a private bath.

Breakfast is a full country repast, with whole-wheat, sunflower seed pancakes the house specialty. Honey is available, but in Vermont most guests opt for maple syrup.

Besides being a warm, fun place for adults, the Hugging Bear is going to be a part of the pleasant memories of childhood for a lot of youngsters fortunate enough to spend some magical nights in Bear Country, Vermont style. The Thomases belong to the Good Bears of the World, an international organization that provides teddy bears for children and the elderly in hospitals and homes.

Goodness, even the house dog is named—you guessed it—Bear!

THE HUGGING BEAR INN, Main St., Chester, VT 05143; 802-875-2412. A 6-guestroom (all private baths) bed-and-breakfast inn and shoppe on Rte. 11, 8 mi. from Springfield, Vt. Breakfast (full) the only meal served, but there are restaurants nearby. Open all year. Antique and craft stores all around; skiing nearby. Children welcome (cribs and teddy bears available). Special advance arrangements necessary for pets. No smoking. Georgette and Paul Thomas, Proprietors.

Directions: From I-91 take Exit 6. Go north on Rte. 103, which becomes Main St., Rte. 11, in Chester.

For B&B rates, see Index.

THE INN AT WEATHERSFIELD
Weathersfield, Vermont

On Route 106, which plies between Springfield and Woodstock, Vermont, passing to the west side of Mt. Ascutney, just a few minutes west of I-91, I discovered The Inn at Weathersfield.

It is a beautiful old white clapboard building, set well back from the road. Oddly enough, Mt. Vernon-like pillars (a rarity in New England) add to its grace and serenity. I learned that these had been added around 1900 by a Southern minister who became homesick.

Originally it was a homestead and farm and later it became a tavern and stagecoach stop on the road between Rutland, Vermont, and Nashua, New Hampshire.

From stem to stern the inn has been lovingly furnished with beautiful antiques by the innkeepers, Mary Louise and Ron Thorburn. There are nine large guest rooms and two two-room suites. Each room has a private bath and most, to the joy of the traveler, have working fireplaces. In fact, there are eleven fireplaces in the building, as well as an 18th-century beehive brick bake oven, still in working order.

Normally in the morning guests have the option of having an early breakfast in their rooms. This includes a sterling silver coffee service and freshly squeezed orange juice, a croissant, and coffee, tea, or cocoa. Later they may come downstairs for the rest of the breakfast which includes eggs Benedict, eggs Weathersfield (too complicated to explain), Scottish eggs, waffles, and other unusual breakfast treats. Incidentally afternoon tea is also a daily occurrence at this out-of-the-way inn.

If at all possible, plan to arrive for dinner.

THE INN AT WEATHERSFIELD, Weathersfield, Vermont 05151; 802-263-9217. An 11-room country inn just a few minutes from the town of Perkinsville, and within a short distance of Mt. Ascutney. Open all year. Mod. Amer. plan also available. Closed for dinner Mon. and Tues. Hiking, backroading, swimming, boating, fishing, xc and downhill skiing, berrying, golfing, and horseback riding nearby. Not suitable for children under 8. No pets. Mary Louise and Ron Thorburn, Innkeepers.

Directions: If traveling north on I-91 use Exit 7 at Springfield and Rte. 106 and turn west. From Boston, leave I-89 and follow Rte. 103 across New Hampshire west into Vermont, where it becomes Rte. 131. Continue west to Rte. 106, then south on Rte. 106.

For B&B rates, see Index.

THE INN AT WESTON
Weston, Vermont

The beguiling twists and turns of Route 100 now lead into Weston, Vermont, where the village inn is located, and where the Weston Playhouse has been offering summer theater fare to visitors for many, many years. Just off the green is the Orton Family Country Store, which features many gadgets from the past. Other attractions are the 1797 Farrar Mansur House Museum, the restored Gristmill Museum, the Fudge Shop, the Weston Bowl Mill, several crafts shops, and the Weston Priory (Benedictine monastery, known for its own special music). Pleasant day trips to several quaint towns can be arranged at the inn.

There are thirteen typical country inn bedrooms at Sue and Stu Douglas's Inn at Weston. Each room has its own diffcrent color scheme and they're all done in Vermont country-inn furniture. The inn consists of the main house, converted stable and hayloft, and attached barn. Portions of it go back to the 1840s.

There's a very wide lawn on the south side, which is suitable for croquet, and because this is an inn that accommodates many young people, there's lots of space for them to move around.

The dinners were especially noted for their excellence by *Gourmet Magazine*.

A full breakfast is included in the B&B rate, with lots of emphasis on natural foods, including whole-wheat pancakes. Sue also does something special with country granola. The Sunday brunch on the inn's sunny porch is a special treat.

THE INN AT WESTON, Box 56NS, Rte. 100, Weston, VT 05161; 802-824-5804. A 13-guestroom village inn (7 with private baths). Dinner and Sunday brunch also served. Open from Memorial Day Weekend to Thanksgiving; Dec. 15 to Easter. All of the central Vermont four-season recreation nearby, including downhill and xc skiing (Viking Touring Center), bicycling, backroading, swimming, hiking, etc. Summer theater, museums, and many craft shops within walking distance. No pets. No credit cards. Stu, Sue, and Molly Noel Douglas, Innkeepers.

Directions: Weston is north of Londonberry and south of Ludlow on Rte. 100.

For B&B rates, see Index.

THE INN ON THE COMMON
Craftsbury Common, Vermont

The village of Craftsbury Common in Vermont's North East Kingdom was founded in 1789. It's one of Vermont's most remarkable hill towns. The most impressive feature is the Common which dwarfs the surrounding old homes, church, and Academy. A white-rail fence surrounds the Common area.

The inn is composed of three restored 19th-century houses, all handsomely wallpapered and furnished with antiques, original and folk art, hooked rugs, and colorful custom quilts. There are all varieties and sizes of rooms, some with fireplaces; many with private baths. Well-stocked bookshelves and a library of films on tape offer quiet entertainment.

Basically, the inn is on the American plan because there is all manner of sports, recreation, and entertainment available in all four seasons. However, there are a few B&B accommodations available. I would strongly advise telephoning considerably ahead in order not to be disappointed.

Big breakfasts are the order of the day, with a full measure of approval from the Colonial portraits in the dining room. It's possible to order almost anything, and the omelets are especially good.

THE INN ON THE COMMON, Craftsbury Common, Vt. 05827; 802-586-9619. A 17-room (most with private baths) resort-inn in a remote Vermont town 35 mi. from Montpelier. Modified American plan omits lunch. Breakfast and dinner served to houseguests only. Open all year. Attended pets allowed. Swimming, tennis, croquet, xc skiing, snowshoeing, on grounds. Golf, lake swimming, sailing, canoeing, fishing, xc and downhill skiing, skating, hiking, and nature walks nearby. Michael and Penny Schmitt, Innkeepers.

Directions: From Exit 7, I-89N, take Rte. 2 east to Rte. 14 north until 8 mi. north of Harwick. Watch for marked right hand turn, go 2 mi. to inn. From Canada and points north, use Exit 26 and I-91 and follow Rte. 58W to Irasburg. Then Rte. 14 southbound 12 mi. to marked left turn, 3 mi. to inn.

For B&B rates, see Index.

INWOOD MANOR
East Barnet, Vermont

East Barnet is quite a ways north in Vermont, although still south of the famous North East Kingdom. The Connecticut River separates most of Vermont and New Hampshire, but at this point veers off to the east, and travelers along Route 5, which runs parallel to I-91, are treated to the sights along the Passumpsic River.

Inwood Manor is just over the bridge at East Barnet to the east of Route 5, and was once the main site for the world's largest croquet factory. It is situated on a plateau overlooking the river and it's a very short walk to the delightful waterfalls.

The hosts here are Peter Embarrato and Ron Kaczor who are both Vermont transplants and feel that they've finally found a home. It's obvious that they've put a great deal of work and consideration into this building whose original integrity is now preserved for many generations to come.

The nine guest rooms all have shared baths and have been furnished with early attic beds and tables and generous helpings of good humor. It is old Vermont come to life again.

It's worth noting that travelers can be accommodated for lunch and dinner if advance notice is given.

Included with the room rate is a continental breakfast featuring home-baked breads and homemade jams. A full Vermont breakfast is available at an additional charge.

The Inwood Manor is one of the inns on the upper Connecticut River that is cooperating in a canoeing program, making it possible for participants to enjoy the river and float from inn to inn spending a night in each, if desired. A telephone call or letter will fill in more details.

INWOOD MANOR, East Barnet, Vermont 05821; 802-633-4047. A 9-bedroom inn (shared baths) in one of the most beautiful natural sections of Vermont, quite convenient to both the White and Green Mountains and all of the recreational opportunities. A light lunch and dinner is served upon advance request. Open year-round. Closed Christmas. Cross-country and downhill skiing nearby. No pets. No credit cards. Peter Embarrato and Ron Kaczor, Innkeepers.

Directions: From I-91 use Exit 18 (Barnet), follow Rte. 5 north and turn east on the Lower Waterford Road across the railroad tracks. Turn left at inn sign.

For B&B rates, see Index.

IRASBURG GREEN BED & BREAKFAST
Irasburg, Vermont

The upper section of Vermont has been traditionally called the North East Kingdom, and for the traveler in search of a unique type of independent remoteness some of the villages in this part of the state are choice discoveries.

Such a discovery is Irasburg, where there are some extremely interesting late 18th- and early 19th-century houses built around a village green, and where the town meeting place is the general store.

To add to the intrigue even more, the Irasburg Green Bed & Breakfast is owned by a most interesting German woman named Steffi Stackelberg who has a lively sense of humor, is an excellent conversationalist, and, as the creator of silver jewelry, has a more-than-average interest in crafts. Furthermore, she maintains a very brisk business in local crafts, which are displayed throughout the house.

Steffi has three second-floor bedrooms which share the family bathroom on the first floor, so it is a good idea to bring a bathrobe. The season starts around May first and ends about the middle of October.

The breakfast is most generous with a choice of bacon, eggs, toast, juice, and coffee. This would be a good basis for the vigorous summertime activities in the area, which include swimming, hiking, fishing and golf. Steffi will serve the evening meal on request.

Irasburg is not for the traveler who has become accustomed to being pampered and spoiled by exotic accommodations. It is a slice of Vermont the way it was more than 100 years ago, but I think visitors would be most intrigued, not only with the village and the accommodations, but also with the proprietress.

IRASBURG GREEN BED & BREAKFAST, Irasburg, Vt. 05845; 802-754-6012. A 3-bedroom bed-and-breakfast home in one of the remote villages of Vermont's North East Kingdom. Full breakfast included in the cost of the accommodations. Open May 1 to mid-Oct. Plenty of outdoor activity available nearby. No pets. Steffi Stackelberg, Proprietress.

Directions: Leave I-91 at Orleans, follow Rte. 58 to Irasburg. House is located on village green and includes sign in front for craft shop.

For B&B rates, see Index.

JUNIPER HILL LODGE
Windsor, Vermont

Juniper Hill Lodge is not your run-of-the-mine accommodation. For example, stately white columns greet the visitor to this sizable mansion, which includes, among other things, twenty-four bedrooms, thirteen baths, and fourteen fireplaces. It was built by Maxwell Evarts, who was a descendant of one of the signers of the Declaration of Independence.

In 1980, Maurice and Alma Gilbert, owners of the Oaks Maxfield Parrish Museum, purchased it and began the restoration process. It is located high on a hill amidst trees that are ablaze with color in the fall. The entrance is through a Georgian doorway and the unusually large reception area is about half the size of a tennis court. At the time of my visit it featured original oils by the contemporary Spanish artist, Puyet.

It might be called a "mansion in transition" and like a really good thoroughbred racehorse who hasn't raced in a few years, it is now being brought back up to peak condition. At the time of my visit, refurbishing and redecorating were still being done on the top floor.

Windsor is literally the birthplace of Vermont and has the longest covered bridge in the United States. There's much to see and do of historic and cultural interest in the area.

JUNIPER HILL LODGE, P.O. Box 1, Juniper Hill Rd., Windsor, Vt. 05089; 802-674-5273. A 24-room (8 private baths) bed-and-breakfast mansion. Continental breakfast. Open all year. Conveniently located for visits to the Vermont State Crafts Center, St. Gaudens National Historic Site, Maxfield Parrish Museum, Mt. Ascutney Ski Area, and Vermont and New Hampshire back roads and antique shops. Alma and Maurice Gilbert, Proprietors.

Directions: From Rte. 5 turn west on Juniper Hill Rd. (opposite Bottle Gas Co.); go ¼ mi. and then take left fork signposted Juniper Terrace.

For B&B rates, see Index.

KEDRON VALLEY INN
South Woodstock, Vermont

Nestled in a gentle valley surrounded by the hills and forests of the Green Mountains, this venerable old 1828 inn offers its guests both a comfortable stay and all sorts of diversions.

Surrounded by beautiful woodland trails and with a stable of over thirty horses, the inn arranges trail rides, sleigh and surrey rides, private riding lessons, and can provide mounts for beginners and experts.

The spring-fed pond is wonderful for a cool dip on a hot day and ice skating in the winter. There are lovely walks and hikes (which become cross-country ski trails in the winter) through the woods and past old farms and beautifully restored 18th-century homes. The inn is within minutes of seven downhill ski areas, including Killington Peak and Mt. Ascutney. Golf, tennis, and fishing are all available nearby. Or you can just sit in a rocking chair on the wide verandah and wave at the occasional passing car.

Paul and Barbara Kendall have been involved for many years in providing both comfort and enjoyment for their guests. Paul always cooks the breakfasts, which might include such hearty fare as red flannel hash, McKenzie's whole hog sausage, griddle cakes with the inn's own maple syrup, and, of course, eggs. Breakfast is à la carte, unless you want to take advantage of the modified American plan rates, which include an excellent dinner topped by a mouth-watering piece of one of Paul's mother's pies.

There are roomy lounge areas with fireplaces, and the bedrooms are nicely furnished with private baths; some rooms have their own fireplaces or stoves, and there are various sizes of beds.

KEDRON VALLEY INN, Rte. 106, South Woodstock, Vt. 05071; 802-457-1473. A 31-room rustic resort-inn (all private baths), 5 mi. south of Woodstock, and near Killington, Mt. Ascutney ski areas. European and mod. American plans. No B&B rate. Breakfast, lunch, and dinner served daily from early May to Nov. 1; closed Sun. eve. Nov. to mid-Mar. Closed from last Sun. in Mar. to first Fri. in May. Christmas Day buffet served 1 to 5 P.M. Horseback riding, trail rides, sleigh and surrey rides, swimming, paddle tennis, hiking, and xc skiing on grounds. Tennis, golf, downhill skiing, and bicycles nearby. Paul and Barbara Kendall, Innkeepers.

Directions: Take Exit 1 from I-89 and follow Rte. 4 to Woodstock. Proceed south on Rte. 106 for 5 mi. Or, take Exit 8 from I-91, and follow Rte. 131 for 8 mi. Proceed north on Rte. 106 for 12 mi.

For Lodging rates, see Index.

THE LAKE HOUSE
Thetford, Vermont

Sunday morning breakfast at the Lake House (just a few steps from the shores of Lake Fairlee in Vermont) features delicious, made-from-scratch waffles with real Vermont maple syrup, and also home-made muffins and scones. In the summertime guests can take breakfast on the porch and enjoy the wonderfully clear Vermont air and verdant countryside.

Originally built as an inn in 1870, the Lake House's tradition of innkeeping is being continued by Charles and Betty Pemberton.

The antiques and furnishings in some of the bedrooms are really quite exceptional. I saw a platform rocker, many tufted bedspreads, and flowered wallpapers that reflect a real country feeling.

There are eight bedrooms, one with a king-sized bed and private bath, in this old Vermont country house. There are lots of opportunities to sit in the living room and become acquainted with other guests, some of whom may be staying longer than just one night. There are many activities nearby, including golf, tennis, boating, fishing, and swimming in the lake. Dartmouth College sports and cultural activities are just a few minutes away as well.

With numerous country roads, cyclists may enjoy easy scenic rides around the shores of Lake Fairlee and Lake Morey. Scenic flights over Vermont can be enjoyed from Post Mills Airport, only a short walk from the inn. Just watching the sailplanes and airplanes come and go can be fun, too.

THE LAKE HOUSE, Rte. 244, P.O. Box 65, Post Mills, VT 05058; 802-333-4025. An 8-guestroom (1 private bath) bed-and-breakfast inn just off I-91 a few miles north of Norwich, Vermont. Open all year. Many outdoor activities and country recreation available including bike riding, horseback riding, apple picking, downhill and xc skiing, snowshoeing, snowmobiling, and ice fishing available. The countryside has many covered bridges and leisurely drives. No pets. Charles and Betty Pemberton, Innkeepers.

Directions: From I-91 take exit No. 14 west, drive approx. 7 mi. on Rte. 113, turn right 1/4 mi. beyond Baker's General Store on Rte. 244 and go exactly 9/10 mi. to the inn on the left.

For B&B rates, see Index.

LAKE ST. CATHERINE INN
Poultney, Vermont

Lake St. Catherine is another of the wonderful places in the world in which I have a proprietary interest. When my sons were growing up we spent many summers and many Thanksgivings and Christmases on the lake, which is one of the most beautiful and purest in Vermont. It is circled with a ring of low hills and the lake water provides marvelous swimming, canoeing, fishing, and sailing. We all learned to water-ski and sail on it.

That's why I was delighted when I learned from John Kenny, the innkeeper of the Lake St. Catherine Inn, that although it is basically a modified American plan inn, special arrangements can be made for bed-and-breakfast guests. Be sure to indicate this when you make your reservation.

The inn is at the lakeside and has all of the water sports mentioned above.

The 35 rooms all have private baths and some of them have very pleasant lake views. It's a great place for young and old alike. One diversion that has grown in popularity in recent years is bicycle touring, which provides more intimate views of the wonderful scenery.

Besides the rooms in the main section of the inn, there are cottages that are spread out among the campuslike grounds.

On the basis of the wonderful aromas coming from the dining room, I would advise anybody staying even for one night to arrive in time for dinner.

LAKE ST. CATHERINE INN, Poultney, Vt. 05764; 802-287-9347. A 35-room resort inn on beautiful Lake St. Catherine in western Vermont. All rooms have private baths. Open May to Oct. A full breakfast is included. Modified American plan, but arrangements can be made for bed and breakfast with advance notification. All of the Vermont summer and winter attractions are nearby, including excellent fishing, xc skiing, backroading, swimming, tennis, bicycling, antiquing, and the like. No pets. No credit cards. Patricia Marks and Raymond Endlich, Innkeepers.

Directions: From I-87 (Northway) take Exit 20. Go east on Rte. 149 to Rte. 4 at Ft. Ann. Take left on Rte. 4 for 4 mi. and then right on Rte. 22 (across bridge) for 9 mi. to Rte. 22-A. Turn left at flasher, and right over bridge 2 mi. to Rte. 149 at red flasher which is Granville. Turn left on Rte. 149 for 2 mi. to Rte. 30 (flasher). Turn left on Rte. 30 and proceed 6 mi. to turn-off on the left to the inn.

For B&B rates, see Index.

LAREAU FARM COUNTRY INN
Waitsfield, Vermont

"We had a country wedding last week right over there in the meadow," Susan Easley said, pointing to a particularly lush part of the forty-five green acres that belong to the inn. Lucky bride and groom, I thought, to begin married life knee-deep in daisies.

More commonly, visitors arrive to enjoy the pleasure of all four seasons in the Mad River Valley that runs north and south along the Green Mountains near Sugarbush. In winter, there are three major downhill ski areas minutes away, and that meadow is a great start for cross-country and for horsedrawn sleigh rides available through the inn. In summer, consider the fact that the Mad River runs right through the inn's front yard, and the fishing is easy. Autumn in Vermont is so special it has become a cliché, and as for spring—well, in spring there are wildflowers and fresh maple sugar.

This 150-year-old farm-cum-inn is on the State Register of Historic Buildings with a barn that is officially listed as one of the few wood stanchion dairy types left in the state.

Traveling families will find the rooms bright and sunny, each individually decorated with interesting old pieces and homemade quilts. There is a homey living room for guests, and rocking chairs on the porch. A full country breakfast, cooked on a wood stove, is served in the informal dining room, and when you come back to the inn after a day of activity, Susan will probably offer you a nice cup of tea or après ski hors d'oeuvres.

LAREAU FARM COUNTRY INN, Box 563, Rte. 100, Waitsfield, VT 05673; 802-496-4949. A 10-room (4 with private bath) bed-and-breakfast inn in Sugarbush Valley, Vermont. Full country breakfast included; no other meals served. Many excellent restaurants in the area. Open all year. Skiing, swimming, canoeing, fishing, tennis, horseback riding, shopping all nearby. Crib and rollaways available. No smoking in bedrooms. No pets. Susan and Dan Easley, Proprietors.

Directions: Rte. 100 runs north and south in the middle of Vermont. The Lareau Farm Country Inn is set back on the western side of the road, and there is a large sign. It is south of the Rte. 17 junction, 1/4 mi. from the Waitsfield shopping areas.

For B&B rates, see Index.

MAPLE CREST FARM
Cuttingsville, Vermont

This is the Vermont you've always dreamed about—a farm in a stand of maple trees on a country road with a sweeping view of the valley that has been in the same family for five generations.

The parlor, bedrooms, dining room, and kitchen are like a Norman Rockwell illustration. Sharing space with dozens of family photographs, diplomas, and hundreds of well-read books and magazines are blue ribbons won by various members of the Smith family in recent years for canning, vegetables, and cattle-raising at the Vermont State Fair.

The furnishings in this farmhouse reflect the five generations that have grown up here. There are wonderful high beds, platform rockers, old prints and paintings, and many colorful quilts.

Besides the bedrooms there are also efficiency apartments with separate accommodations for children, if you prefer. Each has its own entrance leading to the lawn and the great barn where there are over a hundred cows.

Breakfast is the time when everyone sits around the big table in the kitchen and, while Donna Smith turns out endless stacks of pancakes and plates of scrambled eggs, guests share the table with members of the family, including three strapping sons.

One of the most interesting times to visit would be during maple sugaring time which starts around the 18th of March and runs for a month. Chances are there would be some cross-country skiing as well.

When you visit Maple Crest Farm be prepared to wish you could have stayed longer.

MAPLE CREST FARM, Cuttingsville, Vt. 05738; 802-492-3367. (An American Bed & Breakfast host.) A beautiful old 6-bedroom Vermont farmhouse with two efficiency apartments. Ideal for longer stays. Open year-round. A full breakfast is the only meal served; however, there are good restaurants nearby for the evening meal. Downhill and xc skiing, backroading, walking, antiquing abound. No credit cards. No pets. Donna Smith, Proprietor.

Directions: Cuttingsville is on Rte. 103 between Ludlow and Rutland. Once in Cuttingsville turn east on a country road that runs next to the green bridge in the middle of town. Drive about two miles to the top of the hill where you can see the red buildings of the farm and a sign on the side of the barn.

For B&B rates, see Index.

MAY FARM LODGE
Waterbury Center, Vermont

It was the "Antiques" sign that caught my eye from the road, then the "1790" on the house that made me turn around and pull into the parking area of the May Farm Lodge. I was traveling north on the Stowe Road (also known as Route 100) out of Waterbury, and was almost too distracted by the Green Mountain scenery to notice things close at hand. Fortunately, I glanced to the right at the serendipitous moment.

Antiques do not end at the door of the crowded shop. They spill into the kitchen, up the stairs, and through the four big bedrooms. However, you don't have to be a dedicated antiquer to enjoy these spacious, sunny quarters, to sit out on the neatly clipped back lawn, or to appreciate the full country breakfast served every morning in the dining room.

The location is excellent, too. The inn is just two miles south of the Stowe town line. Cross that and you are in an area world-famous for its skiing, dining, and shopping. There is golf, hiking, biking, theater, and either a gondola or an automobile ride to the top of Mount Mansfield for the fabulous views. There are galleries and a flea market every Sunday all summer long.

May Farm Lodge doesn't advertise or put out a brochure. Many of the returning guests were directed here in the first place by the pricey inns when they ran out of space. Alas for the big ones, they last their customers forever to this home-away-from- home.

MAY FARM LODGE, Rte. 100, P.O. Box 161, Waterbury, VT 05677; 802-244-7306. A 4-guestroom (2 shared baths) bed-and-breakfast lodge just south of Stowe in north-central Vermont. Breakfast the only meal served, but it is a full country one. Open year-round. All restaurant, resort, and shopping facilities nearby. Off-street parking. Antique store attached. No pets. No credit cards. During foliage season (mid- Sept. to early Oct.) reserve far in advance. Rose and Joseph Lukowich, Proprietors.

Directions: Rte. 100 is the north-south road that bisects Vermont. If you are coming south from Morrisville, the inn will be on your left about 2 mi. after crossing the Stowe/Waterbury town line. If you are going north (take the Waterbury exit from Hwy. 89), start looking for the inn on your right about 7 mi. out of Waterbury. There is a sign, and the driveway is on Rte. 100.

For B&B rates, see Index.

THE MIDDLETOWN SPRINGS INN
Middletown Springs, Vermont

Lovers of Vermont back roads will cherish their knowledge of Middletown Springs and only share it with their most treasured friends. I imagine that inn-lovers also will feel the same way about The Middletown Springs Inn.

First of all, the roads leading to Middletown Springs from Rutland, Poultney, or Pawlet are some of the most enticing in Vermont. They ramble past wonderful farms, run alongside merry brooks and rivers, and reflect a rural remoteness that is becoming more rare with each passing year.

Situated on the village green along with several interesting shops, the inn is an old Victorian building that is remarkably well preserved, considering its many proprietors of the past.

Innkeepers Jean and Mel Hendrickson have not only created a warm country inn atmosphere, but also designed what I'm sure is one of the most unique doll museums in North America. Jean's grandmother started the collection and it was continued by her mother, and now by Jean. There are dolls of every description, shape, ethnic origin, and occupation.

The inn has ten very tastefully decorated Victorian bedrooms with many interesting and unusual touches.

A full breakfast is served with fresh fruit, blueberry pancakes, Vermont maple syrup, sausage, and coffee as typical offerings. The evening meal is offered to houseguests only on request.

THE MIDDLETOWN SPRINGS INN, Middletown Springs, Vermont 05757; 802-235-2198. A 10-bedroom (private baths) Victorian mansion on the green of a lovely 18th- and 19th-century village. Full breakfast included; arrangements can be made for dinner. Open year-round; however, call in advance for reservations. Within easy driving distance of all central Vermont summer and winter recreation in Mt. Killington, state parks, summer theater, etc. Trout fishing, hiking, xc and alpine skiing, bicycling, swimming, golf, tennis nearby. Museum quality doll and miniature collection on display. Not suitable for young children. Jean and Mel Hendrickson, Innkeepers.

Directions: From Manchester Center, Vermont, follow Rte. 30 to Pawlet and turn north on Rte. 133 to Middletown Springs. From Poultney, Vermont, follow Rte. 140 to East Poultney and on to Middletown Springs.

For B&B rates, see Index.

NORTH HERO HOUSE
North Hero, Vermont

Unlike some of the places mentioned in this book that are not on the road to anywhere, North Hero, Vermont, is on the way to a great many "somewheres."

It is located on North Hero Island on Lake Champlain just a few miles south of the Canadian border and 65 miles south of Montreal. The traveler-in-a-hurry can reach it from New York City in a day's drive by taking the New York State Thruway and the Northway. (See directions below.)

Once arrived I don't know how anyone could leave without staying at least two days. The North Hero House is an early American Champlain inn that has been offering hospitality to travelers since the mid-19th century. It has a magnificent view across Lake Champlain to Mt. Mansfield, and has motorboating, canoeing, sailing, a lakeside sauna, swimming, and fishing for the considerable varieties of finny denizens in the lake.

Comfortable bedrooms are to be found in the main house and in several waterside buildings, all painstakingly restored by the owners, Roger Sorg, and his wife, Caroline, along with their now-grown children, David and Lynn.

Guests may enjoy a full Lake Champlain à la carte breakfast of juice or fresh fruit cup, blueberry waffles or eggs with bacon or sausage, bread doughnuts with maple syrup, country-inn french toast, pancakes, or omelets.

Lunch and dinner are also served.

NORTH HERO HOUSE, Champlain Islands, North Hero, Vt. 05474; 802-372-8237. A 23-room New England resort-inn on North Hero Island in Lake Champlain, 35 mi. north of Burlington and 65 mi. south of Montreal. European plan. Breakfast, lunch, and dinner served daily to travelers. Open from mid-June to mid-Oct. Swimming, fishing, boating, waterskiing, ice-house game room, sauna, bicycles, and tennis on grounds. Horseback riding and golf nearby. No pets. No credit cards. Roger and Caroline Sorg, Innkeepers.

Directions: Travel north from Burlington on I-89, take Exit 17 (Champlain Islands) and drive north on Island Rte. 2 to North Hero. From N.Y. Thruway (87 north), take Exit 39 at Plattsburg and follow signs "Ferry to Vermont." Upon leaving ferry, turn left to Rte. 2, then left again to North Hero. Inn is 15 min. from ferry dock on Rte. 2.

For Lodging rates, see Index.

THE OLD BARN INN
West Wardsboro, Vermont

It was the sign on the west side of Route 100 in West Wardsboro that first attracted my attention to this inn and caused me to back up twenty-five yards after I passed it. The sign is actually a painting into which the words, "Old Barn," have been carefully designed.

Investigation proved that this was, indeed, not only a bed- and-breakfast inn, but one that serves dinner as well. It is the result of loving attention and hard work by Denis and Kathy Smith, who manage to have the best of all possible worlds, wintering on the Florida coast, where they maintain a charter boat business and summering here in glorious central Vermont.

The inn is really a barn, built in 1797 and moved to its present location in 1935. Weathered beams and wide floor- boards are complimented by antiques, old photographs of the barn in its various stages, and a twelve foot fireplace, which is an exact duplicate of one found in the Jared Coffin House on Nantucket. There is a deck off the main sitting room affording a glorious view of this hidden valley.

Bedrooms are all furnished in a wonderful Vermontish style, accented by colorful quilts. Kathy refers to the furnishings as "early flea market."

Originally the Smiths established a restaurant in the barn seven years ago; however, dinner guests came, loved the rooms, and wanted to remain overnight, so it was decided to add the guest bedrooms.

As far as breakfast is concerned, guests are invited to rise at their leisure, come down into the kitchen and cook breakfast themselves. Coffee has been set up in advance as well as homemade breads and juices. There are always plenty of fresh eggs and cereals so guests can fend for themselves.

It may have been the sign that attracted my attention, but I can assure the reader that it is the ambience, the spirit of friendliness and warmth, that would bring me back to this inn many times.

THE OLD BARN INN, Rte. 100, West Wardsboro, VT 05360; 802-896-6100. A 4-guestroom (sharing 2 baths) country inn in the central Vermont fastness. Make-your-own-breakfast is included in the room rate. Dinner is served. Open from the last week of June thru the third week in Oct. Conveniently located to enjoy all of the wonderful summer and fall delights of the Vermont mountains and countryside. Denis and Kathy Smith, Innkeepers.

Directions: West Wardsboro is a few miles north of Mt. Snow on Rte. 100.

For B&B rates, see Index.

PARTRIDGE HILL
Williston, Vermont

Partridge Hill is an ideal bed-and-breakfast home. It sits on the top of a hill with a commanding view of the northern Vermont countryside, Mt. Mansfield, and Camel's Hump.

Roger and Sally Bryant (he is the head athletic trainer at the University of Vermont) furnished and decorated their home, including the two guest bedrooms, with quiet good taste. There are many prints, photographs, and watercolors used to great advantage.

There is one room with queen-sized bed, and the other has two single beds. Both of these share a private guest parlor, bath, and private entrance.

Sally serves a typical Vermont breakfast of orange juice, pancakes made with wholewheat flour or french toast made with Sally's homemade bread, sausage or bacon, their own maple syrup, real cream, and real butter. Even the plates are heated.

In summer, breakfast is often taken on the deck overlooking the beautiful view to the east, and in winter, in the main dining room where there is a fireplace.

It is ideal for a summer visitor with the Shelburne Museum close by. During the winter guests may enjoy cross-country skiing right on the property or downhill skiing at Stowe, only 35 minutes away.

PARTRIDGE HILL, P.O. Box 52, Williston, Vt. 05495; 802-878-4741. (an American Bed & Breakfast Host.) A 2-bedroom private bed-and-breakfast home located 8 miles from Burlington and 25 miles from Stowe. Open year-round. A full breakfast is included in the price of the room. Conveniently located for all the northern Vermont recreational, historical, and cultural activities. Xc skiing on grounds. No smoking, please. Roger and Sally Bryant, Proprietors.

Directions: From Burlington use the Essex Junction, Rte. 2A Exit 12 from I-89. Follow to Essex Junction, turning right on Rte. 2 to Williston Village. Turn right at the Federated Church onto Oak Hill Road and continue .5 mile to just past the Thomas Chittenden Health Center. Turn right where the road up to Partridge Hill is clearly marked with a fancy sign. Inn is at the top of the hill.

For B&B rates, see Index.

THE QUECHEE INN AT MARSHLAND FARM
Quechee, Vermont

Travelers on I-89 and I-91 in eastern Vermont will only have to take a few minutes' side trip to be at the Quechee Inn, and what a surprise it will be.

For one thing it's just minutes away from Quechee Gorge which is called the Grand Canyon of the East, and imagine how refreshing it would be to go for a swim before settling down to a very pleasant country inn dinner.

The inn is a 1793 farmstead near Woodstock, Vermont, and Dartmouth College at Hanover, New Hampshire.

The original carriage house is now a comfortable lounge where period furniture, wide pine-board floors, and braided rugs help to recreate the atmosphere of the past.

Nestled in the beautiful Ottauquechee Valley and bordering a wildlife preserve, the inn enjoys a panorama of lake, river, and mountains that is exceptional.

Guests pour their own coffee at the continental breakfast and also toast the English muffins to the exact degree of doneness they prefer. It's a good opportunity to chat with other guests over fruit juices, homemade coffee cake, and fresh fruit. In the winter, breakfast is taken in the dining room, but on sunshiny days, even when there's snow on the ground, the terrace makes a wonderful place to enjoy breakfast.

THE QUECHEE INN AT MARSHLAND FARM, P.O. Box 457, Quechee, Vermont 05059; 802-295-3133. A 22-room country inn just a few miles from Woodstock, Vermont, and Hanover, New Hampshire. Within a short drive of both the Green Mountains and the White Mountains. All types of summer and winter recreation available, including downhill and cross-country skiing, hiking, and backroading, canoeing, sugaring, bird watching, and cider making. Closed 3 wks. in April and from just after Thanksgiving for 2 weeks. Closed Mon. and Tues. most of the year for dinner, Mon. only mid-July to mid-Oct., but rooms are available. Please check for seasonal changes. Within a short drive of both the Green Mountains and the White Mountains. All types of summer and winter recreation available, including tennis, golf, fishing, swimming, downhill and xc skiing, hiking, biking, backroading, canoeing, sugaring, bird-watching, and cider making. No pets. The Yaroschuk Family (Michael and Barbara), Innkeepers.

Directions: From the intersection of I-89 and I-91, take I-89 north for one exit (No. 1), follow Rte. 4 toward Woodstock and Rutland. After 1.2 miles turn right on Clubhouse Rd. for ½ mile. Inn is on right.

For B&B rates, see Index.

RABBIT HILL INN
Lower Waterford, Vermont

Lower Waterford, Vermont, on the edge of the North East Kingdom, is one of the most picturesque, and hence photographed, villages in Vermont. Across the street from the Rabbit Hill Inn is the village church, built in 1859, and around the corner is the 150-year-old post office that is also an "honor system" library. There is a glorious view of New Hampshire's White Mountains and many enticing outdoor activities nearby, including fishing, sailing, canoeing, nature walking, mountain climbing, and skiing, both downhill and cross-country.

The main building of the inn was built in 1825 and was located on the main route from Portland to Montreal.

All of the inn's twenty bedrooms have their own private baths, and all but two have a view of the mountains. There is a comfortable lounge, a book nook, and dining rooms.

The inn is kept by the Charlton family, originally from England, who are adding new dimensions to American innkeeping.

The continental breakfast features homemade oatmeal toast, orange juice, and homemade muffins. Hearty breakfasts are available at à la carte prices.

RABBIT HILL INN, Pucker St., Lower Waterford, Vt. 05848; 802-748-5168. A 20-room country inn with a view of mountains on Rte. 18, midway between St. Johnsbury, Vt., and Littleton, N.H. Modified American, European plans. Open all year except April and November. Breakfast and dinner served to travelers. Fishing, xc skiing on grounds. Tennis, swimming, walking, alpine skiing, sailing, backroading nearby. The Charlton Family, Innkeepers.

Directions: From I-91: Exit 19 onto I-93, then Exit 1 onto Rte. 18 south. From I-93: Exit Rte. 18 junction, turn north (left) on Rte. 18.

For B&B rates, see Index.

ROWELL'S INN
Simonsville, Vermont

If you are traveling on Route 11, which cuts east and west across Vermont from Manchester to the Connecticut River Valley, I hope you'll keep your eye peeled for Rowell's Inn. It is a beautiful red brick building with a three-tiered front porch and a most graceful enclosed arch on the third story. I have admired this building literally scores of times, and now I am happy to say that it is not only a historic five-bedroom country inn, but has also been placed on the National Register of Historic Places.

The interior is equally as impressive as the exterior, and rather than listing all of its virtues, including the beautiful floors, carved mantel pieces, and many family antiques, let me say that true inn lovers will be delighted even to stop in for a quick look.

The more I wandered around this inn, which started out as a stagecoach stop built in 1820 by Major Edward Simons, the founder of this tiny village, the more I felt myself being absorbed into the past of Vermont. Today, its role is being lovingly continued, probably better than ever, by Beth and Lee Davis, who became enchanted with the idea of owning an inn during a New England inn-hopping trek. I burst with pride to say that they became interested in inns as a result of reading *Country Inns and Back Roads* a number of years ago.

Breakfast is a full country repast with everything from bacon and eggs to ham and cheese soufflés, omelets, and pancakes. Something is baked fresh every morning from sticky buns to bread and muffins. A single entrée, fixed-price dinner is served to houseguests on request with advance notice.

Rowell's Inn is not only a warm, cozy country in, it's a prime example of the rewards in store for anyone who is lucky enough to find such a building and faithfully restore it.

ROWELL'S INN, Simonsville, Vt. 05143; 802-875-3658. A 5-bedroom (3 rooms with private bath, 2 rooms sharing 1 bath) restored stagecoach stop, now a welcoming country inn. Full breakfast included in room rate. Dinner on advance request to houseguests only. Open all year, except 2 wks. in April. Convenient for the splendid recreational, cultural, and scenic attractions in both southern Vermont and New Hampshire. Major ski areas nearby. Children over 6 welcome. No pets. Beth and Lee Davis, Innkeepers.

Directions: Simonsville is located between Londonderry and Chester on Route 11.

For B&B rates, see Index.

SAXTONS RIVER INN
Saxtons River, Vermont

The Saxtons River Inn is about midway between New York City and Montreal. It is just a few miles west of I-91, and is a most engaging stopover.

Saxtons River is an almost-hidden Vermont village where a group of people from some of our larger cities have decided to create a new lifestyle. There's a community interest in music, arts, crafts, and improving the environment.

The center for much of this activity is found in the Saxtons River Inn on the main street, right in the middle of town. You can't miss it because it has a tower section that extends about two-and-a-half stories above the main building.

The front porch, tavern, and dining rooms always find an interesting mix of both locals and travelers enjoying the hospitality. Although there is a fascinating collection of Victoriana throughout the inn, the feeling is somewhat contemporary because of a great many art gallery posters. It is an excellent collection and I must say blends in very well with the entire atmosphere.

In her brochure, Averill Larsen, the innkeeper, points out that inns express their individuality in many ways, and in the case of the Saxtons River Inn, no two bedrooms are alike and each is individually decorated, varying in size and decor. There are nineteen altogether; eight do not have private baths. One in particular would make a very nice honeymoon room. Each of these rooms is generously supplied with a packet of information about everything that can be done in both southern Vermont and nearby New Hampshire.

A continental breakfast is served in the front dining room and is included in the room rate. Dinner is also served every night except Tuesdays.

SAXTONS RIVER INN, Saxtons River, Vt. 05154; 802-869-2110. A 19-bedroom most interesting and casual village inn about 4½ hrs. from NYC and 2½ hrs. from Boston. (Some shared baths.) Breakfast included in room rate. Dinner served every night except Tues. Inn closed Jan., Feb., and Mar. Most conveniently located for guests to enjoy all of the scenic, recreational, and cultural attractions in southern Vermont and New Hampshire. Children welcome. No pets. No credit cards. Averill Larsen, Innkeeper.

Directions: Leave I-91 at Exit 5, turn left off the exit ramp, travel about ¼ mile to T intersection, and turn right on Route 121. This continues on into Saxtons River.

For B&B rates, see Index.

THE SHIRE INN
Chelsea, Vermont

Interstate 89 crosses the Connecticut River at Lebanon, New Hampshire, and goes north to Barre and on to Burlington before continuing to Canada. If the traveler will pause for a moment and join me in examining the Vermont map, he will note that Route 14 begins at Lebanon and follows the White River north through some exceptionally beautiful Vermont countryside and villages, including West Hartford, South Royalton, Randolph Center, Brookfield, and Williamstown. There are several alternate parallel routes, including Route 110 which could include a stop at Chelsea and an overnight stay at the Shire Inn.

Chelsea itself is well worth a visit if for nothing else than the two commons, or open spaces, and a visit to Ackerman's Store, said to be the oldest in Vermont.

In a little village that has many outstanding houses and homes, the Shire Inn is one of the most attractive. Built of Vermont brick in 1832, it has a fan doorway, black shutters, and a pleasant garden and lawn. Inside the entranceway, a curving staircase leads to the second floor and there's a very pleasant sitting room with a cozy fireplace, wide floorboards, and tons of books.

Innkeeper Jackie Arundell is happy to explain that this was the ancestral home of the Davis family and there are many photographs of the family members adorning the walls. The six bedrooms have all been most tastefully furnished and provide an excellent opportunity "to sleep in the past."

The full breakfast consists of as many local viands as possible, including the eggs, honey from the local bees, tomatoes from the garden, jellies made from the local fruit trees, and of course real Vermont maple syrup.

SHIRE INN, Chelsea, Vermont 05038; 802-685-3032. A 4-room village inn (two with private bath) in a beautiful central Vermont setting. Open all year. The Justin Morgan horse farm, the Joseph Smith memorial, cross-country skiing, fishing, walking, and bicycling are all available. No pets. Jackie Arundell, Innkeeper.

Directions: From I-89 use Exit 4, proceed to East Randolph and Brookfield Center. Ask directions for the unmarked road over the mountain to Chelsea. From I-91; exit at Rte. 113 proceeding northwest to Chelsea. Both of these roads are extremely picturesque.

For B&B rates, see Index.

STONE HOUSE INN
North Thetford, Vermont

Here's a suggestion for the I-91 traveler on the east side of Vermont: momentarily abandon the interstate at St. Johnsbury or Norwich, follow the Connecticut River villages on the Vermont side, and see some of the loveliest sights in New England. The farms, barns, river views, and fields will enchant.

In North Thetford, Vermont, a few miles north of Norwich, the Stone House Inn is set on the river side of Route 5 in a little jog off the highway. Six guest rooms are comfortable and cheerful, with views toward the mountains, river, and pond. There's a wide screened veranda, an armchair by one of the fireplaces, and a pleasant walk through the woods alongside the pond to create a wonderful country mood.

The bedrooms are typical farmhouse style, well furnished, clean, and very inviting. The parlor has an upright piano, a fireplace, and there's ample opportunity for guests to become acquainted.

Dianne Sharkey, innkeeper, along with her husband Art, bakes great sticky buns for breakfast, and all the bread, muffins, and sourdough English muffins. These are served with coffee, tea, and fruit juice and during the summertime can be taken on the porch, which overlooks the pond.

Of even further interest, is the fact that there is a canoeing program among inns located on the Connecticut River, and Dianne and Art have all the information.

STONE HOUSE INN, North Thetford, Vermont 05054; 802-333-9124. A 6-bedroom (3 shared baths) guest house located on the banks of the Connecticut River just a few miles north of Norwich, Vermont. Open every day of the year. There is much to offer in both the Green and White Mountains nearby. Within a short distance of Hanover, New Hampshire and Dartmouth College. No pets. Dianne and Art Sharkey, Innkeepers.

Directions: From I-91 take Exit #14 (Thetford). Turn right on Rte. 113 and left after one mile on Rte. 5. The inn is two miles on the right-hand side of the road.

For B&B rates, see Index.

THREE CHURCH STREET
Woodstock, Vermont

Woodstock, Vermont, is a picture-book village that is still unspoiled by its growing reputation. The oval-shaped village green, the new covered bridge, the Historical Society, the DAR Historical Museum, and the Paul Revere bells in the churches make it a memorable experience in any season.

This elegant early 1800s bed-and-breakfast inn on three acres in the heart of the village joins many other fine village residences listed in the National Historic Registry.

The extra-large rooms, swimming pool, and tennis court have provided ample growing space for innkeeper Eleanor Paine's brood of eight children.

Guests enjoy the beautiful music room, cozy library, spacious living and dining rooms, and the gallery overlooking the Ottauquechee River and Mt. Tom.

Each of the bedrooms has a distinct personality with emphasis on individual decorations and furnishings—they have a "Georgetown feeling."

The full breakfast runs the gamut from juices to hot and cold cereal, home fries or grits, eggs cooked in many ways, bacon, corned beef hash, pancakes, and french toast with maple syrup.

From the 4th of July to mid-Oct., simple lunches will be served by the pool or on the porch (weather permitting) on Wednesday through Saturday, and there will be Sunday barbecues from July 7 to August 25.

THREE CHURCH STREET, Village Green, Woodstock, Vt. 05091; 802-457-1925. A 10-bedroom (5 rooms with private baths; 5 rooms share one bath) bed-and-breakfast guest house in a stately home. Closed during April. A full breakfast is included in room rate. Simple lunches available in season. Conveniently located for xc and downhill skiing, golf, horseback riding, backroading, antiquing, fishing, and hiking. Swimming pool and tennis court on grounds. No pets. The Paine Family, Innkeepers.

Directions: Woodstock is on the east side of Vermont, just a short distance from I-91 and I-89.

For B&B rates, see Index.

THREE MOUNTAIN INN
Jamaica, Vermont

Our journey on Route 100, the road that runs up the backbone of Vermont, finds us still in the ski country just outside the entrance to Stratton Mountain and within twenty minutes of Bromley and Magic Mountain. Our objective is the very interesting old village of Jamaica which has been tucked away in this mountain fastness since at least 1780.

In the middle of the village at one of the crossroads stands the Three Mountain Inn with a history dating back to the late 18th century. The living room has a roaring fire in the large fireplace, wide-plank pine walls and floors and the original Dutch oven fireplace.

The innkeepers are all members of the Murray family—Elaine and Charles, and their three vivacious daughters.

The bedrooms have the hallmarks of real country Vermont with candlewick spreads, old prints, framed needlework, and some country furniture made in one of the nearby villages.

The menu in the main dining room with the pink tablecloths changes every night and the modified American plan rates include dinner on the night of arrival and breakfast on the following morning.

Breakfast menus vary according to what is fresh and in season. Starting with June and July there are freshly picked strawberries and red raspberries. These are followed by blueberries, melons, peaches, and apples. Among the breakfast offerings there's a special recipe for light pancakes served with pure Vermont maple syrup, and also Vermont scrambled eggs served with local cheddar cheese. B&B rates are available for readers of this book.

THREE MOUNTAIN INN, Jamaica, Vermont 05343; 802-874-4140. A 7-room village inn (4 with private baths) in the mountains of southern Vermont. Closed from the 15th of April to the 15th of May. Dinner is also served. Swimming pool on the grounds. Fishing on the West River, with special fishing packages available. Downhill skiing at Stratton, Bromley, and Magic Mountains, a short distance away. Cross-country skiing, snowshoeing, hiking, tennis, and wonderful Vermont backroading at the doorstep. No pets. The Murray Family, Innkeepers.

Directions: From I-91 take the second exit at Brattleboro and follow Rte. 30 to Jamaica. From Rte. 7 take Rte. 5 east to Wilmington and follow Rte. 100 north.

For B&B rates, see Index.

THE VERMONT MARBLE INN
Fair Haven, Vermont

If you're traveling from the south via New York's Interstate 89 ("The Northway") to reach Burlington, Stowe, Pico, or Killington, U.S. Route 4 is a convenient road to take into Vermont. And just after entering Vermont, at the junction of U.S. 4 and Route 22A, is the pleasant town of Fair Haven, where the Vermont Marble Inn is located. It is an 1867 Italianate Victorian mansion with a porte cochere, and almost the entire exterior is of golden marble, hewn in neaby Proctor, Vermont. It was built by descendents of Ira Allen, brother of Ethan Allen. Inside there are seven hand-carved marble fireplaces, high ornate ceilings, and windows of etched glass.

The mansionlike bedrooms have been furnished with old-fashioned beds, tables, and chairs, and the somber Victorian theme has been relieved by colorful bedspreads and curtains.

The full breakfast includes a quiche in a homemade pie shell, waffles, fresh-baked muffins, and a buffet of freshly cut fruit. Everything is home-baked. Lunch and dinner are also served in the two spacious dining rooms, one featuring marble fireplaces.

Fair Haven is nestled in the rolling hills between New York's Adirondacks and the Green Mountains of Vermont. It is picturesque in the manner of many of New England's smaller villages, with church steeples surrounding a shaded village green.

The Fair Haven village green is registered in the National Register of Historic Places, as are many of the surrounding homes and churches, including the Vermont Marble Inn. The inn is near Lake Bomoseen, Lake St. Catherine, and Lake Champlain, and is about forty minutes west of the Pico and Killington ski areas. There are golf courses nearby.

THE VERMONT MARBLE INN, 12 West Park Place, Fair Haven, VT 05743; 802-265-4736. A 10-guestroom mansion converted into a bed-and-breakfast inn. Breakfast, lunch, and dinner are served. Open year-round. Sailing, canoeing, fishing, hunting, hiking, bicycling, golf, antiquing, historic tours, skiing, horseback riding, summer theater, museums, and cultural events nearby. Jerry and Margaret Henkel, Innkeepers.

Directions: Fair Haven is 1 mi. south of Rte. 4 on Rte. 22A, west of Lake Bomoseen, Rutland, Pico, and Killington.

For B&B rates, see Index.

THE VILLAGE INN
Landgrove, Vermont

Here's an overnight (or possibly longer) stop for families that might be traveling with children or young people, because this small somewhat secluded inn has several rooms that would be adaptable for whole families, as well as bunk rooms for children.

Landgrove, near Bromley Mountain ski area, is a few miles north of Route 11 which goes east and west across southern Vermont.

The Village Inn has been owned and operated by Jay and Kathy Snyder and assorted members of their families for the past twenty years. It is an all-season resort. Some of the outdoor recreation to enjoy without leaving the inn grounds includes cross-country skiing, sledding, skating, snowshoeing, archery, swimming, and tennis.

The atmosphere is very much that of a country inn and guests awaken to an aroma of a full breakfast which might include the "J-bar special," which Kathy Snyder says is a little bit of everything. Other favorites for the morning meal include blueberry pancakes and toast "Paree."

The Village Inn might well be included on an itinerary that has overnight stays at several other of the Vermont and New Hampshire accommodations mentioned in this book.

THE VILLAGE INN, Landgrove, Vt. 05148; 802-824-6673. A 20-room rustic resort-inn in the mountains of central Vermont, approximately 4½ mi. from Weston and Londonderry. Lodgings include breakast. Breakfast and dinner served to travelers by reservation during the summer except Wed. dinner. Open from Dec. 15 to April 1; June 25 to Oct. 20. Children most welcome. No pets. Swimming, tennis, volleyball, pitch and putt, xc skiing, skating, fishing, and hot tub on grounds. Downhill skiing, riding, indoor tennis, paddle tennis, antiquing, backroading. Alpine slide, golf, summer theatre nearby. Jay and Kathy Snyder, Innkeepers.

Directions: Coming north on I-91 take Exit 2 at Brattleboro, follow Rte. 30 to Rte. 11 and turn right. Turn left off Rte. 11 at signs for Village Inn. bear left in village of Peru. Coming north on Rte. 7 turn east at Manchester on Rte. 11 to Peru. Turn left at signs for Village Inn. Bear left in village of Peru.

For B&B rates, see Index.

THE WALLINGFORD INN
Wallingford, Vermont

Wallingford is north of Manchester and south of Rutland on Route 7, one of the well-traveled ways to go north to Burlington, Stowe, or even all the way north to Canada.

Wallingford Inn is a beautiful old Victorian mansion on the west side of Route 7, about a half-block from the center of the town. It was built in 1876 and the interior has oak woodwork, arched marble fireplaces, elegant chandeliers, and polished wood floors. The architecture of the inn, the gazebo, carriage house, and broad lawns brings to life the grandeur of a time past.

Because it's a mansion, all six of the bedrooms have impressive high ceilings and are attractively furnished. All have private baths, some with tubs and others with showers. I was particularly impressed by the good, heavy-weight towels.

Bed and breakfast is available here, and dinner is also served in the candlelit, rather formal dining room. The small lounge provides a pleasant place in which to relax before or after dinner. Innkeepers Frank, Netia, Debbie, Scott, and Todd Groggett keep the Wallingford inn open year-round, but it is always preferable to make reservations in advance.

Nestled in the Green Mountains, Wallingford is near historic sites, antique shops, covered bridges, the Green Mountain National Forest, and unspoiled scenery that is a photographer's paradise in every season. During the spring and summer wooded trails and mountains, swimming and canoeing are a bicycle ride away. The Battenkill River offers excellent trout fishing each spring, with guides available. Golf and tennis are nearby, as are concerts and theaters in the summer.

THE WALLINGFORD INN, Box 404, 9 No. Main St., Wallingford, Vt. 05773; 802-446-2849. A 6-bedroom restored Victorian mansion nestled in the Green Mountains. Open all year. Continental breakfast included with the price of the room. Dinner also served. Centrally located for swimming, canoeing, bicycling, antiquing, backroading, downhill and cross-country skiing, golf, and tennis. No pets. The Groggett Family, Innkeepers.

Directions: Wallingford is about 10 minutes south of Rutland on Rte. 7.

For B&B rates, see Index.

WAYBURY INN
East Middlebury, Vermont

The Waybury Inn is a great deal more than a bed-and-breakfast inn. It's a traditional New England inn, built in 1810 at the foot of the Green Mountains as a stagecoach stop on one of the major passes through the mountains. Much of the atmosphere of almost 175 years ago still prevails and is reflected in the furnishings of the bedrooms and public rooms with their massive hand-hewn beams.

It's just down the road from the Middlebury Snow Bowl and a short distance from the Breadloaf Writers' Conference, which is held each summer. Lake Dunmore is nearby and there is lots of good Green Mountain backroading, walking, and hiking, as well as both downhill and cross-country skiing. Middlebury College is just a few miles away.

Besides breakfast, which features on occasion absolutely scrumptious blueberry pancakes, dinner and Sunday brunch are also served. The inn has a local reputation for the roast rolled leg of lamb and fresh, homemade breads, desserts, and entrées.

There are scores of nearby attractions, including the Vermont State Craft Center at Frog Hollow in Middlebury, the Sheldon Museum, the UVM Morgan Horse Farm, the Fort Ticonderoga Ferry, the New England Maple Museum in nearby Pittsford, the Vermont Marble Exhibit and Gift Shop in Proctor, Wilson Castle, and the Middlebury College campus and activities that abound there.

You'll recognize the Waybury Inn at a distance because of the beautiful maple trees, which are gorgeous during the fall foliage season.

WAYBURY INN, Rte. 125, East Middlebury, VT 05740; 802-388-4015. A 12-guestroom (8 with private bath) traditional village inn 5 mi. south of Middlebury. Open year- round. Breakfast for house-guests only. Dinner is served daily to the public. Located just a few miles from Lake Dunmore on a mountain-pass road. Conveniently located for all of the Green Mountain recreational, historical, and cultural attractions. Hiking, swimming, fishing, downhill and xc skiing, golf, antiquing, backroading all nearby. Jim and Betty Riley, Innkeepers.

Directions: East Middlebury is just off Rte. 7 on Rte. 125, 29 mi. north of Rutland and 5 mi. south of Middlebury.

For B&B rates, see Index.

WEATHERVANE LODGE
West Dover, Vermont

For the traveler with kids and young people, the Weathervane Lodge is ideal. There are all types of accommodations—apartments, suites, rooms with bunk beds, shared and private bathrooms, and plenty of diversions for holiday-seekers of all ages.

To the above virtues, I guess we had better add the fact that it's open year around, which is quite convenient, because during the winter there are several nearby ski areas, including Mt. Snow, and during the other seasons, a wide variety of central Vermont recreational opportunities.

The first two things that impressed me on a chance visit were the many flags flapping in the breeze on the deck of the Weathervane and a large, well-tended lawn, accented by both vegetable and wild flower gardens.

A very impressive lounge sports a ping-pong table, lots of sofas and chairs, hundreds of magazines, a popcorn machine where you can make your own, and a sort of rumpus room atmosphere that encourages everybody to get acquainted very quickly.

What innkeeper Ernie Chabot describes as a "full hearty breakfast" is served every day as a part of the room rate. The evening meal is served only on Saturdays and holidays during the winter.

As is the case with many of the accommodations mentioned in this book, the Weathervane Lodge not only is a friendly overnight stop, but also would provide an excellent vacation of longer duration.

WEATHERVANE LODGE, West Dover, VT 05356; 802-464-5426. A 12-guestroom inn (several shared baths) situated in the Mt. Snow area of central Vermont. Open year-round. Dinner served on Sat. and holidays in winter only. Breakfast included in room rate. Suitable for young people of all ages. Located within a short distance of many recreational opportunities in all seasons, including downhill and xc skiing. No credit cards. No pets. Liz and Ernie Chabot, Innkeepers.

Directions: From Wilmington follow Rte. 100 north 6 mi., turn right over a concrete bridge and follow this unmarked road 1 mi. Inn is on left.

For B&B rates, see Index.

WEST MOUNTAIN INN
Arlington, Vermont

High on a hill above the Battenkill River, this comfortable, roomy, seven-gabled country estate has an air of easy informality and friendliness, due, in no small part, to the engaging personalities of innkeepers Mary Ann and Wes Carlson. They and their two teenagers keep things humming, not only with warmth and hospitality inside, but also with all manner of outside diversions on the 150 acres of meadows and hills where wilderness trails abound. There is spring trout fishing and summer swimming in the Battenkill and cross-country skiing and tobogganing in the winter.

The thirteen guest rooms, one of which is fully equipped for the handicapped, come in all shapes and sizes; some with outside porches, one with a cedar-lined bathroom, one with a working fireplace, one with a bed loft for children, two with high, pine-paneled cathedral ceilings, and all attractively and comfortably furnished.

A continental or full à la carte breakfast is available.

Truly, as the Carlsons say, a place where one can rest, play, and/or work—but most of all—enjoy.

WEST MOUNTAIN INN, Arlington, Vt. 05250; 802-375-6516. A 13-bedroom comfortable hilltop country estate with a view of the Green Mountains. Private and shared baths. European plan. Open year-round. Breakfast and dinner served to travelers daily except Sun.; a Sun. brunch served 9 to noon. Swimming, canoeing, hiking, fishing, nature walks, xc skiing, and tobogganing on grounds. Special weekend programs from time to time; call for information. Children welcome. No pets. Mary Ann and Wes Carlson, Innkeepers.

Directions: Take Historic Rte. 7 to Arlington. Follow signs for West Mountain Inn, ½ mi. west on Rte. 313; bear left after crossing bridge.

For B&B rates, see Index.

WHETSTONE INN
Marlboro, Vermont

This inn, which is right next door to a beautiful white-spired church, is one of the most photographed locations in Vermont. Marlboro is located about midway between Interstate 91 and Route 100—a very tiny village which has excellent cross-country skiing in the winter and the Marlboro Music School and Festival during the summer.

The inn was built around 1800 and was used as a tavern in stagecoach days. There are inviting living rooms with open fires and books and music. The bedrooms, most of which have private baths or lavatories, are large and cheerful. There is a beautiful little pond to the rear of the inn which sits on the top of a very high hill with a beautiful view across the valleys to the east.

This is a four-season inn, but I must point out that during the summer Marlboro concert season and fall foliage-time, reservations are made far in advance.

The full Vermont breakfast frequently includes waffles, popovers, and pancakes. It is served in the antique dining room where there's a huge old fireplace with a crane holding an iron cauldron.

Dinner is served most Saturday nights, and with varying frequency on other nights, depending upon the season.

Innkeepers Harry and Jean Boardman make a stop at the Whetstone Inn a very memorable experience.

WHETSTONE INN, Marlboro, Vermont 05344; 802-254-2500. An 11-room (7 with private baths) mountaintop inn located in southern Vermont. Open all year. Breakfast is not included with room. Marlboro, Hogback Mt. Ski Area, Vermont backroading, hiking and walking, and cross-country skiing available from the inn's doors. No credit cards. Harry and Jean Boardman, Innkeepers.

Directions: From I-91 follow Rte. 9 west to top of the mountains and turn left at the signs for Marlboro.

For Lodging rates, see Index.

WOODCHUCK HILL FARM
Grafton, Vermont

In an era when bed-and-breakfast homes are popping up like dandelions in the springtime, Anne and Frank Gabriel at Woodchuck Hill Farm, with sixteen years of experience behind them, can certainly be classified as veterans.

My good friends at the Chester Inn, Tom and Betsy Guido, told me that the Woodchuck would be a perfect entry for this book, and Betsy pointed out that the Gabriels will even serve dinner to their houseguests with advance notice.

The location is exceptional. It is about two miles from the village of Grafton at the end of a real dirt road in a deep forest. The views of the mountains and mowings are enchanting.

The farmhouse is one of the oldest buildings in Grafton—a circa 1780 Colonial, furnished in antiques with accommodations for as many as fourteen guests. One of the special features is a large open porch with cushioned wicker furniture and hanging plants overlooking the seventy-five-mile view of the mountains of Vermont and New Hampshire. The atmosphere is most informal and guests are always encouraged by the Gabriels to make themselves at home.

An additional, attractive feature of Woodchuck Hill Farm is their own antique shop located in the old barn. This is filled with some of the most enticing and attractive small antique furnishings I have ever seen.

Behind the barn is a large pond surrounded by attractive lawns—most inviting for swimming and getting a good Vermont tan—and it sometimes provides the trout for dinner.

There are guest rooms appropriately furnished in the main house as well as two additional apartments, some with fireplaces.

WOODCHUCK HILL FARM, Middletown Rd., Grafton, Vt. 05146; 802-843-2398. A 9-bedroom B&B home located high in the mountains near Grafton village. Open May through Nov. 1. Continental breakfast included with room. Dinner available by advance request. Afternoon tea is also offered. Exceptional back-roading abounds in the area, swimming on grounds, other active outdoor sports within a short drive. Frank and Anne Gabriel, Proprietors.

Directions: From Grafton Village drive to the end of the main street, ignore right turn on Rte. 121 and continue about 200 yds. Take the right fork at the sign for Gabriels' Barn Antiques; continue about 2 mi. through forest.

For B&B rates, see Index.

THE ALEXANDER-WITHROW HOUSE
Lexington, Virginia

Lexington, Virginia, just a few minutes from I-81, is one of the most interesting and off-the-beaten path areas in the South. Besides the campuses of Virginia Military Institute and Washington and Lee University, it contains much memorabilia connected with Stonewall Jackson and Robert E. Lee.

The surrounding countryside has beautiful scenery and Natural Bridge, a towering limestone structure 215 feet high, the Blue Ridge Parkway, Goshen Pass, and Cyrus McCormick's farm and workshop are nearby.

The Alexander-Withrow House is an exquisite guest house now included in the National Register of Historic places. It was built in 1789, just two years after the founding of the town.

There are seven rooms and suites in the A-W House, and in the McCampbell Inn, another historic house across the street, there are now sixteen rooms. They are all beautifully furnished with antiques and the little touches that make a country inn. Each suite has its own sitting room, bedroom, and refreshment area equipped with a hot pot and and refrigerator, with coffee, tea, and orange juice provided.

In addition to the coffee and orange juice supplied to each room, Alexander-Withrow guests may now enjoy, compliments of the house, freshly baked muffins and coffee or tea from 8:30 to 10 every morning in the Great Room of the McCampbell Inn, which affords an opportunity for some pleasant conversation with other guests.

THE ALEXANDER-WITHROW HOUSE, 11 No. Main St., Lexington, Va. 24450; 703-463-2044. Two historic houses with 23 elegant bedrooms and suites. Continental breakfast included. Advance reservations recommended. Open year-round. Within walking distance of Virginia Military Institute, Washington and Lee University, and the George C. Marshall Research Library. Natural Bridge, Blue Ridge Parkway nearby. Golf, hiking, Appalachian Trail, canoeing also available. No pets. Mr. and Mrs. Peter Meredith and sons, Owners; Don Fredenburg, Innkeeper.

Directions: Take any Lexington Exit from I-64 or I-81. Follow signs into Lexington. The Alexander-Withrow House is on the corner of Main and Washington Streets.

For Lodging rates, see Index.

GRISTMILL SQUARE
Warm Springs, Virginia

Gristmill Square is a village within a village. It is set in southwest Virginia in a sequestered valley with hills on both sides. The brook running through the middle of the town still turns the great mill wheel which was built in 1900. The Mill House is now a rustic restaurant.

Around Gristmill Square are an antique and a country store and fourteen guest accommodations, some with a kitchen, living room, balcony or sundeck and a wood-burning fireplace. There are also double rooms and small suites.

This section of Virginia has been a playground for outdoor sports since the 1880s and guests at the inn can enjoy tennis and swimming on the grounds as well as golf at the famous Cascades Club.

B&B guests at Gristmill Square are served a continental breakfast in their rooms.

The Waterwheel Restaurant is located in what used to be the old mill and the atmosphere is enhanced by the pervading scent of grain.

Even a hasty traveler intent on covering as many miles as possible every day will find the side trip to Gristmill Square most rewarding. I can only warn that the temptation to stay on longer is very great.

GRISTMILL SQUARE, P.O. Box 359, Warm Springs, Va. 24484; 703-339-2231. An unusual restoration which includes a restaurant and 14 guest rooms in a small country town in the Allegheny Mountains 19 mi. north of Covington. European plan. Restaurant open for dinner daily Tuesday-Sunday. Also open for Sunday buffet; luncheon Tues. thru Sat., May to Oct. Closed Mondays. Suggest telephoning for details. Tennis courts, swimming pool on grounds. Golf at neaby Cascades or Lower Cascades. Skiing at the Homestead and Snowshoe, West Va., a little over an hour away. Skating, riding, hiking, fishing, hunting, antiquing, and backroading nearby. Children welcome. Jack and Janice McWilliams, Innkeepers.

Directions: From Staunton, Va. follow Rte. 254 to Buffalo Gap, Rte. 42 to Millboro Spring, Rte. 39 to Warm Springs. Turn left on Rte. 692 in Warm Springs. From Lexington, take Rte. 39 to Warm Springs. From Roanoke, take Rte. 220 to Warm Springs; turn left on Rte. 619.

For B&B rates, see Index.

MEADOW LANE LODGE
Warm Springs, Virginia

Meadow Lane Lodge, owned by my good friends, Cathy and Philip Hirsh, is a small bed-and-breakfast inn of gracious charm situated in the beautiful Allegheny Mountains of southwest Virginia. It is an integral part of an estate comprising approximately 1600 acres of woods, fields, and streams.

The accommodations consist of three suites and four double bedrooms all with private baths. The decor of the entire lodge is that of an earlier period of American life, coupled with all modern conveniences. The rooms are liberally furnished with lovely antiques.

A short stroll from the lodge will bring animal lovers to the barnyard and pastures where the sheep and goats graze and gambol. Chickens, ducks, guinea fowl, geese, and turkeys inhabit the old horse stalls and large stable, and freely wander about in the surrounding areas. Cats and kittens mingle, as do farm dogs. There is a full breakfast prepared by Phil. He has already made his mark as a morning chef and specializes in all kinds of egg dishes, delicious pancakes, and french toast.

Besides the tennis court, and all of the wonderful walks and rides in the mountains, and the trout fishing in the river, guests have the advantage of being close to the Cascades and Lower Cascades golf courses.

MEADOW LANE LODGE, Star Route A, Box 110, Warm Springs, Va. 24484; 703-839-5959. Meadow Lane Lodge is a portion of a large estate where guests are accommodated in the main building as well as in a comfortable outbuilding. Additional lodgings are in a historic building in the village of Warm Springs. There are eight lodging room in all. Open April 1 to Jan. 31. A full breakfast, the only meal served. Dinners are available at nearby restaurants 10 min. away. Tennis court and excellent fishing on grounds. Also, miles of hiking and walking trails. Golf, riding, skeet and trap shooting, swimming pool nearby. Philip and Cathy Hirsh, Innkeepers; Hella Armstrong, Manager.

Directions: From Staunton, Va., follow Rte. 254 west to Buffalo Gap; Rte. 42 south to Millboro Spring; Rte. 39 west to Warm Springs. From Lexington, take Rte. 39 west. From Roanoke, take Rte. 220 north to Warm Springs and Rte. 39 west to Meadow Lane Lodge. From Lewisburg, W. Va., take I-64 to Covington; Rte. 220 north to Warm Springs. Lodge is on Rte. 39, four miles west of Warm Springs.

For B&B rates, see Index.

PEAKS OF OTTER LODGE
Bedford, Virginia

The Blue Ridge Parkway is one of the truly remarkable motoring experiences in North America. It starts at the Skyline Drive near Front Royal in northern Virginia and continues on to North Carolina. There are no commercial intrusions for the entire course of the road, and the effect of being in a truly natural setting is enhanced by the absence of guard rails.

There are just a few accommodations on this road, among which is the Peaks of Otter Lodge. Even though it is a motel, everything has been kept in harmony with nature with a very pleasant lakeside setting and a decor of natural woods and subtly blended textures, tones and colors.

The guest accommodations are in spacious rooms with two double beds and private baths. Each has its own secluded balcony and terrace, and features a truly spectacular view.

Although the lodge is open year-round, reservations are always advisable and it is practically impossible to book a room in September and October during the fall foliage season. A "winter special" is available from December through March.

Peaks of Otter Lodge and Restaurant is an authorized concessioner operation in the National Park System. Facilities for the handicapped are available.

PEAKS OF OTTER LODGE, P.O. Box 489, Bedford, Va. 24523; 703-586-1081. A 58-bedroom motel at the intersection of Blue Ridge Parkway and Rte. 43, ten miles south of I-81 and ten miles north of Bedford. Breakfast, lunch, and dinner served daily. Open all year. Hiking, fishing, nature trails, and exceptional mountain motoring. No pets. Reservations absolutely, positively, necessary.

Directions: From Rte. 460 in Bedford follow Rte. 43 north with the Peaks of Otter in plain view. Turn north for one half mile on the Blue Ridge Parkway. It is located on milepost 86.

For Lodging rates, see Index.

PROSPECT HILL
Trevilians, Virginia

The "American Style" in our title also includes a few authentic southern plantation houses. Prospect Hill dates to 1732, and in 1793 additional slave quarters were added, some of which are being used as lodging rooms today. Part of its history involves one of the owners who returned from the War Between The States to find his family plantation overgrown and his slaves gone.

If the history is intriguing, the setting is even more so, for Prospect Hill begins where the boxwood hedge along the entrance-way ends. It's in the midst of an English tree garden, shaded by rare magnolias, tall tulip poplars, and giant beeches. Innkeeper Bill Sheehan says, "This is the way Prospect Hill was two centuries ago, and the way it is today."

It is within a convenient distance of Charlottesville, Monticello, and the University of Virginia campus, and just off the main highway from Charlottesville to Richmond.

This is the place where breakfast in bed is the rule rather than the exception. On the groaning tray, which is brought directly into each room, there is homemade french bread and croissants, breakfast souffles, and such specialties as crêpes w/fried apples, all of which are homemade.

PROSPECT HILL, Route 613, Trevilians, Va. 23070; 703-967-0844. A 7-room country inn on a historic plantation 15 mi. east of Charlottesville, Va.; 90 mi. southwest of Washington, D.C. Bed and breakfast-in-bed Sun. thru Tues. Mod. American plan with full breakfast-in-bed and full dinner Wed. thru Sat. Dinner served Wed. thru Sat. by reservation. Dining room closed Sun., Mon., and Tues. Breakfast always served to houseguests. All accommodations have private baths. Near Monticello, Ashlawn (Pres. Monroe's home), Univ. of Virginia, Castle Hill, and Skyline Drive. Swimming pool. Children welcome. No pets. Bill and Mireille Sheehan, Innkeepers.

Directions: From Washington, D.C.: Beltway to I-66 west to Warrenton. Follow Rte. 29 south to Culpeper, then Rte. 15 south thru Orange and Gordonsville to Zion Crossroads. Turn left on Rte. 250 east 1 mi. to Rte. 613. Turn left 3 mi. to inn on left. From Charlottesville or Richmond: take I-64 to Exit 27; Rte. 15 south ½ mile to Zion Crossroads; turn left on Rte. 250 east 1 mi. to Rte. 613. Turn left, 3 mi. to inn on left.

For B&B rates, see Index.

RED FOX INN AND TAVERN
Middleburg, Virginia

Middleburg is in the famous horse country of Virginia and there are large estates and farms along Route 50 that have some beautiful animals grazing in the fields bordered by fences.

The Red Fox Tavern, which has been in the same building for more than 200 years, is at the crossroads in Middleburg, adjacent to some very excellent shops offering country clothes and saddlery.

There are twelve tastefully decorated lodging rooms in the Red Fox and in another building called the Stray Fox. Some have sitting rooms and 18th-century documented wallpapers and paint colors. Each room is furnished with period antiques and has canopied beds, and most have working fireplaces.

On the second floor of the tavern there is a most attractive pine-paneled dining room with two fireplaces. This had been a lounge that was converted, by popular demand, into a dining room and is now one of the seven dining areas in which guests may enjoy their meals. Dinner is served every evening.

A continental breakfast is included in the room rate for the Red Fox only. The full breakfast, served in one of the dining rooms, features homemade buttermilk pancakes or waffles, cappuccino or espresso coffee, and a selection of country jams and jellies.

It's just 40 miles to Washington and an ideal distance for a stop the night before a few days in the nation's capital.

RED FOX INN AND TAVERN, Middleburg, VA 22117; 703-687-6301. A 12-guestroom historic village inn (8 of the rooms in the Stray Fox) near the Blue Ridge Mountains, approx. 40 mi. from Washington, D.C. Near Manassas Battlefield, Oatlands, and Oak Hill (President Monroe's White House). European plan. Complimentary continental breakfast included in room rate for Red Fox only. Breakfast, lunch, and dinner served to travelers. Open every day of the year. Spectator sports such as polo and steeplechasing available nearby. No activities available for small children. Consult innkeeper for policy on pets. The Reuter Family, Innkeepers.

Directions: Leave the Washington, D.C. Beltway (495) at Rte. 66 west, to Rte. 50. Follow Rte. 50 west for 22 mi. to Middleburg.

For B&B rates, see Index.

SOJOURNERS BED AND BREAKFAST
Lynchburg, Virginia

Lynchburg, on the James River at the gateway to southwest Virginia and the Blue Ridge Mountains, is in a rural countryside rich in heritage and history. It is the home of Randolph-Macon Women's College and Lynchburg College, and is just a short distance from Sweet Briar College in nearby Amherst.

Sojourners is located in one of the most attractive residential areas of this small city and, in fact, when guests call to make the required advance reservations, a special map is sent with the confirmation.

The larger of the guest rooms has a double and a single bed, private bath, individual heat, TV, and semi-private entrance. The other guest room is small, with a single bed and shared bath. Actually, Sojourners is a bed-and-breakfast home, so the entire atmosphere is one of being in a home away from home.

The proprietors, Clyde and Ann McAlister, are both gracious, contemporary-minded hosts, and the conversations at breakfast or over an afternoon cup of tea could run the gamut from Algiers to Zoroaster. Both are professional genealogists.

Breakfast is a veritable feast and always has some of Ann's or Mac's homemade breads. Grits, eggs, and sausage are available on request.

Besides the natural beauty and educational establishments in and around Lynchburg, the community also has Westminster-Canterbury, a retirement home nearby, and Sojourners would be an excellent place for visitors to stay.

SOJOURNERS BED AND BREAKFAST, 3609 Tanglewood Lane, Lynchburg, VA 24503; 804-384-1655. A 2-guestroom bed-and-breakfast home in a quiet, residential section of Lynchburg, Virginia. Breakfast, included in the room rate, is the only meal served. Situated conveniently for a vacation in the Blue Ridge Parkway section of Virginia, an area rich in history. No credit cards. No pets. Clyde and Ann McAlister, Proprietors.

Directions: Please telephone Sojourners for full information.

For B&B rates, see Index.

WAYSIDE INN
Middletown, Virginia

Interstate 81 is one of the principal north-south roads in the East. It starts (or ends if you wish) at the Canadian border in upper New York State at the famous Thousand Island Bridge and zooms its way across Pennsylvania and Virginia into the heartland of the South.

Middletown, Virginia, is on I-81 and is just south of Winchester. It is also about 1½ hours west of Washington on I-66.

The Wayside Inn dates from at least 1797. It is referred to as a historic restoration and is an antique-lover's paradise. All of the dining rooms, sitting rooms, and bedrooms have been furnished with a potpourri of tables, chests, paintings and *objets d'art* which, while serving a serious function, sometimes indicate that the designer has an interesting sense of humor.

In earlier days the Wayside served as a way station where fresh teams of horses waited to be harnessed up to arriving stagecoaches traveling the Shenandoah Valley Turnpike. Soldiers from both the North and South frequented the inn during the War Between the States.

Today Middletown is just a few miles from the northern entrance to the beautiful Blue Ridge Parkway (Skyline Drive) which is still another way of traveling from Virginia to North Carolina.

Guests notifying the front desk in advance may enjoy, for an additional charge, the continental breakfst featuring freshly squeezed orange juice, a choice of homemade apple strudel, muffins, or biscuits, and freshly ground coffee. The Colonial dining room usually is the scene of breakfast-time conversation among guests.

Since this inn is such a short distance from the interstate, I hope many of our readers take the opportunity to stop for dinner and overnight and enjoy a unique, country inn experience before continuing on their way.

WAYSIDE INN, Middletown, Va. 22645; 703-869-1797. A 21-room country inn in the Shenandoah Valley, about 1½ hrs. from Washington, D.C. European plan; breakfast, lunch, and dinner served Monday through Saturday. Sunday: breakfast and dinner. Open every day of the year. Professional Equity Theater, Belle Grove, Cedar Creek Battlefield, Blue Ridge Parkway, Crystal Caverns, Hotel Strasburg, Washington's Headquarters, and Wayside Antique Warehouse nearby. Convenient to Apple Blossom Festival. Chuck Alverson, Innkeeper.

Directions: Take Exit 77 from I-81 to Rte. 11. Follow signs to inn.

For Lodging rates, see Index.

WELBOURNE
Middleburg, Virginia

As trite as it may sound, visiting Welbourne is indeed like stepping into the past. Located in the Piedmount hunt country, this stately colonial mansion with five graceful pillars was built in 1775. The Morison family made it their home in 1820 and have lived there continuously since then. Major additions and wings were added as late as 1870.

The accommodations are exactly what one would expect in such stately surroundings. The bedrooms are extremely large and the furniture extremely antique. There are sleigh beds, four-posters, free-standing full-size mirrors, and many pieces that could never be duplicated. The house, grounds and gardens have a remarkable air of genteel antiquity.

Most impressive are the oil portraits of members of the Morison family who have occupied this home. Some of them are in the dress of colonial times and others in uniforms of the War Between the States. One of them is of Major John Pelham, the boy hero of the Confederacy.

The hostess of this 600-acre farm, which is on the list of Virginia Historic Landmarks and the National Register of Historic Places, is Sally Holmes Morison who is the seventh generation of her family. Her son Nat and his wife Sherry are also part of the gracious hospitality. The most appropriate thing I can say is that they belong with the house.

WELBOURNE, Middleburg, Va. 22117; 703-687-3201. A 7-bedroom antebellum mansion, and 3 cottages, in the heart of the Virginia hunt country a short distance from the center of Middleburg, and 30 mi. from Dulles Airport. Full breakfast is the only meal served, but there are restaurants in nearby Middleburg. Centrally located for beautiful backroading and walking. No credit cards. Mrs. N. Holmes Morison, Innkeeper.

Directions: From blinker light in Middleburg take U.S. 50 west for 3½ mi. Turn right on Rte. 611; go 1½ mi; turn left on 743. Welbourne is 1¼ mi. on the left.

For B&B rates, see Index.

THE ASHFORD MANSION
Ashford, Washington

Mount Rainier National Park is one of the great attractions of the Pacific Northwest, so finding a historic house offering bed and breakfast only six miles from the Paradise entrance is good news for travelers. Ashford town took its name from the family who built the elegant frontier home at the turn of the century, though they called the place "Twin Brook Estate," for the streams that still cross it.

Guests get a big Northwest breakfast: juice, fresh fruit, eggs, homemade bread, biscuits, and huckleberry muffins. The variety of jams always includes wild blackberry from fruit gathered on the side of the mountain. "You need a good start if you're going to hike in the park all day," Jan Green says.

The Greens can tell you what there is to see and do in this picturesque area both in and outside the park. They can advise on hiking trails and fill you in on the history and topography of the park. They have the menus of the local restaurants, so you can preplan dinner while resting on the veranda in summer or before the roaring fire in winter.

The mansion is off the main highway, a peaceful as well as a beautiful place to stay.

THE ASHFORD MANSION, Old Mountain Rd., Ashford, WA 98304; 206-569-2739. A 2-guestroom (shared bath) bed-and-breakfast home on the slopes of Mt. Rainier, 6 mi. from the Paradise entrance to the park. Breakfast only. Open all year. Advance reservations necessary. Restaurants, sightseeing, craft shops, hiking, mountain climbing, xc skiing, tubing, nature walks, nearby. Children should be at least 12 years old. Pets O.K. if kept outside on leash. No smoking. Jan and Walt Green, Owners.

Directions: Old Mountain Rd. is an arc that both joins and parallels busy Hwy. 706. The big white mansion sits well back from the road on the north side.

For B&B rates, see Index.

THE CAPTAIN WHIDBEY INN
Coupeville, Whidbey Island, Washington

Whidbey Island is about 50 miles north of Seattle and 6 miles south of Everett. It is the largest of the 172 islands in Puget Sound and is reached by ferry systems and the scenic Deception Pass Bridge. A most unusual holiday of island-hopping that can last hours or even days may be enjoyed via the ferries that travel to several different islands.

The Captain Whidbey Inn, built of the famous madrona logs, is as fetching a piece of New England as can be found west of Cape Cod.

The natural center of the inn is the living room with its massive fireplace made of round stones. Here everyone sits around leafing through the dozens of magazines and chatting. There's a fire almost every evening. The Chart Room features nautical decorations and an occasional view of an errant whale in Penn Cove.

Some of the lodging rooms are upstairs in the main house which overlooks Penn Cove and others are hidden away in a number of rustic lodgings built in the woods across the road overlooking a pastoral pond.

The continental breakfast allows guests to get off to a good start with sweet rolls, english muffins, juice, coffee and tea.

By the way, the New England flavor of this Puget Sound inn is entirely authentic, as the Stone family is from Nantucket Island, off the coast of Massachusetts.

THE CAPTAIN WHIDBEY INN, 2072 W. Capt. Whidbey Inn Rd., Coupeville, Wash. 98239; 206-678-4097. A 25-room country inn, 50 mi. north of Seattle, 3 mi. north of Coupeville. European plan. Four cottages with private bath; 12 rooms with private bath. Breakfast, lunch, and dinner served daily to travelers. Open year-round. Boating and fishing on grounds. Golf nearby. Pets allowed in cottages only. Geoff and John Stone, Innkeepers.

Directions: Whidbey Island is reached year-round from the south by the Columbia Beach-Mukilteo Ferry, and during the summer and on weekends by the Port Townsend-Keystone Ferry. From the north (Vancouver, B.C. and Bellingham), take the Deception Pass Bridge to Whidbey Island.

For B&B rates, see Index.

INN OF THE WHITE SALMON
White Salmon, Washington

The famous Columbia River Gorge with its many well-known dams and fish ladders is one of the most popular attractions in the Northwest. There are excursions available on the river and the views are most impressive.

The Inn of the White Salmon is located in the village above the river and the entrance is through beveled glass doors into a small reception area where a brass-decorated cash register and a carefully framed mirror, a real old-style guest register, and old-fashioned wallpaper take the guest backward in time.

Several lodging rooms have been completely redecorated and refurnished in a warm accommodating style with good beds, pastel sheets, wool blankets, fluffy comforters, and extra large towels in the bathrooms. Second-floor rooms have a bird's-eye view of the Columbia Valley and the mountains beyond.

The Inn of the White Salmon has one of the most impressive "continental breakfasts" I've ever enjoyed. There are three or four different varieties of juices, fruits, breads, and over twenty different breakfast pastries every morning. Everything is homemade and the breakfast sweets are delicious.

To make this entire breakfast seem more unique there is a continuous large-screen showing of color slides of scenes along the Columbia River Gorge, ski areas, the orchards, Mt. Hood, Mt. Adams, and Mt. St. Helens. The photography is spectacular and this is an interesting and novel way of presenting the story of recreational and scenic advantages in this very beautiful part of the world.

INN OF THE WHITE SALMON, Box 1446, White Salmon, Wash. 98672; 509-493-2335. A 21-room village inn 60 mi. east of Portland, Oregon. Near the Columbia River Gorge, Mt. Adams, Mt. Hood, Mt. St. Helens. Breakfast only meal served. Open all year. Hot tubs, swimming pool (planned) on grounds. River-raft and backpack trips arranged. Golf, steelhead and salmon fishing, hiking, skiing, berry picking, backroading nearby. No pets. Loretta and Bill Hopper, Innkeepers.

Directions: From Portland: follow I-84 east to Hood River, Ore., take White Salmon exit, cross toll bridge over Columbia River. Follow large green signs to White Salmon; inn is 4 mi. from Hood River, Ore., on west side of town.

For B&B rates, see Index.

SHELBURNE INN
Seaview, Washington

Sleep in an antique bed! Such is the claim of the one-hundred-year-old Shelburne Inn in southern Washington.

The fourteen guest rooms are decorated in Early American comfort—bright, cheerful rooms with brass beds, braided rugs, and beautiful old quilts. Baths are shared.

The Shelburne Inn is a restoration of a Victorian hostelry built by Charles Beaver as an overnight rest stop for travelers in 1896, and is now listed in the National Register of Historic Places.

The caring innkeepers, Laurie Anderson and David Campiche, have carefully restored the Shelburne Inn inside and out, returning it almost perfectly to its original state. The dark green shingled exterior is crisply outlined by white trim.

The interior is completely covered with warm, dark woods. The decor is Victorian, with English and American antiques. At the time of this writing, renovation of the first floor had just been completed. The lobby was enlarged, and beautiful stained glass windows, newly imported from England, fronted the street.

The Shelburne Inn's restaurant has received national acclaim. In addition to its regular meals, there are Sunday brunches and English-style teas on Saturday and Sunday. In spring the menu may feature sautéed chicken breasts served with raspberry sauce. In fall, rabbit may be the choice with fresh chanterelles from the surrounding hills. The wine list is lengthy and designed for people with a real interest in wine.

SHELBURNE INN, Box 250, Seaview, WA 98644; 206-642-2442. A 14-guestroom (shared baths) antique-filled Victorian inn, just north of the Oregon border in a small, oceanside village. Breakfast available, but not included with room. Open year-round. Lunch served Mon. thru Sat., dinner served nightly except Wed. Sun. brunch, 9:30 to 2:00 P.M. No television or telephones. Children welcome. No pets. Laurie Anderson and David Campiche, Innkeepers; Tony and Ann Kischner, Restaurateurs.

Directions: From Portland, Oregon take I-5 to Longview, Washington—turn west on Hwy. 4 to Johnson's Landing, take Hwy. 101 to Seaview, which is 15 mi. Inn is on Pacific Hwy. 103 and J St., left side—watch for large inn sign.

For B&B rates, see Index.

GENERAL LEWIS INN
Lewisburg, West Virginia

It takes about an hour and a quarter to drive from Lexington, Virginia, to Lewisburg, West Virginia, through the beautiful mountains which look very much like a color guard on parade. The hues and tones of the skies and the silhouettes of the mountains are a beautiful and thrilling experience. It's possible to take I-64 all the way to Lewisburg, but White Sulphur Springs is well worth a short visit.

The General Lewis Inn is like a primitive flashback of old West Virginia. It is furnished in old antiques. There's a sizable collection of old kitchen utensils, spinning wheels, churns, and other tools used many years ago, as well as an unusual collection of chinaware and old prints.

The parlor has a friendly fireplace flanked by some of the many different types of rocking chairs that are scattered throughout the inn. The atmosphere is made even more cozy by the low-beamed ceilings.

The inn is surrounded by broad lawns, and in the rear there are fragrant flower gardens, tall swaying trees, and even a small rock garden.

Some of the rooms have waist-high four-poster beds with rope springs which are comfortable and unusual.

The full breakfast included in the B&B rate includes two eggs served in any style, sausage or bacon, fried apples, juice, toast and jelly or apple butter, and coffee, tea, cocoa, or milk. I understand that for a small surcharge it can be served in your bedroom.

GENERAL LEWIS INN, Lewisburg, W. Va. 24901; 304-645-2600. An antique-laden 30-room village inn on Rte. 60, 90 mi. from Roanoke, Va. European plan. Breakfast, lunch, and evening meal served daily. Dining room closed Christmas Day. Famous golf courses nearby. John McIlhenny, Innkeeper.

Directions: Take Lewisburg exit from I-64. Follow Rte. 219 south to first traffic light. Turn left on Rte. 60, two blocks to inn.

For B&B rates, see Index.

OLD RITTENHOUSE INN
Bayfield, Wisconsin

The northwest corner of Wisconsin is pinched between Minnesota on the west and that inexplicable portion of western Michigan on the east. On a peninsula stretching out into Lake Superior are the town and county of Bayfield, the Redcliff Indian Reservation, and the Apostle Islands National Lakeshore. As a vacation and resort area, it may be one of the best-kept secrets in North America.

One of the most fascinating aspects is that in this unspoiled but still accessible area, the Old Rittenhouse Inn is a model of Victorian style and elegant grace.

Although the main stress of this book is on excellent accommodations and succulent breakfasts, I just can't imagine visiting the Old Rittenhouse Inn without arriving in time for dinner.

Innkeepers Jerry and Mary Phillips told me that the house had been built in 1890 as a summer home. The basic form was there, but it was necessary to find appropriate Victorian furniture.

Guest rooms have four-poster beds, marble topped dressers and commodes to add to the Victorian atmosphere. There are fireplaces in three of the five lodging rooms, and Lake Superior can be seen from rooms facing the southeast. Breakfast is served every morning in the same dining room where the dinner menu is recited to guests each night. Among the unusual offerings are wild rice pancakes, sourdough pancakes, omelets, and freshly baked english muffins. The Old Rittenhouse is one of the few inns I have ever visited where there is a sweet course served at breakfast, which could be tortes, crêpes, or small cakes.

OLD RITTENHOUSE INN, 301 Rittenhouse Ave., Bayfield, Wis. 54814; 715-779-5765. A 5-bedroom Victorian inn in an area of historic and natural beauty, 70 mi. east of Duluth, Minn., on the shore of Lake Superior. European plan. Breakfast and dinner served to travelers. Open May 1 to Nov. 1. Advance reservations most desirable. Extensive recreational activity of all kinds available throughout the year, including tours, hiking, and cycling on the nearby Apostle and Madeline Islands. Not comfortable for small children. No pets. Jerry and Mary Phillips, Innkeepers.

Directions: From the Duluth Airport, follow Rte. 53-S through the city of Duluth over the bridge to Superior, Wisconsin. Turn east on Rte. 2 near Ashland (1½ hrs.), turn north on 13-N to Bayfield.

For Lodging rates, see Index.

THE RENAISSANCE INN
Sister Bay, Wisconsin

One of the very agreeable things about Door County, Wisconsin, besides the occasional glimpses of distinctive local architecture and the pleasant shoreline drives, is the fact that everything is within an easy driving distance.

For example, from Sturgeon Bay there is a choice of roads that eventually will lead to Sister Bay, and it's possible to go up one side and down the other and enjoy a very pleasant drive.

I must say that I was very much surprised to find a bed-and-breakfast inn with a Renaissance theme located in this part of the world. It has seven smallish guest rooms on the second floor, all with private baths, and each room is decorated differently with European furniture and Renaissance prints. This Renaissance theme is carried out with reproductions of various well-known pieces of art by easily recognizable Renaissance artists. Oddly enough, there are also some French impressionist touches as well, mixed in with some late 19th-century American wrought-iron bedsteads.

The best one-word description for this inn is "neat." That's the first and most lasting impression I had during my visit with JoDee Faller, who with her husband John, is the new innkeeper.

It was also a surprise to find that a rather intimate dining room provides guests with the evening meal, which is basically seafood cuisine, including crab legs and various shrimp dishes. I also noticed the sirloin tips and a chicken dish as well. Breakfast could be described as limited but interesting.

Situated in a residential area, the Renaissance Inn is within walking distance of numerous shops, galleries, boat docks and the public beach. Of course, there is much to do in Door County within convenient driving distance.

THE RENAISSANCE INN, 414 Maple Dr., Sister Bay, WI 54234; 414-854-5107. A 7-guestroom (private baths) modest inn located in the upper end of the Door County peninsula. Breakfast and dinner served daily. Open all year except for the inclement weeks of the winter. Conveniently located to enjoy the cultural and recreational advantages of Door County. No credit cards. No pets. JoDee and John Faller, Innkeepers.

Directions: Follow Rte. 42 to Sister Bay and turn left at the Bundas Department store. The inn is just a few rods farther on the right.

For B&B rates, see Index.

SEVEN PINES LODGE
Lewis, Wisconsin

Although overnight lodgings including breakfast are available at this sophisticated rustic lodge in the Wisconsin deep woods, I feel it only fair to warn the prospective guest that it will be very difficult to leave after a single night's stay. One of the attractions is a trout stream that meanders through the tree-shaded grounds. In fact, freshly-caught trout from that stream are a main entrée on the dinner menu—and on the breakfast menu, upon request.

Accommodations at Seven Pines Lodge are in the main building, where there are five year-round bedrooms, and also in unique out-buildings that are used during the temperate seasons.

Everybody gathers around the fireplace in the living room after dinner and, among other things, there are many albums of photographs of the earlier days at this lodge which at one time played host to Calvin Coolidge.

Although a full breakfast is available at an additional charge, I find that the continental breakfast, included in the room rate, consisting of homemade breads, danish aebleskiver or carmel roll, juice, and coffee is quite enough for me. It is served, when the weather permits on the porch overlooking the stream. Otherwise it is served in the rustic dining room, where dinner is also served.

SEVEN PINES LODGE, Lewis, Wis. 54851; 715-653-2323. A 10-room rustic resort inn (3 rooms have shared baths) in the Wisconsin woods about 1½ hrs. from Minneapolis. Open year-round. Closed Thanksgiving and Christmas Day. St. Croix Falls, Taylors Falls, National Wild River Scenic Waterway nearby. Tennis, swimming, golf woodswalking, downhill skiing, backroading nearby. Xc ski pkgs. available. Very attractive for children of all ages since the innkeepers also have children. No pets. No credit cards. Joan and David Simpson, Innkeepers.

Directions: From Minneapolis/St. Paul: follow 135 W or 135 E north to US 8 at Forest Lake, Minn. East on US 8 through Taylors Falls, Minn./St. Croix Falls, Wis., to Wis. 35 north to Lewis. Turn right at 76 gas station to "T," right 1 mi. to fork in road and turn left ½ mi. to Seven Pines Lodge entrance.

For B&B rates, see Index.

THE WHITE GULL INN
Fish Creek, Wisconsin

Our midwestern readers are probably very familiar with the term "Fish Boil," which is, as far as I know, a tradition limited to Wisconsin. The Fish Boil at the White Gull Inn features freshly caught lake fish, boiled potatoes, homemade cole slaw, fresh-baked bread and cherry pie. The wood-smoked fire combined with the aroma of Lake Michigan fish creates truly gargantuan appetites. Fish Boil dinners are served every Wednesday, Friday, Saturday, and Sunday evening during the summer and fall. On non-Fish-Boil nights, the inn serves candlelight dinners for its regular menu.

The White Gull Inn is also open during the winter, when the Fish Boil is served on Saturday and Wednesday nights only, and a bed-and-breakfast rate is available.

Lest I give the impression that the only thing there is to do in Door County, Wisconsin, is to eat, let me explain that the location of Fish Creek along the shores of Lake Michigan provides ample four-season recreational activity plus a generous helping of attractions for those inclined to the theater and the arts.

During the winter season breakfast is included with the room rate. In the summer, it is additional.

THE WHITE GULL INN, Fish Creek, WI 54212; 414-868-3517. A 13-guestroom inn with 3 cottages, many fireplaces, in Door County, 23 mi. north of Sturgeon Bay. Rooms with and without private baths. Open year-round. European plan. Breakfast and lunch daily year-round. Fish Boils: Wednesday, Friday, Saturday, Sunday nights throughout the season. All meals open to travelers. Reservations requested for evening meals. Golf, tennis, swimming, fishing, biking, sailing, and other summer and winter sports nearby. Excellent for children of all ages. No pets. Andy and Jan Coulson, Joan Holliday, Nancy Vaughn, Innkeepers.

Directions: From Chicago: take I-94 to Milwaukee. Follow Rte. I-43 (141) from Milwaukee to Manitowoc; Rte. 42 from Manitowoc to Fish Creek. Turn left at stop sign at the bottom of the hill, go 2½ blocks to inn. From Green Bay: take Rte. 57 to Sturgeon Bay; Rte. 42 to Fish Creek.

For B&B rates, see Index.

WHITE LACE INN
Sturgeon Bay, Wisconsin

In many ways the White Lace Inn, a Queen Anne Victorian with a big, wide porch and green shingles on the third floor, is a wonderful introduction to Door County. On a quiet street in the residential area of Sturgeon Bay, it is within five blocks of the bay, and two blocks of the National Historic downtown district.

At the time of my visit, Dennis Statz who, with his wife, Bonnie, is the innkeeper, was busy working on the newest addition, the Garden House, a simple Victorian "cottage," circa 1885, behind the main house. Bonnie declared there were going to be many, many perennials planted to give it a real garden feeling. (The latest news is that over 300 have now been planted.)

As I wandered through the main house, admiring the extremely well-preserved interior woodwork, hardwood floors, and other Victorian embellishments, Bonnie explained to me that although Door County is certainly well known in the summertime for all of the water-oriented activities on the lake, cross-country skiing is extremely popular during the wintertime. Particularly on the weekends between January and March.

"Very often our guests ski for about an hour or two and then mostly just relax and read and do a bit of driving around. There's also a small downhill slope in Sturgeon Bay," she told me.

There is a total of eleven guest rooms, all with private baths. There are many antiques, flowered wallpaper, down pillows, cozy comforters and quilts, live plants, and lace curtains. There is a fireplace in each of the guest rooms in the new Garden House.

"Our breakfast is continental with muffins, juice, and coffee, and is served on plates rather than self-served. Coffee and tea are available at any time during the day."

For the first-time visitor, the White Lace Inn, like Door County, is a very pleasant surprise.

WHITE LACE INN, 16 N. Fifth Ave., Sturgeon Bay, WI 54235; 414-743-1105. An 11-guestroom (private baths) bed-and-breakfast inn in one of Wisconsin's attractive resort areas. Breakfast to guests only is the only meal served. Open year-round. Conveniently located near all of the cultural and recreational attractions in Door County. Special three- and five-day packages available during the winter. No pets. No credit cards. Dennis and Bonnie Statz, Innkeepers.

Directions: From the south take the Rte. 42-57 bypass across the new bridge, turn left on Michigan and go right on Fifth Ave.

For B&B rates, see Index.

PANSY PATCH
St. Andrews, New Brunswick, Canada

What a surprise this was! I visited it originally because I found a fetching little brochure for the Pansy Patch Shop, and discovered not only an enticing collection of fine furniture, antiques, rare and out-of-print books, prints, silver, glass, china, paintings, maps, quilts, baskets, primitives, and many other items, but also a very pleasant bed-and-breakfast inn.

The proprietors are Kathleen and Michael Lazare, who live in Sherman, Connecticut, in the wintertime and operate Pansy Patch during the summer.

The shop is very attractive and greatly resembles some excellent shops of the same nature that I have visited in England. The living room is filled with fine furniture, antiques, and prints. The sun porch is lined with bookcases of volumes on virtually every subject; the dining room sparkles with silver and glass, and there are maps and books in the library. Even the butler's pantry is open, with a large selection of cookbooks, books on gardening, antiques, and Colonial living.

A breakfast of homemade biscuits, muffins or rolls—especially blueberry muffins in season—with homemade jams and coffee and fresh fruit in season can be enjoyed on a terrace looking down across a beautiful lawn and into the streets of the town of St. Andrews.

There are three very tidy guest rooms on the second floor and breakfast is included in the room rate.

There is an Old Welsh quotation carved into the mantelpiece: *"Now faire betyde who here abyde / and merrie may they be and / faire befalle who in this halle / repaire in courtesie. From morne till nighte / be it darke or brighte / we banish dole and dree / come sitte besyde our hearthe tis wide / for gentle companie."*

PANSY PATCH, 59 Carleton St., St. Andrews, New Brunswick, Canada EOG 2XO; 506-529-3834. A 3-guestroom bed-and-breakfast inn situated in a delightful shop located immediately behind the Algonquin Hotel. Breakfast the only meal served. Open from June until early Oct. Most conveniently located to enjoy all of the recreational, historical, and cultural advantages of St. Andrews. Not particularly suited for children. No pets. Michael and Kathleen Lazare, Inn- Shopkeepers.

Directions: Pansy Patch is immediately behind the Algonquin Hotel.

For B&B rates, see Index.

SEASIDE INN
St. Andrews, New Brunswick, Canada

For many travelers St. Andrews, New Brunswick, is going to be a unique, "first-time" experience—it is an area rich in history. Dochet's Island in the St. Croix River is where the famous French explorer, Samuel de Champlain, established a colony in 1604. The island can be seen easily from a high point on Highway 127, five-and-a-half miles from St. Andrews, on the road to St. Stephen. As the first governor of French Canada, Champlain's history is closely linked to that of St. Andrews, and the story is detailed in a small booklet presented to me by Marjorie Richardson of the Seaside Inn. Among other interesting information in the Chamber of Commerce booklet is the fact that the tides of Passamaquoddy Bay rise as much as twenty-eight feet at certain times.

Marjorie is a wonderful example of the hospitality and generosity I found throughout the Canadian Maritimes. Her father built this home when she was five years old, and since 1923 it has been a most accommodating guest house set at the far end of the main street in St. Andrews within expansive gardens and lawns.

This is an experience in an old Canadian home, and sitting in the parlor, the traveler has many reminders of Canada and Canadians at the turn of the century. There are all kinds of wonderful, glass-covered prints and portraits on the walls, and the kind of furniture that has been reserved for front parlors and sitting rooms in North America for over a century.

The eighteen immaculately clean guest rooms of many sizes and shapes almost all have chenille bedspreads with the legend "Seaside Inn" woven into the design. Baths are mostly shared, and rooms without private baths have sinks in the bedroms.

The front porch is one of the very nice features at Seaside Inn, and perhaps Marjorie will find the opportunity to sit and talk about the St. Andrews that she knows and loves so well.

SEASIDE INN, St. Andrews, New Brunswick, Canada EOG 2XO; 506-529-3224 An 18-guestroom guest house in a conservative Canadian atmosphere. Open all year, but check ahead if you're coming in the winter months. Breakfast is not served. Within convenient walking distance of St. Andrews' many interesting shops and restaurants. Please note a time-change when crossing the USA-Canada border at Calais, Maine—set clock ahead one hour. Marjorie Richardson, Owner

Directions: Seaside Inn is at the end of the main street in St. Andrews.

For B&B rates, see Index.

TARA MANOR
St. Andrews, New Brunswick, Canada

St. Andrews has many historical connections with the remainder of the North American continent. For example, at the time of the American Revolution in Portland, Maine, there were many who decided they would move to British North America and establish a settlement at Castine, Maine, on the north shore of the Penobscot River.

However, following the war, the British and American governments negotiated a boundary that still placed Castine south of British North America, and these British Empire Loyalists, as they were known, loaded their homes on sailing ships and transported them to St. Andrews.

Today St. Andrews is a most pleasant resort town and certainly a favored stop on the long road across the Maritimes to New Brunswick, Prince Edward Island, and Nova Scotia.

Tara Manor, set in several acres of beautifully manicured grounds, was built by Norman Ryall as a home for his family. In recent years it has been converted into a most attractive small resort with a heated swimming pool and a splendid panoramic view of Passamaquoddy Bay.

The guest rooms are generous in size, and have sun rooms or balconies looking out over the grounds to the sea. Incidentally, Tara is considerably removed from the main road and enjoys a welcome peace and quiet.

Both breakfast and a sumptuous evening meal are offered in the dining room.

Tara's broad lawns and sculptured hedgerows provide a welcome respite for vacationing families, for here youngsters can run and play in safety.

TARA MANOR, St. Andrews, New Brunswick, Canada EOG 2XO; 506-529-3304. A 19-guestroom resort inn in a historic Canadian town overlooking Passamaquoddy Bay. Breakfast is not included in the room rate. Breakfast and dinner served from May 1 to mid-Oct.; guestrooms available until the end of Oct. Swimming pool on grounds. Golf, sailing, boating, walking, ice skating, (even in the summer) available nearby. Norman and Sharon Ryall, Innkeepers.

Directions: Follow the signs from Rte. 1 to New Brunswick, and then the inn signs, turning left at the Irving Station.

For rates, see Index.

BLOMIDON INN
Wolfville, Nova Scotia, Canada

Distances in the Canadian Maritimes are deceiving. Just try driving from Yarmouth to Cape Breton and you'll see what I mean. Fortunately, it's now possible to make a very pleasant overnight or even longer stop at the Blomidon Inn in Wolfville, about halfway between the two points. Or, if you're coming around the land route via New Brunswick, it also will serve as a diverting stopping-off place.

The inn was built in 1877 by Captain Rufus Burgess, a descendant of New England planters, and was one of the grandest houses in the beautiful Annapolis valley. Much of the fine mahogany and walnut was brought as ballast on his ships. Captain Burgess imported two Italian craftsmen who fashioned the lovely cornices and dadoes.

Set back from the road in very spacious grounds, this Victorian beauty has working fireplaces, and all of the eleven bedrooms are furnished with low poster beds and quilts. The views are of the two acres of terraced lawns shaded by huge elms, maples, and chestnuts.

The innkeepers here are Gale and Peter Hastings, who are Maritimers themselves and have spent many, many months of painstaking and loving care restoring the inn and adding even much more to its luster.

In addition to being a bed-and-breakfast stopover, the Blomidon is also a full-service inn. Gale describes her cooking as "sophisticated country." Travelers should plan on taking dinner.

Wolfville is surrounded by countless beautiful trails leading to delightfully small farming and fishing communities, and both the inn and the area invite much longer stays.

BLOMIDON INN, 127 Main St., P.O. Box 839, Wolfville, N.S., Canada, B0P 1X0; 902-542-9326. An 11-room Victorian mansion on Main St. in Wolfville. Nine rooms with private baths; 2 share a bath. Continental breakfast included in room rates. Full breakfast available. Licensed dining room serving travelers daily. Golf, xc skiing, hiking, tennis, swimming nearby. Close to Provincial and Federal parks and museums. Gale and Peter Hastings, Innkeepers.

Directions: Take either Exit 10 or 11 from Hwy. 101 and proceed to the eastern end of Wolfville. Located on Main Street.

For B&B rates, see Index.

HIGHLAND HEIGHTS INN
Iona, Nova Scotia, Canada

Many of the early settlers to Nova Scotia came from Scotland and the people of Iona are dedicated to building a fitting memorial to their Scottish ancestors. They have built a museum depicting the history of the Scot in America, and the village pipe band and dancers perform on an outdoor stage and amphitheater built under the side of a hill, giving a most beautiful view of Bras d'Or Lake.

The Highland Heights Inn was opened in 1973 to accommodate visitors to this area. It, too, overlooks Bras d'Or Lake, an extraordinary "salt-water lake" carved naturally from the entire central area of the island.

There are sixteen bedrooms, all with a lake view, and the dining room is open from 8 A.M. to 9 P.M. every day. The seafood and the steaks are a specialty; particularly the local salmon. This inn is listed in *Where to Eat in Canada*.

HIGHLAND HEIGHTS INN, P.O. Box 66, R.R. 2, Iona, Cape Breton Island, Nova Scotia; 902-622-2360. A 16-room bedroom pleasant motel in the scenic area of Cape Breton Island. Dining room open daily from 8 A.M. to 9 P.M. Breakfast is not included in room rate. Conveniently situated to enjoy fishing, swimming, boating, and hunting. Also convenient for visits to Fortress Louisbourg and the Alexander Graham Bell Museum. The Cabot Trail is just a few minutes away. Scott MacAulay, Innkeeper.

Directions: From Trans-Canada 105, take the Little Narrows Ferry (operating every 10 min., 24 hrs. a day) to Rte. 223, and continue 15 mi. to inn. From Sydney, turn left off Trans-Canada 125 at Leitches Creek on Rte. 223 and continue 30 mi. to inn.

For B&B rates, see Index.

INVERARY INN
Baddeck, Nova Scotia, Canada

Baddeck, on the Bras d'Or Lakes on Cape Breton in Nova Scotia is an exciting nautical paradise for sailboat and yachting enthusiasts because of its sparkling clear water, many sheltered anchorages, and the superb highland scenery.

Most of the early settlers came to Baddeck from the highlands of Scotland. Gaelic language and Scottish culture are preserved here in a number of ways.

Alexander Graham Bell's life and inventions are commemorated at the museum in Baddeck and include Dr. Bell's successful efforts toward powered flight, telephone communication, early X-ray, and a first attempt to use an iron lung.

The North American traveler intent on covering the Canadian Maritimes in as quick a fashion as possible errs in not remaining at least two nights at the Inverary Inn. It takes at least a full day to traverse the Cabot Trail which runs along next to the sea among the fishing villages, and then plunges into the Great Nova Scotia forests.

The inn is an old farmhouse with a barn, wagon house, and pine-paneled cottages situated on the outskirts of Baddeck overlooking the lake. The winding paths lead through the trees past the children's playground to the bathing wharf.

It's quite a drive from the southern end of Nova Scotia or the New Brunswick-Nova Scotia border to Baddeck so it is well to plan on enjoying an Inverary dinner.

A full Scottish breakfast of hot spiced applesauce, oatmeal porridge with brown sugar and cream, crisp fried Scottish sausage and home fries, and a basket of Scottish oat cakes and bannock, is offered as part of the B&B rate. It is served in the dining room, which itself has a most pleasant view of the lakes. It's almost the same as being in Scotland.

INVERARY INN, Box 190, Baddeck, Cape Breton, N.S. Canada 902-295-2674. A 40-room village inn on the Cabot Trail, 52 mi. from Sydney, N.S. On the shores of Lake Bras d'Or. European plan. Some rooms with shared baths. Breakfast and dinner served to travelers daily. Open from May 15 to Nov. 1. Bicycles and children's playground on grounds. Boating and small golf course nearby. Isobel MacAulay, Innkeeper.

Directions: Follow Trans-Canada Hwy. to Canso Causeway to Baddeck.

For B&B rates, see Index.

MILFORD HOUSE
South Milford, Nova Scotia, Canada

Milford House is very frequently the first stop for travelers using the ferry between Bar Harbor, Maine and Yarmouth, Nova Scotia.

More than a century ago, Abraham Thomas established this way-station at South Milford, Nova Scotia, on the long, bumpy coach ride from Liverpool, on the Atlantic Coast, across the province to Annapolis Royal on the Bay of Fundy. Even before the turn of the century, his hotel had begun to draw, not just weary travelers, but tourists and sportsmen who came for the fishing and the solitude.

For a number of years, even before my first visit in 1973, the inn has been expertly managed by Margaret and Bud Miller.

Accommodations at Milford House are in cottages spread along the shores of two lakes; each of them has its own dock and living room with a fireplace, electricity, and a bathroom with hot and cold running water and a shower or tub.

The guests take their breakfasts and dinners at the main lodge where there are homebaked breads and pastries, vegetables from the garden, roasts, fresh fish, and blueberries and raspberries.

Everyone walks through the woods up to the main dining room to enjoy a full homemade breakfast featuring griddle cakes, corned beef hash, kippers, homemade bread, which is toasted to just the right color, and lots of steaming coffee. It is at this time that guests make new friends and perhaps plan some outdoor activity together. The next stop could be the Cabot Trail.

MILFORD HOUSE, South Milford, R.R. #4, Annapolis Royal, N.S., Canada, BOS 1AO; 902-532-2617. A rustic resort-inn with 27 cabins on 600 acres of woodlands and lakes, 90 mi. from Yarmouth, N.S., near Kejimkujik National Park. Modified American plan. Breakfast and dinner served daily with picnic lunches available. Open from June 15 to Sept. 15; fall and winter by special reservation. Tennis, fishing, croquet, canoeing, birdwatching, and swimming on grounds. Deep-sea fishing and golf nearby. Warren and Margaret Miller, Innkeepers.

Directions: From Yarmouth follow Rte. 1 to traffic lights in Annapolis Royal. Turn right and continue on to Rte. 8, 15 mi. to inn.

For B&B rates, see Index.

GRANDVIEW FARM
Huntsville, Ontario, Canada

Basically, Grandview Farm is a resort-inn and does not accept advance reservations for less than a two-night stay. However, at certain off-season times of the year, it might be possible to telephone the same day and get a room and breakfast for one night.

Travelers crossing Canada, either east and west, or north and south, will find it a very pleasant experience and enjoy the brand of personal hospitality which has been offered for many years by the Craik family.

For one thing, Grandview Farm is located in the Muskoka resort area of Ontario and there is much to entice the traveler to remain for extra days, including tennis, swimming, sailing, wind surfing, water skiing, cross-country skiing, and the like.

The farm was originally settled in 1874 and portions of it are still cultivated. The lodging rooms are located in the rather elegant main house and also in a series of lakeside chalets and cottages.

There is a sumptuous full Canadian breakfast which leads off with fruit and juices. This is followed by porridge and cereals, bacon, sausage, eggs, pancakes, homebaked Chelseas, toasts, muffins, and other surprises. This is served in the dining room, the sun room, or the patio, depending on the weather.

It is possible for the overnight traveler to get an excellent dinner, which might include London broil, chicken, butterfly lamb, or ribs. Lunch is also served.

GRANDVIEW FARM, Huntsville, Ontario, Canada POA 1KO; 705-789-7462. A 29-room resort-inn on Fairy Lake, 142 mi. (227km) north of Toronto in a beautiful lake and mountain resort area. American and modified American plans. Breakfast, lunch, and dinner served to travelers daily. Open mid-May to mid-Oct.; Dec. 26 to Mar. 31. Closed Christmas Eve and Christmas Day. Minimum stay during July and Aug.: 3 nights; rest of year: 2-night minimum. Tennis, swimming, sailing, windsurfing, waterskiing, canoeing, xc ski trails (10km), alpine skiing close by. No pets. The Craik Family, Innkeepers.

Directions: From Niagara Falls, N.Y. (I-95): take Rainbow Bridge, Rte. 420 to Queen Elizabeth Way, north to Toronto, Rte. 427 north to Rte. 401 east to Rte. 400 north to Barrie, then Rte. 11 north to Rte. 60 (just north of Huntsville), then right for 4½ mi. (7km.). Grandview Farm is on your right. Hwy. 60 is the main route to Ottawa from this part of Ontario.

For B&B rates, see Index.

THE OPINICON
Chaffey's Locks, Elgin, Ontario, Canada

Guests can arrive at the Opinicon not only by car, bus, train, and taxi, but also by boat because it is located on the Rideau Canal which was opened in 1832 to connect Kingston, Ontario, with Ottawa and thus avoid the rapids of the St. Lawrence River.

The Opinicon had a simple beginning as a family residence in the early 19th century and became in succession, a boarding house, a men's fishing club, and now has evolved into one of eastern Ontario's oldest and most respected resorts. It's been owned and operated by the same family since 1921, and while retaining its style, has been updated to offer every convenience. It's a good place for children.

Accommodations are in the friendly old main building and in cottages that are scattered around the campuslike grounds which extend to the lake shore.

I should warn all my readers that one of the temptations to stay on for further days is the excellent fishing.

B&B guests who can bear to tear themselves away from this idyllic scene can console themselves with a large breakfast of assorted juices, fruits, dry cereals, and porridge. After that, there's a choice of any style of eggs that they can imagine, broiled maple leaf bacon, ham, pork sausages, hash-brown potatoes, french toast with maple syrup, and griddle cakes. An extra feature seldom found these days is a glass of cold buttermilk.

THE OPINICON, Chaffey's Locks, RR #1, Elgin, Ontario, Canada K0G 1C0; 613-359-5233. An 18-room resort-inn on Opinicon Lake, part of the Rideau Canal System of eastern Ontario; 38 accommodations also available in rustic cottages. Full American and modified American plan. Open April 4 to Nov. 26. Fishing, boating, tennis, heated swimming pool, shuffleboard, bicycles on grounds; golf course nearby. Excellent for children of all ages. No credit cards. Personal checks accepted. Albert and Janice Cross, Innkeepers.

Directions: From south: Interstate 81 to 1000 Island Bridge to Ontario Rte. 401 west. Turn off exit No. 106 at Rte. 32 (right), go north to Rte. 15, turning right (north). Follow to 2 miles beyond Elgin (bypassed). Turn left on Chaffey's Locks Road. From east: Rte. 401 west to exit No. 112 (Brockville), turn north (right) on Rte. 42, follow Rte. 42 to Crosby, turn south (left) on Rte. 15 for 2 miles and turn right on Chaffey's Locks Road.

For B&B rates, see Index.

SHAW'S HOTEL
Brackley Beach, Prince Edward Island, Canada

Prince Edward Island is one of the great surprises of North America. For one thing, ocean water temperatures along the wide P.E.I. beaches average 68 to 70 degrees in summer and the sun is excellent for tanning. It has one of Canada's finest national parks stretching 25 miles along the Gulf of St. Lawrence.

I might suggest that the traveler to and from Nova Scotia detour for an extra night (please call ahead for reservations) at Shaw's Hotel on Brackley Beach. With ferries at each end of the island, an extra night in this Elysian province may suggest a longer stay on the next trip.

Operating since 1860, Shaw's Hotel is a typical resort experience. There are quite a few accommodations including cottages with fireplaces, which have two, three, and four bedrooms.

Fortunately, the overnight B&B guest can also enjoy dinner here.

Whether the day is spent driving from New Brunswick or upper Nova Scotia, or possibly sunning on the nearby beach, the full breakfast, which is served every morning with an unusual number of menu choices, is most welcome.

Shaw's Hotel is well booked at the height of the season; however, if it's for one night only, try telephoning the day before—maybe you'll be lucky.

SHAW'S HOTEL and Cottages, Brackley Point Road, Brackley Beach, Prince Edward Island, Canada COA 2HO; 902-672-2022. A 24-room country hotel within walking distance of Brackley Beach, 15 mi. from Charlottetown. Mod. American plan. Some rooms with shared baths; 10 guest cottages. Breakfast and dinner served to travelers daily. Open from June 15 to Sept. 15. Tennis, golf, bicycles, riding, sailing, beach, and summer theatre nearby. Pets allowed in cottages only. No credit cards. Personal checks accepted. Gordon Shaw, Innkeeper.

Directions: Prince Edward Island is reached either by ferry from Cape Tormentine, New Brunswich (near Moncton), or Caribou, Nova Scotia. In both cases, after arriving on P.E.I. follow Rte. 1 to Charlottetown, then Rte. 15 to Brackley Beach. P.E.I. is also reached by Eastern Provincial Airways, Canadian National Railways, and Air Canada.

For B&B rates, see Index.

HANDFIELD INN (AUBERGE HANDFIELD)
St. Marc-sur-le-Richelieu, Quebec, Canada

The Handfield Inn is a great many things: a venerable mansion that has seen a century and a half of history; an enjoyable French restaurant; a four-season resort; and perhaps best of all, it is an opportunity to visit a French-Canadian village which has remained relatively free from the invasion of developers.

Accommodations are in rustic rooms decorated and furnished in the old Quebec style, but with touches of modern comfort including tile bathrooms and controlled heating.

The village of St. Marc is wonderfully French and when I was there I had animated communication with the village baker, he in French, I in English, while the aroma of his bread and rolls sent my gastronomic senses reeling. St. Marc stretches along the Richelieu River, and has a twin village on the opposite side called St. Charles, which is reached by ferry.

Visitors during the summer can enjoy summer theater on the converted ferry boat *l'Escale* from June 15 to September 15. There is also a marina with a 300-foot pier for pleasure boats. Visitors between March 1 and the end of April can also take part in the maple sugar parties in the nearby woods.

A full French-Canadian breakfast is served in the old-fashioned dining room. It includes homemade beans, omelettes and bacon, maple-smoked ham, buckwheat pancakes, and eggs cooked in maple syrup. Special B&B rates are available to readers of this book.

HANDFIELD INN (Auberge Handfield), St. Marc-sur-le-Richelieu (Saint Marc on the Richelieu River), Quebec, JOL 2EO, Canada; 514-584-2226. A 45-room French-Canadian country inn about 25 miles from Montreal. Different lodging plans available. Please consult with the inn in advance. Some rooms have shared baths. Breakfast, lunch, and dinner served daily to travelers. Ladies are expected to wear a skirt or dress and gentlemen, a coat at dinner. Open every day all year. All summer and winter active sports easily available. Many handcrafts, antique, and historical tours in the area. No pets. M. and Mme. Conrad Handfield, Innkeepers.

Directions: From Champlain, Victoria, or the Jacques Cartier bridges, take Hwy. 3 to Sorel, turn right at Hwy. 20. From the east end of Montreal go through the Hyppolite LaFontaine Tunnel. Rte. 20 passes through St. Julie, St. Bruno, and Beloeil. Leave Hwy. 20 at Exit 112 turning left on Rte. 223 north. Handfield is 7 miles distant.

For B&B rates, see Index.

HOTEL MANOIR d'AUTEUIL
Quebec City, Canada

In the account of my visit to Chateau de Pierre, a companion hotel to this very pleasant accommodation, I have explained in some detail why the North American visitor to Quebec City will find it a most interesting adventure. At this moment I have listed only two small hotels in Quebec City; however, the tourist bureau of the city can supply the traveler with many others, both in and out of the Old City.

The Manoir d'Auteuil is out of the more heavily traveled river-front area of Quebec, but visitors should be warned that during the high summer season tourists from all over North America are great in number. I found it very intriguing that the atmosphere of the entire city is predominantly French, and it makes it that much more attractive to me.

The Manoir d'Auteuil is just inside the walls of the Old City across from the Esplanade Park. In a city that has quite a few examples of Victorian architecture, it seemed rather interesting to me that Art Deco should be the prevailing theme of the decor here. I learned that one of the previous owners of the hotel had become interested in this particular style, and the present owners, the Couturier Family, have preserved the circa 1930 look. Some rooms were being redecorated during my stay.

The bedrooms basically are quite comfortable in size. Mine in particular had a bathroom big enough for a half-court game of basketball. There are showers and tubs in every bathroom—my shower had seven water spouts.

Parking is available at a reduced rate for hotel guests in the underground public parking garage.

HOTEL MANOIR d'AUTEUIL, 49 rue d'Auteuil, Vieux-Quebec, (Quebec) QC, G1R 4C2; 418-694-1173. A 17-guestroom (private baths) small hotel within the walls of the Old City of Quebec. All rooms have color TV and direct-line telephones. Breakfast is not included in the room rate and is not served during the summer months. Most conveniently located to enjoy all of the touristic sights of the Old City. (See section on Le Chateau de Pierre). Parking nearby. George Couturier, Hotelier.

Directions: Stop at one of the many tourist information bureaus en route to Quebec City and you'll get good directions and a good map.

For B&B rates, see Index.

HOVEY MANOR
North Hatley, Quebec, Canada

Elsewhere in this book I have written about Routes 100 and I-91, both of which run the full north-south length of Vermont. They meet in Newport and continue on to Quebec, Canada, where the road is known as Autoroute 55. This is the main road into the Eastern Townships and to Three Rivers and Quebec City.

Just a few miles to the east of Route 55 is North Hatley, Quebec, on the shores of Lake Massawippi. Hovey Manor sits on a height of land directly on this beautiful lake.

Hovey Manor's Colonial atmosphere is unique in Quebec. This is a year-round resort-inn. In the summer the guests enjoy sailing, canoeing, paddleboating, water-skiing, fishing, and tennis. There are also ten golf courses within a short drive of the inn, many art centers, and summer theater. There's cross-country skiing from the front door and five downhill ski areas within a reasonable drive.

Accommodations are within the main house and in a series of smaller houses and cottages which are strung out along the shore of the lake.

A choice of full Canadian breakfasts is offered on the bilingual menu. Freshly squeezed orange juice, as well as farm-fresh eggs (any style) are served with Nichol's famous dry-cured bacon or sausages and toast. I enjoy the French crêpes stuffed with blueberries or apples and served with local "AAA" maple syrup.

HOVEY MANOR, North Hatley, Quebec, Canada JOB 2CO; 819-842-2421. A 29-room resort inn (8 with woodburning fireplaces) on Lake Massawippi, 25 min. from U.S./Canada border. Modified American and European plans. Breakfast, lunch, dinner served every day. Open all year. Lighted tennis court, two beaches, sailing, canoeing, paddleboats, water-skiing, fishing, cross-country skiing on grounds. Downhill skiing, horseback riding, golf (10 courses) nearby. Many scenic and cultural attractions nearby. Happy experience for children of all ages. Pets allowed in cottages but not in Manor House. Stephen and Kathryn Stafford, Innkeepers.

Directions: From Vermont/Quebec border follow Rte. 55 to No. Hatley Exit (No. 29). Follow Rte. 108E for 5 mi. to "T" junction at Lake Massawippi in North Hatley. Turn right for ¾ mi. to Hovey Manor sign and private drive on left—this is only 25 min. from Vermont.

For B&B rates, see Index.

LE CHATEAU DE PIERRE
Quebec City, Canada

First of all, I would like to encourage everybody to visit Quebec City. It is one of the most unusual, instructive, entertaining, and joyful experiences I've ever had. Like Victoria, its counterpart in British Columbia on the west coast of Canada, it has a wonderful, natural feeling.

Incidentally the term "Quebec" can refer either to the city or the entire province.

I cannot go into great detail here because we do want to tell our readers about Le Chateau de Pierre; however, sufficient to say that the old section of the city (Vieux-Quebec) is the big attraction. Dominated by the really tremendous Hotel Chateau Frontenac, it sits high up on the bluffs above the St. Lawrence River. The old streets and shops and the general atmosphere is quite like Paris, and I found the entire experience most delightful. It's a good idea to make a short stop at the Museum du Fort, which will provide an entire historical background of the city.

For a complete booklet on the region, contact: Tourisme Quebec, Ministere de l'Industrie, du Commerce et du Tourisme, Case postale 20 000, Quebec, Qc Canada G1K 7X2.

LE CHATEAU DE PIERRE, 17, Avenue Ste-Genevieve, Quebec City, Canada, G1R 4A8; 418-694-0429. A 15-guestroom (private baths) conservative, clean, Victorian-style hotel in the Old City, just a few steps from the river. Open year-round. Breakfast is not served. No credit cards. English, French, and Spanish spoken. Mme. L. Couturier, Proprietress.

Directions: Stop at one of the many tourist information bureaus en route to Quebec City and you'll get good directions and a good map.

For B&B rates, see Index.

CALIFORNIA GUEST HOUSE
Nelson, New Zealand

I have never been to New Zealand, but I thought it would be fun in response to two letters I have received from out-of-the-way places (the other one is Alaska) to at least include a listing in this book. If any of my readers visit, I would be very much interested in hearing your opinions.

The California Guest House is presided over by two young Americans who fell in love with New Zealand as tourists. They explain that the climate in Nelson is similar to that of California's Santa Clara Valley where they both grew up—warm sunshine day after day, very little rain, mild winters with occasional frost. Nelson is a popular tourist spot because of its sunshine and beaches and it is also on the main route around South Island.

The house is registered with the New Zealand Historic Places Trust, and contains 24 stained glass windows, beautiful old wood paneling, three fireplaces, eleven-foot ceilings, a veranda on two sides, large lawn and gardens, and is set well back from the street in a residential area about five minutes' walk from the town center.

There are six guest rooms, five in the house and one in a small cottage on the grounds.

The specialty of the house is a homebaked California breakfast that includes freshly squeezed orange juice, fresh fruit, and such goodies as apple blintzes, omelets, and apricot-nut bread. Finnish pancakes with fresh fruit and pure Canadian maple syrup are also served.

The California Guest House in Nelson, New Zealand is open for six months a year during the winter (summer in New Zealand), closing down after Easter for six months. I would be delighted if every reader who visits Carol and Alan would send me a postcard. It's possible to make reservations in the United States after May 15th for the following November to May by telephoning the California number given in the following paragraph.

CALIFORNIA GUEST HOUSE (Mailing address, May to Nov.: P.O. Box 166, Elk, Ca. 95432; 707-877-3417). The address in New Zealand is 29 Collingwood St., Nelson, New Zealand: (Tel.): Nelson 84173. A 6-bedroom guest home in a scenic section of New Zealand on the road to the Southern Alps. A full breakfast is the only meal served. Open for six months in the winter and closing after Easter. Carol Glen, Innkeeper.

For B&B rates, see Index.

INDEX/RATES

(These are approximate rates for lodgings and breakfast for two people for one night and may include low, off-season rates, as well as high-season rates. In some cases, tax and service charge are additional.)

INN	RATE	PAGE
ALASKA		
GUSTAVUS, Gustavus Inn	$150†	11
ARIZONA		
TUCSON, Lodge on the Desert	$40-$106	12
CALIFORNIA		
ARROYO GRANDE, Rose Victorian Inn	$85-$115†	47
BERKELEY, Gramma's Bed & Breakfast	$61-$88	27
BOONVILLE, Toll House Inn	$60-$86	54
CALISTOGA, Larkmead Country Inn	$85	41
CARMEL, Happy Landing	$60-$85	31
CARMEL, San Antonio House	$85-$115	48
CARMEL, Sandpiper Inn	$65-$105	49
CARMEL, Vagabond's House	$65-$95	56
CLOVERDALE, Vintage Towers	$38-$68	58
DEL MAR, Rock Haus B&B Inn	$70-$100	46
EUREKA, Carter House	$40-$135	20
FERNDALE, Gingerbread Mansion	$47-$75	23
FERNDALE, Shaw House Inn	$55-$85	51
FORT BRAGG, Grey Whale Inn	$45-$75	30
FORT BRAGG, Pudding Creek Inn	$40-$63	44
GEYSERVILLE, Hope-Merrill House	$50-$60	35
GUALALA, Whale Watch Inn by the Sea	$75-$175	60
HEALDSBURG, Grape Leaf Inn	$45-$95	28
IONE, Heirloom, The	$45-$65	32
JACKSON, Gate House Inn	$45-$80	22
LITTLE RIVER, Glendeven	$60-$80	25
LITTLE RIVER, Victorian Farmhouse	$63	57
MENDOCINO, Big River Lodge	$86-$150	17
MENDOCINO, Hill House Inn	$56-$105	34
MENDOCINO, Joshua Grindle Inn	$56-$68	39
MONTEREY, Jabberwock, The	$75-$125	38
MUIR BEACH, Pelican Inn	$95	42
NAPA, Beazley House	$70-$100	15
NAPA, La Residence	$60-$115	40
NEVADA CITY, Red Castle Inn	$45-$85	45
PACIFIC GROVE, Gosby House Inn	$70-$125	26

INN	RATE	PAGE
PACIFIC GROVE, Green Gables Inn	$80-$135	29
PACIFIC GROVE, House of Seven Gables	$75-$110	36
SACRAMENTO, Amber House	$65-$75	13
ST. HELENA, Chalet Bernensis	$55-$95	21
ST. HELENA, Wine Country Inn	$80-$130	61
SAN DIEGO, Britt House	$65-$95	18
SAN FRANCISCO, Bed & Breakfast Inn	$58-$165	16
SAN FRANCISCO, Hermitage House	$65-$95	33
SAN FRANCISCO, Inn at Union Square	$90-$155	37
SAN FRANCISCO, Petite Auberge	$85-$185	43
SAN FRANCISCO, Spreckel's Mansion, The	$78-$175	52
SAN FRANCISCO, Union Street Inn	$75-$165	55
SAN FRANCISCO, Washington Square Inn	$70-$135	59
SANTA BARBARA, Bath Street Inn	$70-$85	14
SANTA BARBARA, Glenborough Inn	$40-$120	24
SEAL BEACH, Seal Beach Inn	$45-$120	50
SUTTER CREEK, Sutter Creek Inn	$55-$75	53
YOUNTVILLE, Burgundy House	$35-$120	19

COLORADO

BOULDER, Briar Rose Bed & Breakfast	$65-$75	62
COLORADO SPRINGS, Hearthstone Inn	$55-$95	63
GREEN MOUNTAIN FALLS, Outlook Lodge	$28-$40	64

CONNECTICUT

CHESTER, Inn at Chester	$70-$80*	71
EAST HADDAM, Bishops Gate	$60-$85	66
ESSEX, Griswold Inn	$55-$75	69
GREENWICH, Homestead Inn	$91-$135	70
GROTON LONG POINT, Shore Inne	$35-$45	73
KENT, Candlelight, The	$30*	67
NORWALK, Silvermine Tavern	$62-$67	74
OLD LYME, Bee and Thistle Inn	$50-$75	65
RIDGEFIELD, West Lane Inn	$90	75
RIVERTON, Old Riverton Inn	$48-$78	72
SALISBURY, White Hart Inn	$60-$120*	76
WOODBURY, Curtis House	$25-$50	68

DELAWARE

BETHANY BEACH, Homestead Guests	$20-$25	77
BETHANY BEACH, Sea-Vista Villà	$45	78

*Breakfast additional or unavailable

Rates are approximate for 2 people for 1 night

INN	RATE	PAGE
DEER ISLE, Goose Cove Lodge	$50-$60	109
DEER ISLE, Pilgrim's Inn	$70-$130†	128
DENNYSVILLE, Lincoln House Inn	$45-$55*	119
EAST MACHIAS, Breeze Inn	$25	96
EAST WATERFORD, Waterford Inne, The	$50-$70	133
KENNEBUNKPORT, Captain Lord Mansion	$79-$99	98
KENNEBUNKPORT, English Meadows	$50-$60	108
KENNEBUNKPORT, Old Fort Inn	$65-$105	125
NAPLES, Charmwoods	$80-$95	101
NEWCASTLE, Captain's House, The	$35	99
NEWCASTLE, Elfinhill	$35-$45	107
NEWCASTLE, Mill Pond Inn	$45-$60	120
NEW HARBOR, Bradley Inn	$45	94
NORTHEAST HARBOR, Grey Rock Inn	$85-$100	111
OGUNQUIT, Hartwell House	$85-$95	113
PROUTS NECK, Black Point Inn	$90-$100	91
RANGELEY, Country Club Inn	$62-$70	103
SEARSPORT, Carriage House Inn	$49	100
SEARSPORT, Homeport Inn	$50-$60	116
SOUTHWEST HARBOR, Harbor Lights	$25-$30*	112
SOUTHWEST HARBOR, Moorings, The	$30-$60	122
SURRY, Surry Inn	$42-$48	131
WISCASSET, Roberts House	$36-$40	129
WISCASSET, Squire Tarbox Inn	$65-$75	130
YARMOUTH, Homewood Inn	$47-$83*	117
YORK, Dockside Guest Quarters	$35-$60	105
YORK HARBOR, Moorelowe	$22-$25*	121

MARYLAND

ANNAPOLIS, Historic Inns of Annapolis	$65-$110*	134
NEW MARKET, Strawberry Inn, The	$50-$65	136
OXFORD, Robert Morris Inn	$31.50-$105	135

MASSACHUSETTS

BARNSTABLE VILLAGE, CAPE COD, Beechwood	$65-$85	139
BARNSTABLE VILLAGE, CAPE COD, Cobb's Cove	$98-$109	149
BASS RIVER, Captain Isaiah's House	$25-$30	144
BREWSTER, CAPE COD, Bramble Inn, The	$50-$70	140
BREWSTER, CAPE COD, Captain Freeman Inn	$40-$58	143
BREWSTER, CAPE COD, Old Manse Inn	$40-$60	176
CHATHAM, CAPE COD, Captain's House Inn of Chatham	$60-$95	146

†AP or MAP   *Breakfast additional or unavailable

INN	RATE	PAGE
CHATHAM, CAPE COD, Queen Anne Inn	$86-$116	180
CONCORD, Hawthorne Inn	$65-$85	162
DEERFIELD, Deerfield Inn	$65-$70*	154
DENNISPORT, CAPE COD, Innisfree of Dennisport	$55	166
EAST ORLEANS, Nauset House Inn	$33-$65*	173
EDGARTOWN, Charlotte Inn	$90-$275	148
FALMOUTH, Mostly Hall	$39-$70	172
GLOUCESTER, Gloucester Traveler	$35-$55*	158
GLOUCESTER, Gray Manor	$30-$45*	159
GREAT BARRINGTON, Elling's Guest House	$35-$50	155
GREAT BARRINGTON, 500 So. Main Street	$45-$65	157
GREAT BARRINGTON, Seekonk Pines	$40-$57	186
GREAT BARRINGTON, Turning Point	$55-$70	191
LAKEVILLE, Pistachio Cove	$30-$45	179
LEE, Haus Andreas	$45-$140	161
LEE, Morgan House	$25-$75	170
LEE, 1777 Greylock House	$50-$75	187
LENOX, Village Inn	$40-$105	193
LENOX, Walker House	$45-$110	194
MONUMENT BEACH, CAPE COD, Bay Breeze Guest House	$20-$35*	138
NEWBURYPORT, Morrill Place	$30-$35	171
NEWBURYPORT, Windsor House	$60-$80	199
NEW MARLBOROUGH, Old Inn on the Green	$50	175
NORTHAMPTON, Autumn Inn	$46-$58	137
NORTHFIELD, Centennial House	$30-$35	147
NORTHFIELD, Northfield Country House	$50-$100	174
PITTSFIELD, La Maison du Pothier	$45-$55	167
PLYMOUTH, Colonial House Inn	$40-$55*	151
PRINCETON, Country Inn at Princeton	from $95	152
PROVINCETOWN, Hargood House	$52-$94*	160
PROVINCETOWN, Windamar House	$45-$55	198
ROCKPORT, Captain's House, The	$34-$55	145
ROCKPORT, Inn on Cove Hill	$28-$60	165
ROCKPORT, Ralph Waldo Emerson	$52-$90	181
ROCKPORT, Rocky Shores	$56-$68	183
ROCKPORT, Seacrest Manor	$48-$72	185
ROCKPORT, Yankee Clipper	$50-$75	200
SALEM, Salem Inn, The	$55-$65	184
SANDWICH, CAPE COD, Summer House, The	$50	189
SHEFFIELD, Darr Antiques and Guest House	$65-$70	153
SHEFFIELD, Staveleigh House	$60-$65	188
SHELBURNE, Parson Hubbard House	$30	178

Rates are approximate for 2 people for 1 night

INN	RATE	PAGE
SOUTH ASHFIELD, Bull Frog Bed & Breakfast	$35	142
SOUTH EGREMONT, Weathervane Inn	$60-$65	195
SOUTH LEE, Federal House Inn	$40-$125	156
SOUTH LEE, Merrell Tavern Inn	$45-$95	169
STOCKBRIDGE, Inn at Stockbridge	$50-$150	164
STURBRIDGE, Colonel Ebenezer Crafts	$65-$75	150
TOPSFIELD, History House	$34-$36	163
WEST BROOKFIELD, Brookfield House Inn	$55-$95	141
WEST HARWICH, CAPE COD, Lion's Head Inn	$38-$50	168
WEST HARWICH, CAPE COD, Tern Inn, The	$40-$50	190
WESTMINSTER, Westminster Village Inn	$38-$55*	197
WESTON, Webb-Bigelow Place, The	$55	196
WHITINSVILLE, Victorian, The	$79-$98	192
WILLIAMSTOWN, River Bend Farm	$40-$45	182
YARMOUTH PORT, One Centre Street Inn	$39-69	177

MICHIGAN

DOUGLAS, Rosemont Inn	$50-$70	202
MARSHALL, National House Inn	$48-$81	201
PETOSKEY, Stafford's Bay View	$70-$80	203
SAUGATUCK, Wickwood Inn	$55-$110	204

MINNESOTA

MINNEAPOLIS, Nicollet Island Inn	$65-$115	206
NEW PRAGUE, Schumacher's	$60-$80*	207
STILLWATER, Lowell Inn	$69-$119*	205

MISSOURI

STE. GENEVIEVE, St. Gemme Beauvais Inn	$40	208

NEW HAMPSHIRE

ASHLAND, Cheney House	$34	211
BRIDGEWATER, Pasquaney Inn	$36-$45	228
CAMPTON VILLAGE, Campton Inn, The	$22-$50	210
CENTER SANDWICH, Corner House Inn	$32-$40	213
CHOCORUA, Stafford's in the Field	$62-$92	233
DANBURY, Inn at Danbury	$28-$38	223
ETNA, Moose Mountain Lodge	$56	227
FRANCESTOWN, Inn at Crotched Mountain	$35-$50*	222
FRANCONIA, Lovett's	$44-$86*	225
GORHAM, Pinkham Notch Camp	$21	230
HANCOCK, John Hancock Inn	$55-$60*	224

*Breakfast additional or unavailable

INN	RATE	PAGE
HAVERHILL, Haverhill Inn	$50	218
HENNIKER, Colby Hill Inn	$45-$70	212
JACKSON, Dana Place Inn	$56-$88	215
LACONIA, Hickory Stick Farm	$42-$48	219
LITTLETON, Beal House Inn	$32-$70*	209
LYME, Lyme Inn	$55-$70	226
NEW LONDON, Pleasant Lake Inn	$32-$40*	231
NORTH CHARLESTOWN, Indian Shutters Inn	$28*	220
NORTH SUTTON, Follansbee Inn	$25-$40*	217
NORTH WOODSTOCK, Woodstock Inn	$34-$65	234
PORTSMOUTH, Inn at Christian Shore	$50	221
SHELBURNE, Philbrook Farm Inn	$50-$55	229
SUGAR HILL, Southworth's B&B	$30-$35	232
SUNAPEE, Dexter's Inn	$60-$90	216
WEST PLYMOUTH, Crab Apple Inn	$45-$55	214

NEW JERSEY

BAY HEAD, Conover's Bay Head Inn	$45-$95	236
CAPE MAY, Mainstay Inn	$50-$84	238
SPRING LAKE, Kenilworth, The	$54-$90	237
SPRING LAKE, Normandy Inn	$55-$81	239
STOCKTON, Colligan's Stockton Inn	$65-$115	235
STOCKTON, Woolverton Inn	$55-$80	240

NEW MEXICO

LAS VEGAS, Plaza Hotel	$45-$65*	242
SANTA FE, Grant Corner Inn	$45-$100	241
SANTA FE, Preston House	$40-$95	243

NEW YORK

AMAGANSETT, Mill-Garth, The	$75-$200*	267
AUBURN, Springside Inn	$46	278
BERLIN, Sedgwick Inn, The	$40-$55	273
CANAAN, Shadowbrook Farm	$50	275
CAZENOVIA, Hillside Bed & Breakfast	$35	262
CAZENOVIA, Lincklaen House	$45-$100	264
CHESTERTOWN, Balsam House	$100-$140	247
CHESTERTOWN, Friends Lake Inn, The	$48	257
CLARENCE, Asa Ransom House	$60-$65	245
COLD SPRING-ON-HUDSON, Mews, The	$55-$75	266
EAST AURORA, Roycroft Inn	$40-$60	271
EAST HAMPTON, Bassett House	$35-$95	249

Rates are approximate for 2 people for 1 night

INN	RATE	PAGE
EAST HAMPTON, 1770 House	Call In	274
ELKA PARK, Redcoat's Return	$65-$75	270
FREDONIA, White Inn, The	$49-$59	282
GARRISON, Bird & Bottle, The	$95-$120	251
GHENT, Cedar Hill Inn	$72	254
GREENPORT, Bartlett House Inn	$30-$55	248
GREENVILLE, Greenville Arms	$60-$80	261
HENDERSON HARBOR, Gill House Inn	$34-$40*	259
HIGH FALLS, Captain Schoonmaker's B&B	$55-$60	253
HIGH FALLS, House on the Hill	$45-$65	263
HILLSDALE, Swiss Hutte	$48-$95	280
LAKE PLACID, South Meadow Farm	$46-$52	277
LAKE PLACID, Stagecoach Inn, The	$30-$35	279
NORTH RIVER, Garnet Hill Lodge	$46-$62	258
RHINEBECK, Beekman Arms	$50-$85	250
SARATOGA SPRINGS, Adelphi Hotel	$45-$75	244
SENECA FALLS, Gould, The	$40-$60*	260
SHELTER ISLAND, Bowditch House, The	$45-$68	252
SHELTER ISLAND, Ram's Head Inn	$50-$125	269
SKANEATELES, Sherwood Inn	$35-$65	276
STEPHENTOWN, Millhof Inn	$65-$90	268
STONE RIDGE, Baker's Bed and Breakfast	$58	246
STONY BROOK, Three Village Inn	$60-$75*	281
TUCKAHOE, 82 Vermont Terrace	$40-$46	256
WARRENSBURG, Merrill Magee House	$50-$60	265
WESTHAMPTON BEACH, Seafield House	$40-$60	272
WINDHAM, Christman's Windham House	$50-$70	255

NORTH CAROLINA

INN	RATE	PAGE
BLACK MOUNTAIN, Red Rocker Inn	$30-$45*	292
BLOWING ROCK, Ragged Garden Inn	$50-$85	291
BREVARD, Womble Inn	$32	294
BRYSON CITY, Hemlock Inn	$53-$70	287
BURNSVILLE, Nu-Wray Inn	$22-$42	289
FRANKLIN, Buttonwood Inn	$25-$35	285
HENDERSONVILLE, Havenshire Inn	$65	286
MARS HILL, Baird House	$40-$45	283
PISGAH FOREST, Mountain Key Lodge	$56	288
ROBBINSVILLE, Blue Boar Lodge	$60†	284
ROBBINSVILLE, Snowbird Mountain Lodge	$87†	293
SALUDA, Orchard Inn	$68	290

†AP or MAP   *Breakfast additional or unavailable

Rates are approximate for 2 people for 1 night

INN	RATE	PAGE
NEWPORT, Brinley Victorian, The	$45-$150	328
NEWPORT, Captain Samuel Rhodes Guest House	$68-$78	329
NEWPORT, Ellery Park House	$45	330
NEWPORT, Inn at Castle Hill	$40-$175	331
NEWPORT, Inntowne	$85-$120	332
NEWPORT, Queen Anne Inn	$35-$60	335
NEWPORT, Sunnyside Mansion	$45-$110	337
NEWPORT, Wayside	$45-$60	338
NEWPORT, Willows of Newport, The	$78-$98	339
WAKEFIELD, Larchwood Inn	$40-$60*	333

SOUTH CAROLINA

CHARLESTON, Swordgate Inn	$84-$98	340

TENNESSEE

GATLINBURG, Riverhouse	$35-$95	342
NORMANDY, Parish Patch Inn	$55-$75	341

VERMONT

ARLINGTON, Hill Farm Inn	$46-$52	356
ARLINGTON, West Mountain Inn	$40-$65*	388
BENNINGTON, Colonial Guest House	$18-$22	349
BONDVILLE, Bromley View Inn	$44-$68	346
CHELSEA, Shire Inn	$45-$65	379
CHESTER, Chester Inn	$42-$84	348
CHESTER, Hugging Bear Inn, The	$60	358
CRAFTSBURY COMMON, Inn on the Common	$90-$140	361
CUTTINGSVILLE, Maple Crest Farm	$28-$35	369
DORSET, Barrows House	$82-$116	343
EAST BARNET, Inwood Manor	$30-$40	362
EAST MIDDLEBURY, Waybury Inn	$35-$75	386
FAIR HAVEN, Vermont Marble Inn	$45-$70	383
GRAFTON, Woodchuck Hill Farm	$45-$85	390
GUILFORD, Capt. Henry Chase House, The	$35	347
IRASBURG, Irasburg Green B&B	$28-$35	363
JAMAICA, Three Mountain Inn	$50-$60	382
LANDGROVE, Village Inn	$30-$58	384
LOWER WATERFORD, Rabbit Hill Inn	$44-$69	376
LUDLOW, Governor's Inn	$80	354
MANCHESTER, Birch Hill Inn	$32-$44	344
MANCHESTER, 1811 House	$75-$125	353
MARLBORO, Whetstone Inn	$35-$55*	389

*Breakfast additional or unavailable

INN	RATE	PAGE
MIDDLETOWN SPRINGS, Middletown Springs Inn	$65-$75	371
MORETOWN, Camel's Hump View Farm	$36-$42	346
NEWFANE, Hobby Hill	$40	357
NORTH HERO, North Hero House	$35-$65*	372
NORTH THETFORD, Stone House Inn	$35	380
POULTNEY, Lake St. Catherine Inn	$60-$78	367
QUECHEE, Quechee Inn	$65-$140	375
SAXTONS RIVER, Saxton's River Inn	$30-$60	378
SIMONSVILLE, Rowell's Inn	$45-$55	377
SOUTH WALLINGFORD, Green Mountain Tea Room	$18-$22*	355
SOUTH WOODSTOCK, Kedron Valley Inn	$30-$85*	365
THETFORD, Lake House	$45-$55	366
WAITSFIELD, Lareau Farm Country Inn	$50-$70	368
WALLINGFORD, Wallingford Inn	$50-$60	385
WATERBURY CENTER, May Farm Lodge	$27-$32	370
WEATHERSFIELD, Inn at Weathersfield	$68-$76	359
WEST DOVER, Deerhill Inn	$85-$105	352
WEST DOVER, Weathervane Lodge	$45-$75	387
WEST WARDSBORO, Old Barn Inn, The	$35	373
WESTON, Colonial House Inn	$40-$60	350
WESTON, Inn at Weston	$35-$65	360
WILMINGTON, Darcroft's Schoolhouse	$25-$50	351
WILLISTON, Partridge Hill	$36	374
WINDSOR, Juniper Hill Lodge	$35	364
WOODSTOCK, Three Church Street	$40-$52	381

VIRGINIA

INN	RATE	PAGE
BEDFORD, Peaks of Otter Lodge	$50*	394
LEXINGTON, Alexander-Withrow House	$52-$67	391
LYNCHBURG, Sojourners B&B	$36	397
MIDDLEBURG, Red Fox Tavern	$65-$175	396
MIDDLEBURG, Welbourne	$85	399
MIDDLETOWN, Wayside Inn	$50-$95*	398
TREVILIANS, Prospect Hill	$85-$110	395
WARM SPRINGS, Gristmill Square	$60-$90	392
WARM SPRINGS, Meadow Lane Lodge	$69-$90	393

WASHINGTON

INN	RATE	PAGE
ASHFORD, Ashford Mansion, The	$34-$42	400
COUPEVILLE, Captain Whidbey Inn	$40-$80	401
SEAVIEW, Shelburne Inn	$40-$60*	403
WHITE SALMON, Inn of the White Salmon	$65-$70	402

Rates are approximate for 2 people for 1 night

	INN	RATE	PAGE

WEST VIRGINIA
LEWISBURG, General Lewis Inn — $45-$55 — 404

WISCONSIN
BAYFIELD, Old Rittenhouse Inn — $40-$75 — 405
FISH CREEK, White Gull Inn — $44-$76 — 408
LEWIS, Seven Pines Lodge — $42-$58 — 407
SISTER BAY, Renaissance Inn — $59 — 406
STURGEON BAY, White Lace Inn — $49-$68 — 409

CANADA
NEW BRUNSWICK, Pansy Patch — $45-$55 — 410
NEW BRUNSWICK, Seaside Inn — $35-$50* — 411
NEW BRUNSWICK, Tara Manor — $56-$68* — 412
NOVA SCOTIA, Blomidon Inn — $35-$65 — 413
NOVA SCOTIA, Highland Heights — $55* — 414
NOVA SCOTIA, Inverary Inn — $65 — 415
NOVA SCOTIA, Milford House — $55-$60* — 416
ONTARIO, Grandview Farm — $80 — 417
ONTARIO, Opinicon, The — $27-$38 — 418
PRINCE EDWARD ISLAND, Shaw's Hotel — $50-$60* — 419
QUEBEC, Handfield Inn — $37-$55* — 420
QUEBEC, Hotel Manoir d'Auteuil — (Canadian) $60-$85* — 421
QUEBEC, Hovey Manor — $57-$90 — 422
QUEBEC, Le Chateau de Pierre — (Canadian) $60-$85* — 423

NEW ZEALAND
NELSON, California Guest House — $24-$30 — 424

The rates for lodgings mentioned in this book (see Index) are intended as general guidelines only and are not to be considered as firm quotations. Naturally, with the fluctuating inflation rate and the high cost of doing business, they are subject to change.

In order to avoid any misunderstanding, when making reservations, please indicate that you wish the B&B rate. Some of the accommodations listed also have American plan and modified American plan rates.

*Breakfast additional or unavailable